Politics, Power, and Bureaucracy in France

POLITICS, POWER, AND BUREAUCRACY IN FRANCE

The Administrative Elite

Ezra N. Suleiman

PRINCETON UNIVERSITY PRESS
PRINCETON, NEW JERSEY

COPYRIGHT © 1974 BY PRINCETON UNIVERSITY PRESS

ALL RIGHTS RESERVED
LCC: 72–6524
ISBN: 0–691–07552–2 (clothbound edn.)
ISBN: 0–691–1022–5 (limited paperback edn.)

LIBRARY OF CONGRESS CATALOGING IN PUBLICATION DATA WILL
BE FOUND ON THE LAST PRINTED PAGE OF THIS BOOK.

COMPOSED IN LINOTYPE JANSON

PRINTED IN THE UNITED STATES OF AMERICA BY
PRINCETON UNIVERSITY PRESS, PRINCETON, NEW JERSEY

for Susan

CONTENTS

Contents

ix

Conclusion   369

XIV. Bureaucracy, Technocracy, and the
      Stalemate Society   372
      Bureaucracy or Technocracy?   374
      A Stalemate Society?   383

      Appendix: Questionnaire   391

      Bibliography   417

      Index   433

TABLES

GRAPHS

DIAGRAMS

ACKNOWLEDGMENTS

Although the responsibility for this study is exclusively mine, I am deeply aware of how much others have contributed to it. It would have been difficult to contemplate undertaking this work, much less completing it, without the cooperation of the many French higher civil servants who gave very generously of their time and who agreed to subject themselves to hours of interviewing. Whether in the Elysée, in ministerial cabinets, or in the ministries, they were always ready to answer my questions. Because they were assured of total anonymity, I can do no more than express my gratitude to them collectively.

In addition to interviews, this study called for research in many libraries and I want to thank, for their help, the staffs of the Archives Nationales, the Bibliothèque Nationale, the Bibliothèque de la Documentation Française, and the Bibliothèque de la Fondation Nationale des Sciences Politiques.

At the early stages of my research I benefited greatly from the advice of Michel Crozier, Bernard Gournay, Catherine Grémion, and Jean-Pierre Worms.

I am especially grateful to a number of scholars who have taken an interest in this study and who have read the manuscript in various versions. Lewis J. Edinger was always ready to offer his guidance, and his advice saved me from numerous errors. Stanley Hoffmann not only made invaluable criticisms and suggestions but also provided me with the opportunity to air a number of the themes in this study at a conference on France held at Harvard University in May 1971. I have discussed different aspects of this work with Allan Silver on so many occasions that I would be hard put to isolate his contributions. Blanche Blank, Thomas Cassilly, Roger Errera, and Robert O. Paxton all gave the manuscript a thorough reading and I have profited enormously from their suggestions. My thanks also go to J. David Greenstone for his incisive criticism of an earlier version of Chapter XII.

xvii

My debt to Juan Linz stands out above all others. He has taught me most of what I know about social science and his generosity and deep commitment to scholarship have been a source of constant encouragement and intellectual stimulation. He has been associated with this study from its inception and my profound indebtedness to him is both intellectual and personal.

I wish to record my thanks to the French Government and to the Foreign Area Fellowship Program of the Social Science Research Council and the American Council of Learned Societies whose Fellowships made possible a lengthy residence in Paris. I am also grateful for the computer facilities and the technical assistance I received from the Bureau of Applied Social Research at Columbia University. Mrs. Mary Heston, of Woodstock, Vermont, typed the manuscript with admirable skill and rare dedication.

Finally, I thank my wife, Susan Madeleine Suleiman, who, despite pressures on her own time, spent innumerable hours pointing out errors and contradictions. Without her support and devotion, this study would have taken many more years to complete.

It goes without saying that I alone am responsible for all the errors and misjudgments that remain.

Ezra N. Suleiman

Paris, October 20, 1973

POLITICS, POWER, AND BUREAUCRACY IN FRANCE

INTRODUCTION

This is not a study in what is traditionally known as public administration, a vast field that gives rise to hundreds, perhaps thousands, of monographs and texts every year. In the United States, the central preoccupations of this field have been what might be called "managerial," whereas in Europe they have been largely juridical. It is hardly surprising, therefore, that we should know so little about the role of bureaucracy in a political system. Hitherto, we have had to content ourselves with certain a priori assertions which have come to be regarded as basic verities, even though these assertions have lacked empirical documentation.

Two views concerning the role of the bureaucracy in different political systems have gained especially wide currency. The first, which is applicable mostly to the Anglo-Saxon countries, holds that the bureaucracy is totally subordinate to the political institutions. In other words, the bureaucracy is not recognized as having any degree of autonomy. All the literature on the British civil service has accepted this point of view.[1] In the United States, study of the bureaucracy's role in society and in the political process has only recently begun to receive attention. Again, this is in large part because the Federal bureaucracy has usually been regarded as unquestionably subordinate and obedient to the directives of the political elites. Mills, indeed, denying any importance to the bureaucracy in America, went so far as to write that "the civilian government of the United States never has had and does not now have a genuine bureaucracy."[2] He concluded his discussion of the absence of a bureaucracy in the United States thus: "There is no civil service career that is secure enough, there

[1] See J. Donald Kingsley, *Representative Bureaucracy* (Yellow Springs, Ohio: The Antioch Press, 1944); C. H. Sisson, *The Spirit of British Administration* (London: Faber and Faber, 1959); and Henry Parris, *Constitutional Bureaucracy* (London: George Allen and Unwin, 1969).

[2] C. Wright Mills, *The Power Elite* (New York: Oxford University Press, 1959), p. 237.

3

is no administrative corps that is permanent enough, to survive a change-over of political administration in the United States. Neither professional party politicians nor professional bureaucrats are now at the executive centers of decision. Those centers are occupied by the political directorate of the power elite."[3]

Mills accepted the widespread belief that there exist in Europe permanent and neutral bureaucracies which find no counterpart in the United States. Yet, as Parsons pointed out some years ago, Mills tended "to under-estimate the real influence of 'nonpolitical' government officials on long-run policy."[4] A recent study has shown that certain departments are staffed by a permanent body of civil servants, while others—Treasury, Commerce—continually have a large influx of people from the private sector. This same study also shows that it is only at the very outset of their terms that Presidents tend to appoint to political executive posts persons from outside the Federal service. In every administration (except Truman's), from Franklin Roosevelt to Lyndon Johnson, the percentage of those appointed to political executive posts from among Federal officials was shown to have increased.[5] It might be added that in addition to underestimating the power and the number of permanent officials in the American Federal bureaucracy, Mills also overestimated the permanence and the neutrality of the European bureaucracies.

In the case of the United States, Mills' view is actually the classical textbook view of the totally subordinate bureaucracy; whether it is permanent or whether it undergoes major changes in personnel with successive presidents, the bureaucracy is not regarded as having any autonomy. It may be that the revelations of the Pentagon Papers will stimulate students of American public administration to look more closely at the power of the permanent officials in the Federal bureaucracy—hitherto, they have pretty much ignored the political and social impact of governmental agencies. They have been more concerned with "scientific" questions of "management," "communication," "personnel,"

[3] *Ibid.*, p. 241.
[4] Talcott Parsons, "The Distribution of Power in American Society," in G. William Domhoff and H. B. Ballard, eds., C. *Wright Mills and The Power Elite* (Boston: Beacon Press, 1969), p. 79. Parsons' essay first appeared in *World Politics*, xi, no. 1 (1957).
[5] David T. Stanley, Dean E. Mann and Jameson W. Doig, *Men Who Govern: A Biographical Profile of Federal Political Executives* (Washington, D.C.: The Brookings Institution, 1967), pp. 51–52.

"efficiency," and so forth. Important as these questions are, undue emphasis on them has tended, as James Q. Wilson has pointed out, to make the study of organizations more concerned with their own internal mechanism than with their relationship to and their impact on their clientele.[6]

If the bureaucracy has been regarded as a totally subordinate, hence secondary, institution in the United States and in Britain, it has often been seen as being all-powerful in Continental European countries. One of the first things that a student of French politics learns is that while the politicians had their fun and played their games in the Third and Fourth Republics, the country was held on an even keel and actually prospered under the guidance of a permanent body of dedicated officials. Thus Herbert Luethy could write in the 1950's that "France is not ruled, but administered"[7] by a group of civil servants who have seldom been affected by changes in regimes. Karl Deutsch and Lewis Edinger wrote in a similar vein of the power of the German administrative elite. They noted that the extent of the administrative elite's "influence over policy making has varied more or less inversely with the power of the political elite," and that it was only "under the strong political leadership of Hitler [that] the influence of the professional administrative elite was practically eliminated as a factor in policy making."[8] The theory that the administration's power has varied in inverse proportion to the power of the political elite has a deceptive logic about it. When applied to France, it makes little sense, as will be seen in this study,[9] and when applied to Germany, it appears equally deceptive since the administrative elite was neither all-powerful under the Empire and under Weimar, nor was its power totally crushed under Hitler.[10]

[6] James Q. Wilson, *Varieties of Police Behavior* (New York: Atheneum, 1970), p. 2.

[7] Herbert Luethy, *France Against Herself* (New York: Meridian Books, 1954), p. 40.

[8] Karl Deutsch and Lewis Edinger, *Germany Rejoins the Powers* (Stanford: Stanford University Press, 1959), p. 80.

[9] Doubts have been shed on this theory in Ezra N. Suleiman, "The French Bureaucracy and Its Students: Toward the Desanctification of the State," *World Politics*, XXIII, no. 1 (1970), pp. 126–129.

[10] See Ralf Dahrendorf, *Society and Democracy in Germany* (New York: Doubleday and Co., 1967), pp. 249–254; and Karl Dietrich Bracher, *The German Dictatorship* (New York: Frederick A. Praeger, 1970), pp. 330–349.

These two extreme views—subordination and autonomy—of the role of the bureaucracy in a political system have had an unfortunate consequence: they have hindered the study of the bureaucracy as an integral, and dynamic, part of the political system. In other words, the bureaucracy has seldom been seen as an institution that operates within the larger politico-administrative framework. If the bureaucracy is seen as an institution that interacts with other institutions in a society, it becomes easier to understand why a governmental bureaucracy cannot be characterized as either totally subservient or totally autonomous. As usual, reality is far more complex. The principal aim of this study is to examine the French higher civil service as an integral part of the politico-administrative system. I have concentrated on the highest officials—the Directors of the central administration and the members of ministerial cabinets—and I have chosen to study the interaction of these men not merely with their immediate superiors and subordinates, but with their clientele, broadly defined. Such an approach has, I believe, a certain significance in that it shows the extent to which the higher civil service can or cannot be regarded as a homogeneous institution, and the extent to which changes in regimes either do or do not affect the functioning of certain institutions. Thus, for example, in studying the ministerial cabinet in France we find that every argument that has been offered about its functioning has been in some way linked to the type of regime in existence. Yet it appears very clear from the data I have been able to gather that the central purpose and role of this institution has varied not at all from the Third to the Fourth to the Fifth Republics.

It may appear somewhat paradoxical that, while the bureaucracy in France has been generally regarded as an all-powerful institution, it has remained perhaps the least studied of all political institutions. The reasons for this curious fact are many, and it would require a rather lengthy digression to go into them.[11] In recent years some effort has been made to study local administration and politics in France but, with regard to the central administration, the last important study was by Walter Rice Sharp, and appeared in 1931.[12]

The present book aims to fill only a small part of this lacuna.

[11] See Suleiman, "The French Bureaucracy and Its Students," pp. 151–155.
[12] Walter R. Sharp, *The French Civil Service: Bureaucracy in Transition* (New York: Macmillan, 1931).

A forthcoming study dealing with the relationship between public and private elites in France will be largely concerned with the formulation of public policy, a subject that I have touched on here but have not been able to treat fully. Even so, my aims may appear at once too narrow and too broad—too narrow because the book treats only the civil servants who occupy the highest posts in the politico-administrative system, thus excluding other high civil servants lower in the hierarchy; too broad because, unlike a monographic study, it treats their recruitment, their role perception, their relation to the larger society, and the degree to which their administrative functions can be said to impinge upon the formulation of public policy. It could be argued that the study attempts to cover too many aspects of the higher civil service, and such a criticism would not be entirely unjustified. Moreover, in treating the administration's relationship with deputies and with interest groups, I have examined these relationships only from the administration's side. Clearly, more detailed studies are required that would take account of how the deputies and the interest groups view their own relationships with the bureaucracy. Given, however, that little has been written on the subjects treated here, I felt it necessary to attempt to paint as large a picture as possible, rather than concentrate on one particular aspect of the subject.[13] Often I will do little more than raise questions and suggest areas that require more detailed investigation.

The data in this study are based, in the main, on interviews which I conducted in Paris in 1968–70 with Directors of the central administration and with members of ministerial cabinets.[14] It should be emphasized that a survey cannot always provide answers to all questions. Sometimes it can do little more than point to certain possible answers, and this only when account has been taken of all available historical material. In researching and writing this study, I have been particularly conscious of the fact that the problems treated here did not originate shortly before I decided to investigate them. They have existed for a long time, and

[13] No matter how broad the scope of the study is, it has not been broad enough to include certain important institutions of the public sector. The chief omission in this regard is the growing importance of para-administrative institutions, which have yet to be studied.

[14] All the interviews were conducted personally by the author. See questionnaire in Appendix.

7

I have often searched for historical similarities and explanations.

Many of the conclusions reached here, as well as certain re-formulations of standard interpretations of French politics, were suggested by the surveys that I carried out. They generally had to be followed up in further interviews and necessarily had to be examined in the light of published sources.[15] I have attempted throughout to make judicious use of the survey data and to place this data within a theoretical, and where possible, a comparative context. It is perhaps worth noting that had the interviews been carried out by a group of interviewers rather than by the author alone, it is very likely that the study would have reached different conclusions. This is because, in a survey, respondents tend to suggest certain themes that are not indicated by the questionnaire. If these themes recur over and over again in the responses, they may suggest patterns that cannot be accommodated in a structured questionnaire and so are not likely to be followed up. A very telling example of this is provided in Chapter XII.

At the outset of the research, the aim was to study only the Directors. It soon became evident, however, that the ministerial cabinets had to be included because they constituted a crucial part of the politico-administrative system. As I will show at length, it is not possible to examine the French central administration or the relationship between politics and administration without as-signing a primordial role to the ministerial cabinets. I inter-viewed 90 Directors (out of a total of slightly over 100) and 45 members of ministerial cabinets. The interviews with Directors lasted from two to five hours, averaging three and one half hours each, while those with members of ministerial cabinets lasted from one and one half to two and one half hours. In both surveys a structured questionnaire was used, which would indicate that elites are by no means averse, as is generally thought, to sub-mitting themselves to structured interviews. So long as the ques-tions are addressed in the language to which the persons being interviewed are accustomed, and so long as they remain perti-nent and specific, they will be willingly responded to by an elite regardless of how structured or "closed" they are. This would suggest that in interviewing elites it is preferable to avoid using professional interviewers and to rely more heavily on those bet-

---

[15] All translations from the French, as well as the occasional ones from German, Spanish, and Italian, are my own.

ter versed in the subject matter. It may well be, therefore, that the difference is not between elite and mass interviewees, but between elite and mass interviewers.

In Part One I attempt to present an overall view of the place of the State in French society, emphasizing the aura of sanctity with which the modern State has been imbued since its creation by Napoleon, as well as the recent questioning of the State's traditional role. Part Two deals with the recruitment of higher civil servants. In addition to documenting what is generally well known —the high social origin of the French administrative elite—I attempt to explain, using comparative data for other French elites and for other Western administrative elites, why the social origin of French higher civil servants has remained fairly constant despite repeated attempts to democratize their recruitment. I then briefly relate the social origin variable to administrative behavior. I have thought it important to discuss the many ramifications of the problem of recruitment at length in order to provide a context for the later discussions on administration and politics. A reader who is primarily interested in the problems of administrative and political interactions, however, may wish to skip Part Two.

In Part Three I deal with the important institutional mechanisms of the central administration, examining the role perception of the higher civil servants, their relation to their political chiefs—the ministers—and to the ministerial cabinets, as well as the role of the Grands Corps in the politico-administrative system. I have tried to emphasize that even a centralized and powerful bureaucracy, such as exists in France, must be seen as a complex of institutions rather than as a monolithic organization. The role conflicts experienced by higher civil servants illustrate this clearly. Such conflicts, if and when they are recognized, are often treated lightly. But to the extent that they have a bearing on public policy, they should be accorded greater importance.

As I have already indicated, this is not a clinical study of the French bureaucracy. The final portion deals with the relation of the higher civil servants to other groups in the society—deputies, interest groups, and the regime of the Fifth Republic. This part of the study shows the extent to which the higher civil service reflects the desire of the regime to deal with large groups who are linked to the Gaullist government. The examination of the relationship between the bureaucracy and the Gaullist regime shows

9

that a novel situation may be in the making: namely, the use of the bureaucracy and the governmental machine by a relatively cohesive political force. Ultimately, and this is indicated at various points in the study, the existence of a majority party, or of a party government, has had a far greater impact on the bureaucracy than has ministerial stability or instability.

PART ONE

State and Society in France

CHAPTER I

The Administrative State

Je veux constituer en France l'ordre civil. Il n'y a jusqu'à présent dans le monde que deux pouvoirs: le militaire et l'ecclésiastique. . . . Je veux surtout une corporation parce qu'une corporation ne meurt point . . . [une corporation] n'a d'autre ambition que celle d'être utile et d'autre intérêt que l'intérêt public. Il faut que ce corps ait des privilèges, qu'il ne soit pas trop dépendant des ministres ni de l'Empereur. . . . Je veux un corps dont l'administration et les statuts deviennent tellement nationaux qu'on ne puisse jamais se déterminer à y porter légèrement la main.

—*Napoleon*[1]

The structure of the modern French State owes more to Napoleon than to any of his predecessors or successors. He intended the bureaucracy that he created to be at once at the service of the State and the representative of the State. To understand the role of the bureaucracy in French society, therefore, it is necessary to grasp the importance that has been ascribed to the State ever since Napoleon gave it its modern form. This chapter will deal with the rise of what Dwight Waldo has called the "administrative state."[2] After ascribing the origins of this State to Napoleon rather than to the monarchs of the *ancien régime*, we will examine some of the arguments that have been used to justify the need for a strong state, arguments that continue to be reiterated today. That it was the State's own servants that had to be the first to submit to the exigencies of the powerful State will also be seen. Finally, it will be argued that the bases of the Napoleonic State are now questioned as they never have been before.

[1] Cited in Roger Grégoire, *La Fonction publique* (Paris: Armand Colin, 1954), p. 39.

[2] Dwight Waldo, *The Administrative State* (New York: The Ronald Press, 1948).

13

TREND TOWARD CENTRALIZATION

De Tocqueville's thesis that administrative centralization in France was a creation of the *ancien régime* and not of the Revolution has had a profound impact on historical, sociological, and political studies of French institutions. The reverence accorded to this thesis is best evidenced by the uncritical and universal acceptance it has enjoyed ever since it was first expounded more than a century ago. It is hardly surprising, therefore, that the term "centralization" should today be used as a catch-all phrase that subsumes and explains all the complex phenomena of the French political and social system. More important, however, Tocqueville's analysis of the origins and consequences of the trend toward centralization appears to have obviated the need for his followers to search for other explanations of the workings of the political system, of patterns of social behavior and interactions, and of cultural norms.[3]

One has only to see how some of the most influential sociological studies on France have sought to document their own observations by invoking the analysis of Tocqueville. In *The Bureaucratic Phenomenon*, perhaps the most influential of the recent studies, Crozier's conclusions about French society probably owe more to Tocqueville than to Crozier's own remarkable empirical investigations in two administrative agencies.[4] Greenstein and Tarrow have recently noted, with considerable justification, that most of the explanations that have been handed down to us by students of French society have been based largely on impressionistic observations rather than on serious empirical in-

---

[3] It suffices only to glance at Tocqueville's chapter headings to see how little has been added to his analysis by contemporary students of French politics and society: "How administrative centralization was an institution of the old regime and not, as is often thought, a creation of the Revolution or the Napoleonic period" (Part II, Ch. 2); "How paternal government, as it is called today, had been practiced under the old regime" (Part II, Ch. 3); "How France had become the country in which men were most like each other" (Part II, Ch. 8); "How, though in many respects so similar, the French were split up more than ever before into small, isolated, self-regarding groups" (Part III, Ch. 9). *The Old Regime and the French Revolution* (New York: Doubleday, Anchor Books edition, 1955).

[4] See Michel Crozier, *The Bureaucratic Phenomenon* (Chicago: University of Chicago Press, 1964), pp. 213–269. Crozier himself has been called a "latter-day Tocqueville." See Henry Ehrmann, *Politics in France* (Boston: Little, Brown & Co., 1968), p. 131.

vestigations. "When applied by a Tocqueville, or, more recently, a Luethy or a Wylie," they note, "unsystematic procedures for considering evidence can lead to brilliant speculations. But the speculations of such writers are too often treated as final verities, rather than being subjected to rigorous assessment."[5]

These authors also note that the study of French institutions has tended for the most part to emphasize their uniqueness, which is precisely what Tocqueville, Crozier, Luethy, Wylie, Pitts and others have done. Thus, for example, one study of French local politics has been largely based on the observation that the pattern of consensus that obtains locally in France, as well as voter turnout, is markedly different from that which obtains nationally.[6] Yet a recent study on British local government has shown that similar differences prevail between local and national politics in Britain.[7]

Quite apart from the remarkable influence that Tocqueville's analysis of French society has had on students of French politics, his central thesis concerning the origins of the modern centralized State is now in need of revision. His emphasis on an ineluctable historical process underestimates the very powerful and determined role played by those who came to power in the wake of the Revolution of 1789, particularly Napoleon, without whom the structure of the French State would have turned out very different from what it is today. One need only look at the gamut of administrative institutions and the educational system to see the clear imprint of Napoleon. Indeed, it can be argued that, without the educational system that Napoleon established, the structure of French society would have taken a very different shape during the course of the nineteenth century. While it is impossible to deny an important role to the *ancien régime* in the shaping of the modern French State, it is now equally impossible to underestimate the decisive part played by Napoleon. As a British historian has recently noted: "The first prerequisite for fully centralized government was . . . the suppression of any rival influence in the

---

[5] Fred I. Greenstein and Sidney G. Tarrow, "The Study of French Political Socialization: Toward the Revocation of Paradox," *World Politics*, XXII, no. 1 (1969), p. 98.

[6] Mark Kesselman, *The Ambiguous Consensus* (New York: Alfred A. Knopf, 1967).

[7] I. P. MacKintosh, *The Devolution of Power* (Middlesex: Penguin Books, 1968), pp. 9–38.

provinces. This was achieved by the abolition of privileges, territorial and corporate as well as personal, after the night of Fourth August, and by the subsequent division of France into departments, areas of more or less uniform size, uniformly administered. By eliminating the administrative anomalies of the *ancien régime* the Assembly made a centralized system of government possible. It was left to Napoleon to make it a reality."[8]

If the origins of the trend toward State centralization are open to debate, so must the evolution of the trend also be debated. It should, of course, first be recognized that at stake are two separate questions: the origins of the process and the process itself as it evolved. Historians must address themselves not only to the first question, which concerns the genesis of the centralized State, but they must also explain how and why the process of centralization continued unabated throughout the nineteenth century; in other words, why no forces sprang up to counter the centralizing trend. Was this merely because the authoritarian nature of governments prohibited the formation of associations? Is it not possible that the State was gradually undertaking to fill social needs that were shunned by the private sector? If France is a country of shopkeepers, and if Malthusianism is the characteristic French attitude toward commerce,[9] is this the result of an inexorable process of State centralization that stifled private initiative? Or, on the contrary, did the Malthusianism of the French bourgeoisie encourage or oblige the State to fulfill tasks that it might have preferred to leave to others? Did not the bourgeoisie in the early nineteenth century, as many historians have noted, adopt the values of the waning aristocracy and "put money gained in commerce, manufacturing, finance and state service into land"?[10]

It has been variously argued that France is basically a country in which peasant or bourgeois or aristocratic values predominate, but which set of values have made the greatest imprint on French society is not at all clear. What is clear is that all those

[8] Nicholas Richardson, *The French Prefectoral Corps, 1814–1830* (Cambridge: Cambridge University Press, 1966), p. 1.

[9] See John E. Sawyer, "Strains in the Social Structure of Modern France," and David S. Landes, "French Business and the Businessman: A Social and Cultural Analysis," both in Edward M. Earle, ed., *Modern France: Problems of the Third and Fourth Republics* (Princeton: Princeton University Press, 1951).

[10] Norman Birnbaum, *The Crisis of Industrial Society* (New York: Oxford University Press, 1969), p. 29.

who have argued for one or another of these values have arrived at the same conclusion: that there is among Frenchmen a fear of and resistance to change.[11] This conclusion becomes highly significant when it is applied to the elites of French society and compared to the responsiveness of the elites in other societies. Consider, for example, the reaction of the British aristocracy to the demands for universal suffrage in the early nineteenth century. As W. L. Guttsman has shown, the British cabinet that was responsible for the Reform Act of 1832 was the most artistocratic in British history.[12] The British aristocracy, like that of Germany, shifted to politics and to industry and did not retire to its castles as did the French aristocracy. All this suggests that a centralized state depends on a complex of historical factors, foremost among which is the responsiveness of elites to the increasing demands of society.

The important point is that the State did not, over a period of two hundred and fifty years, purely and simply seize power from the society. Rather, a dialectical process was unfolding, a process in which the State and the society were responding to one another. Today, for example, we find instances of institutions having a good deal more power than they choose to use. This is particularly evident at the local level where institutions are not only deprived of power but essentially deprive themselves of what power they possess. A good example of this is given in Worms' description of the cooperation between the prefect and the mayor, which more often than not depends on the abdication of responsibility on both their parts in favor of the central authorities.[13] The verticalization of decision-making is thus not merely the result of an imperialist and usurpationist predisposition on

[11] See Crozier, *The Bureaucratic Phenomenon*; Herbert Luethy, *France Against Herself* (New York: Meridian Books, 1954); André Siegfried, *France: A Study of Nationality* (New Haven: Yale University Press, 1930); Jacques Fauvet, *La France dechirée* (Paris: Fayard, 1957); Stanley Hoffmann, "Paradoxes of the French Political Community," in Hoffmann et al., *In Search of France* (Cambridge, Mass.: Harvard University Press, 1963).

[12] W. L. Guttsman, *The British Political Elite* (New York: Basic Books, 1963), p. 36. Allan Silver has analyzed the Whig government's reactions to the demand for universal suffrage. See his "Social and Ideological Bases of British Elite Reactions to Domestic Crisis in 1829–1832," *Politics and Society*, 1 (February 1971), 179–201.

[13] See Jean-Pierre Worms, "Le Préfet et ses notables," *Sociologie du Travail*, Special Number VIII, no. 3 (1966).

17

the part of the central authorities, but is encouraged by the peculiar need for cooperation and the maintenance of peace among institutions.[14] In other words, while Napoleon may have fashioned the institutions upon which the centralized State is predicated, the reasons for the acceptance and continuance of this State must be sought in the behavior and particular political disposition of local and other elites in French society.

If local and national elites have been reluctant to entertain changes that entail decentralization, it is also necessary to note that champions of a strong State, like de Gaulle and Pompidou, have sought to impose reforms from above rather than encourage local participation in the formulation of reforms. In *Les Institutions régionales et la société locale*,[15] Worms and Grémion show how, after having opposed the decreed administrative reform of 1964, the local elites directly affected by it were able to re-create the same institutional patterns and relationships that had existed prior to the reform and thus render the reform nugatory. As Crozier has shown, the French bureaucratic mode of authority is resistant to change because decisions are made by men too far removed from those who are affected by these decisions.[16] But, according to Crozier and others, just as the State does not encourage participation, neither do the citizens seek a greater voice in their own affairs. This can only aggravate the problems involved in decentralization. It also suggests that a very complex relationship exists between State and society, a relationship in which it is neither the one nor the other that continually has the upper hand, but in which they interact to form an elaborate system of reinforcements which are, ultimately, conducive to preserving the structure of the existing State. In effect, Pompidou is not far wrong when he says that it is false to think of French life as being a permanent battle between the French people and the "monster" [the State].[17]

If I have raised some questions about the genesis of the centralized State and about the evolution of the trend toward

[14] It strikes us as slightly odd, though by no means insignificant, that in a plea for decentralization one was able to argue toward the end of the nineteenth century that the French mayor possessed too much power, that he was in fact "a small constitutional monarch." See Paul Deschanel, *La Décentralisation* (Paris: Berger-Levrault, 1895), p. 10.

[15] Paris: C.N.R.S., 1969.

[16] Crozier, *The Bureaucratic Phenomenon*, pp. 193–194.

[17] *Le Monde*, January 4, 1972.

18

centralization, I have not questioned the fact that there exists in France a centralized State administration that is wholly or partly responsible for conducting almost every activity in the nation. That this administration is located almost entirely in Paris is not without importance, for it symbolizes the capital's monopoly of the nation's intellectual, scientific, financial, and political activities, a monopoly that has been admirably documented in J.-F. Gravier's *Paris et le désert Français*.[18] So evident is the tremendous gap between Paris and *province* that it has not been unusual to liken the provinces to France's former colonies and to demand the "decolonization of France."[19]

At the beginning of this chapter I quoted Napoleon's desire to create "a corporate body that does not die" and that "must have privileges," a desire that has been fully realized and that has shaped the structure of the French State throughout the past century and a half. But the creation of the corporate body entailed, first of all, the total subservience and subordination of its employees to the higher aims of this body. The tyranny of the official is often invoked; what has been less frequently invoked has been the tyranny *over* the official. The power of the State had, therefore, to manifest itself first over its agents and then over those whom it was intended to serve.

THE SUPERIORITY OF THE STATE

In his study of administrative syndicalism in France, Harold Laski wrote that "the civil servant is not an actor in the events of which he is the administrator."[20] The French civil servant has always been placed in a "situation réglementaire," which has meant that the rules governing his employment were in no way analogous to those affecting the employee of a private institution, but were to be determined unilaterally by the State.[21] Prior to the

---

[18] Paris: Flammarion, 2nd ed., 1958.

[19] See Charles Brindillac, "Décoloniser la France," *Esprit*, xxv (December 1957), 799–812. See also J.-F. Gravier, "Les Parisiens sont-ils colonialists?" *La Table Ronde*, Special Number, no. 245 (June 1968), 18–27.

[20] Harold J. Laski, *Authority in the Modern State* (New Haven: Yale University Press, 1919), p. 344. It will be seen in the present study how the higher civil servant is very much an *actor* in the affairs he administers.

[21] P. Chatenet, "The Civil Service in France," in W. A. Robson, ed., *The Civil Service in Britain and France* (London: The Hogarth Press, 1956), p. 162.

Revolution of 1789, public employees were regarded as servants of the Monarch whose commands were their duties. The State and the Monarch, as Louis XIV proclaimed, were one. To be in the employ of the Monarch was to be serving the State, just as to be serving the State was to be in the employ of the Monarch.[22]

The Revolution, it has been argued, altered the hitherto prevailing monism very little, for it merely substituted the abstraction of the State for the Monarch. As Laski has observed, "The *ancien régime* implied a monistic state; and when for the crown was substituted the nation, the worship of a unified indivisibility underwent no change."[23] The new element that was born with the Revolution was that of the "national will." Although this concept was wholly incompatible with the absolutist age, its democratic implications were obscured after the Revolution; for, as Barker has noted, "If Louis XIV had simply said 'I am the State,' Napoleon could say, more subtly but with greater force, 'I am the nation, and *therefore* the State.' "[24] More significantly, there was henceforth to be a distinction between the State and the Nation, sanctioned by law and having serious ramifications for the development of public power in France.

The concept of the State forming a separate entity, at once within and outside the Nation, was born with the Revolution, and the particular meanings attached to this concept from the beginning of the nineteenth century have constituted the cardinal elements in the State's relations to its agents. The State could justify the possession of arbitrary power on the grounds that public and private employment are wholly different. The State cannot be compared to a private employer, since it is entrusted with responsibilities that cannot be transferred to any other institution. Its unique role therefore justifies its unique power.

What set the State apart from other institutions was not only the uniqueness of the functions it performed but also the indispensability of these functions. Consequently, being in the service of the State was not analogous to being in the service of a private institution. Even in the France of today, one hears of the unique role of the State and of the honor of being its employee. "The State is not an employer like others. It is an honor and a vocation

---

[22] Ernest Barker, *The Development of Public Services in Western Europe, 1660–1930* (Hamden, Conn.: Archon Books, 1966), p. 6.

[23] Laski, *Authority in the Modern State*, p. 321.

[24] Barker, *The Development of Public Services*, p. 14.

to serve the Nation."[25] Like Debré, many jurists and other champions of the integrity of the State have claimed not only superiority for the State over all other institutions, but also legitimacy, based on the indispensable functions it performs. "The considerable extension," we read in a modern text, "of the power of the State is accepted by the citizens because it appears, on the whole, as the necessary condition for the rendering of services needed by society. In other words, public service is the contemporary legitimacy of power. Is it also the *raison d'être* of the State?"[26] This assumption is peculiarly French, and to some extent continental, in that it sees the State's role of providing services as an indispensable element of its *raison d'être*. Brian Chapman has noted that, although in Britain the State may provide as many services as do any of the European states, there is nonetheless a general feeling that these services should *not* be provided by the State.[27] The difference is basically one of attitude and carries with it wide ramifications as far as those responsible for the conduct of the State's affairs are concerned.

What above all distinguishes the State from the other institutions in society is that it alone can take account of the "general interest." "The State represents the national collectivity. The services under its charge are tasks it performs on behalf of the general interest."[28] Only the State can be expected to have no selfish interests. In other words, only the State can have a disinterested view of what is good for the nation as a whole. Clearly, this poses serious questions for the philosophers, for defined as such the State becomes an abstraction. I shall return a number of times to this theme during the course of this study, and I will suggest some explanations for the persistent invocation of the "general interest" on the part of those who serve the State. I will also examine, particularly in Chapter XII, the circumstances under which the invocation of the "general interest" may sometimes be a mere rationalization for serving particular interests.

Paradoxically, the superiority of the State finds a further jus-

[25] Michel Debré, *Au Service de la nation* (Paris: Edition Stock, 1963), p. 251.

[26] Gérard Belorgey, *Le Gouvernement et l'administration de la France* (Paris: Armand Colin, 1967), p. 11.

[27] Brian Chapman, *British Government Observed: Some European Reflections* (London: George Allen and Unwin Ltd., 1963), p. 17.

[28] Debré, *Au service de la nation*, p. 261.

21

tification in democratic theory. The Napoleonic theory of the supremacy of the State was found to be perfectly compatible with the theory of democracy. The State was supreme because it was the representative of the people. Hence, ". . . Only unquestioning acceptance by public employees of the commands of their superiors can assure the responsibility of the bureaucracy to the representative branches of the government. Thus the administrative apparatus of a democratic society ironically is denied the possibility of organizing itself democratically by virtue of the alleged imperatives of representative government."[29]

The sharp differentiation between private and public law in France has been at once the basis of the democratic concept and of the inequality between the administration and the *administrés*. Because the law represents the sovereignty of the people, there has come to exist what has been called "juridical dualism"; that is, "the right of the individual, which forms private law, and the right of the State, which is public law. The latter is autonomous and has its own rules of jurisdiction."[30] The consequence of this juridical dualism has been the construction of a sharp and unequivocal line of demarcation between the principles that govern the relations between the State and its agents and those that govern the relations between the private employer and the private employee. The latter depended for the most part on common law. As for the former, it was maintained that, "since the administration is organized according to a principle of authority, its relations with its agents cannot be founded on equality. Therefore, they cannot be determined by contractual agreements."[31]

Perhaps the most important justification for the superiority of the State has been the unquestionable need for its continuity. Only the continuity of the State in the face of wars, depressions, or political upheavals could guarantee its superiority as well as its eternal nature. This is what Napoleon meant when he stated his intention to create "a corporate body, because a corporate body does not die." As M. Bouère has noted: "First and above all, the *raison d'être* of the public service is its continuity: it is to permit the normal functioning of an activity that is essential to the State, and to assure in a permanent manner the satisfaction of a

[29] M. R. Godine, *The Labor Problem in the Public Service* (Cambridge, Mass.: Harvard University Press, 1951), p. 47.
[30] Chatenet, "The Civil Service in France," p. 162.
[31] *Ibid.*

22

collective need. . . . This law of continuity concerns, in the final analysis, the perpetuity of the State itself, the cluster of public services."[32]

In order to assume the role of a civil servant, one had therefore to submit to all the strenuous obligations that public service entailed. This meant, above all, renouncing any private interests. For implicit in the classical concept of the *fonction publique* was the assumption that the agent of the State could not, and perhaps need not, have any interests outside the interests of the State. "If it appears to him, in effect, that he finds himself in this respect in a situation inferior to that of other citizens, he alone is responsible for it; for he knew, when he entered the *fonction publique*, that he was abandoning certain liberties and that he was submitting his own individual interest to the superior law of the general interest."[33]

The law of October 19, 1946, which sets down regulations concerning the status of civil servants states that "le fonctionnaire est vis-à-vis de l'administration dans une situation statutaire et réglementaire" (Article 5). In theory, this merely constitutes a statutory reaffirmation of the classical doctrine of the *fonction publique*. In practice, however, the syndicalists' struggle has in large measure modified the classical doctrine.

That the State refused to grant the civil servant the liberties which it was making available to the private citizen was due to a persistent and fundamental disagreement between the administrative syndicalists and the government: the syndicalists maintained that the relationship of the civil servant to the State was a contractual one. As Proudhon had expressed it, "Contracts are what we put in the place of laws."[34] The government, on the other hand, maintained that in no way could the civil servant be considered as having a relationship to the State similar to that between the private citizen and his employer. Hence contractual arrangement with the State was incompatible with the duties and responsibilities with which the State was charged. The State came gradually to relax its adamant position with regard to granting civil servants the rights it had been obliged to grant other workers. The rights granted to the civil servants by the

[32] Jean-Pierre Bouère, *Le Droit de grève* (Paris: Librarie Sirey, 1958), p. 92.
[33] *Ibid.*, p. 94.
[34] Quoted in Godine, *The Labor Problem in the Public Service*, p. 52.

various governments, rights which eventually came to be greater than those granted to workers in private employment, were finally codified in the 1946 *Statut de la Fonction Publique.*

THE CENTRALIZED STATE AND THE GENERAL INTEREST

Today there is scarcely an activity in France which the State does not either totally control or markedly influence. Just as civil servants fought for and ultimately obtained a certain degree of independence from the State, so now the cry of the society for a loosening of the State's grip is daily heard. As a distinguished group of French citizens recently demanded: "It is necessary, in the strict sense, to nationalize the State, that is, to make certain that its identification with the Nation is no longer through the exclusive intermediary of civil servants possessing all the powers, charging themselves with all the responsibilities and attempting to domesticate the citizens, who possess a liberty that is more and more devoid of content. The entire Nation must recognize itself in the State. In a word, it is necessary to give back the State to the Nation."[35]

Or, as M. Bloch-Lainé, a member of this group, expressed the same point in a different context: "The citizens who constitute the nation must be able to say: *L'Etat, c'est nous*—as Louis XIV used to say: *L'Etat, c'est moi.* We believe that this is not the case at the present time."[36] Those, however, who have always argued for a strong State have been accustomed to regard the State as "expressing the nation,"[37] ever fearful of the various sectional demands for autonomy that have largely remained dormant. "The State is not an inert body [wrote Debré] but a living being, because it is the expression of a community living like a person, living like a family: the nation. To be sure, the nation is composed of individuals and of groups. But this composition gives birth to an independent and animated body which is, in fact, the nation and, in law, the State."[38]

The major bone of contention between what we might call the

---

[35] C. Alphandery et al., *Pour nationaliser l'Etat* (Paris: Seuil, 1968), p. 24.

[36] François Bloch-Lainé, interview with Albert du Roy, Europe No. 1, *Europe-Soir*, December 27, 1968, p. 2.

[37] Michel Debré, *La Mort de l'Etat Republican* (Paris: Gallimard, 1947), p. 35.

[38] *Ibid.,* pp. 31-32.

étatistes and the *décentralisateurs* has to do with reconciling the preservation of the general interest with a wide participation in government by the citizenry. The former see mass participation as being fundamentally incompatible with upholding the general interest. They argue that citizens form part of, and are represented by, groups which seek only their own interests and which always remain oblivious to the general interest. This argument has been extended in France to the point where, as we shall see, the deputy's function has sometimes been called into question because he is elected by, and represents only, a fraction of the nation. The *étatistes* have always used the argument that the State stands above all of society's conflicts. The State arbitrates society's conflicts and it denies the existence of conflict within its own ranks. As President Pompidou stated in a speech to the Conseil d'Etat: "For more than a thousand years . . . there has been a France only because there was a State, the State to keep it together, to organize it, to make it grow, to defend it not only against external threats but also against collective egotism, the rivalry of groups. Today, more than ever, the State's force is indispensable not only to assure the nation's future and its security, but also to assure the individual his liberty."[39]

Like de Gaulle before him, Pompidou recognizes that the preponderant role of the central administration in the economic and social life of the country has had at times a strangulating effect. Consequently, he too has called for decentralization and for regional reform. But his conception of decentralization has much in common with the passionate plea for decentralization that Debré made in his *La Mort de l'Etat Républicain* in 1947:[40] it seeks a deconcentration of power, by which is meant greater delegation of authority and initiative to the State's local representatives. It strongly denies the opposition's plea for decentralization, by which is meant greater local autonomy, relative financial independence, and regional assemblies elected by universal suffrage. Such autonomy, according to the *étatistes*, would fragment the nation and would constitute a serious threat to the authority of the State. Taking account of the Italian regional reform, Pompidou noted, in an important speech in Lyon, that he did not wish to create a regional level with a political character.[41] Despite some of the unfortunate consequences of centralization, he observed

[39] *Le Monde*, 29 April 1970.   [40] See pp. 66–79.
[41] *Le Monde*, 31 October 1970.

in another speech before the Conseil d'Etat, only the State can "have a complete and disinterested vision of the general interest" and only the State can "preserve the welfare of all against particular and contradictory appetites." Rather than constituting a threat to the liberty of the citizen, the State constitutes "the most solid and the best guarantee" of this liberty.[42]

The *décentralisateurs*, on the other hand, see the State as being placed in the hands of men who, if they do not constitute a self-serving class, are at any rate conservative; and to the extent that they seek above all order and stability, they are also defending certain established interests to the detriment of the national interest. The *décentralisateurs* also argue that a centralized State overburdens itself with decisions that it either cannot make or can make only badly, and that no viable reforms can be introduced without greater citizen participation. The imposition of reforms from above cannot, they maintain, be successful, and a general disillusionment with the State institutions therefore occurs. Taking cognizance of the authoritarian disposition of French institutions, General de Gaulle planned, after the uprising of May–June 1968, to devote the remainder of his term in office to introducing a greater degree of participation into these institutions.[43]

Those who have been most vocal in calling for decentralization have generally tended to regard the invocation of the preservation of the general interest by the *étatistes* as nothing more than an attempt to disguise their partiality and service to a particular class. They have therefore concluded that a greater degree of group participation would best be able to ensure the general interest. In other words, they believe that the general interest will emerge from the various competing interests.

It is evident from our own experiences in the United States, however, that there is no simple equation between group influence and wide citizen participation, or between group interest

[42] *Le Monde*, 29 April 1970. As he put it in another context: "Decentralization does not have as its aim the dismantling of the State but the very contrary, to reinforce its means where its presence is necessary and irreplaceable." *Le Monde*, 3–4 January 1971.

[43] That General de Gaulle was aware of the strangulating effect of the centralized State seems clear. There is nothing to indicate, however, that the remedies he proposed—as evidenced by his desire to introduce the profit-sharing principle to workers in their plants and his plans for regional reform —would have significantly altered the basic structure of French institutions.

26

and the national interest. The case for decentralization in France derives its major arguments, if only imperceptibly, from the pluralist theory and the Federal structure of government prevalent in the United States.[44] Paradoxically, the recent attacks in the United States on the pluralist system of democracy have based their case on the fact that a decentralized federal structure has afforded groups undue influence in policy-making, has excluded a large segment of the population from having any influence on the decisions that affect their lives, has diluted national values, has denied the existence of a national interest and, finally, has wiped out the distinction between public and private. As Grant McConnell has noted in his analysis and indictment of American democracy, excessive decentralization has kept government informal and has led to "the fragmentation of rule and the conquest of pieces of governmental authority by different groups."[45] It is not surprising, therefore, that the *étatistes* have argued that a higher authority is needed, one that is above narrow and selfish interests, in order to preserve the public interest. This is certainly not as absurd as it has been made out to be: the principle of centralization has simply been extended beyond its optimum point in France, just as in the United States the principle of decentralization has been extended to a point where the national interest cannot any longer be said to exist. As McConnell has noted: "Far from providing guarantees of liberty, equality, and concern for the public interest, organization of political life by small constituencies tends to enforce conformity, to discriminate in favor of elites, and to eliminate public values from effective political consideration. The service of a multitude of narrowly constituted political associations is often genuine. However, this service lies in the guarantee of stability and the enforcement of order, rather than in support for the central values of a liberal society."[46]

[44] Many of those in France who argue for decentralization tend to confuse the decentralized administrative structure of the United States with the economic efficiency of large American corporations. For an example of this, see Jean-Jacques Servan-Schreiber, *Le Pouvoir régional* (Paris: Grasset, 1971), pp. 68–69.

[45] Grant McConnell, *Private Power and American Democracy* (New York: Vintage Books, 1970), p. 7. We shall see in Chapter XII how even within a centralized, unitary structure that prides itself on the distinction between the public and the private, the existence of informal relations and well-organized groups may lead to a distortion of the national interest.

[46] *Ibid.*

27

The central thesis of McConnell's *Private Power and American Democracy* is that in the United States the public interest is always sacrificed to narrow interests. And it is not difficult to see why the arguments he adduces would provide powerful ammunition to the most die-hard *étatistes* in France, who are loath to see the State relinquish any of its powers.[47] Nor, as I have indicated, are the fears of the *étatistes* totally unfounded. Decentralized decision-making strengthens the power of local elites and renders them less accountable for their actions. That is why the groups that "get most of what there is to get," to paraphrase Lasswell, have recently joined the champions of primary democracy in the United States in their opposition to the power of the Federal government. We shall see in greater detail why local elites in France have been able to thwart reforms and how they have managed, despite the power of the central government, to oppose change. It is highly significant that no less a foe of oligarchy than Michels could see the dangers inherent in decentralization which, as he noted, might prevent the rise "of a single gigantic oligarchy" but which leads to "the creation of a number of smaller oligarchies, each of which is no less powerful within its own sphere."[48] While opposing the oligarchical tendencies of all forms of organization, Michels was not blind to the dangers of the movements toward decentralization. It is worth quoting the following passage from his *Political Parties*:

In the modern labor movement . . . we see decentralizing as well as centralizing tendencies at work. The idea of decentralization makes continuous progress, together with a revolt against supreme authority of the central executive. But it would be a serious error to imagine that such centrifugal movements are the outcome of the democratic tendencies of the masses, or that

[47] There have been numerous attacks in recent years on American democracy and its pluralist foundations, though McConnell's remains perhaps the most learned. For a concise and interesting critique of pluralist theory, see Robert Paul Wolff, "Beyond Tolerance," in R. P. Wolff, Barrington Moore, and Herbert Marcuse, *A Critique of Pure Tolerance* (Boston: Beacon Press, 1965), pp. 3–54. See also George D. Beam, *Usual Politics* (New York: Holt, Rinehart, and Winston, 1970); Henry S. Kariel, *The Decline of American Pluralism* (Stanford: Stanford University Press, 1961); William E. Connolly, ed., *The Bias of Pluralism* (New York: Atherton Press, 1969); Theodore J. Lowi, *The End of Liberalism* (New York: Norton, 1969).

[48] Roberto Michels, *Political Parties* (New York: Dover Publications, 1959), p. 201.

these are ripe for independence. Their causation is really of an opposite character. The decentralization is the work of a compact minority of leaders who, when forced to subordinate themselves in the central executive of the party as a whole, prefer to withdraw to their own local spheres of action (minor state, province, or commune). A group of leaders which finds itself in a minority has no love for strong national centralization. Being unable to rule the whole country, it prefers to rule at home, considering it better to reign in hell than serve in heaven.[49]

Given the evident problems posed by both administrative centralization and decentralization, the question, at once theoretical and practical, that remains may be stated in the following terms: how to achieve the desired degree of citizen participation in policy-making without permitting the fragmentation of government so that it becomes the domain of well-organized elites? A number of solutions have been offered. One has proposed the institution of primary or participatory democracy.[50] Another has concentrated on the need to alter the political system. Still a third has advocated the revamping of the economic system. It is doubtful whether any of these solutions is backed by a well-developed political theory. As Robert Nisbet recently observed with regard to the United States, the poverty of political theory and philosophy in this country has meant that critiques of society have hardly ever been accompanied by well-founded proposals for reform.[51] The same is undoubtedly true of the case against administrative centralization in France. That it is, a priori, a strong case can hardly be denied. It remains, however, to be made.

THE ADMINISTRATIVE STATE CHALLENGED

If I have pointed to some of the dangers of decentralization, as they have developed in the United States, it is not to sanction the ills that emanate from a centralized state. This study will in fact emphasize certain problems posed by rigid centralization. But,

[49] *Ibid.*, pp. 196–197.

[50] For an interesting discussion of this solution, see Robert A. Dahl, *After the Revolution?* (New Haven: Yale University Press, 1971).

[51] Robert A. Nisbet, "The Grand Illusion: An Appreciation of Jacques Ellul," *Commentary*, August 1970, p. 44.

whereas the nature of the French State has by and large gone unquestioned—save during periods of crisis—in recent years the authority of this State has been challenged incessantly. The veneration of the past has given way to the kind of criticism hitherto reserved only for the State's enemies. "Future revolutions," writes an authority on the French administration, "will doubtless be directed against the administration and not against the political system."[52]

The institution in France that today bears the brunt of attacks from the entire range of the political, economic, and social spectrum is the French administration—the State bureaucracy that, since the early part of the nineteenth century, has been charged with directing most of the State's affairs. Today the parties of the Left, Right, and Center; big business, small business, and the propertyless; the privileged and unprivileged; the intellectuals, the students, and the Unions—in effect, the French people—are agreed on what they regard as the excessive and nefarious role that the bureaucracy plays in French life. One has only to recall the attacks delivered against the "bureaucrats" and the "technocrats" during the May 1968 uprising. The cry of "dix ans, ça suffit" was aimed as much at those who administered de Gaulle's policies as at de Gaulle himself. Few Frenchmen would agree with François Gazier, former Director of the Ecole Nationale d'Administration, when he writes that "the French administration, thriving under praise and criticism alike, can at least be credited with one success: it has known how to keep in tune with its times."[53] One is tempted to say, after taking account of contemporary criticisms of the French bureaucracy, that were these words not merely the manifestation of hyperbolic tendencies commonly found in preface-writing, some courage would have been needed to write them. It is hard to conceive in present-day France of an attempt to sustain the thesis that the administration is in tune with its times.

The scorn, criticism, and vilification previously heaped on politicians and political parties appears now to have converged on the bureaucracy, which is accused of overcentralization, of technocratic power and arrogance, of bureaucratic high-handedness

[52] Charles Debbasch, *L'Administration au pouvoir: fonctionnaires et politiques dans la V*^{e} *République* (Paris: Calmann-Lévy, 1969), p. 9.

[53] François Gazier, "Introduction" to Belorgey, *Le gouvernement et l'administration de la France*, p. 7.

and inefficiency, of inefficient management of the State's affairs, and of constituting a closed caste and a ruling class—all these accusations are made by groups that have little else in common.[54] No longer is it possible to maintain, as does one student of administrative reform, that the demand for such reform is a theme of the political opposition.[55] It is, today, a theme that both the government and the opposition attempt to exploit.

The ministers of the Fifth Republic have been among the foremost critics of the administration. Albin Chalandon was among those leading the government's attacks on the State bureaucracy. "France is stifled," he once has said, "by an excessive hold of the State."[56] Even while he was a minister in the government he engaged in a war with the administrators—particularly with the corps of civil engineers—of his own ministry. "Every civil servant considers himself the owner of his post. The head of a business can give orders. A minister is obliged to convince his own Directors. This leads to an administrative totalitarianism, in the face of which public power is struck by impotence."[57]

The severe criticism directed at the administration by Couve de Murville at the time he was Prime Minister is another example. In a speech before the Alumni Association of the Ecole Nationale d'Administration, he delivered a scathing attack on the insensitivity of the French administration and on its basically un-

---

[54] The administration, so long neglected, is now the subject of innumerable books and attacks. See particularly, Club Jean Moulin, *L'Etat et le citoyen* (Paris: Seuil, 1961) and *Les Citoyens au pouvoir* (Paris: Seuil, 1968); Jean Meynaud, *La Technocratie: mythe ou réalité* (Paris: Payot, 1964); Octave Gelinier, *Le Secret des structures compétitives* (Paris: Hommes et Techniques, 1966); Philippe Bauchard, *Les Technocrates et le pouvoir* (Paris: Arthaud, 1966); Julian Cheverny, *Les Cadres* (Paris: Juillard, 1967); Jacques Mandrin, *L'Enarchie ou les mandarins de la société bourgeoise* (Paris: La Table Ronde du Combat, 1967); Philippe Bernard, *La France au singulier* (Paris: Calmann-Lévy, 1968); Edgard Pisani, *La Région . . . pour quoi faire? ou le triomphe des jacondins* (Paris: Calmann-Lévy, 1969).

[55] Albert Lanza, *Les Projets de réforme administrative en France de 1919 à nos jours* (Paris: Presses Universitaires de France, 1968), p. 160.

[56] Cited in *L'Express*, 29 September–5 October 1969, p. 62.

[57] Quoted in Michel Boyer, "M. Albin Chalandon s'en prend au corps des ponts et chaussées," *Le Monde*, 12 May 1969. In addition to having been an Inspecteur des Finances, Chalandon has also been a banker and a secretary-general of the UDR party. For his particular philosophy of the role of the state, see his article, "Comment je conçois le rôle de l'Etat," *Preuves*, 2ème trimestre (1970), and his exchange with Michel Rocard in *L'Expansion*, XXVIII (March 1970).

31

democratic character.[58] Gone, perhaps, are the days when the
leading politicians of the country told the students of this school
that they were, as General de Gaulle called them, "an elite in
every respect, an intellectual elite, a moral elite,"[59] or that their
school was, in the words of Michel Debré, "a wheel in a mechanism, the mechanism of French Democracy."[60] Far be it from any
Prime Minister or President of the Republic to praise the administration today. Only a few months after he entered the Elysée,
Georges Pompidou denounced before a solemn session of
the Cour des Comptes what he called the "administrative
labyrinths."[61]

That far-reaching administrative reforms are urgently needed
in France today is a matter that hardly anyone questions. All the
governments of the Fifth Republic have started their terms with
eloquent pledges to carry out a reform of the administrative system. Prime Minister Chaban-Delmas' celebrated characterization
of France as a *société bloquée*—a term borrowed from Stanley
Hoffmann—had the administrative system in mind; in presenting
the outlines of his planned reforms, Pompidou's former Prime
Minister attacked primarily the cumbersome State bureaucracy.[62]
Future historians of the Fifth Republic will undoubtedly see the
inertia of the Gaullist regime in this domain as one of its more
serious shortcomings. But, as M. Lanza has justly noted, "Administrative reform must be wanted, not merely wished for, by the
political bodies, which must consent to devote themselves to reforms even at the risk of meeting with difficulties and unpopular-
ity."[63] It is evident that these requirements were absent during
General de Gaulle's period of office. Nevertheless, it is well to
note that the outcry against the current state of French administration is not matched by any serious agreement on the kinds of
reforms needed.

To be sure, "Administrative reform is a political act that slow

[58] *Le Monde*, 9–10 February 1969.

[59] General Charles de Gaulle, Speech at ENA, in *Promotions*, no. 52 (1962),
11.

[60] *Michel Debré*, "Naissance et perspectives d'une institution," *Promotions*, no. 35 (1955), 27.

[61] *Le Monde*, 26 September 1969.

[62] See his speech delivered before the National Assembly on October 16,
1969. The text of this speech is printed in full in *Le Monde*, 17 October 1969.

[63] Lanza, *Les projets de réforme administrative en France*, p. 100.

32

and lengthy studies prepare but will never replace."[64] But the opposite is also true: namely, the "political act" does not negate the need for reflection and profound study. The regional reform proposal, for example, that led to the downfall of General de Gaulle was hastily prepared and ill-conceived, and demonstrated a remarkable blindness to some of the most pressing problems confronting French society, some of which it was more likely to aggravate than alleviate. Its motivations were "political" and it was not preceded by detailed study. The institutions that were to be created by this reform would not have altered the basic nature of the centralized State, would have allowed only a token participation and would, like the CODER (Commission régionale de développement économique) created in the 1964 reform, have been token institutions with no more than consultative and advisory powers. Consequently, the proposed reform appeared further to complicate the administrative system by introducing regional institutions without giving them any powers. It also left untouched the entire structure of local government, merely adding a layer without removing any of the bottom layers.[65] Finally, the claims of decentralization and participation notwithstanding, the projected reform, through the creation of Regions and regional assemblies composed of designated rather than elected personnel and lacking even rudimentary financial powers, would have served only to augment the centralized character of the State. The inertia of the Fifth Republic regarding administrative reform has also played its part in other domains—education, tax reform[66]—that have long been in need of reform. It is not at all certain, therefore, that "authoritarian regimes have originated more fundamental transformations of society and State

[64] *Ibid.*

[65] The existence of 38,000 communes in France poses numerous problems, most of which have been recognized. This has not, however, induced any government, under either the Fourth or the Fifth Republic, to undertake a thoroughgoing reform that aims at a more rational, efficient, and equitable division of the French local structure. See Club Jean Moulin, *Les citoyens au pouvoir*, and *Quelle réforme? Quelles régions?* (Paris: Seuil, 1969).

[66] An educational reform was instituted only in the wake of the May 1968 uprisings, and some measures to check fiscal fraud—which no government had dared attempt since Edgar Faure's experience in 1955—have recently been put into effect by Finance Minister Giscard d'Estaing. See *Le Monde*, 21 November 1970.

than representative regimes."[67] In fact, as Philip Williams has pointed out, the ministerial instability that characterized the Fourth Republic had the advantage of providing repeated opportunities for initiating new measures.[68]

One of the major causes cited for the general disillusionment with the Gaullist regime that led to the events of May 1968, and culminated in the downfall of General de Gaulle a year later, was that the regime was not responding to the demands of the society. Moreover, despite its authoritarian disposition and its desire to represent the *nation* through its powers of arbitration, the regime rapidly lost the impartial posture it had sought so desperately to cultivate. It became identified with certain interests. While undermining all the formal representative institutions it imperceptibly strengthened, as we shall see in this study, the power of well-organized groups; foremost among these groups was the Gaullist party itself. The regime thus came to place an increased value on "informal" government. It is perhaps not surprising that a recent survey on "Les Français et L'Etat," undertaken by SOFRES (poll) on behalf of the Interministerial Committee on Information, should find that 47 percent of the respondents regarded the State as defending the rich, against 8 percent who saw it as defending the poor. Also, 24 percent placed the State to the right of the political spectrum (as against 3 percent who placed it to the left) and 42 percent considered the State unjust or intolerant.[69]

The incessant attacks now directed at the administration can be seen as attacks on the authority of the State. In other countries the symbol of the State's authority may be the police or the army —in France the presence of the State is made evident by the ubiquitous power of its civilian representatives. The revolt against "authority" may well be a universal phenomenon that has its social, cultural, economic, and political bases. But in France the rejection of the authority of the State is perhaps more specifically a political phenomenon than it is elsewhere. Thus, for example, although the events of May 1968 originated in the universities and were (in their early phase) directed at the appall-

[67] Henry Ehrmann, *Politics in France*, p. 12.

[68] Philip M. Williams, *Crisis and Compromise: Politics in the Fourth Republic* (New York: Doubleday Anchor, 1966), p. 457.

[69] A summary of its findings may be found in Alain Duhamel, "Les Français n'aiment pas l'Etat mais ils en attendent tout," *Le Monde*, 10 October 1970.

ing conditions of French universities, it cannot be said that the main thrust of the revolt was purely pedagogic or academic. The university, as it existed in France, was undeniably related to the French political and social system. That is why the revolt spilled over so rapidly from the university to the entire society. This *political* phenomenon of the attack against authority is what Stanley Hoffmann referred to, in his analysis of protest movements in France, as the "total" nature of protests in France.[70]

If the reasons above are of a general nature and affect the State as a whole rather than the administration proper, there are other factors that pertain specifically to the bureaucracy and that explain the attacks of the last decade on the institution that "has been one of the main driving forces, if not *the* driving force, in French life."[71]

First, the distinction between politics and administration, or between politicians and administrators, appears to have been effaced under the Fifth Republic. General de Gaulle's appointment of civil servants (Couve de Murville, Chenot, Pisani, Sudreau, Chirac, Giscard d'Estaing, Chalandon, Guéna) to key ministerial posts,[72] as well as the stable nature of a regime that appeared to do away with politics and politicians,[73] brought the administration to prominence as never before. The Fourth Republic had been called "La République des députés,"[74] and the Fifth Republic has come to be seen as "La République des fonctionnaires."[75] That this is a superficial distinction between the two

---

[70] Stanley Hoffmann, "Protest in Modern France," in Morton A. Kaplan, ed., *The Revolution in World Politics* (New York: John Wiley and Sons, Inc., 1962), pp. 72–73.

[71] F. Ridley and J. Blondel, *Public Administration in France* (New York: Barnes and Noble, 1965), p. 54.

[72] A distinction needs to be made between those who, like Chalandon, Chirac, and Guéna, were elected to parliament before becoming ministers and those who, like Chenot, Couve de Murville, and Ortoli, came to occupy ministerial posts without first being elected to parliament. The former are continuing a venerable tradition that began with the Third Republic. The latter represent an innovation of the Fifth Republic.

[73] It became quite common, before May 1968, to speak of "depoliticization" in France. See Georges Vedel, ed., *La dépolitisation, mythe ou réalité* (Paris: Armand Colin, 1962).

[74] See Roger Priouret, *La République des députés* (Paris: Grasset, 1959).

[75] See Pierre Avril, *Le gouvernement de la France* (Paris: Editions Universitaires, 1968), pp. 139–154; and Debbasch, *L'Administration au pouvoir*, pp. 25–101.

will be seen later. But its superficiality as an explanation of the distinctions that characterize the two regimes does not detract from the powerful images that it has projected of them, images with which they have come to be indelibly associated.

Another related factor responsible for attacks on the administration has been the ubiquity of civil servants not only in the State apparatus, where they are naturally to be found, but in the para-administrative sector, the political sector, and the private sector. All the attacks on the administration may be regarded as in some way emanating from this one factor. It has revived the old "200 families" argument and all the charges of nepotism, personal gain, collusion, etc. It has brought into sharp focus the class divisions in French society. It has pointed to the undemocratic recruitment of French elites and to the undemocratic structure of French society. Finally, it has been seen as one of the more important explanations of the inefficiency of French institutions. Thus the training, recruitment, and career patterns of the administrators have recently been subjected to the most vigorous criticism.

Still another important reason for the persistent questioning of the administration's traditional authority has to do with the decline of representative institutions, particularly the political parties and parliament. The impotence of parliament and of the political parties is in sharp contrast to the power that the UDR (Union of Democrats for the Republic) party has come to enjoy in the past decade. Because France today has many of the features of a single-party State, the State is in some measure associated with the Gaullist party. Thus, insofar as the society is concerned, the authoritarian nature of the administration has been mirrored in the authoritarian disposition of the Fifth Republic. In attacking the government and the administration, one attacks the State.

The State's influence on society has not changed much over the past century. And if Frenchmen feel powerless to exert any influence on decisions taken on their behalf,[76] it is not at all certain

---

[76] The survey quoted above, "Les Français et l'Etat," showed that 69 percent of the respondents feel the weight of the State on their daily lives (against 27 percent who did not); 73 percent said that they felt incapable of exercising any influence on decisions affecting them, as opposed to 23 percent who felt that they could influence decisions.

that the citizen feels very differently in England, Germany, or the United States. What I have tried to suggest in this chapter is that the tensions that have characterized the relations of State and society in France have resulted from a complex dialectical relationship and not from a systematic attempt on the part of the State, dating back two hundred and fifty years, to spread its tentacles throughout society. That the State, ever since it was imbued with the Napoleonic concept of authority, has fashioned an ideology of centralized power has been shown at length. It may also be possible, however, that the Napoleonic concept of the State was more widely accepted than we have hitherto been prepared to admit. And if today the State appears reluctant to see itself in a less rigidly centralized posture, this is the result of the vested interests of its agents, of an adherence to the ideology of a centralized State, and of a profound skepticism toward the alternative, pluralist model.

PART TWO

The French Administrative Elite

CHAPTER II

Background and Recruitment of the Administrative Elite

Bureaucracy inevitably accompanies modern mass democ-
racy in contrast to the democratic self-government of small
homogeneous units. . . . Mass democracy makes a clean
sweep of the feudal, patrimonial, and—at least in intent—
the plutocratic privileges in administration. Unavoidably
it puts paid professional labor in place of the historically in-
herited avocational administration by notables.

—*Max Weber*[1]

Studies of elites in Western and non-Western societies have emphasized the crucial role of education in the recruitment of these elites.[2] The centralized nature of the French educational system and the selection procedure that characterizes it consti-tute the most important factors in the recruitment of French elites. Thus recruitment into the French higher civil service is restricted to those few who are able to overcome the rigorous selection mechanism which conforms, in all its outward manifesta-tions, to democratic norms. It is ostensibly objective and egali-tarian, depending as it does on merit and not on birth, nepotism, or patronage. In this chapter, I shall do little more than suggest the particular relationship that exists between the French educa-tional system and the background of the French administrative elite. In the next chapter, however, we will adopt a comparative perspective, attempting to view the recruitment of this elite in an

[1] Max Weber, "Bureaucracy," in H. H. Gerth and C. Wright Mills, eds., *From Max Weber: Essays in Sociology* (New York: Oxford University Press, 1958), pp. 224–225.

[2] The author of a book on the Turkish political elite, for example, begins his study with an analysis of the educational background of this elite and sees education as being the "hallmark" of the Turkish elite. See Frederick W. Frey, *The Turkish Political Elite* (Cambridge, Mass.: The M.I.T. Press, 1965), pp. 29–72.

41

intranational and cross-national perspective. Only after having presented this comparative material will we be able to deal with the crucial question of the relationship between the educational system and the social system that obtains within a society.

CONDITIONS PRECEDING THE 1945 REFORM

The candidate's rank in the *concours*, the national examination, determines his success or failure in being admitted to the select group of higher civil servants. The general *concours*, long used in recruiting the members of other French elites—teachers, scientists, engineers—came to be employed in the recruitment of French higher civil servants at a relatively late date. It was only after World War II, when the entire recruitment procedure into the upper ranks of the civil service was modified, that a certain unity was achieved.

Prior to the reform of 1945, recruitment into the French civil service was effected by means of numerous *concours*.[3] Each ministry and each corps administered its own examinations, set its own standards and steadfastly withstood attempts to curb its jurisdiction over the selection of those desiring to enter its ranks. The four most important criticisms of this system were directed against the degree of specialized training it forced on the candidates, the degree of cooptation inherent in this selection procedure, the consequent undemocratic nature of the recruitment, and the compartmentalization of the administration that resulted from numerous standards, qualifications, and loyalties. We will later explore the attempts of the 1945 reform to meet these criticisms, but it would be helpful to look at them more closely at this stage.

The qualifications necessary for passing the *concours* of a small sector of the administration required a candidate to be a rather narrow specialist. Having passed the *concours* and having been admitted to a particular corps, one was, it was felt, little qualified to serve elsewhere in the administrative sector. Consequently, narrow specialization also meant that much potential talent was inevitably lost. Moreover, the reformers argued, the training itself, because of its specialization, had to be revamped and an at-

---

[3] It has been estimated that there were about 1,200 different *concours* before 1945. See Walter R. Sharp, *The French Civil Service: Bureaucracy in Transition* (New York: Macmillan, 1931), p. 124.

tempt had to be made to give a wider and more "useful" education to those destined to serve the State.

The pre-1945 system of recruitment also led to cooptation because, as Michel Debré noted in 1945, "each *concours* [was] prepared and judged in accordance with a certain 'esprit de chapelle.' "[4] The examining jury of a corps was composed of members of that corps,[5] and there is sufficient evidence to show that more candidates whose fathers belonged to the Grands Corps gained entry into these corps before 1945 than under the new system of recruitment established after the war.[6] The pre-1945 system, which lent itself so readily to cooptation, did not lend itself to widening the social bases of the administration. Democratizing recruitment was not one of its principal preoccupations.

The fourth serious malady from which the French administration suffered was that of compartmentalization. The formation of fiefdoms, or closely-knit groups, which all analysts of French society from De Tocqueville to Crozier have seen as characterizing French society, was as evident, if not more so, within the administration as in the society at large. The existence of innumerable closed and impenetrable groups within the administrative system, all fighting for their autonomy and jurisdictions, was seen as having a detrimental effect on the formulation, coordination, and execution of policy. It gave rise to what Walter Rice Sharp referred to in 1931 as "centralization minus integration."[7] In our discussion of the Grands Corps, we shall see how some of these groups function within a centralized administrative system which, despite its pyramidal structure, nevertheless makes room for numerous, relatively autonomous groups, each with its own monopoly over a given domain. For the moment, suffice it to say that the idea of instituting a single *concours*, as a means of giving uniform training to higher civil servants destined to serve the State rather than a particular corps, was not entirely novel.[8] The

[4] Michel Debré, *Réforme de la fonction publique* (Paris: Imprimerie Nationale, 1946), p. 15.

[5] For more details on admission into the corps, especially the Grands Corps (Inspection des Finances, Cour des Comptes, and Conseil d'Etat), see Chapters IV and X.

[6] Pierre Lalumière, *L'Inspection des finances* (Paris: Presses Universitaires de France, 1959), p. 45.

[7] Sharp, *The French Civil Service*, p. 27.

[8] Although a number of politicians had expressed a desire to end the innumerable *concours* within the French bureaucracy, few were able to see

Liberation merely provided a propitious moment for such a reform. Given the characteristics of the higher civil service at that time, it was possible to describe it as constituting "a supreme and self-recruiting body immune from political intervention, responsible to no one outside its own hierarchy, a rock against which all political storms beat ineffectively and in vain; a completely closed mandarin system, even in the social choice it exercises in reproducing itself; its *esprit de corps*, the sense of belonging to a chosen elite fostered from childhood in the great boarding schools which prepare pupils for *la carrière*. These have to demonstrate their suitability to be received into the caste in the entry examination prescribed by the hierarchy."[9]

AIMS OF POSTWAR REFORM

It has been remarked that most attempts at administrative reform in France have taken place in the wake of a national crisis.[10] It took the Second World War and the Vichy experience to institute the first major administrative reform since the early part of the nineteenth century. The chief elements were the codification of regulations pertaining to the civil servant's rights, embodied in the *Statut Général des Fonctionnaires*, and the overhauling of the recruitment procedure into the upper ranks of the civil service, henceforth to be the monopoly of the newly created Ecole Nationale d'Administration. Despite its important measures, the

---

the needed reform through. Joseph Caillaux, for example, himself an Inspecteur des Finances, was very critical of the recruitment methods that existed in this day. "For a long time it has seemed to me," he wrote, "that we could have an elite of civil servants beyond compare if we were to recruit, at the same time and by the same *concours*, for all the major administrative careers; if, in other words, the Inspecteurs des Finances, the *auditeurs* at the Conseil d'Etat or at the Cour des Comptes, the officials of embassies were all interchangeable. This is how the British civil service, which has provided the British Empire with a first-rate structure, is constituted." Joseph Caillaux, *Mes Memoires*, I. *Ma jeunesse orgueilleuse, 1863–1907* (Paris: Plon, 1942), 74.

9 Herbert Luethy, *France Against Herself* (New York: Meridian Books, Inc., 1954), p. 17. It should be noted that Luethy was writing of the French civil service after the reform of 1945, yet he appears to be describing the system as it existed prior to the reform.

10 Raymond Isay, "Grands Corps et Grands Commis—Introduction," *Revue des Deux Mondes*, 15 June 1958, p. 633.

reform was scarcely a major event in the post-Liberation period. Nor was the interest of French scholars aroused. When, for example, a few years after World War II, leading American and French experts on France surveyed every aspect of French society, there was not the slightest attention paid either to the 1945 reform of the civil service or to the role of the bureaucracy in French society.[11]

It is significant that the promulgation of the *statut* was undertaken by regular legislative means, whereas the revolutionizing of the recruitment procedure, which entailed, among other things, the nationalization of the Ecole Libre des Sciences Politiques and the creation of the Ecole Nationale d'Administration, was promulgated by Ordinance. The question may legitimately be raised as to why ENA was created in 1945 by means of an Ordinance, whereas the *statut* was incorporated into a law voted by the Assembly. In the first place, it is necessary to make a distinction between 1945 and 1946. In the earlier year the regroupment of political forces, including the unions, had not been fully accomplished. Consequently, the pressure to pass a law granting extensive rights to civil servants could not be as powerful as it was to become a year later when de Gaulle had left the political scene, when the Communist party was firmly installed in the Government, and when the unions had renewed their strength.

Second, de Gaulle's decision to create ENA by means of an Ordinance was undoubtedly based on a keen awareness of the fact that no Assembly would be willing to vote into law the creation of such an institution. As he wrote in his War Memoirs, "The school, springing full-fledged from the brains and the labors of my adviser, Michel Debré, saw the light of day . . . in an atmosphere of skepticism on the part of the major bodies of public service and the parliamentary milieus."[12] The use of the Ordinance was, therefore, dictated by important tactical considerations. Nevertheless, the creation of ENA, occurring so soon after the war, must surely have appeared out of step with the priorities of the times. But, for de Gaulle, the creation of this school was an

[11] See Edward Mead Earle, ed., *Modern France: Problems of the Third and Fourth Republics* (Princeton: Princeton University Press, 1951).

[12] Charles de Gaulle, *The Complete War Memoirs of Charles de Gaulle* (New York: Simon and Schuster, 1967), p. 983. Debré himself has called ENA "mon enfant." See his *Une Certaine idée de la France* (Paris: Fayard, 1972), p. 88.

45

indispensable complement to the reforms and measures that were to follow. As he wrote in a revealing passage of his War Memoirs:

> I regarded the state . . . [as] an institution of decision, action and ambition, expressing and serving the national interest alone. In order to make decisions and determine measures, it must have a qualified arbitrator at its head. In order to execute them, it must have servants recruited and trained so as to constitute a valid and homogeneous corps in all public functions. Of these two conditions, the first was fulfilled today, and I was ready to make certain it would be so tomorrow as well; the second led me to establish the National School of Administration. . . . If the structure thus outlined became definitive, the new levers in the hands of the state would give it sufficient control over French activity for it to be able to make the nation stronger and happier.[13]

Moreover, it is important to add that, in bypassing the legislature, de Gaulle's measure allowed the Ecole Libre des Sciences Politiques, which had become a most controversial institution, to be saved by being nationalized. It is extremely doubtful whether this institution could have continued to exist, given the prevailing sentiments, had its fate been left to the Assembly.

Neither the *statut* nor the creation of ENA elicited widespread public interest. Indeed, the *statut* was passed in the Assembly almost without debate, and even outside the Assembly hardly a voice was raised to contest any of its measures.[14] Both these reforms were passed very hastily and at a moment of quasi-national unity. They were pushed through by the joint effort of Gaullists and Communists, and their chief architects were the most unlikely of bedfellows, Michel Debré and Maurice Thorez. One might wonder how Thorez was able to accept the creation of an institution whose chief function was to train higher civil servants, few of whom would come from the disadvantaged groups

[13] De Gaulle, *ibid.*, p. 780.

[14] As in a number of other areas it was left to the Vichy government to make the break with the past, for the codification of rules and regulations pertaining to civil servants was undertaken by Vichy in 1941. The *Statut des Fonctionnaires* of 1941 was abrogated by the Provisional Government in 1944. See *Journal Officiel*, Débats Parlementaires, Assemblée Nationale, October 5, 1946.

of French society. If we bear in mind, however, the enormous gains in job security, pay increases, unionization rights, and other guarantees that the *statut* promised for the majority of civil servants, we might conclude that the acceptance of ENA was a small concession that Thorez was obliged to make in order to procure these gains. For Debré the *statut* was a necessary concession in exchange for the establishment of an institution representing the fulfillment of the Napoleonic dream, a uniformly trained cadre of *grands commis*. While Debré, therefore, reserved his praise almost entirely for the recruitment aspect of the reform,[15] Thorez concerned himself solely with the *statut*,[16] which represented a remarkable achievement for him personally and for his party, the culmination of the long struggle of administrative syndicalism in France. The unity of the two major opposing forces in the France of the Liberation period undoubtedly served to depoliticize the issue of administrative reform, an issue that throughout the years of the Third Republic had been highly sensitive and political. But the agreement of the Gaullists and the Communists was not of a general nature; it was manifested on the issue of administrative reform because both sides were prepared for give-and-take. It was not repeated in the Liberation period, for even on the question of nationalization the Gaullists and Communists were severely divided.[17] It may be suggested that had the reforms inspired greater interest at the time of their implementation many pitfalls might have been avoided.

The reform brought about by the Ordinance of October 9, 1945, sought, according to the *Exposé des Motifs*, to "transform completely the method of recruitment of the categories of civil servants affected by it. It [the reform] also organizes their training, creating toward this end university institutes of political studies situated in Paris and in the provinces, a national school of administration and a center of higher administrative studies."[18] This reform was seen as merely the prelude to a much wider administrative reform to which most subsequent governments have

[15] See his *Réforme de la fonction publique*.

[16] See Maurice Thorez, *Le Statut général des fonctionnaires* (Paris, n.d.). This pamphlet was published at about the same time as Debré's *Réforme de la fonction publique*.

[17] See Georgette Elgey, *La République des illusions* (Paris: Fayard, 1965), pp. 31–35.

[18] *Journal Officiel*, Ordinances et Décrets, October 10, 1945, p. 6378.

paid lip service, but which still remains to be undertaken. The reform of 1945 sought, at any rate, to widen the training of future servants of the State and to establish "a recruitment system which opens access to State service to all who show themselves capable, without distinction of rank or fortune and without cooptation or favoritism."[19]

In addition to giving a more solid training to those destined to serve the State, the reform claimed, as Napoleon had done a century and a half earlier, to make possible the "carrière ouverte aux talents." Prior to the creation of ENA, it was the Ecole Libre des Sciences Politiques in Paris that trained the administrative elite. The Ecole Libre was a private institution—born of another disaster, the Franco-Prussian war—that had as its chief aim to provide the State with well-trained and dedicated civil servants. Almost all the highest ranking civil servants, as Table 2.1[20] shows,

TABLE 2.1

Recruitment into the Grands Corps from the Ecole Libre, 1901-1935

Corps	Total Number Admitted	Attended Ecole Libre	
		No.	%
Inspection des Finances	232	228	98.4
Conseil d'Etat	122	119	97.5
Cour des Comptes	101	88	87.0
Diplomatic Corps	285	250	87.5
Total	740	685	92.5

were trained at the Ecole Libre. Because of the particular type of training needed for passing a *concours*, a candidate was almost obliged to attend the Ecole Libre. As Lalumière noted in his study of the *Inspection des Finances*, "In fact, a serious preparation for the entrance examinations into the Grands Corps could only be undertaken in Paris. To have a real chance of passing, it

[19] Debré, *Réforme de la fonction publique*, p. 7.
[20] The figures in this table were supplied in an Ecole Libre pamphlet in 1936. See T. B. Bottomore, "Higher Civil Servants in France," in *Transactions of the Second World Congress of Sociology*, II (1954); and Pierre Lalumière, *L'Inspection des Finances*, p. 28.

was indispensable to spend one or two years at the School of the rue Saint-Guillaume. The students who studied in Paris possessed a considerable advantage over their provincial comrades. Ultimately, these preparation requirements for the entrance examinations into the Grands Corps had a foreseeable consequence: they favored the candidates with a Parisian background and they affected the social recruitment of the Grands Corps and particularly of the Inspection [des Finances]."[21]

Because of the restricted nature of its student body—a necessary consequence of high tuition fees and its Paris location—the Ecole Libre always had its share of detractors, and as early as 1881 Ferry had expressed the desire to nationalize the school. In one of the rare debates that took place in the Consultative Assembly in 1945 concerning the proposed reform, one deputy, Pierre Neumeyer, elicited a good deal of applause all around the hemicycle when he noted: "Doubtless it is necessary to do away with, as soon as possible—I think that we will all agree on this point—this school of political science which has, to be sure, provided us with fine civil servants, but whose special training was such that it did not always, to say the least, contribute to the general interest of the nation. After having served the State, the graduates of this school used to go to serve the large economic and financial organizations, if they did not already serve them while they were serving the State."[22]

The reform of 1945 nationalized the Ecole Libre, which became the Institut d'Etudes Politiques, and eleven similar institutes were to be established in the provinces.[23] Being State institutions, these institutes were to be incorporated into the universities, be tuition-free and give a wider training to their students, not all of whom were destined for an administrative career. But for those seeking such a career, recruitment, or so it was held at the time, was to be democratized by being regionalized. "We wish," said Pierre Cot, the *rapporteur*, "that they should come from every region of France and from every class of the French nation. This is why we have insisted that the Government, in its decrees, regard the Paris Institute, like the others,

[21] Lalumière, *ibid.*, p. 28.

[22] *Journal Officiel*, Débats de l'Assemblée Consultative Provisoire, June 21, 1945, p. 1166.

[23] Only seven other institutes were eventually created.

49

as a university institute and as a State institute."[24] It was therefore no longer necessary to be Parisian, or to have the means for a Paris education in order to prepare for the higher civil service. Preliminary preparation could now be undertaken at any of the Instituts d'Etudes Politiques in France, all of which were to be equipped for giving the requisite training to those wishing to take the *concours* for the newly created Ecole Nationale d'Administration.

The creation of ENA was the most important single feature of the new reform,[25] as important for what it abolished as for what it created. All higher civil servants were now to be recruited through ENA, and the various ministries and corps could no longer do their own recruiting, with each employing its own standards. The general *concours* established a uniform standard. The reform, having overcome the power of the various fiefdoms to do their own recruiting, sought to follow the traditional method by which other French elites were recruited: long and hard preparation for an examination at which all was won or lost. It is a selection system that claims to minimize subjective criteria and to maximize objective and impersonal ones,[26] so that poor and rich, Parisians and non-Parisians are on an equal footing. It is not unusual for societies like France and England, where access to education is fairly restricted, to employ selection criteria of the most objective type. We will examine the implications of this phenomenon in the next chapter.

[24] *Journal Officiel*, Débats de l'Assemblée Consultative Provisoire, June 21, 1945, p. 1175.

[25] Pierre Bouffard, "Le recruitement des cadres de la nation: l'Ecole nationale d'administration," *Revue de défense nationale*, x (January 1950), 78.

[26] The distinguished jurist, Jèze, gave the following definition of a *concours* in his *Cours de droit public*: "The *concours* is a complex operation comprising a series of acts of which the principal are the following: (1) the decision that there shall be a *concours*, fixing the date, and the period in which candidates may enroll; (2) the designation of the members of the examining board; (3) the fixing of the list of those admitted to the examinations; (4) the board's decision determining the conditions under which the tests shall be held; (5) the drawing up of the list of those successfully surviving the preliminary tests, if any, and therefore eligible to take the final group; (6) the determination of the definitive list of successful candidates to be presented, in order of merit, to the appointing authority; (7) the approval of the list by this authority, or its rejection on grounds of irregularity; (8) the appointment itself." Quoted in Sharp, *The French Civil Service*, pp. 122–123.

The uniform preparation for State service was seen as shifting loyalties from a particular corps to the State. The reformers appear to have been very much influenced by the Administrative Class of the British civil service, that is, by a group that did not have an overriding loyalty to one specialized branch of the administration but that allowed its capacities to be exploited, as the need arose, by the entire bureaucracy. Interchangeability of personnel was to be the new order of the day in the French administrative system. But if the single *concours* was instituted in the name of democracy and administrative efficiency, it was also needed to satisfy the deep urge for a uniformly trained cadre of loyal and dedicated servants of the State. All the stronger was the desire to create this cadre in view of the turmoil that characterized French politics at the Liberation. As Debré noted at the time: "The training—one need not hide this—also has a moral objective. It is not one of the missions of the school to play politics or to impose a particular doctrine. But the school must also teach its future civil servants 'le sens de l'Etat'; it must make them understand the responsibilities of the Administration, make them taste the grandeur and accept the servitudes of the *métier*."[27]

Even at the time of the reform it was apparent that the creation of ENA and the elite to which it would give rise were in contradiction with the temper of the times, which was characterized by profound disillusionment with the prewar elites. As one deputy observed: "We have not forgotten either Vichy or other periods of our history. Our organizations fear the preparation and birth of a new mandarinate—modern, no doubt, but mandarinate all the same—and we ought all to be agreed on condemning it."[28] But the government rejected the charge that its project threatened to create, or re-create, a caste system or a group of mandarins. It believed in its attempts to diversify recruitment into the administrative elite. Implicit in this optimism was the belief that an elite not wholly composed of Parisians from the upper-bourgeoisie would not strictly speaking be an elite. The State, it was believed at the time, could have its uniformly trained elite and could democratize it. As the *rapporteur* for the government's project noted in his reply to the charge that the new school might in fact turn out to be no more than a train-

[27] Debré, *Réforme de la fonction publique*, pp. 24–25.
[28] *Journal Officiel*, Débats de l'Assemblée Consultative Provisoire, June 21, 1945, p. 1116.

51

ing ground for yet another elite: "It is therefore absolutely necessary to accomplish a reform which permits France to dispose of a corps of higher civil servants closely tied to the country, as well as insure a more democratic recruitment into the higher civil service. Consequently, we congratulate the Government for having studied this problem and for having presented us with a project. We also congratulate it for having found solutions that appear to be particularly ingenious."[29]

These "ingenious" solutions were, as we have indicated, the nationalization of the Ecole Libre, the creation of the provincial Instituts d'Etudes Politiques, and the abolition of separate *concours* for entry into the higher civil service. There was one other reform that was intended to go a considerable way toward enlarging—socially rather than numerically—entry into the higher civil service. It concerned entry into ENA, which could be effected by one of two methods: the first method was reserved for students who had completed their higher education and who could present themselves at the first *concours* (*concours d'étudiants*); the second was reserved for civil servants who had completed at least five years of State service and who were under thirty years of age. They could take the second *concours* (*concours fonctionnaires*). If some of the reformers did not place much hope in the first *concours* for democratizing the civil service, they undoubtedly believed that if intelligent and enterprising civil servants who had not had the means to obtain a higher education or who had not attended, for one reason or another, the Ecole Libre, were permitted to enter the higher civil service by means of a special *concours*, the social, educational, and regional backgrounds of the upper ranks of the civil service would be greatly diversified and made more representative of the society as a whole. We turn now to an examination of the extent to which this goal was fulfilled.

CONSEQUENCES OF THE REFORM

The attention currently centered on the school is, as a former student of ENA has observed, in marked contrast to the "discreet life" the school led for many years.[30] ENA today has few admirers,

29 *Ibid.*, p. 1172.
30 Jean-François Kesler, "Les Anciens élèves de l'Ecole Nationale d'Administration," *Revue française de science politique*, XIV, no. 2 (1964), 243.

and even some of its students have recently called for its abolition,[31] thus going beyond the most bitter attack directed at the school, in 1967, by three former graduates.[32] Although much of the recent criticism has come from its students or former students, it is widely shared by the society in general. Disillusionment with the school and its curriculum is undoubtedly part of the general disillusionment with the entire French educational system. We have already noted that those who created the school sought to mold it into the traditional educational pattern; they accepted this pattern as a given and did not seek to go beyond it. A second reason for the deep malaise that now characterizes the school is that it continues to operate under the laudable principles proclaimed twenty-five years ago, principles, however, that have not been put into practice. A third reason is that the school has for the past several years been on the verge of another reform that never seems to be specified or implemented. Thus, although the goals proclaimed at the Liberation have not materialized—and this is hardly questioned any longer—no government has been willing to undertake the necessary corrective measures.[33]

As concerns the intellectual diversification of the pre-*concours* training, Table 2.2 shows at a glance the preponderant position played by the Institut d'Etudes Politiques of Paris. Just as the forerunner of this school, the Ecole Libre, prepared its students for an administrative career, so now does the IEP; and if to become a

[31] A group of students presented a series of demands in a letter to *Le Monde*. They noted: "Given these conditions, why should one be surprised at these defects of our administration: 'esprit de caste,' that is, the tendency to regard the principal administrative posts as the jealously guarded domain of a selected, in reality coopted, minority; technocracy, that is, the inability of this caste to conceive of its action within a living totality; feudalism, that is, the predisposition to conceive of the administration in terms of hierarchy and not of animation. . . . The Ecole Nationale d'Administration as it now exists must be abolished" (*Le Monde*, 22 April 1970). The class of 1972, for example, circulated a petition among its ranks asking the students in the school to refuse to accept entry into the Grands Corps. The petition was signed by two-thirds of the student body. This is discussed in Chapter III.

[32] Jacques Mandrin, *L'Enarchie ou les mandarins de la société bourgeoise* (Paris: La Table Ronde de Combat, 1967).

[33] The government of Chaban-Delmas instituted a reform of the school in September 1971. The reform aims at enlarging the social, geographic, and intellectual bases of recruitment into the higher civil service. See *Journal Officiel*, September 23, 1971, p. 9347.

53

higher civil servant under the Third Republic it was necessary to obtain a diploma from the Ecole Libre, now it is necessary to obtain one from the IEP of Paris. The danger of replicating the ills of the pre-1945 reform were evident early in the life of ENA, although it was maintained at the time that the danger would be averted by the impending educational reform. Indeed, the entire 1945 reform of the recruitment procedure was predicated on the vague but determined aspiration to reform the French educational system—an aspiration to which all politicians subscribed, but which somehow seems never to have been real-

TABLE 2.2

Educational Background of ENA Students

Year	Total No. of Candidates Admitted (First Concours)	Students with IEP Diploma		Students with Paris IEP Diploma		Students with Provincial IEP Diploma	
		No.	%	No.	%	No.	%
1949	52	41	78.9	38	73.1	3	5.8
1950	67	50	74.6	48	71.6	2	3.0
1951	71	55	77.5	47	66.2	8	11.3
1952	62	47	75.8	40	64.5	7	11.3
1953	53	37	69.8	31	58.5	6	11.3
1954	39	32	82.1	30	76.9	2	5.1
1964	62	56	90.0	53	85.7	3	4.8
1965	65	57	87.6	54	83.1	3	4.6
1966	67	57	85.0	52	77.5	5	7.5
1967	66	55	83.4	50	75.8	5	7.6
1968	70	51	72.9	48	68.6	3	4.3
1969	62	55	88.8	53	85.6	2	3.2

Source: For 1949-1954, Ecole Nationale d'Administration, *Concours d'Entrée, Statistiques*, 1954. For 1964-1969, the figures are calculated for each year separately from the appropriate annual *Statistiques*.

ized. Even in 1964, when the aura of sanctity surrounding the school had not yet diminished, its alumni noted in their journal: "The 'monopoly' exercised by the I.E.P. of Paris seems difficult to avoid. That this monopoly exists was proven recently by the results of the *concours* which showed that candidates coming from the Faculty of Law and the Faculty of Letters were at a distinct disadvantage when compared with those coming from the I.E.P. The *Institut* is in fact continuing an old tradition, for ever since Hippolyte Taine founded the Ecole Libre in 1871, Science Po's avowed aim has been to educate the political and administrative cadres of the State."[34]

It follows that in order to aspire to a career in the higher civil service, one must either be born in Paris or possess the means for studying in Paris. Table 2.3 shows the extent to which candidates for entrance into ENA are drawn from the Paris region. In his study of the Inspection des Finances, Lalumière found that for the eighty-five year period 1870–1954, 40 percent of the members of the corps were born in Paris. "It is necessary," he writes, "first to note the stability of the 40 percent figure. In particular, the transformation of the method of recruitment in 1946 has not modified it in the least. The diminution of the Parisian influence, so deeply sought by the reformers of the Liberation, has not heretofore manifested itself."[35] Moreover, Lalumière notes that two-thirds of the Inspecteurs des Finances were born in the 6th, 7th, 8th, and 16th *arrondissements*—the areas inhabited by the more well-to-do. Table 2.4 shows that the majority of those admitted into ENA through the first *concours* were educated exclusively in Paris.

The reform of 1945 has notably failed in what was considered at the Liberation its most important single feature: democratization of the higher civil service. Table 2.5 shows the extent to which higher civil servants are recruited from the upper-middle classes. It would be rash to conclude, however, that ENA has brought about no changes in the social composition of the administrative elite. As Lalumière has noted with regard to the Inspection des Finances, the *petite* bourgeoisie has profited most from the new system of recruitment, although the system has not permitted a single person whose father was either a qualified worker, a farmer, or an unqualified worker to enter the Inspection des Finances.[36] By excluding the aristocracy and the lower class (workers and farmers), the administrative elite has become strongly middle and upper-middle class in composition. As I shall argue in Chapter III, the social composition of the French admin-

---

[34] "L'Accès a l'Ecole Nationale d'Administration," *Promotion*, Special Number, no. 70 (1964), 21.

[35] Lalumière, *L'Inspection des finances*, p. 31.

[36] *Ibid.*, p. 40.

TABLE 2.3

Regional Origin of ENA Students Admitted by First Concours

| Year | Region | No. of Candidates by Region of Birth | | | | No. of Candidates by Region of Residence | | | |
| | | All Candidates | | Successful Candidates | | All Candidates | | Successful Candidates | |
		No.	%	No.	%	No.	%	No.	%
1953	Paris	215	29.8	21	39.6	452	62.5	39	73.6
	Other	508	70.2	32	60.4	271	37.5	14	26.4
	Total	723	100.0	53	100.0	723	100.0	53	100.0
1954	Paris	235	32.3	16	41.1	497	68.3	35	89.7
	Other	492	67.7	23	58.9	230	31.7	4	10.3
	Total	727	100.0	39	100.0	727	100.0	39	100.0
1955	Paris	181	34.6	8	25.0	353	67.5	22	68.7
	Other	343	65.4	24	75.0	171	32.5	10	31.3
	Total	524	100.0	32	100.0	524	100.0	32	100.0
1956	Paris	176	39.4	40	50.1	315	70.7	66	83.5
	Other	270	60.6	39	49.9	131	29.3	13	16.5
	Total	446	100.0	79	100.0	446	100.0	79	100.0
1959	Paris	116	35.6	24	52.1	233	71.4	39	84.8
	Other	210	64.6	22	47.9	93	28.6	7	15.2
	Total	326	100.0	46	100.0	326	100.0	46	100.0
1965	Paris	136	27.0	21	32.3	417	82.9	58	89.2
	Other	369	73.0	44	67.7	86	17.1	7	10.8
	Total	505	100.0	65	100.0	503	100.0	65	100.0
1966	Paris	183	31.7	30	44.7	442	76.6	55	82.1
	Other	394	68.3	37	55.3	135	23.4	12	17.9
	Total	577	100.0	67	100.0	577	100.0	67	100.0
1967	Paris	202	32.2	24	36.4	478	76.0	59	89.4
	Other	427	67.8	42	63.6	151	24.0	7	10.6
	Total	629	100.0	66	100.0	629	100.0	66	100.0
1968	Paris	276	36.4	25	35.7	566	74.6	59	84.3
	Other	482	63.6	45	64.3	192	25.4	11	15.7
	Total	758	100.0	70	100.0	758	100.0	70	100.0
1969	Paris	307	40.5	38	61.2	547	72.2	57	91.4
	Other	451	59.5	24	38.8	211	27.8	5	8.6
	Total	758	100.0	62	100.0	758	100.0	62	100.0

Source: Calculated from annual, Ecole Nationale d'Administration, *Concours d'Entrée, Statistiques*, 1953-1959 and 1965-1969.

istrative elite differs not at all from the composition of other French elites, nor does it differ in this respect from the administrative elites of other countries.

The social composition of the French administrative elite becomes narrower as one approaches the apex of the pyramid. Lalumière notes that 84 percent of the 165 Inspecteurs des Finance who entered the corps before 1947, and 68 percent of those who entered through ENA, came from the highest social classes in the country.[37] The same is true of the other corps. Prior to

TABLE 2.4

Educational Origin of First Concours *Candidates: Paris vs. Provinces,*
1953-1969

Year	Total No. of Candidates Admitted		Educated in Paris		Educated in Provinces		Unaccounted for[1]	
	No.	%	No.	%	No.	%	No.	%
1953	53	100.0	35	66.0	6	11.3	12	22.7
1954	39	100.0	31	79.5	2	5.1	6	15.4
1955	32	100.0	21	65.5	3	9.5	8	25.0
1956	32	100.0	23	71.9	2	3.8	7	24.3
1958	33	100.0	26	78.6	1	3.2	6	18.2
1959	46	100.0	40	86.9	2	4.4	4	8.7
1960	43	100.0	33	76.7	6	14.0	4	9.3
1961	60	100.0	52	86.6	7	11.7	1	1.7
1962	71	100.0	69	97.2	2	2.8	0	0.0
1963	70	100.0	67	95.7	1	1.4	2	2.9
1964	62	100.0	57	91.9	3	4.8	2	3.3
1965	65	100.0	60	92.2	3	4.6	2	3.2
1966	67	100.0	59	88.0	5	7.5	3	4.5
1967	66	100.0	57	86.3	3	4.6	6	9.1
1968	70	100.0	57	81.4	2	2.9	11	15.7
1969	62	100.0	56	90.3	2	3.3	4	6.4

[1]This column includes those who obtained only a *licence*. Although the source from which these data are derived does not specify the university from which the diploma was obtained, it is highly probable that it was obtained in Paris.

Source: Calculated from Ecole Nationale d'Administration, *Concours d'Entrée, Statistiques*. The figures in the table are calculated for each year from the appropriate annual *Statistiques*.

[37] *Ibid.*

TABLE 2.5
Social Origin of Students Entering ENA by First Concours (number)

Social Origin	1953 Candi-dates	1953 Ad-mitted	1956 Candi-dates	1956 Ad-mitted	1959 Candi-dates	1959 Ad-mitted	1962 Candi-dates	1962 Ad-mitted	1965 Candi-dates	1965 Ad-mitted	1969 Candi-dates	1969 Ad-mitted
Administration: A1	24	2	21	4	19	5	19	9	45	7	36	13
A2	140	15	104	8	68	5	79	11	78	7	134	5
B	63	–	26	1	12	–	16	3	17	–	72	6
C	13	–	8	–	5	1	6	–	10	–	16	1
D	2	–	3	–	4	–	2	–	2	–	–	–
Total Administration	242	17	162	13	108	11	122	23	152	14	258	25
Artisans & shopkeepers	126	6	57	4	29	1	52	6	65	9	53	3
Heads, industrial enterprises	23	3	20	4	13	3	23	6	21	2	40	6
Commercial employees (cadre)	128	11	83	3	74	16	73	11	115	18	165	6
Industrial employees (low-level)	50	1	30	2	18	5	26	4	22	2	23	–
Technicians	–	–	1	–	3	–	2	–	1	–	43	6
Liberal professions	97	10	73	5	58	5	84	19	93	17	134	15
Workers	13	1	2	–	4	1	7	–	4	–	6	–
Farmers	29	2	11	1	12	4	13	–	18	2	20	1
Landowners, proprietors, or without profession	12	2	7	–	5	–	3	2	6	1	–	–
Profession not indicated	3	–	–	–	2	–	4	–	6	–	16	–
Total other than Adm.	481	36	284	19	218	35	287	48	351	51	500	37
Total, all social origins	723	53	446	32	326	46	409	71	503	65	758	62

Source: Calculated for each year separately, from Ecole Nationale d'Administration, Concours d'Entré, Statistiques.

1939, for example, the diplomatic corps contained not one person with a working-class background, and only a small percentage whose parents were deputies, teachers, or members of one of the liberal professions.[38]

The widening of the geographic and social origins of members of the higher civil service results from allowing civil servants to enter ENA by means of a special second *concours*. Table 2.6 shows that members of this group do not tend to be Parisian to the same degree as those who enter through the first *concours*, although here again those whose "residence," as opposed to "region of birth," is Paris have a greater chance of being admitted than those who are born and continue to reside in the provinces. Table 2.7 shows that the social background of the second *concours* entrants is not only more diversified than that of the first *concours* entrants, but is distinctly less upper-class. To some extent, then, the institution of a special *concours* for officials has widened the class basis of the higher civil service. One should not, however, exaggerate the significance of the evident contrast in background.

In the first place, as Table 2.8 indicates, the number of those entering ENA by the second *concours* has declined in proportion to those who enter by the first.[39] Second, the number, in both relative and absolute terms, of those entering ENA by the second *concours* is simply too small to make much difference to the social composition of the higher civil service as a whole. Third, it is not at all certain that the second *concours* now attracts the type of official it was intended to attract. That many officials are discouraged from the outset may be inferred from the small numbers of those who now present themselves as candidates when compared to the large numbers who presented themselves in the first decade of the school's existence. Recruitment through the second *concours* puts undue pressure on civil servants, who are

---

[38] H. Langier, Weinberg and Charretier, "Le Recrutement du personnel du Ministère des Affaires Etrangères avant la guerre de 1939," in Alain Girard, *Le Réussite sociale en France* (Paris: Presses Universitaires de France, 1961), p. 299.

[39] There is no longer a fixed number of places for civil servant entrants into ENA. If, as a group, they do not perform as well as the students taking the first *concours*, then the latter come to occupy more of the vacant places. Originally, it was planned that civil servants would account for half the student body of ENA.

TABLE 2.6
Regional Origin of Civil Servants Admitted into ENA by Second Concours

Year	Region	No. of Candidates by Region of Birth				No. of Candidates by Region of Residence			
		All Candidates		Successful Candidates		All Candidates		Successful Candidates	
		No.	%	No.	%	No.	%	No.	%
1953	Paris	101	18.9	11	26.2	255	47.5	19	45.3
	Other	435	81.1	31	73.8	281	52.5	23	54.7
	Total	536	100.0	42	100.0	536	100.0	42	100.0
1954	Paris	61	13.2	10	24.4	205	46.0	25	61.0
	Other	384	86.8	31	75.6	240	54.0	16	39.0
	Total	445	100.0	41	100.0	445	100.0	41	100.0
1955	Paris	53	18.5	9	29.1	142	49.5	20	64.5
	Other	234	81.5	22	70.9	145	50.5	11	35.5
	Total	287	100.0	31	100.0	287	100.0	31	100.0
1956	Paris	45	20.6	5	17.8	98	44.8	17	60.7
	Other	174	79.4	23	82.2	121	55.2	11	39.3
	Total	219	100.0	28	100.0	219	100.0	28	100.0
1959	Paris	20	20.2	2	14.3	54	54.5	7	50.0
	Other	79	79.8	12	85.7	45	45.5	7	50.0
	Total	99	100.0	14	100.0	99	100.0	14	100.0
1965	Paris	27	21.8	4	12.9	76	61.3	20	64.5
	Other	97	78.2	27	87.1	48	38.7	11	35.5
	Total	124	100.0	31	100.0	124	100.0	31	100.0
1966	Paris	37	26.4	7	24.2	99	70.7	22	75.8
	Other	103	73.6	22	75.8	41	29.3	7	24.2
	Total	140	100.0	29	100.0	140	100.0	29	100.0
1967	Paris	33	28.2	10	30.4	104	69.3	24	72.7
	Other	117	71.8	23	69.6	46	30.7	9	27.3
	Total	150	100.0	33	100.0	150	100.0	33	100.0
1968	Paris	41	24.8	6	17.2	116	70.3	29	82.9
	Other	124	75.2	29	82.8	49	29.7	6	17.2
	Total	165	100.0	35	100.0	165	100.0	35	100.0
1969	Paris	43	25.9	13	42.0	107	64.4	26	83.9
	Other	123	74.1	18	58.0	59	35.6	5	16.1
	Total	166	100.0	31	100.0	166	100.0	31	100.0

Source: Calculated from annual, Ecole Nationale d'Administration, *Concours d'Entrée, Statistiques,* 1953-1959 and 1965-1969.

TABLE 2.7

Social Origin of Civil Servants Entering ENA by Second Concours (number)

Social Origin	1953 Candidates	1953 Admitted	1956 Candidates	1956 Admitted	1959 Candidates	1959 Admitted	1962 Candidates	1962 Admitted	1965 Candidates	1965 Admitted	1969 Candidates	1969 Admitted
Administration: A1	10	2	2	–	1	–	2	1	8	3	10	3
A2	84	11	32	6	20	2	17	4	21	7	17	3
B	68	8	23	5	14	5	8	1	8	2	31	4
C	37	–	23	2	15	1	14	3	11	3	10	2
D	12	1	4	–	4	–	5	1	4	–	–	–
Total Administration	211	22	82	13	54	8	46	10	52	15	68	12
Artisans & shopkeepers	94	6	38	3	7	1	17	1	26	5	14	–
Heads, industrial enterprises	4	–	–	–	–	–	2	–	–	–	5	1
Commercial employees (cadre)	36	5	20	6	7	2	9	2	8	2	6	1
Industrial employees (low-level)	59	2	23	1	11	1	24	3	14	4	9	1
Technicians	–	–	6	1	1	1	–	–	2	–	19	5
Liberal professions	14	4	13	–	3	–	7	3	8	2	15	3
Workers	23	1	13	4	4	–	12	1	6	1	12	2
Farmers	6	2	15	–	7	–	10	2	7	2	16	6
Landowners, proprietors, or without profession	4	–	4	–	2	1	2	–	1	–	–	–
Profession not indicated	2	–	3	–	3	–	1	–	–	–	2	–
Total other than Adm.	453	20	217	15	45	6	84	12	72	16	98	19
Total, all social origins	664	42	299	28	99	14	130	22	124	31	166	31

Source: Calculated for each year separately, from Ecole Nationale d'Administration, *Concours d'Entrée, Statistiques.*

obliged to spend several years studying for an examination under less than ideal circumstances. They are older than the first *concours* students, they hold full-time jobs, and they tend to be married and have larger families than their first *concours* counterparts. Table 2.9 shows, in effect, that those with smaller families are more inclined to undergo the long preparation for the examination, as well as more likely to be successful in the examination.

TABLE 2.8

Number of ENA Entrants by Method of Entry, 1952-1969

Year	Total Candidates Admitted	Admitted through First Concours		Admitted through Second Concours	
		No.	%	No.	%
1952	129	62	48.1	67	51.9
1953	95	53	55.8	42	44.2
1954	80	39	48.7	41	51.3
1955	63	32	50.8	31	49.2
1956	60	32	53.4	28	46.6
1958	60	33	55.0	27	45.0
1959	60	46	76.5	14	23.5
1960	60	43	71.5	17	28.5
1961	78	60	76.9	18	23.1
1962	93	71	76.3	22	23.7
1963	93	70	75.3	23	24.7
1964	81	62	76.5	19	23.5
1965	96	65	67.7	31	32.3
1966	96	67	69.7	29	30.3
1967	99	66	66.6	33	33.4
1968	105	70	66.6	35	33.3
1969	93	62	66.6	31	33.4

Source: Ecole Nationale d'Administration, *Concours d'Entrée, Statistiques, 1952-1969.*

The State does not make adequate provision for civil servants who wish to prepare for the ENA examination, nor do these officials receive, on the whole, much encouragement from their peers or superiors. They are often looked upon with a good deal of suspicion because their preparation for the *concours* and their desire to enter ENA is taken as an indication of dissatisfaction with their present positions. Consequently, if civil servants wish to prepare for the second *concours* they must generally accept

TABLE 2.9

Family Situation of ENA Entrants by Method of Entry, 1960-1969

Marital Status	First Concours				Second Concours			
	No. of Candidates	%	No. Admitted	%	No. of Candidates	%	No. Admitted	%
Bachelor	4,358	87.9	557	87.5	363	26.2	52	20.2
No children	367	7.4	49	7.7	266	19.1	50	19.5
1 child	208	4.2	28	4.4	313	22.5	64	24.9
2 children	22	.4	2	.4	280	20.2	65	25.3
3 "	3 } .1		—	—	119	8.6	19	7.4
4 "	1 }		—	—	23	1.7	7	2.7
5 "	—	—	—	—	16	1.2	—	—
6 "	—	—	—	—	4	.3	—	—
7 "	—	—	—	—	1 }		—	—
8 "	—	—	—	—	1 } .2		—	—
12 "	—	—	—	—	1 }		—	—
Total	4,959	100.0	636	100.0	1,387	100.0	257	100.0

Source: Calculated from annual, Ecole Nationale d'Administration, *Concours d'Entrée, Statistiques,* 1960-1969.

a considerable amount of tension in their everyday working relations with their colleagues. And even when they have been admitted to ENA, these civil servants come to be regarded in some sense as second-class citizens because they managed "to slip in through the back door" by means of a "special" examination.

BACKGROUND OF TOP ADMINISTRATORS

Since this study bears largely on those who occupy the highest posts within the administration proper—the Directors and Directors General of the central administration—a brief examination of the backgrounds of those who occupied these posts between 1946 and 1969 is in order.[40]

Geographic origin

Of the 440 Directors who occupied their posts between 1946 and 1969, approximately one-third were born in the Paris region,

[40] Some additional data are provided by a cohort analysis.

which accounts for only 18 percent of the nation's population (see Table 2.10). This accords with the data available on all elites in French society. In his study of over 2,500 members of diverse elites in France—the "Contemporary Personalities," as they are referred to in the study—whose names figured in the *Dictionnaire bibliographique français contemporain*, Girard found that Paris was the birthplace of 34 percent of this group.[41] Our cohort analysis indicated that Paris, as the birthplace of those occupying the highest posts in the administration, has been gaining in importance (Table 2.11 and Graph 2.1), and that the

TABLE 2.10

Regional Origin of Directors Compared to Total Population

Region of Birth	(A) Population in Millions	(B) Percent of Total Population	(C) Number of Directors[1]	(D) Percent of Directors	(E) Index of Representativity[2] B/D
Paris	8	18.0	42	35.0	+ 0.32
Center	5	11.2	9	7.5	- 0.20
East	4.5	9.0	10	8.4	- 0.03
West	6	13.5	14	11.6	- 0.08
North	7	15.6	5	4.2	- 0.58
Northeast	4	9.0	6	5.0	- 0.28
Northwest	1	2.2	0	0.0	- 1.00
South	3	6.8	9	7.5	+ 0.05
Southeast	3	6.8	7	5.8	- 0.05
Southwest	3	6.8	12	10.0	+ 0.19
Corsica	.5	1.1	3	2.5	+ 0.39
Outside Metropole	—	—	3	2.5	—
Total	45	100.0	120	100.0	

[1] Occupied post in 1963.
[2] Index derived as follows: $\left(E = \dfrac{D-B}{D+B} \right)$

administrative elite is being recruited to a greater extent than before from large urban centers. Table 2.11 shows that the percentage of those born in large towns, including Paris, increased from a low of 10 percent during the 1897–1900 period to a

[41] Girard, *La Réussite sociale en France*, p. 78.

high of 78.7 percent in 1921 and after. During the same periods, on the other hand, the percentage of those born in towns of under 10,000 inhabitants decreased from a high of 70 percent to a low of 7.1 percent. There appears to be an unequivocal trend toward the recruitment of Directors from large towns. The bias in favor of the Paris region is equally evident (Graph 2.1). This bias is undoubtedly greater than our data indicate for, as in the case of those entering ENA (Tables 2.3 and 2.4), the Paris area is adopted as the place of residence by a large proportion of those who are born outside it.

TABLE 2.11

Correlation of Directors' Age with Size of Birthplace (percent)

Population	71 and over	70-67	66-63	62-59	58-55	54-51	50-47	46-43	42 and under
Over 100,000 (including Paris)	50.0	0.0	10.0	45.5	32.0	38.4	42.0	58.5	78.7
50,000-100,000	50.0	0.0	10.0	0.0	12.0	19.2	5.3	0.0	0.0
10,000-50,000	0.0	50.0	10.0	9.0	12.0	0.0	21.0	33.3	7.1
Under 10,000	0.0	50.0	70.0	45.5	40.0	42.4	26.4	8.2	7.1
Outside Metropole	0.0	0.0	0.0	0.0	4.0	0.0	5.3	0.0	7.1
Total	100.0	100.0	100.0	100.0	100.0	100.0	100.0	100.0	100.0

The conclusion Girard reached in his Contemporary Personalities study, that "in each region, the *département* that includes the largest urban center is always the most highly represented," neither wholly confirms nor contradicts our data. Girard divided France into regions and examined only the subject's *département* of birth, not the actual town. In our own study, however, in addition to dividing France into regions and *départements*, we examined the subject's actual place of birth and its size (Table 2.12). Nevertheless, taking an overall view, we are bound to concur in Girard's conclusion that "a large diffusion across the country can be observed."[42] Our analysis of the place of birth of the 440 Di-

[42] *Ibid.*, p. 89.

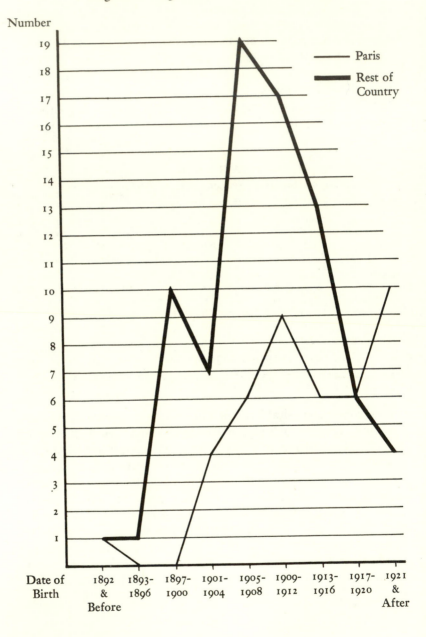

Graph 2.1 Number and Age of Directors According to
Region of Origin: Paris vs. Rest of Country

TABLE 2.12

Percent of Directors, According to Size of Birthplace

Size of Town	%
Born in Paris or Paris region	35.0
Born in town with population of 100,000 or over (except Paris)	7.5
Born in town with population of 50,000-100,000	9.2
Born in town with population of 10,000-50,000	11.7
Born in town with population of under 10,000	34.7
Born outside France	2.5
Total	100.0

rectors showed that every *département* was represented, however minimally.[43]

Educational background

In the educational background of the Directors there is greater homogeneity than in geographical origin, owing primarily to the preeminence of Paris as the educational and intellectual capital. This can be seen not only in the case of a university education (Table 2.13), but also in the case of *lycée* education (Table

TABLE 2.13

Place of Secondary and Higher Education of Directors

Place	%
Attended university in Paris, but not *lycée*	35.8
Entire education in Paris	42.0
Educated in Paris and provinces	3.7
Attended *lycées* in Paris and in provinces, but university only in Paris	4.1
Educated only in provinces	6.2
Unaccounted for	8.2
Total (N=440)	100.0

[43] We might add that, in general, the diversity of birthplaces of the administrative elite is slightly greater than that of other elites in French society. See *ibid.*, p. 80.

2.14). It is highly significant that one-third of the administrative elite attended one of the elite Parisian *lycées*, and over half had received all or part of their secondary education in Paris. Moreover, only 6 percent of this group received its entire (secondary and higher) education in the provinces. Consequently, whether one is born in Paris or not, it is well-nigh indispensable to be educated in Paris if one is to succeed. This is as true for a career in the administration as it is for other fields of endeavor. There is little need to dwell on the data presented in Tables 2.13 and 2.14.

TABLE 2.14
Paris Lycées Attended by Directors

Lycée		%
Louis-le-Grand		12.3
Henry IV		6.2
Janson-de-Sailly		9.9
Saint-Louis		3.7
Lycée Montaigne		1.2
Lycée Condorcet		3.7
Other Parisian *lycées*		19.8
Total	(N = 440)	56.8

They raise, however, a crucial question that will be treated in detail in the next chapter: the relationship between social origins and academic success. As Girard noted in his Contemporary Personalities study: "In order to achieve real success, birth into a favorable milieu constitutes a very useful, if not an almost indispensable springboard. If privileges have been legally abolished, French society has substituted for them a certain number of selective tests, the examinations and the *concours* which presuppose a higher education. Now, the great majority of people studied, 85 per cent, have acquired precisely such an education, which they have been able to obtain because they belong to a milieu where this is considered a rule. Herein lies the problem of social recruitment of students, a problem posed in an indirect way."[44]

[44] *Ibid.,* p. 103.

Social Origin

We have already noted the high social origin, based on father's occupation, of entrants into ENA. The social background of the present generation of Directors differs slightly from the above (Table 2.15), since not all of them are ENA graduates. In the next generation, however, this difference will be eliminated, since the highest administrative (nontechnical) posts will come to be occupied exclusively by ENA graduates. When we examine the social origins of Directors based on grandfathers' occupations (Table 2.15, cols. B and C) we get a different picture: the highest social categories are markedly less represented, the lowest much more so. This would indicate that a certain upward mobility has taken place within two generations. From the information we obtained

TABLE 2.15

Social Origin of Directors, According to Occupations of Father, Grandfather, and Father-in-Law

Occupation	(A) Father		(B) Paternal Grandfather		(C) Maternal Grandfather		(D) Father-in-law	
Civil Servant:								
Higher	12.2		2.5		5.1		9.0	
Medium level	5.8	22.6	3.8	14.0	2.5	19.0	2.5	16.6
Lower	4.6		7.7		11.4		5.1	
Business:								
Big	13.8		11.4		8.8		15.1	
Small	4.9	22.0	6.3	30.5	5.1	24.9	6.3	25.2
Shopkeeper	3.3		12.8		11.0		3.8	
Teaching:								
Professor	9.4		3.8		3.8		3.8	
Secondary-school	2.7	12.1	3.8	7.6	1.2	5.0	2.5	6.3
Liberal professions	20.9		15.1		15.0		18.8	
Military	—		—		3.8		12.8	
Low-level employee:	7.9		5.1		7.7		7.7	
Worker	0.7		11.4		11.0		—	
Artisan	2.4		6.3		5.1		2.5	
Peasant	2.7		7.7		9.0		2.5	
Artist	2.1		—		1.2		2.5	
No occupation	6.6		2.3		—		2.6	
Total	100.0		100.0		100.0		100.0	
	(N = 440)		(N = 78)		(N = 78)		(N = 78)	

on the occupations of the maternal and paternal grandfathers of a sample of the Directors, we are able to conclude that the administrative elite has profited, as much as the society as a whole, from a cross-generational upward mobility. The classical three-generational climb to high social status may be speeded up by marrying above one's class, as is the case with a small proportion of the administrative elite (Table 2.15, col. D). It is difficult to compare this data with Girard's Contemporary Personalities study because he obtained no information on the grandfathers'

TABLE 2.16

Distribution According to the Father's and Grandfather's Occupation of Persons Belonging to the Highest Social Categories

Profession	Industrialists & Liberal Professions		Executives & Higher Civil Servants	
	Father %	Grand-father %	Father %	Grand-father %
Industrialists and liberal professions	32	16	12	7
Executives and higher civil servants	11	6	17	11
Shopkeepers and artisans	23	25	22	20
Employees and medium and low-level civil servants	17	11	27	13
Workers and unskilled laborers	10	12	10	14
Farmers	7	28	8	30
Farm workers	0	2	4	5
Total	100	100	100	100

Source: Population, no. 3 (1950), and Girard, *La Réussite sociale en France,* p. 339.

occupations. However, using the data of a study completed in 1950 on the highest social category of French society (Table 2.16), Girard noted that the comparison between the father's and grandfather's occupation did indeed indicate a clearly discernible upward mobility, and he concluded that "one or two generations, and perhaps more, were therefore incontestably necessary for a large number of people in the highest social categories to attain their present position."[45]

We have examined the background of the French administrative elite and have seen that ENA has brought about few of the desired changes in the composition of this elite. We must now attempt to explain why the administrative elite, like other elites in French society, is always recruited from the same social classes.

[45] *Ibid.*, p. 340.

CHAPTER III

Education and Social Structure

"Democracy" takes an ambivalent attitude towards the system of examinations for expertise. . . . On the one hand, the system of examinations means, or at least appears to mean, selection of the qualified from all social strata in place of the rule by notables. But on the other, democracy fears that examinations and patents of education will create a privileged "caste," and for that reason opposes such a system.

—*Max Weber*[1]

The Administrative Class type was not created by Open Competition. Open Competition served to perpetuate a type which had already come to the top.

—*Henry Parris*[2]

The data presented in the last chapter illustrate an irrefutable fact: the French administrative elite is undemocratically recruited because it does not adequately reflect the society's groups and classes. In and of itself this fact tells us little about (a) whether this is peculiar to the administrative elite or whether it is true of other elites in French society; (b) whether administrative elites in other societies are more representative of these societies' social classes than is the French one; and (c) whether the social background of the French administrative elite circumscribes and defines a priori its mode of behavior. This chapter will be concerned with the first two questions, and the third will be discussed in Chapter IV.

ELITES IN FRENCH SOCIETY

In comparing the background of the administrative elite with that of other elites in French society, we find that there is

[1] Max Weber, *Economy and Society: An Outline of Interpretive Sociology*, III (New York: Bedminster Press, 1968), 999.

[2] Henry Parris, *Constitutional Bureaucracy* (London: George Allen and Unwin Ltd; 1969), p. 159.

a marked homogeneity in origins. In other words, the administrative elite is no more unrepresentative of the society than are the others. The available evidence suggests that all elites in French society are equally unrepresentative of that society.

In the Contemporary Personalities study, Girard found that "there exists a large homogeneity in the social recruitment of the various elites" and he concluded that "*success comes above all to those who, from the start, were blessed with advantages inherent in their milieu.*"[3] Thus, taking the various elites together, 81 percent represented groups comprising no more than 15 percent of the population. In effect this figure is slightly higher than that for the administrative elite.

TABLE 3.1

Social Origin of Contemporary Personalities, According to Father's Occupation (percent)

Workers	2
Peasants	6
Shopkeepers and artisans	11
Employees, civil servants, and medium-level executives	19
Executives, liberal professions, and higher civil servants	62
Total	100

Source: Girard, *La Réussite sociale en France*, p. 91.

Girard also undertook, in addition to the Contemporary Personalities survey, a study of a sample of students from four *grandes écoles*—Polytechnique, Ecole Normale Supérieure, Ecole Centrale and the Institut Agronomique. Again the results show that two-thirds of these students came from the most favored groups of French society.

In comparing the social origins of the students of ENA with those of the Grandes Ecoles students, Girard noted: "The conclusion is clear. The Ecole Nationale d'Administration recruits its students, from a social point of view, as do the other grandes écoles; that is, from the most favored segment of the population."[4] Since our purpose here is to compare the background of

[3] Alain Girard, *La Réussite sociale en France* (Paris: Presses Universitaires de France, 1961), p. 93. Italics in original.
[4] *Ibid.*, p. 309.

73

TABLE 3.2

Social Origin of Grandes Ecoles Students (percent)

Workers	2
Peasants	6
Shopkeepers and artisans	11
Employees, low and medium-level civil servants	15
Upper cadres, liberal professions, executives, and higher civil servants	66
Total	100

Source: Girard, *La Réussite sociale en France*, p. 191.

the administrative elite with that of other elites in French society, we may observe that the recruitment of the former is no more socially restricted than is the case for the other elites. In fact, a close look at Table 3.3 shows that the percentage of those re-

TABLE 3.3

Social Origin of Grandes Ecoles Students,
According to School and Father's Occupation (percent)

Father's Occupation	Poly-tech-nique	Cen-trale	Agro	Normale Supe-rieure	Combined Four Schools	ENA 1952-1958
Workers	2	3	3	2	2.3	3.7
Peasants	2	3	19	2	6.0	3.1
Shopkeepers and artisans	11	12	10	12	11.2	12.7
Employees	5	4	4	6	4.5	6.4
Low and medium-level civil servants	11	9	10	16	10.6	12.3
Medium and upper cadres	22	26	21	16	22.7	18.1
Liberal professions	7	8	7	11	7.4	9.7
Higher civil servants	21	9	18	28	16.5	27.8
Heads of private enterprise	19	26	8	7	18.8	4.0
Rentiers, proprietors, and without profession	–	–	–	–	–	2.2
Total	100	100	100	100	100.0	100.0

Source: Girard, *La Réussite sociale en France*, p. 309.

cruited from the lower social strata (the first five occupations listed in the table) is highest for the Institut Agronomique and second highest for ENA. We can, however, conclude that the recruitment of all five schools, as of the various elites, is socially restricted and may, to a considerable extent, be accounted for by the hereditary factor. As Girard observes: "The schools are differentiated by the varying proportions of students belonging to a given milieu—depending on the particular vocation of the school—but in each case, only high social categories are involved: there are more sons of civil servants at ENA and at Normale Supérieure, of farmers at the Institut Agronomique, of engineers and heads of enterprises at Centrale and Polytechnique. To the strictly social aspect is always linked, with regard to the choice of a career, a hereditary aspect, which itself is linked to the milieu."[5]

Lest the presentation of these data be misinterpreted, it is important to emphasize that a case is not being made here, by what may inadvertently appear to be the use of a relativist argument, for the democratic recruitment of the French administrative elite. The data presented in the last chapter, as in this one, show the contrary. But the data presented above also show that if the recruitment of the administrative elite is characterized by undemocratic traits, it shares these traits with all other elites in French society. Why this should be the case will be explained presently.

I have used the terms "democratic" and "representative" recruitment more or less interchangeably because the attempt to democratize the recruitment of elites in France has usually meant no more than the desire to insure more equal representation of the various social classes. Yet any elite should be judged by the dual criteria of representativeness of and responsiveness to the society. This chapter is concerned solely with the first of these.

CROSS-NATIONAL COMPARISONS OF ADMINISTRATIVE ELITES

Given that the French administrative elite, like other elites in France, is not representative of the society, we may ask whether this reveals some important traits of French society or whether it indicates characteristics that inhere in the recruitment of elites in general. The answer is both: the socially restricted nature of

[5] *Ibid.,* p. 310.

the French elites is grounded, as we shall see presently, in a severely selective educational system, a system in which social
status is closely related to academic success. But while other societies may possess less restrictive educational systems, they, too,
exhibit a correlation between social status and academic success.
To illustrate this point, brief references to the recruitment of administrative elites of other countries will be helpful.

In his study of the recruitment of British higher civil servants,
Kelsall noted that the higher the rank the more socially restricted
was its recruitment. "The gulf separating the Administrative
Class from the lower classes of the Service was a social one. . . ."[6]
The social status of the members of the Administrative Class was
related to the types of schools they attended and to their academic success. Cambridge and Oxford, for example, provided
about 85 percent of open competition entrants.[7] There was, moreover, a correlation between the type of school attended and performance on the examinations: those who succeeded, by a far
greater proportion than those who failed, had attended boarding
schools.[8] The high social origins of the Administrative Class of
the British civil service have been adequately documented by
others[9] as well as Kelsall. But here again, a student of British administration has recently argued, in his castigation of the Fulton
Commission's Report, that the British civil service has actually
mirrored British society, so that if the service has defects,
it shares them with other institutions in the society. "If there is
an excessive proportion of Oxbridge graduates in the Administrative Class," writes Henry Parris, "so is there in the House of Commons. The electorate ought to be blamed for making the wrong
choice just as much as the Civil Service Commissioners. If too
few higher civil servants have scientific and technological
backgrounds, the same criticism can be made of industrial
managers."[10]

In the United States, where the most significant distinguishing
feature, in comparison with European countries, is the spread of
mass education, elites cannot, in any sense, be said to be repre-

---

[6] R. K. Kelsall, *Higher Civil Servants in Britain* (London: Routledge and
Kegan Paul, Ltd., 1955), p. 154.

[7] *Ibid.*, p. 142.   [8] *Ibid.*, p. 131.

[9] See Anthony Sampson, *The Anatomy of Britain Today* (New York:
Harper and Row, 1966), pp. 259–261.

[10] Parris, *Constitutional Bureaucracy*, p. 315.

sentative of the society as a whole. Lloyd Warner and his associates have shown in important studies the upward mobility that characterizes American society.[11] In their study of the American Federal executives, however, Warner et al. summarized their findings as follows: "Thus we can say that, compared to the general population, most of these men . . . come from the more highly placed occupational levels; that their fathers tended to be in disproportionately high numbers from the executive or owner of large business class or from the comparable high position of professional men, including doctors, lawyers, ministers and engineers."[12]

While the Warner study included over 10,000 Federal executives, a study of a more select Federal executive elite, the Assistant Secretaries, showed that a high proportion of this group—one-fifth compared to one-tenth of the total population—attended private schools, and that there was a heavy concentration in the Ivy League institutions. "The 'Big Three'—Yale, Harvard and Princeton—alone supplied the undergraduate education of nearly a quarter of the executives, as against only 4 per cent of the total 1921 college graduate population. This emphasis was even more pronounced at the graduate level. About two-thirds of these public officials with post graduate experiences attended a group of seven schools. Harvard was clearly in the lead, primarily because of the Harvard Law School which trained one in ten of all the political executives who served during this period."[13]

The author draws the portrait of this group as follows: Most of them, he observes, ". . . went to the best known schools (especially at the undergraduate level), joined the important clubs, and generally preferred town life to the country. These executives did not constitute an elite in the sense that entry into their ranks was closed to those who lacked those precise qualifications;

[11] Lloyd Warner and James C. Abegglen, *Occupational Mobility in American Business and Industry* (Minneapolis: University of Minnesota Press, 1955); and *Big Business Leaders* (New York: Harper and Row, 1955).

[12] Lloyd Warner et al., *The American Federal Executive* (New Haven: Yale University Press, 1963), p. 31.

[13] Dean E. Mann, *The Assistant Secretaries: Problems and Processes of Appointment* (Washington, D.C.: The Brookings Institution, 1965), p. 20. The group studied by Mann includes the 650 Assistant Secretaries who held their posts in the administrations of Presidents F. D. Roosevelt, Truman, Eisenhower, and Kennedy.

but they did reflect the characteristics of many other leadership groups throughout the country."[14]

In a more recent study that included the leading Federal executives—undersecretaries, assistant secretaries, general counsels of ten cabinet departments, administrators of major agencies, and members of regulatory commissions—as well as the cabinet secretaries, Stanley and his associates have shown how unrepresentative of the population as a whole this elite is. Like the assistant secretaries, the members of these groups attended the best schools (20 percent attended a private school) and colleges, thus enjoying advantages available to other elites but not to the general population.[15] In other words, despite the widespread availability of higher education in the United States, what distinguishes the American administrative elite is also what distinguishes their British and French counterparts: the quality of education. That the undemocratic recruitment of administrative elites is a nearly universal phenomenon can be seen from Table 3.4, which gives comparative data for six countries. In the case of Germany, one study notes that "both in education and in social origin, the members of the higher civil service are clearly stamped as belonging to the upper classes of society. The proportion of higher civil servants belonging to the so-called 'best families' is ten times greater than would be expected of a random sample of the population."[16] As Ralf Dahrendorf has noted, however, "so far as the proportion of members recruited from the upper class is concerned, there is little difference between the administrative elite and other German elites."[17] Similarity in the social backgrounds of the various elites is also found in Spain.[18] The one significant exception to the upper-class phenomenon of adminis-

[14] *Ibid.*, p. 61.

[15] David T. Stanley et al., *Men Who Govern* (Washington, D.C.: The Brookings Institution, 1967), pp. 9–30.

[16] Wolfgang Zapf, *Beiträge zur Analyse der deutschen Oberschicht* (Munich: Piper, 1965), p. 82. See also Lewis J. Edinger, *Politics in Germany* (Boston: Little, Brown & Co., 1968), pp. 181–182.

[17] Ralf Dahrendorf, *Society and Democracy in Germany* (New York: Doubleday, 1965), p. 252.

[18] See Juan J. Linz and Amando de Miguel, "La Elite Funcionarial Espanola Ante La Reforma Administrativa," in Anales de Moral Social y Economica, *Sociologia de la Administracion Publica Espanola* (Madrid: Raycar, 1968), p. 217.

trative elites is Italy, where it was found in a comparative analysis that "the percentage of . . . civil servants who are sons of upper-level executives and members of liberal professions is less than in any other country considered."[19] The regional and social origin of Italian civil servants is for the most part southern and *petit bourgeois*,[20] in marked contrast to the regional and social origin of other Western administrative elites.

TABLE 3.4

Comparison of the Occupations of the Fathers of Higher Civil Servants in Six Countries (percent)

| | Middle Classes | | | | | | Others | |
Name of Country	Shopkeepers, Businessmen, etc.	Governmental (incl. Army Employees)	Business Employees	Professionals	Skilled Workers	Total for Middle Classes	Unskilled Workers	Agricultural Workers and Farmers
Denmark (1945)	19.5	25.1	4.3	38.3	–	87.2	4.3	8.5
Gr. Britain (1949-52)	17.8	27.0	13.3	30.4	8.7	97.2	1.5	1.3
France (1945-51)	11.4	50.2 (41.8)	8.3	23.1	3.3	96.4	–	3.6
U.S.A. (1959)	20.0	?	24.0	20.0	17.0	81.0	4.0	15.0
Turkey (1960)	16.0	45.5	–	29.0	–	90.5	1.0	8.5
India (1947-56) (a) I.A.S.	12.0	50.6	4.5	29.2	–	96.3	–	4.7
(b) A/cs Services	7.5	46.7	5.2	28.2	–	87.6	4.2	8.6

Source: V. Subramaniam, "Representative Bureaucracy: A Reassessment," *The American Political Science Review,* LXI (December 1964), 1016.

EDUCATION, SOCIAL STRUCTURE, AND THE
DEMOCRATIZATION OF ELITES

In a recent and monumental decision, the United States Supreme Court ruled that the requirement of an educational diploma for a job constituted a form of discrimination that the Court held un-

[19] Paolo Ammassari, "L'Estrazione sociale dei funzionari dello Stato e degli enti locali," in Ammassari et al., *Il Burocrate di Fronte Alla Burocrazia* (Milan: Giuffre, 1969), p. 25.
[20] *Ibid.,* pp. 12–21.

constitutional.[21] In its decision in *Griggs vs. Duke Power Company*, the Court dealt a severe blow to one of the most enduring and cherished myths of modern democratic societies: that a society becomes more egalitarian and democratic as a result of the institution of educational criteria as the chief means of selection. As one writer, attempting to summarize this general point of view, notes, "Among Western nations, education is the great socializer, the great leveller, the great homogenizer. One study after another in political sociology has reported that this or that cross-national or cross-class differential is eliminated by controlling for education."[22] This faith in the democratic potential of education is hardly justified, if only because it is oblivious to the central problem of access to educational opportunities. Indeed, it can be shown that the contrary is closer to the truth: that is, whenever the avowed aim is to democratize a particular elite or institution and whenever academic criteria are instituted as the sole means of ensuring this democratization, it is practically certain that little or no democratization will occur. The reason lies in the undeniable correlation that exists between high social status and academic success.

Weber believed that bureaucracy accompanied mass democracy because "the qualitative extention of administrative tasks" meant that plutocratic privileges would give way to the professional. The chief merit of the triumph of competence over inherited privilege was its egalitarian and democratic aspects. Yet Weber was profoundly aware of the potential dangers that specialized examinations posed for democracy. The first danger was that the prestige derived from diplomas could be turned to economic advantage. But, more significantly, Weber's skepticism regarding educational qualifications was largely based on the fear that such qualifications would give rise to simply another type of caste system. As he noted in an important passage that is worth quoting at length:

> The role played in former days by the "proof of ancestry," as prerequisite for equality of birth, access to noble prebends and endowments and, wherever the nobility retained social power,

---

[21] *Griggs vs. Duke Power Company*, March 8, 1971; *The United States Law Week*, no. 124, LW 4317.

[22] Harvey Waterman, *Political Change in Contemporary France* (Columbus, Ohio: Charles E. Merril Co., 1969), p. 32.

for the qualification to state offices, is nowadays taken by the patent of education. The elaboration of the diplomas from universities, business and engineering colleges, and the universal clamor for the creation of further educational certificates in all fields serve the formation of a privileged stratum in bureaus and in offices. Such certificates support their holders' claims for connubium with the notables (in business offices, too, they raise hope for preferment with the boss's daughter) . . . and, above all, claims to the monopolization of socially and economically advantageous positions. If we hear from all sides demands for the introduction of regulated curricula culminating in specialized examinations, the reason behind this is, of course, not a suddenly awakened "thirst for education," but rather the desire to limit the supply of candidates for these positions and to monopolize them for the holders of educational patents.[23]

That Weber's fears have been justified can hardly be questioned, for it appears clear that where occupational success depends on academic success, it is also likely to depend on social origin. This is certainly true of France, but it holds even for a more mobile society like the United States. As Warner and his associates have noted: "When we recall the great differences in percentage of men from these various groups in Federal elites, we can see how higher education has functioned as a selective device. There are more men of higher occupational backgrounds precisely because more men from these prestigeful groups are able to attend college. In this manner higher education functions to maintain occupational succession. Sons of men in high occupational status have more than equal opportunity to secure the educational qualifications necessary to maintain or enhance high status in their own lifetimes."[24]

The unequal opportunities inherent in the recruitment of British higher civil servants arise from the educational system, which favors those already more advantaged. That is why it has been argued that the only way in which the restrictive educational system can be circumvented, insofar as entry into the Administrative Class is concerned, is to make promotion through the ranks

[23] Weber, *Economy and Society*, p. 1000.
[24] Warner, *The American Federal Executive*, p. 112.

81

the only means of entry into the upper echelons of British bureaucracy.

While many recent studies have noted, if only in passing, that the high educational level of elites is evidence not merely of high qualifications but of high social status as well,[25] few of these studies have examined in any detail the social and psychological bases of access to educational opportunities. It was left to a French sociological study to document the unmistakable link between access to education and academic success on the one hand, and social origin on the other. That a particular educational system, guided as it may be by democratic ideology, may nevertheless be a hindrance to democratization is the thesis of one of the most influential and controversial studies to have been published in France in the past decade. The authors of this book, *Les Héritiers*, argue that "of all the factors of differentiation, social origin is without a doubt the one whose influence is greatest on the student milieu, greater at any rate than sex or age, and above all greater than any clearly recognized factor such as religious affiliation."[26] Thus, for example, the son of a high-level executive has 85 times more chance of entering a university than the son of a peasant and 40 times more than the son of a worker.[27]

The "inheritors" are the ones who succeed because they have access to and enjoy all the "fine things" of the dominant culture, which they themselves fashion, regulate, and maintain.[28] Raymond Aron has quite rightly noted that Bourdieu and Passeron do not make their position clear, that they leave it up to the reader to make the choice between two possible interpretations of their critique: would they like everyone to be able to share in the culture of "les héritiers," or do they reject this culture altogether?[29] It is true that the authors do not give a direct answer to this question, but their answer may be implied: if everyone *could* somehow accede to a higher education, the system itself would no longer be the same. As the educational system current-

[25] Other elite studies, like Frey's *The Turkish Political Elite*, present solid data that cannot but impress the reader of the high educational attainments, compared to the general population, of the elite. But these studies tend to ignore the central question of access to education.

[26] Pierre Bourdieu and Jean-Claude Passeron, *Les Héritiers* (Paris: Editions de Minuit, 1964), p. 22.

[27] *Ibid.*, p. 12.

[28] *Ibid.*, p. 30.

[29] Raymond Aron, *La Révolution introuvable* (Paris: Fayard, 1968), p. 80.

ly exists, it denies higher education to all except the most advantaged in the society, and the less advantaged, when they do gain access, are apt to be eliminated very rapidly.

A recent study of over 6,000 students in the Faculté des Lettres has shown that those who are eliminated after the first year at the university are those who rank highest on an index of "handicaps": being relatively old, holding a job while at the university, not having obtained honors on the *baccalauréat*, and having pursued the "technical" rather than the "classical" course at the *lycée*[30]—handicaps with which students from the lower classes are saddled. As the author of this study notes: "In order to overcome the considerable handicap of holding a professional job, the students of the lower classes must have two or three other advantages: they must be young, they must have received honors [in their *baccalauréat*] and they must have followed the classical curriculum [at the *lycée*]. Yet, here again, their chances of having these advantages are minimal; for one thing, they have often interrupted their studies after the *baccalauréat* and are therefore older; for another, they rarely pursue the classical curriculum."[31]

The chief criterion for selection and elimination, a criterion which characterizes and maintains the system, is that of the examination. The examination is premised on what Bourdieu and Passeron have called "the ideology of givens"[32]—aptitude, initiative, work. All candidates are equal before an objective examination where no personal factors enter into the final decision. Particular emphasis is generally put on formal equality where entry into a particular elite is restricted.[33] As Bourdieu and Passeron

[30] As Bourdieu and Passeron have shown in *Les Héritiers*, social origin not only determines the chances of obtaining a higher education but also circumscribes the choice of courses to be pursued. The children of lower-class families cannot allow themselves the luxury of a classical education (the proportion of those who studied Latin at secondary school varies from 41 percent for the sons of workers and peasants to 83 percent for the sons of higher executives and members of liberal professions) or "educational dilettantism" (pp. 25-30).

[31] Noelle Bisseret, "La 'naissance' et le diplôme: Les processus de sélection au début des études universitaires," *Revue française de sociologie*, IX, Special Number (1968), 199.

[32] *Les Héritiers*, p. 103.

[33] For an analysis of the examination as a selective device see Bourdieu and Passeron, "L'Examen d'une illusion," *Revue française de sociologie*, IX, Special Number (1968), 222-253.

observe: "It is understandable that the system should find its ultimate expression in the *concours*, which assures perfectly the formal equality of the candidates but which excludes, through the anonymity of the candidates, the taking into consideration of the real cultural inequalities. The defenders of the *agrégation* can legitimately argue that, in contrast to a system of selection based on statutory rights and on birth, the *concours* gives everyone an equal chance. This is to forget that the formal equality insured by the *concours* does no more than transform privilege into merit, since it allows social origin to continue exercising its effects, but by more covert means."[34]

Although the authors of *Les Héritiers* are, as Aron has pointed out, referring to what is undoubtedly a universal phenomenon, as true of the socialist countries as of the Western countries,[35] if not more so, it would seem difficult to equate the formal examination with the more informal type of selection devices such as interviews, recommendations, and the like. The use of interviews in the recruitment of British higher civil servants has long been a hotly debated issue. Kelsall shows convincingly that the interview did discriminate against those candidates with working-class backgrounds. He quotes the head of the interviewing committee in 1939 as saying: "Directly the young man comes in I try to put him at his ease, by looking at his record, and saying, 'You were at Rugby: you went on from there to Corpus, you got a scholarship there.' . . . One of the others says, 'Have you been abroad much?' . . . You ask him almost anything which occurs to you to find out what his interests are, and how he reacts to other people and things."[36]

As Kelsall himself aptly remarks in this context:

Little perspicacity is required to see how this kind of approach would prejudice the chances of a candidate from the lower social strata, where no point of contact, in his educational career or elsewhere, existed between him and the chairman. . . . The recital of the names of his particular schools and university

[34] Bourdieu and Passeron, *Les Héritiers*, p. 104.
[35] Aron, *La Révolution introuvable*, p. 80. Documentation for Aron's point of view can be found in Suzanne Ferge, "La démocratisation de la culture et de l'enseignement en Hongrie," and in M. Martic and R. Supek, "Structures de l'enseignement et catégories sociales en Yugoslavie," in Robert Castel and J.-C. Passeron, *Education, développement et démocratie* (Paris: Mouton, 1967), pp. 70–74 and 90–100.
[36] Kelsall, *Higher Civil Servants in Britain*, pp. 70–71.

would be unlikely to establish a bond of sympathy between him and the members of the board. His failure to travel abroad would be too easily attributed to narrowness of outlook or lack of the spirit of adventure rather than to the necessity of earning a living during vacations. The hit-and-miss plan of fishing about for a topic would tend, especially as time was invariably short, to press hard on a candidate whose interests did not happen to conform to the Chairman's idea of 'questions on which every young man should have something to say!' And his failure to swallow the early bait thrown to him must itself convey the impression that he lacked two of the principal qualities, alertness and width of interests, for which interview marks were given.[37]

In France the "character" examination has not usually played a major role in the recruitment of higher civil servants.[38] This has undoubtedly permitted the purely formal system of selection to operate, at least to some degee, in accordance with egalitarian criteria, though Bourdieu and Passeron suggest that the formal selection system has no more to recommend it than its egalitarian ideology, which masks all the discriminating elements inherent in such a system. It is a system, as they argue throughout their study, that can "in effect, assure the perpetuation of privilege simply by its own logic; in other words, it can serve the privileged without the privileged having to use it."[39] For the written, anonymous examination must be presented in an eloquent, elegant style that includes a whole range of references. In other words, the same qualities are called for in the written as in the oral (character) examinations.

THE CASE OF THE FRENCH HIGHER CIVIL SERVICE

Discussing the role of education in the recruitment of higher civil servants, one authority recently concluded that "the most important element toward 'democratizing' the European public

---

[37] *Ibid.*, p. 71.

[38] Brian Chapman, a strong critic of the British administration and a great admirer of the French administration, has noted that the "character" examination "is a peculiarly Nordic preoccupation, and probably has something to do with monarchical traditions and the belief that government was the business of the aristocracy." See his *The Profession of Government* (London: Unwin University Books, 1959), p. 93.

[39] *Les Héritiers*, p. 43.

services has been, and no doubt will continue to be, the democratizing of higher education through public universities and fellowship programs whereby students who lack financial resources, and who come from the lower social strata, may be educated. This trend toward democratization of the public service has been observable in Britain, France, and some other European nations since World War II. . . .”[40] But this widely accepted viewpoint is contradicted by all the available data. If anything, the stringent educational requirements, the "diplomania," or what Weber called the "patent of education," has actually retarded the "democratization" of the public services. The United States Supreme Court ruling in *Griggs vs. Duke Power Company* offers a more general refutation of this thesis. And Henry Parris, an authority highly sympathetic to the British civil service, was able to write that "Open Competition served to perpetuate a type which had already come to the top."

In the case of the French administration, the data show an unequivocal correlation between social status and academic (or career) success. Table 3.5 shows that those who gain entry into the most prestigious corps of the administration come from the highest social strata of French society. Table 3.6 shows the discrepancy in the social origins of those who enter the Grands Corps (in other words, those who are academically most successful at ENA) and those who enter the less prestigious corps of *administrateurs civils*. The sons of workers and farmers are almost totally excluded from the Grands Corps, while they have a minimal representation in the corps of *administrateurs civils*. Taking the two groups together, one finds that the sons of administrators have by far the greatest representation, whereas the sons of workers have almost none. The reform of 1945 has not modified in the least the underrepresentation, in both relative and absolute terms, of the working-class population in the higher civil service. The almost total exclusion of the sons of working-class people from high positions is also found in Germany where, as Zapf notes, "To no group are the social and educational paths to higher positions, even in the civil service, so closed as to the industrial workers, who, numerically, represent the largest group of the population."[41] Educational requirements in both France and Ger-

[40] Frederick C. Mosher, *Democracy and the Public Service* (New York: Oxford University Press, 1968), p. 30.
[41] Zapf, *Beiträge zur Analyse der deutschen Oberschicht*, p. 82.

many serve to exclude the sons of workers (and farmers) from holding positions in the higher civil service.

Still another important indicator of the close relationship between social status and academic success is the fate of those civil servants who manage to overcome the entrance hurdles and gain entry into ENA through the second *concours*. Few of them ever manage to graduate near the top of their class, so that the highest

TABLE 3.5

Social Origin of Members of the Grands Corps Entering from ENA,
1953-1968

Father's Profession	Conseil d'Etat	Cour des Comptes	Inspection des Finances
Administration: A1	11	14	15
A2	18	17	18
B	2	6	4
C	–	2	1
D	–	1	1
Total, administrative	31	40	39
Artisans and shopkeepers	8	8	14
Heads of industrial enterprises	1	6	6
Commercial employees (cadre)	20	14	24
Industrial employees (low-level)	4	5	4
Liberal professions	13	15	12
Workers	2	1	–
Farmers (small and large)	1	1	7
Without profession	1	–	–
Total, other than administrative	50	50	67
Total, all professions	81	90	106

Source: Calculated from annual Ecole Nationale d'Administration, *Classement des Elèves, Statistiques, 1953-1968.*

and most sought-after positions in the administration are denied them, and the democratizing influence of the institution of the second *concours* scarcely reaches the Grands Corps. As Table 3.7 shows, the proportion of second *concours* entrants who manage to graduate at the top of their class and thus gain entry into the Grands Corps is remarkably small. In addition to being less socially advantaged, the second *concours* entrants are, as was noted

TABLE 3.6
Social Origin of Entrants into Grands Corps and Corps of Administrateurs Civils from ENA, 1953-1968

Father's Profession	Grands Corps		Administrateurs Civils	
	No.	%	No.	%
Administration: A1	40	14.4	39	5.3
A2	53	19.1	124	16.8
B	12	4.3	57	7.7
C	3	1.1	27	3.7
D	2	.7	3	.4
Total, administration	110	39.6	250	33.9
Artisans and shopkeepers	30	10.1	86	11.6
Heads of industrial enterprises	13	4.7	20	2.7
Commercial employees (cadre)	58	20.9	147	19.9
Industrial employees (low-level)	13	4.7	86	11.6
Liberal professions	40	14.4	87	11.7
Farm owners (large and small)	7	2.5	5	.7
Workers	3	1.2	18	2.4
Farm workers	2	.7	36	4.8
Without profession	1	.3	5	.7
Total, other than administration	167	100.0	490	66.1
Total, all professions	277	100.0	740	100.0

Source: Calculated from annual Ecole Nationale d'Administration, Classement des Elèves, Statistiques, 1953-1968.

TABLE 3.7
Entry into Grands Corps and Corps of Administrateurs Civils by Method of Entry, 1953-1968

Method of Entry into ENA	Grands Corps		Administrateurs Civils	
	No.	%	No.	%
1st Concours (students)	246	92.0	391	53.6
2nd Concours (civil servants)	21	8.0	338	46.4
Total	267	100.0	729	100.0

Source: Calculated from annual Ecole Nationale d'Administration, Classement des Elèves, Statistiques, 1953-1968.

in the last chapter, handicapped by their age, their family responsibilities, and the difficult circumstances under which they are obliged to prepare for the entrance examination.

THE "REVOLT" AGAINST ENA

The general dissatisfaction with the recruitment process into the higher civil service has brought ENA into the center of a large controversy. Among the most vocal critics of the administrative system in general and ENA in particular have been the School's own students. In a letter sent to Prime Minister Chaban-Delmas in September 1971, sixty-eight students of the class "Charles de Gaulle" stated that serious changes were now called for insofar as the distribution of talent among the various sectors of the administration was concerned. The signatories of the letter did not confine themselves merely to a general statement. They wrote quite emphatically that, as a way of expressing their dissatisfaction and as a way of encouraging the Government to undertake a serious reform, they would refuse to accept entry into the Grands Corps regardless of their rank in their class, which was to be graduated in June 1972. As M. Prieur, one of the leaders behind this move, observed, "If we have chosen this method of acting, it is, first, because within the higher administration it is the members of the Grands Corps who on the whole occupy the most privileged positions, and this makes our gesture all the more exemplary. Secondly, it has traditionally been the choice of the Grands Corps that has established the closest and most mechanical link between class rank and career, and this makes our gesture all the more significant."[42]

The students were objecting to what they regarded as the two most flagrant inequalities existing in the administrative system. The first concerns career opportunities—which differ markedly, depending on whether one belongs to the Grands Corps or to the corps of *administrateurs civils*. The second inequality concerns the established hierarchy of various sectors of the administration. Certain sectors, or ministries (the Grands Corps, the ministries of Finance, Interior, Foreign Affairs) have been highly sought after by the top graduates of ENA, whereas others (Social Affairs, Education, Agriculture) have been traditionally shunned by the

[42] D. Prieur, "Reflexions sur un choix," *Promotions* (June 1972), p. 12.

top graduates and left to those in the lowest quarter of the class. The students maintained that this dual inequality has disastrous consequences for the morale of civil servants and for the efficiency of the administration. Why should rank in one's class determine one's entire career? Why, in other words, should those whose high rank in a class put them in the Grands Corps thenceforth be endowed with privileges not available to others? Why should some of the most important ministries (from the point of view of social problems) be scorned and relegated to second-class status? These inequalities have been encouraged not merely by tradition, so the students argued, but by the State, which allows the "noble" ministries to pay bonuses to their officials such that their real salaries are considerably higher than those of officials serving in ministries which are "moins huppés." As M. Prieur observed, "the students of ENA, like all civil servants, are there *to serve the State* where the needs are greatest and where they will be most useful and not to make the State serve them in satisfying their voracious personal ambitions."[43]

What did the students suggest to rectify the inequalities existing within the administrative system? Basically, they called for (1) the creation of a single corps into which all ENA graduates would enter (implying, quite clearly, the abolition of the Grands Corps); (2) an end to the monopoly exercised over certain crucial posts by the Grands Corps; (3) equality in remuneration, and (4) a more reserved use of *détachement* (leaves of absence) from the Grands Corps; that is, the Grands Corps should not be used as mere stepping-stones for glorious careers.

The signatories of the letter did not, of course, expect immediate implementation of their program, if indeed it can be said that they had a program. What they aimed to accomplish, above all, was to dramatize the personal and administrative inequalities. So, for the first time in ENA's history, those graduating in June 1972 chose to deviate from tradition and to adhere to the commitment they had proclaimed in their letter to the Prime Minister the previous year. Of the sixty-eight who had signed the letter, six were in a position to choose the Grands Corps, four refused to do so and two found it impossible to resist the temptation. Nevertheless, it was only with the choice of the twenty-second in the class that the twelve Grands Corps posts were filled. In any

---

[43] *Ibid.*

previous year they would have been filled by the top twelve graduates.

It is difficult to estimate what the consequences of this action will be. Much depends on whether future graduating classes will follow in the footsteps of the "Charles de Gaulle" class, on whether the Government will take more seriously than it has done hitherto the criticisms of the existing system, and on how the Grands Corps will react. At present it appears that the Government and the Grands Corps tend to regard the actions of the "Charles de Gaulle" class as an aberration. They find it hard to believe that potential recruits into the Grands Corps will sacrifice brilliant careers and advantages for the sake of a vain hope of "changing the world." The Government will probably continue trying to gain electoral votes by criticizing the civil service, while at the same time refusing to contemplate far-reaching reforms.

The position of the Grands Corps in this controversy is clearer than that of the Government. What differences and conflicts exist among these corps all but disappear when they are threatened or attacked as a unit. They maintain that entry into any of the major corps has always been the result of a free choice and that no ENA graduate has ever been obliged to enter the Grands Corps.

The Grands Corps are unwilling to see their prestige eroded and they view unfavorably the prospect of no longer being the choice of those who graduate at the very top of their class. As a member of the Conseil d'Etat observed, "the Grands Corps will not agree to become the garbage bin of ENA." In reaction to their critics, the Grands Corps have gone so far as to propose the re-institution of their own separate *concours*, thus assuring themselves of "brilliant recruits" who are more interested in defending historic institutions than in bringing about their demise. In calling for a return to the system of separate *concours*, the Grands Corps have maintained that, just as it is not necessary to attend the Ecole Normale Supérieure in order to become an *agrégé*, so perhaps it ought no longer to be necessary to attend ENA in order to enter the Grands Corps. One ought, in other words, to be able to prepare for the *concours* of the various corps at other institutions as well as at ENA. This argument does not amount to much; no government is likely to permit a return to the pre-1945 system of recruitment, which was open to the most astounding abuses of objectivity and fairness.[44] The suggestion, however, does indicate that the Grands Corps will not stand idly by while others tamper with their power and prestige.

It may also be pointed out that the impact of the letter from the students of the "Charles de Gaulle" class was considerably tempered by a number of factors. In the first place, while some who had the option of choosing entry into the Grands Corps did not do so, the overall distribution as between ministries varied little—the ministries that had hitherto been considered "less noble" received, as always, a less than noble treatment. Table 3.8 compares the choice of careers of the "Charles de Gaulle" class (1972) with that of the "Stendhal" class (1965).[45] It is evident that with the exception of certain changes in preferences (greater preference for the Ministries of Cultural Affairs and Interior and less for the Ministry of Foreign Affairs), the ministries that have traditionally been on the lower end of the totem pole (Agriculture, Education, Social Affairs, Public Health) remained the least desirable in 1972.

The case of the critical students might have been considerably strengthened had the top graduates chosen careers in some of the less prestigious ministries. Instead, they chose careers in the Prefectoral corps (the Ministry of Interior), the most politicized sector of the administration and the one allowing for the least independence. Indeed, no sector of the administration gained as much from the 1972 "revolt" as did the Ministry of Interior, a fact that seemed at odds with the temper and the political outlooks that inspired the "revolt." The students justified their choice on the ground that they were helping to break the hold of Paris on the higher civil servants.

Still a third factor that tended to reduce the students' impact

[44] It was not difficult for the corps to pick those whom they considered most "suitable," regardless of ability. This sometimes involved fraud. One high-ranking member in the present government sat for the *concours* of one of the Corps in the 1930's. There were two vacancies in that corps in that particular year. He placed second, and in so doing he was about to deny entry to a better-connected candidate, who placed third. The results were altered so that the places of the candidates were actually exchanged, and the candidate who placed second was to be informed that he placed third. When this came privately to his attention, he decided not to make a scandal out of it. He was admitted to the corps the following year.

[45] Another class picked for comparison would have shown the same results.

TABLE 3.8
Choice of Careers Based on Rank at ENA, 1965 and 1972

	1965		1972	
Careers Chosen	No. of Places	Rank in Graduating Class	No. of Places	Rank in Graduating Class
Conseil d'Etat	6	1, 3, 5, 6, 7, 9	4	4, 7, 8, 9
Inspection des Finances	6	2, 4, 8, 10, 11, 12	4	5, 6, 12, 22
Cour des Comptes	7	13, 14, 15, 16, 17, 19, 20	4	10, 16, 17, 21
Administrative Tribunals	3	65, 68, 69	3	31, 46, 58
Foreign Affairs	10	18, 21, 23, 25, 28, 29, 30, 31, 32, 35	8	40, 43, 56, 61, 63, 72, 87, 88
Economic Expansion Corps	2	41, 48	2	55, 86
Inspectorate of Social Affairs	—		1	20
Cultural Affairs	3	76, 82, 87	3	26, 28, 29
Agriculture	4	64, 70, 71, 78	2	91, 92
Defense	—		3	80, 82, 90
Overseas Territories	—		1	96
Caisse de Depots	1	36	2	14, 19
Industry	3	45, 51, 59	3	52, 62
Finance	13	27, 34, 38, 39, 40, 46, 54, 55, 56, 58, 60, 61, 63	16	13, 23, 25, 33, 36, 39, 47, 49, 51, 53, 66, 73, 75, 76, 79, 81
Education	6	75, 77, 79, 80, 81, 83	8	54, 59, 67, 69, 70, 74, 77, 78
Equipment and Housing	2	72, 73	5	32, 35, 41, 42, 44
Interior	11	22, 24, 26, 33, 37, 42, 43, 47, 50, 52, 57	10	1, 2, 3, 11, 15, 18, 30, 37, 48, 60
Social Affairs	6	62, 84, 85, 86, 89, 90	12	27, 68, 83, 84, 85, 93, 94, 95, 97, 98, 99, 100
Transport	3	66, 67, 88	2	38, 45
Secretariat General of Government	1	44	2	64, 71
Paris Administration	—		1	65
Refuse to serve the State	1	74	5	24, 34, 50, 57, 89
Repeating last year at school	2	49, 53	—	
Total	90		100	

was the extreme emphasis they placed on the method by which careers were chosen. Their criticism scarcely touched on the morale of other higher civil servants who were not graduates of ENA. Nor did it deal with the promotion procedure within the higher civil service, a procedure which unquestionably favors ENA graduates.

I have pointed out some factors that tempered the effect of the 1972 "revolt" only to suggest that the actions of the students were not uniformly regarded as altruistic, disinterested, and sacrificial. Nevertheless, the "revolt" was inspired in large part by a recognition that the chief cause of the inequality of careers was the educational system, which gave rise to state-created elites whose interests were fundamentally incompatible with notions of equality.

ENA AND THE FRENCH EDUCATIONAL SYSTEM

In light of the data presented in this chapter, it becomes somewhat easier to understand why the reforms of 1945 brought about so few changes in the composition of the French administrative elite. In the first place, one must bear in mind that the idea of establishing a school to train higher civil servants was over a century old. It had often been argued during the course of the nineteenth century that there were schools charged with the responsibility of training engineers, teachers, scientists, and so on, and there ought to be a school to train higher civil servants. In the end, "the creation of ENA was based on a specific model, that of the scientific *grandes écoles*. The example of the Ecole Polytechnique and its specialized schools (*ponts et chaussées, mines, génie maritime*) clearly inspired the founders of ENA."[46] The idea of establishing a school for civil servants was launched in 1837, and in 1848, at the instigation of Carnot, the first Minister of Public Instruction in the Second Republic, an Ecole Nationale d'Administration was founded. The decree that brought this school into being stated that a "school destined to recruit for the various branches of the administration, which have heretofore been deprived of preparatory schools, ought to be established along lines analogous to those of the Ecole Polytech-

---

[46] *Rapport de la commission d'étude des problèmes de l'Ecole Nationale d'Administration* (Paris, 1968), p. 14.

nique."[47] The school, however, foundered eighteen months later on the internal squabbles of the Second Republic and on the opposition of the Law Faculties, who were anxious to prevent the creation of a school that would deprive them of their students and would give a more comprehensive training. (The creation of the Ecole Libre des Sciences Politiques in 1871 was in no small part a reaction to the narrow training offered by the Law Faculties.) But the initiative for reestablishing an Ecole Nationale d'Administration was revived at various periods in the second half of the nineteenth century and the first half of the twentieth, particularly under the Popular Front government when the Ecole Libre came under severe criticism. In fact, a bill creating an Ecole Nationale d'Administration was presented to Parliament in August 1936. After having languished in various commissions for close to eighteen months, it was overwhelmingly voted (422 votes for, 137 against) into law in January 1938.[48] No credits were voted for the school, however, and the outbreak of the war put an end to the entire project. It is not irrelevant to remark that each time a school to train higher civil servants was created, or was about to be created, it was named the Ecole Nationale d'Administration. The ENA inaugurated in 1945 was not only the namesake of the school of 1848, but conformed to the spirit of the school instituted under the Second Republic. Nor, as the Popular Front project shows, was the desire to create a school for higher civil servants a cherished project of the Right—the Left had often seemed equally eager.

Second, the reform of 1945 contained no radical elements. None of the hallmarks of the administrative system were questioned: the *concours*, the corps, the assignment to posts based on rank. Indeed, the reform was negative in one very important sense: it made no allowance for, and in fact denied the virtues of lateral entry into the upper ranks of the civil service, which had been possible prior to the reform. Kelsall has shown, for example, that to the extent that the British higher civil service has been infused with some diversity and dynamic elements, it has been owing in no small measure to the possibilities of promotion. Some 40 percent of those belonging to the Administrative Class in the

[47] Quoted in Debré, *Réforme de la fonction publique*, p. 9.
[48] For the text of the 1938 law, see André Ferrat, *La République à refaire* (Paris: Gallimard, 1945), p. 244.

period he studied had been promoted through the ranks.[49] It is not surprising that Kelsall concludes his study by noting: "On recruitment, the most far-reaching proposal is to make the only means of entry into the Administrative Class that of promotion from the ranks."[50] Elaborating on this proposal he observes: "The primary aim of promotion from the ranks ought to be to ensure that those whose failure to go to a university was due to factors other than inability to reach the required standard should be given an opportunity to use and develop their talents to the greater benefit of the Service. In the past, as we have seen, this has also, because of the inequalities of educational opportunity, been the principal agency in widening the range of social strata from which higher civil servants are drawn. In the future, this widening ought to be increasingly brought about by the improvement of the educational ladder outside the Service."[51]

The reform of 1945, rather than encouraging and making allowance for promotion through the ranks, ensured that it would no longer be possible. The very idea of civil servants entering ENA by a special examination recognized the impossibility of climbing through the ranks. The reform closed all other avenues of promotion to the top and opened a path only to those who had overcome the most stringent academic requirements. But even those who did gain entry into ENA had either to graduate at the top of their class in order to enter one of the Grands Corps or to resign themselves permanently to less prestigious and glorious careers. Entry into the Grands Corps, now centralized through ENA, remained a once-and-for-all entry. The prewar system actually had the advantage that a candidate could attempt to enter the corps of his choice more than once—he simply took the particular *concours* over again. With the creation of ENA, entering the Grands Corps became a now-or-never affair, depending entirely on one's rank in the graduating class.

No one any longer denies that ENA has failed to widen significantly the social basis of the higher civil service, but all are agreed that the fault lies not with ENA but with the French educational system. ENA, it is now argued, cannot be held responsible for not having widened recruitment; the real culprit is the French system of secondary and, to some extent, higher educa-

---

[49] Kelsall, *Higher Civil Servants in Britain*, pp. 55–57.
[50] *Ibid.*, p. 192. [51] *Ibid.*, p. 193.

tion.[52] It is certainly true that a reform of the entire educational system was promised at the Liberation and it was expected that this reform would have some salutary effects on recruitment into ENA. On the other hand, it should be very strongly emphasized that the philosophy on which ENA was founded conformed so closely and neatly to the traditional French educational model that it is hard to see in what way it anticipated changes, or how it would have accommodated itself to any radical reforms in the educational and administrative sectors. We have already pointed to one important aspect—promotion through the ranks—where the reform of 1945 was regressive, but there is another, which illustrates the degree to which ENA and the administrative reform of 1945 (the part affecting the higher civil service) were embedded in the past. While seeking to attack the bad effects of compartmentalization, the reform actually created another serious division in the upper ranks of the civil service: the division between the Grands Corps and the corps of *administrateurs civils*. Those who could not make it into the Grands Corps would henceforth enter the corps of *administrateurs civils*, whose members—some of whom may have missed entry into the Grands Corps by as little as one or two percentage points—resent the "divine law" which guarantees the members of the Grands Corps "unconditional success."[53] They particularly resent the once-and-for-all aspect of the ranking system, from which there is no reprieve and which leads to different careers, marked by "differences of *nature* and not of degree."[54] The conflict between the members of the Grands Corps and the members of the corps of *administrateurs civils* within particular ministries can become particularly acute, and the result can only be "to disorganize the administration . . . , to diminish its effectiveness, and to precipitate its decline."[55]

Conflicts such as this, as well as difficulties in altering the class

---

[52] See Henri Mounier, "L'Ecole et l'administration," *Promotions*, Special Number, no. 35 (1955), 74; Guy Braibant, "Libres opinions sur l'Ecole Nationale d'Administration," *Promotions*, Special Number, no. 35 (1955), 89; Edmond Michelet, "L'Administration à l'heure des Techniques," Conférences des Ambassadeurs, Nouvelle Série, no. 35 (November 30, 1967), 18.

[53] See the interesting article by Georges Bonin and Pierre Lelong, "Inspecteurs des Finances et Administrateurs Civils au Ministère des Finances," *Promotions*, no. 55 (1960), 17.

[54] *Ibid.*, p. 15. Emphasis in original.   [55] *Ibid.*

basis of the higher civil service, were undoubtedly foreseeable, but the reformers were guided by an attachment to the past and an unmistakable fear of the novel and untried. They fell back on the traditional system for their model: instead of attempting to make the administrative career itself more mobile in addition to improving the training, they relied solely on the traditional methods by which other French elites were recruited. Thus recruitment and training were restricted to a chosen few, as has been the practice of the other *grandes écoles*.[56] The reforms of 1945 thus reaffirmed the belief that those who served the State in the most responsible posts can arrive at these posts by no means other than an educational institution of the strictest academic standards. It is certainly paradoxical that a serious reform, attempted only after the traumatic effects of the Second World War and the Vichy experience, should have looked to the past for guidance. This paradox may help to explain why the past twenty-five years have produced no serious determination on the part of the various governments in power to rectify the negative effects of the post-Liberation reforms.

CONCLUSION: EDUCATION AND ELITE LEGITIMATION

I have tried to show that the recruitment of French elites has not been democratized, principally because the means of democratization have always been linked to severe academic barriers. Academic hurdles exclude a major segment of the population from elite positions and, in effect, perpetuate the class basis of recruitment. I have shown this to be the case with regard to the higher civil service. Some would undoubtedly argue that the only way to ensure a high level of competence is to maintain high academic standards. Others would maintain that the primary goal must be to ensure a more democratic recruitment of elites. Clearly, the dogmatic pursuit of either of these goals is bound to have serious adverse consequences. The first would result in high-quality recruits drawn from similar social backgrounds. The

[56] For example, whereas the student body of the University of Paris has increased fourteenfold in the past seventy years, that of *Polytechnique* and the *Ecole des Mines* has remained unchanged; that of ENA has remained unchanged for the past twenty-five years. See Dominique Dejeux, "Le Corps des mines, ou un nouveau mode d'intervention de l'Etat," mimeo. Centre de Sociologie des Organisations, Paris (October 1970), p. 27.

second, which could easily be achieved, as Andrew Jackson showed,[57] by the introduction of the spoils system, would, when pursued to the exclusion of all other goals, be a remedy worse than the disease. The central question becomes, then, how to reconcile high standards with a democratic representation of the society. The only feasible solution would be to place less heavy emphasis on specific academic criteria and to rely more on promotion from different sectors and through the ranks. What is needed, in other words, is a merit system that, unlike the one that currently prevails, would not be tied to specific educational requirements.

The most important function of the present educational system is its legitimation of elites: one who becomes a member of an elite as a result of specific academic qualifications is able to perform tasks and occupy positions for which he has little or no technical competence, but which fall to him as a result of his having gained the cachet conferred by the educational system. The system as it is presently constituted is far more concerned with conferring lifelong titles than with providing technical expertise. Indeed, as we shall see in Chapter x, the mark of distinction granted by a highly selective educational system leads to careers (privileges?) that have little to do with the actual expertise acquired through that system.

[57] See Leonard D. White, *The Jacksonians* (New York: Macmillan, 1954); and Mosher, *Democracy and the Public Service*, pp. 60–63.

CHAPTER IV

Social Class and Administrative Behavior

The concept of "class-interest" is an ambiguous one: even as an empirical concept it is ambiguous as soon as one understands by it something other than the factual direction of interests following with a certain probability from the class situation for a certain "average" of those people subjected to the class situation.

—*Max Weber*[1]

I have discussed the class basis of the French higher civil service and have attempted to show, in Chapter III, that the persistent predominance of the middle and upper-middle classes is a characteristic shared by other elites in French society as well as by the administrative elites of other societies. It is important now to ask whether the social origin of the French administrative elite defines, in and of itself, the attitudes and behavior of this elite.

CLASS AND BEHAVIOR: AN EMPIRICAL PROBLEM

The question concerning the social origin of an elite must be kept separate from questions having to do with the attitudes and behavior of that elite. Except within the framework of a Marxian analysis there can be no a priori connection between the two. No one will deny that social background data are extremely important in elite studies, if only because they permit an appraisal of the relative representation of a society's groups and classes in its elites. These data help to answer the question of who (socially) occupies the leading positions in the key institutions of society. But it is all too easy, as numerous elite studies have demonstrated, to regard social background as the master key that unlocks all doors. As Edinger and Searing have pointed out, in rely-

---

[1] "Class, Status, Party," in H. H. Gerth and C. Wright Mills, eds., *From Max Weber: Essays in Sociology* (New York: Oxford University Press, 1958), p. 183.

ing heavily on social background data the elite studies of recent years have neglected to concentrate on "intervening attitudes which might provide a link between backgrounds and behaviour."[2] Beyond the question of *who* occupies the key positions there is the no less important question of the behavior and attitudes of these officials, which may or may not be related to their social origins. This is a matter that calls for empirical investigation. The relationship between background and behavior cannot simply be assumed from the socioeconomic status of those who occupy the elite positions in a society. As Dankwart Rustow has justly noted in his review of a number of elite studies, "a study of social backgrounds can furnish clues for a study of political performance, but the first cannot substitute for the second."[3]

Some of the more influential studies of elites in the United States have attempted to draw far-reaching conclusions about the distribution of power in American society by an analysis of the socioeconomic status of those who occupy certain positions in the society. C. Wright Mills' *The Power Elite*, for example, not only strictly delimits the spheres of power in American society but also establishes a connection between these spheres on the basis of the socioeconomic status of those who occupy what Mills calls the "command posts." That Mills himself rejected the Marxist conclusions to which his own conclusions pointed is of little importance.[4] Mills' disciples, however, have tended by and large to assume, more explicitly than Mills did, that there exists a clear correlation between a particular socioeconomic background and a particular mode of thought and behavior. They find more palatable than Mills did not only the Marxian framework of analysis but also the Marxian implications and conclusions of this analysis.[5] They are not frightened by the term "class" in the way that

[2] Lewis J. Edinger and Donald S. Searing, "Social Background in Elite Analysis: A Methodological Inquiry," *The American Political Science Review*, LXI (June 1967), 431.

[3] Dankwart A. Rustow, "The Study of Elites: Who's Who, When and How," *World Politics*, XVIII (July 1966), 699.

[4] Mills wrote in a footnote in *The Power Elite*: " 'Ruling class' is a badly loaded phrase. 'Class' is an economic term; 'rule' a political one. . . . It should be clear to the reader by now that we do not accept as adequate the simple view that high economic men unilaterally make all decisions of national consequence." (New York: Oxford University Press, 1956), p. 227.

[5] See G. William Domhoff, *Who Rules America?* (Englewood Cliffs, N.J.: Prentice-Hall, Inc., 1967), and *The Higher Circles* (New York: Vintage Books, 1971).

Mills was; on the contrary, they insist on it vigorously. And they readily link it to "power,"[6] without much precision as to the exact nature of the link between class and power.

SOCIAL BACKGROUND AND COGNITIVE ATTITUDES OF THE ADMINISTRATIVE ELITE

The research for this study did not have as one of its chief aims a thorough examination of the relationship between social background and behavior and attitudes. This question should, however, be treated, if only briefly. It is clear that a more detailed analysis of the problem is needed, one that would help us to understand the role of education in the socialization of higher civil servants, the role of the work environment and the role of socioeconomic status in molding the behavior and attitudes of the administrative elite. Our conclusions, based as they are on limited data, must be considered tentative. Nevertheless they appear to point in a particular direction: that social origin does not appear to determine the attitudes and behavior of the higher civil servants included in this study. At least I could find little evidence to show that civil servants were divided along class lines on issues and attitudes. This leads to the very important point that Karl Mannheim raised some years ago and that I will take up more explicitly in the final chapter: the relationship or connection between the social basis of an elite and the responsiveness of that elite to the society.

Table 4.1 shows that higher civil servants from the various social strata have roughly the same degree of liberality when it comes to the rights of civil servants. There is a general belief that it is undemocratic to prevent civil servants from belonging to any party to which they choose to belong. As one civil servant put it: "Someone would first have to decide which parties are extremist and which are not and this would pose far more problems than it would solve." The higher civil servants took the view that an official of the State could believe in any political philosophy so long as his politicking was "confined to Saturdays and Sundays and he remembered to leave his ideas home when he came to the

[6] In *The Higher Circles*, Domhoff entitles part one of his study "The Upper Class as a Social Class," and part two, "The Upper Class as Governing Class." For a similar analysis of this view, see Ralf Miliband, *The State in Capitalist Society* (New York: Basic Books, 1969), pp. 23–67.

office on Mondays." This liberality knows, however, certain bounds. Thus, for example, higher civil servants were practically unanimous in their opposition to the lower civil servants' right to strike, and felt that a civil servant should not be granted the right to strike. Thus, to the extent that civil servants hold divergent views on the rights of those who serve the State, these divergencies emanate from one's hierarchical position within the service; differences in attitudes and behavior within the civil service probably have little to do with social background, and a great

TABLE 4.1
Democracy and Membership in Extremist Political Parties[1]

Father's Occupation	N	Acceptable		Not Acceptable	
		No.	%	No.	%
Administration	19	3	15.8	16	84.2
Business	13	5	38.5	8	61.5
Teaching	8	–	–	8	100.0
Liberal professions	16	5	31.2	11	68.8
Military	1	–	–	1	100.0
Low-level occupations	19	6	31.6	13	68.4
Total	76	19	25.0	57	75.0

[1] Question: There are countries where civil servants are forbidden from joining extremist political parties. Do you think that this is acceptable or not?

deal to do with one's position in the administrative organizations. For example, higher civil servants from modest social backgrounds were as opposed to granting civil servants the right to strike as were those coming from the upper-middle class. It is clear that there is a vast gulf that separates higher and lower civil servants. Despite the fact that both are State employees, they have little in common.

With regard to the question of recruitment, it might have been expected that the higher civil servants coming from the lower social categories would have been somewhat more critical of a system that did not favor those coming from their own backgrounds. Yet this was not at all the case. Table 4.2 shows that those coming from the lower classes believed in the present system of recruitment as much as those from the higher social categories. In fact, it was often those who came from the more modest backgrounds who expressed the strongest belief in the recruitment system. To quote one such person: "The system couldn't be more democratic. It's all based on examinations. Look at me, I had no fancy advantages but I was able to make it into Polytechnique." Greater skepticism (not indicated in Table 4.2) was shown by those civil servants whose fathers had been either administrators or had followed a liberal profession. Over a third of each of these groups affirmed that recruitment into the higher civil service was

TABLE 4.2

How Democratic is Recruitment into the Higher Civil Service?[1]

		Very		Fairly		Slightly		Not at all	
Father's Occupation	N	No.	%	No.	%	No.	%	No.	%
Administration	15	5	33.3	2	13.4	5	33.3	3	20.0
Business	12	5	41.6	4	33.0	2	16.7	1	8.3
Teaching	6	2	33.3	2	33.3	2	33.3	–	–
Liberal professions	16	4	25.0	5	31.3	5	31.3	2	12.4
Military	1	–	–	1	100.0	–	–	–	–
Low-level occupations	15	5	33.3	2	13.3	6	40.0	2	13.3
Total	65	17	26.2	17	26.2	20	30.8	8	16.8

[1] Question: Do you think that the present system of recruiting higher civil servants is very democratic, fairly democratic, slightly democratic, or not at all democratic?

"as democratic as the educational system," which is to say that "it is either democratic or undemocratic, depending on how you want to look at it."

The partiality to the recruitment system of those civil servants coming from the lower social categories was not entirely unqualified. This is evidenced by their reaction to the institution of the Grands Corps, as shown in Table 4.3. In fact, it is only with regard to the higher civil servant's reaction to the Grands Corps that some difference based on class can be discerned. This difference is not unimportant, given the general reluctance of higher civil servants to tamper with these venerable institutions. It could be argued, for example, that higher civil servants from the lower

104

classes believe in the present recruitment system because that is how they themselves were recruited, and one would suppose that they would favor the abolition of the Grands Corps because generally only those from the upper classes are able to enter these corps. But such an argument would be unconvincing. First, even if these civil servants favored the present recruitment system as a result of their own experience, it would still show that their thinking was more in line with that of colleagues of a different social background than with members of their own class. Second,

TABLE 4.3

Should the Grands Corps be Abolished?[1]

Father's Occupation	N	Desirable		Not Desirable	
		No.	%	No.	%
Administration	18	3	16.7	15	83.3
Business	11	1	9.0	10	91.0
Teaching	7	—	—	7	100.0
Liberal professions	18	3	16.7	15	83.3
Military	1	—	—	1	100.0
Low-level occupations	18	7	38.9	11	61.1
Total	73	14	19.2	59	80.8

[1] Question: Several critics have suggested that it would be best to abolish the Grands Corps. Do you think that this would be desirable or not?

if these civil servants favored the abolition of the Grands Corps because they did not gain entry into them—an entirely plausible hypothesis—this would still not explain why those civil servants from the middle classes who also failed to enter the Grands Corps did not think likewise. I do not wish to exaggerate the class differences on this issue, if only because the majority of members of the lower social categories favored keeping the Grands Corps. But what differences there are among those who favored abolishing the Grands Corps are due to social origin.

Turning to an examination of some important attitudes toward politics, we find that there are no significant differences in the outlooks of higher civil servants coming from the middle and lower classes. Table 4.4 shows that higher civil servants coming from the lower social categories are as disposed, if not slightly more so, to entertain nonprofessional contacts with politicians as are those coming from the higher classes. Similarly, with regard to the civil servant's rights to hold such posts as General Councillor, Municipal Councillor, or Mayor, or belong to a political club or a political party at the same time that he is a higher civil

TABLE 4.4

Desirability of Contact with Political Milieu[1]

		Yes		No	
Father's Occupation	N	No.	%	No.	%
Administration	19	11	57.9	8	42.1
Business	13	8	61.5	5	38.5
Teaching	7	5	71.4	2	28.6
Liberal professions	17	11	64.6	6	35.4
Military	1	1	—	—	100.0
Low-level occupations	19	14	73.7	5	26.3
Total	76	50	65.7	26	34.3

[1] Question: Do you think that it is a good thing for higher civil servants to maintain nonprofessional contacts with the political milieu?

servant, Table 4.5 shows a remarkable similarity in the views of higher civil servants of high and low social status. The differences are roughly equal in the case of each post mentioned. One may legitimately ask whether there may not perhaps exist such a thing as an "administrative culture." Our data do not, of course, provide a definitive answer to this question, although the similarity in the answers to certain questions was striking. For example, I was repeatedly told by civil servants of various backgrounds that a higher civil servant should be permitted to belong to a political party or a political club, but that "he ought not to militate." There is clearly a strong attachment to democratic principles, which may derive from the emphasis on law that civil servants receive during their training. Nevertheless, while democratic rights cannot be denied a citizen, even a higher civil servant, they must not be fully exercised, for they would clash with the responsibilities and duties of a civil servant. This explains why higher

106

TABLE 4.5

Compatibility of Higher Civil Service Posts with Other Posts[1]

Father's Occupation	Political Club				General Councillor				Municipal Councillor				Mayor				Political Party			
	Yes		No		Yes		No		Yes		No		Yes		No		Yes		No	
	No.	%	No.	%	No.	%	No.	%	No.	%	No.	%	No.	%	No.	%	No.	%	No.	%
Administration	10	26.3	8	20.5	12	22.6	6	26.1	16	23.5	2	25.0	14	22.2	4	28.6	10	27.0	8	20.5
Business	6	15.8	9	23.1	9	17.0	4	17.4	12	17.6	1	12.5	11	17.5	2	14.3	6	16.2	7	18.0
Teaching	4	10.5	3	7.7	5	9.5	2	8.7	6	8.8	1	12.5	6	9.5	1	7.1	4	10.8	3	7.7
Liberal professions	9	23.7	8	20.5	13	24.5	5	21.7	15	22.1	3	37.5	15	23.8	4	28.6	8	21.6	10	25.6
Military	—		1	2.6	1	1.9	—		1	1.5	—		1	1.6	—		—		1	2.6
Low-level occupations	9	23.7	10	25.6	13	24.5	6	26.1	18	26.5	1	12.5	16	25.4	3	21.4	9	24.4	10	25.6
Total	38	100.0	39	100.0	53	100.0	23	100.0	68	100.0	8	100.0	63	100.0	14	100.0	37	100.0	39	100.0

[1] Question: Do you think that a higher civil servant can be a member of a political club, hold the post of general councillor, municipal councillor, or mayor, or belong to a political party while exercising his function as a higher civil servant?

civil servants are so ready to deny the right to strike to the lower ranks. This is a right which once granted will be readily used, since it has always been used in any case and since lower civil servants do not, in the eyes of their superiors, have the same attachment to their posts as do the higher echelons.

A further example of this "administrative culture," about which more will be said in Part Two of this study, is the dichotomy of administration and politics that civil servants tend to establish. Thus, as Table 4.5 shows, the functions of a General Councillor, Municipal Councillor, and Mayor—particularly the last two—are regarded as purely administrative. This viewpoint tends to enlarge the role of the central administration and to narrowly delimit the domain of politics; as we shall see, it has a profound bearing on the behavior of the highest officials in the central ministries.

The belief that a higher civil servant should not "faire de la politique" is not the monopoly of any group of higher civil servants with a common social background. Table 4.6 shows that it

TABLE 4.6

Inevitability and Desirability of Civil Servants Holding Political Posts[1]

Father's Occupation	N	Invitable No.	Invitable %	Not Inevitable No.	Not Inevitable %	N	Desirable No.	Desirable %	Not Desirable No.	Not Desirable %
Administration	19	10	52.6	9	47.4	18	6	33.3	12	66.7
Business	12	4	33.3	8	66.7	13	5	38.5	8	61.5
Teaching	8	4	50.0	4	50.0	8	3	37.5	5	62.5
Liberal professions	16	6	37.5	10	62.5	19	4	21.0	15	79.0
Military	1	1	100.0	—	—	1	—	—	1	100.0
Low-level occupations	18	11	61.0	7	39.0	18	6	33.3	12	66.7
Total	74	36	48.6	38	51.4	77	24	31.2	53	68.8

[1] Question: Many higher civil servants and former students of *ENA* occupy today ministerial posts in the government and other purely political posts. Would you say that this phenomenon is inevitable or not? Is it desirable or not?

is shared, in roughly equal proportions, by civil servants of diverse backgrounds. This apoliticism of the highest officials in the central administration has been raised here because it is so widely shared; that it is of profound importance in the behavior and role perception of these officials will be seen throughout the remainder of this study.

SOCIAL ORIGIN AS AN ISSUE IN REFORM

The data presented above do not by any means prove—they merely strongly suggest—that administrative behavior is not determined by the socioeconomic status of the officials. Greater weight must be ascribed to the training of higher civil servants, the administrative structure itself (for example, the existence of tight units known as corps), and the work environment. The argument against the undemocratic recruitment of the French bureaucracy is a powerful one, but one must avoid the temptation of concluding that the structure of French society, as well as the functioning of the administrative machine itself, would be radically transformed by a proportional representation of the society's classes in its administrative elite. It is interesting to observe that there is scarcely any criticism of the undemocratic character of the Italian bureaucracy, although it is as unrepresentative of Italian society as its French counterpart is of French society. The reason is undoubtedly that the Italian bureaucracy includes a disproportionate number from the relatively underdeveloped southern region who have a relatively low socioeconomic status. Surely it would be going too far to suppose that a larger proportion of northern aristocrats and sons of upper-middle-class professionals and businessmen would render the Italian administration less rigid, more efficient, and more responsive to the society. I do not wish to suggest that the issue of social origin is a phony one, but only that undue emphasis on it has diverted attention from the need for other reforms. This has certainly been the case in France.

In view of the role of the State in French society, it may not be surprising to find so much emphasis placed on the need for reform in recent literature on the French administration. But what has usually been meant by reform? A brief look at the attempts to reform the Grands Corps will help us to answer this question. Perhaps no institution or group symbolizes the power of the State more clearly than the Grands Corps, the elite within the French administrative elite. It is the members of these corps that Bernard Gournay had in mind when he made his important distinction between the "grands fonctionnaires" and the "hauts fonctionnaires."[7] The Grands Corps, to which I will devote Chapter x, constitute, in many respects, the foundation of the French administrative system. By their long tradition, their ubiquity within the State apparatus and their closed nature, they have so entrenched themselves that their basic role and functions have remained unaffected by all proposals for administrative reform made over the past century and a half. They have come to be regarded, in Luethy's words, as "a rock against which all political storms beat ineffectively and in vain."[8] The main reason why these corps have remained impervious to demands for their reform is that such demands have never really gone beyond requiring more democratic recruitment. The Grands Corps were, prior to the 1945 reform, regarded as self-recruiting groups, and it was therefore only natural to direct attacks against their undemocratic character. Implicit in these attacks was the belief that a more widely-based recruitment would somehow radically alter the nature of the power and influence of the Grands Corps in the French State.

Before the 1945 reform, as we have seen, entry into the Grands Corps took place by means of a *concours* which was set by the individual corps for its candidates. The examining jury for both the oral and written parts was composed solely of members of the corps. It was this aspect of the recruitment procedure that was most vehemently criticized because, it was justifiably argued, by having absolute powers of decision over the selection of its recruits, the corps was a self-recruiting and self-perpetuating body. Moreover, preparation for these examinations was offered only at the Ecole Libre des Sciences Politiques, a private school whose tuition fees were high and beyond the reach of those not fortunate enough to be born into the Parisian upper-middle class. No serious attempts were made to democratize recruitment into these corps until the Popular Front government issued a decree requiring a more representative jury. But the decree was a relatively timid one, specifying that of the five members that composed the jury of a corps, only two could be members of that corps. Of the three remaining members, two were to come from the other

---

[7] Bernard Gournay, "Un Groupe dirigeant de la société Française: les grands fonctionnaires," *Revue Française de science politique*, xiv (April 1964), 215–241.

[8] Herbert Luethy, *France Against Herself* (New York: Meridian Books, 1954), p. 17.

Grands Corps and one was to be either a higher civil servant or a professor of law. Thus, for example, the jury of the Inspection des Finances had to be composed of two Inspecteurs des Finances, one member of the Conseil d'Etat, one member of the Cour des Comptes and either a Director of the central administration, a law professor, or a member of one of several other corps.[9] It was only with the administrative reform of 1945 that recruitment was taken out of the hands of the individual corps: all higher civil servants were henceforth to be recruited through the Ecole Nationale d'Administration. The chief motive of this reform was to democratize recruitment, but we have already seen that success was limited.

This limited success has had no major effect in transforming or undermining the essential role of the Grands Corps, and it is not likely that a greater success in democratization would have had a greater impact. For, as we have been bound to conclude, however tentatively, social origin does not appear to constitute a decisive element in the behavior of French higher civil servants. To be a higher civil servant and to aspire to enter the Grands Corps is to accept, a priori, the fundamental goals of these corps. And entrance into a corps means being subject to the statutes of that corps, being molded by the corps, defending it, being promoted by it, and achieving considerable social standing as a result of belonging to it. No reform, least of all that of the Liberation, has ever shown a concern for the impact these corps have upon their members and on the entire administrative process. The reform of 1945 even reaffirmed its faith in these corps and in the whole concept of tightly-knit and competing units within the administration. In fact, the reforms undertaken both before and since 1945 have simply been concerned with enlarging the social bases of these corps, and one suspects that even this concern has not always been diligently embraced, since any noticeable success has yet to manifest itself. Even the Popular Front government seemed eager in 1936 to undertake a serious reform, but ended up by merely enlarging, most modestly, the examining juries of the corps. It should not be forgotten that Léon Blum was himself a member of the Conseil d'Etat, a position to which he attached great importance. In fact, as Claude Julien notes, even when it concerned extending the rights of colonial peoples, Blum refused

[9] Pierre Lalumière, *L'Inspection des finances* (Paris: Presses Universitaires de France, 1959), pp. 15–16.

to undertake measures that the Conseil d'Etat might have regarded as unconstitutional. As Julien put it, "Le Conseiller d'Etat l'emportait sur le politicien."[10]

In our discussion of the conflict among higher civil servants (Chapter IX) we will observe again that socioeconomic status cannot be considered as a decisive factor in orienting their behavior. Greater emphasis will be placed on role perceptions, which are dependent on the positions occupied within the politico-administrative system. In an interesting study on the phenomenon of corps, though this study treats only the technical corps, the authors conclude: "A number of students of bureaucracy have emphasized the enormous role that the work system and the social milieu play with regard to the attitudes and behavior of civil servants. Our study indicates that the influence of these factors, although real, is not central."[11] The profound attachment of members to their corps evidences the compartmentalization, the niches within the administrative system upon which so many students of the French administration have commented. This compartmentalization, which allows great career mobility, prestige, and security to members of the corps, springs from the very existence of the corps phenomenon. That is why the behavior of members of these corps does not vary with social origin. Consequently, emphasis on enlarging the class basis of these corps, however important, has been largely misplaced.

[10] Cited in William Cohen, "The Colonial Policy of the Popular Front," *French Historical Studies*, VII, no. 3 (1972), 380.

[11] Jean Claude Thoenig and Erhard Friedberg, *La Création des directions départementales de l'équipement: phénomènes de corps et réforme administrative* (Paris: C.N.R.S., 1970), p. 55.

CHAPTER V

Administration as a Vocation

M. Phellion . . . destinait son fils aîné à l'administration et le second à l'Ecole Polytechnique. Il disait souvent a son aîné: "Quand tu auras l'honneur d'être employé par le gouvernement."

—*Balzac*, Les Employés

THE ETERNAL RECRUITMENT "CRISIS"

The appeal of the civil service as a career in France is well-nigh legendary. It has been portrayed, and often caricatured, by some of the greatest literary figures of nineteenth century France. Yet this appeal has undoubtedly been subject to ups and downs, affecting different hierarchical levels of the administration to different degrees. Also, the changes in the class basis of the civil service from predominantly aristocratic and upper bourgeois to middle and lower bourgeois—a change that began in the early nineteenth century and was paralleled in the recruitment of other elites in French society[1]—brought variations in the attractiveness of State service as a career to the various classes. But there were other factors that continued to make State service an appealing career; for example, the ever-growing role of the State appealed more and more to the emerging middle class. Similarly, the attractiveness of private employment, affected as this was by the economy, wars, and State policies, did at times influence significantly those who were about to choose a career. But the relative appeal of one sector over another was usually temporary and did not affect the different levels of employment to the same degree. Writing, in 1931, of the post-World War I period, Walter R. Sharp argued that the civil service in France no longer possessed the magic appeal that it had enjoyed throughout the nineteenth century: "The war greatly accentuated this evolution.

[1] See E. Beau de Loménie, *Les Responsabilités des dynasties bourgeoise*, 4 vols. (Paris: Denoël, 1947–1954).

113

What had in 1910 been, in the French vernacular, a mild *crise*, became in 1926 a *véritable crise*. Before the war, the father might say to his son, 'If you don't work at your studies, you will be good only for business'; today, he tends to reverse his admonition: 'If you are not studious you will have to resign yourself to becoming a *fonctionnaire*.' The result has been that in recent years entrance examinations have been 'deserted' wholesale."[2]

Sharp saw three reasons for the decline in the attractiveness of the civil service as a career: the depreciation of the franc and the consequent failure of salaries to keep pace, the loss of income from rents, and the rise of living standards for those engaged in commerce.[3] Those most seriously affected by the changing economic structure were the would-be higher civil servants for whom alternative careers now presented themselves. "It is only in the *subaltern* field staffs of the postal, educational, and similar establishments [wrote Sharp] that recruitment has remained easy. Here the old desire for stability of employment, with prospect of old age pension, is still going strong among the unambitious who do not feel drawn toward any particular vocation. As one goes up the hierarchical scale, however, it may safely be postulated that recruits for the civil service are being drawn in steadily increasing numbers from lower social strata than a generation ago."[4]

Writing almost four decades later, Michel Crozier pointed to a similar *crise*, though this time it was the inverse of what Sharp had seen taking place after World War I: it was not the higher civil service that was failing to attract the bright and ambitious; rather, it was the lower echelons of the bureaucracy that were encountering difficulties in filling vacant posts. Because of its rigid stratification, notes Crozier, the administrative system cannot hold its own in competing for potential recruits. It simply does not offer adequate promotion possibilities: "The recruitment problem constitutes henceforth one of the major weaknesses of the French Administration. The crisis, which began to manifest itself in the 1950's, is becoming more and more acute. The number of *concours* where there are more posts than acceptable candidates can no longer be counted."[5]

[2] Walter R. Sharp, *The French Civil Service: Bureaucracy in Transition* (New York: Macmillan, 1931), p. 87.
[3] *Ibid.*   [4] *Ibid.*, pp. 89–90.
[5] Michel Crozier, *La Société bloquée* (Paris: Seuil, 1970), p. 115.

Sharp and Crozier were referring to a crisis of recruitment that was manifested in the "desertion" of entrance examinations, now of the higher civil service, now of the lower. Both writers were, however, dealing with a phenomenon that is far more complex than they appeared to recognize. For one thing, a recruitment "crisis" must be seen over a period of some years and can be substantiated empirically. Neither Sharp nor Crozier supplies pertinent data. As two students of the French administration noted in their examination of recent arguments concerning disenchantment with the civil service as a career: "The *déclassement* of the civil service in comparison to the nationalized or the private sector is generally regarded as a proven fact. But so far, no significant figures measuring the gaps have been determined or *a fortiori* published."[6] In fact, the statistics that do exist show the very contrary of what Crozier has described for the recent period. The number of candidates has far exceeded the number of vacant posts: for category A, there have been two candidates for every vacant place; for category B, three to five candidates; and for categories C and D, five to ten.[7]

Second, recruitment into the civil service may vary from sector to sector of the administration and from region to region. This is because, as is generally recognized, the relative attractiveness of a particular profession is a function of the economic activity of the nation, or of particular regions. Thus Crozier's assertion that it is the rigid stratification system typical of the administration that has caused general disaffection is significantly ahistorical: the rigidity of the system is not, after all, merely a contemporary problem, so that disenchantment with an administrative career at present cannot simply be ascribed to this one factor. After examining in detail the question of the relative attractiveness of the civil service as a career, Mignot and d'Orsay conclude:

> It would be false to speak of a general disaffection from the civil service. It has occurred only as regards certain careers of an "inquisitorial" nature (fiscal administration, police, magistrature. . . .)

[6] Gabriel Mignot and Philippe d'Orsay, *La Machine administrative* (Paris: Seuil, 1968), pp. 11–12.

[7] Laurent Blanc, *La Fonction publique* (Paris: Presses Universitaires de France, 1971), pp. 59–60. See also the graph on p. 58.

It would be equally false to speak of a general recruitment crisis. There are, in fact, only specific problems concerning certain categories of civil servants, which call for specific solutions.

The difficulties in recruitment were real in the 1960's, and were wrongly considered as a general crisis. Essentially, they were due to two related factors: on the one hand, the graduation of unusually small classes due to the low birth rate during the war; on the other hand, the pressure which existed on the labor market until 1964.[8]

These authors argue, in effect, that where there has been a recruitment crisis it has been a temporary one confined to particular sectors, and related to economic and demographic factors.

It will not be necessary for us to enter into the question of whether today a career in the higher civil service is more or less sought after than previously. Judging from the number of candidates who sit for the annual *concours* of ENA, as well as from the regional origin and university education of these candidates, it would appear that the glories of State service are as much sought after as ever.[9] Moreover, if the recruitment "crisis" to which Sharp and Crozier have alluded had in fact taken place, we should expect to find a significant change in the social composition of the civil service. That a recruitment crisis has taken place in the case of the military, for example, has been substantiated by the changing recruitment patterns and by the social composi-

[8] Mignot and d'Orsay, *La Machine administrative*, pp. 14–15.

[9] It is true, however, that there are some signs of early disenchantment with the administration. In the graduating class of 1969, for example, nine out of 94 students refused to sign the customary commitment to serve the state. All obtained employment in the private sector. This is the highest number ever recorded of departures before entry into the administration proper. All nine students were graduated around the middle of their class (ranks 40–60), a respectable enough rank but one denying them access to the Grands Corps. One of the nine, for example, a former army officer, had aspired to enter the Quai d'Orsay, but having been denied this possibility by his rank in the graduating class he decided to return to a military career. All the others entered banks, industry, and public relations firms. See *Le Monde*, 15–16 June 1969. In general, about five students in every graduating class refuse to sign the commitment to serve the state. Nevertheless, the number of candidates who sat for the ENA *concours* in September 1972 was greater than the previous year, and this despite the "revolt" of 1971. See *Le Monde*, 17–18 September 1972.

tion of the officer corps.[10] A crisis in the recruitment of civil servants would undoubtedly have had similar consequences. Yet, as
our data have shown, one of the significant aspects of recruitment
into the higher civil service has been the remarkable similarity
in the social, regional, and intellectual background of higher civil
servants, before and after the 1945 reform. One important reason, as we shall see, why the administration has been able to hold
its own as a career is the overriding fact that the most prestigious
educational institutions of higher learning are State institutions
that prepare their students for State service. But an examination
of the reasons why civil servants choose to enter public service
will enable us to understand not only the appeal of the State as
an employer, but also the particular attachment to the State that
the civil servant acquires. That this is partly the result of his educational experience will be made clear.

CHOICE OF AN ADMINISTRATIVE CAREER

Why does one become a civil servant? This is a complex question
that cannot be answered simply by an examination of the social
background of the administrative elite—indeed, the data presented in Chapter II contribute little. Many explanations have
been offered for the choice of public service as a career: the centralized nature of the French State; the power and prestige of
public service; a dogmatic pursuance of the general interest, security, etc. Reasons for choosing the administration as a career
clearly vary according to the hierarchical level that one chooses
to enter. The obvious case in point here is that security of employment is more important for the lower grades than for the
higher, particularly in periods of economic crisis. Our concern
here, however, is only with the higher civil servants.

The motivations that eventually determine the choice of public service as a career can be gauged to some extent by the period
in the subject's life when an administrative career was envisaged
or decided upon. It can be seen from Table 5.1 that over 40 percent of the higher civil servants interviewed had chosen to pursue an administrative career before entering a university and a
quarter had decided during or before adolescence. Also, almost

[10] Raoul Girardet, *La Crise militaire française, 1945–1962* (Paris: Armand
Colin, 1964), pp. 20–29.

50 percent chose to enter the administration either while at the university or upon graduation, which would seem to indicate that other alternatives were not as attractive, though they were certainly considered, and half of these decided on an administrative career upon graduation because, as the interviews revealed, the decision was essentially made for them by their rank in their graduating class. From the point of view of their motivations in seeking an administrative career, top-level civil servants fall into two roughly equal categories: the first includes those who were more or less bent on administrative careers from the start, for reasons to be presently examined; the second includes those who saw only the *relative* attractiveness of the administration and

TABLE 5.1

Age of Directors at Decision to Pursue Administrative Career (percent)

Before *lycée*		25.9
At *lycée*		18.0
At, or upon graduation from university		47.0
Other		9.1
Total	(N = 90)	100.0

who might very easily have chosen another career. Chance, as a number of civil servants falling into the second category remarked, often played a major role in their choice. Indeed, for almost a quarter of the total number of respondents, the administrative career was chosen for them by their rank in their graduating class. This was mostly the case of the *polytechniciens* whose rank put them into the more prestigious technical corps (the *corps des mines* or the *corps des ponts et chaussées*) as a result of having graduated at the top of their class.

The similarity of the ages at which French and British higher civil servants choose the administration as a career is striking. In a study carried out in 1966 by Professor Richard Chapman for the Fulton Commission, it was found that of 32 entrants in 1956, only one had decided to enter the civil service before entering the university, and seventeen had decided while undergraduates. In other words, a close look at the data for France and Britain shows that the university had a determining effect on about the same proportion of civil servants in both countries in choosing the administration for a career. It is important to note, however, that the years at the university produce no single motive for joining the administration in either case.

In France:

> At university I was trying to decide on a career, and one of my professors whom I admired very much suggested that I try for the Inspection des Finances.

> When I was at Sciences po., E.N.A. was just being created. I knew what a role E.N.A. was going to play, so I decided to try for the *concours*.

> I had studied law and it seemed pretty clear that you couldn't go very far with this education. I was encouraged to try for the E.N.A. *concours*. Mind you, the administration was always in the back of my mind. That's the trouble—it's always at the back of everyone's mind!

> Had I done less well at X, I probably wouldn't be in the administration today.

In England:

> At university, my tutor suggested that I ought to explore the civil service as a career.

> While at university I decided that I wanted to join the . . . (Ministry), but no other government department.

> As a student . . . I wanted to "serve the community"; I wanted to avoid any scrambling for position, etc. The Civil Service seemed the answer . . . (I also wanted to prove to myself that I could pass those administrative examinations which are spoken of with bated breath).[11]

The role of the university in determining the career choice of its students is, as we can see, of extreme importance. The university does more than provide students who are fortunate enough to be there with a certain type of education ("bourgeois culture,"

[11] Richard A. Chapman, "Profile of a Profession: The Administrative Class of the Civil Service," The Fulton Commission, *The Civil Service*, vol. 3 (2) (London: H.M.S.O., 1968), 11.

119

according to the authors of *Les Héritiers*). The very fact of being at the university in a society not given to providing mass education means that one has a choice of professions, restricted as that choice may be by one's social origin and cultural milieu. The years spent at the university are years of relative freedom where one is open, as the quotations from both French and British higher civil servants indicate, to diverse influences.

Knowing the age at which one chooses to enter the administration does not tell us why the administration is chosen as a career in preference to others. Table 5.2 shows a diversity of factors:

TABLE 5.2
Reasons for Directors' Choice of Administrative Career

Reasons	No. of 1st Choice Mentions	All mentions	All Mentions as % of Total Mentions
Possibilities of all sorts offered	10	17	10.7
Interesting and enjoyable work	5	20	12.7
Political vocation	1	1	.6
Promotion possibilities	1	8	5.1
Security	1	8	5.1
Public service vocation	13	24	15.2
Prestige of administration	5	12	7.6
Salary	1	1	.6
Family tradition	14	17	10.7
Chance	13	16	10.2
Dislike of pecuniary gain	8	9	5.7
Preference for general matters	11	17	10.7
No means for creating own enterprise	4	8	5.1
Total	87	158	100.0

the most prominent are the interest of the work, the various career possibilities that open up as a result of serving in the administration, the desire for public service, chance (having served in the Resistance, taken a certain examination, attained a certain rank in one's graduating class), prestige, and family tradition. A similar constellation of factors accounted for the choice of the civil service as a career in Britain (Table 5.3), although one that appears to play a role in France that is absent in Britain is the influence of family tradition. We have already pointed to the high proportion of sons of higher civil servants who become civil servants themselves.[12] A number of them noted that it was in the nature of things for them to enter the higher civil service:

TABLE 5.3

Reasons for Choice of Administration as a Career in Britain

Interest, important work; being in center of things	20
Belief in public service; working for common good	14
Work with congenial colleagues	11
The intellectual quality of the work	9
Attractive pay	6
Lack of enthusiasm for alternative careers	5
Career prospects	3
Difficulty in getting in	3
The attraction of joining an elite group in society	2
Generous leave allowance	2
Opportunity for travel abroad	2
Security	2

Source: Chapman, "Profile of a Profession," p. 12.

I grew up in an atmosphere filled with politicians and higher civil servants. Throughout my childhood they were in and out of our house. This was the world I was brought up in, so it was only natural for me to enter it.

My mother always wanted me to become an Inspecteur des Finances. We had a cousin who was in the Inspection des Finances, and my father never made it into the Inspection. So I'm certain that this factor played a big role in my desire to enter the Inspection.

My father, grandfather, and father-in-law were all *polytechniciens*. I broke enough of a tradition by choosing E.N.A.

I always wanted to be either a Prefect or an Ambassador.

The diversity of reasons for choosing an administrative career notwithstanding, can it be said that an attachment to State service or a public service vocation is discernible in our data? Do the

[12] The influence of the father's profession on the son's choice of a career was found to be equally important for other professions. See Alain Girard, *La Réussite sociale en France* (Paris: Presses Universitaires de France, 1961), p. 310.

121

higher civil servants have a calling for administration? Thus far we have emphasized the variety of factors that lead one to choose an administrative career. A closer look at the data, however, suggests that something resembling a calling for State service may in fact exist. If we surmise that the sum of the following factors: public service vocation, prestige of administration, family tradition, interesting work, dislike of pecuniary gain, and preference for dealing with general over private affairs, evidences a predilection for or an orientation toward State service as opposed to private employment, we may conclude that an attachment to public service reveals itself in slightly under 50 percent of our group. And it was precisely those for whom an administrative career was a given from the start that did not at any time envisage pursuing another career. Not surprisingly, it was generally those who had entered the administration as a result of "chance" (the war, the Resistance, the rank in class) who were most likely to have considered another career. In this category, as a rule, fall the scientists, agronomists, and other technicians whose training could have been applied to either public or private employment. Often, it was as a result of lack of private means that the choice of an administration career was made.

> I had studied law and I didn't have the means for creating my own law practice. So what else was there to do with my qualifications?

> When I entered Polytechnique, I hadn't any ideas about entering the administration. My rank put me in the corps of *ponts et chaussées*, and from there on my career was pretty much mapped out for me.

> It was pure chance that I entered the administration. I took the *concours* and passed.

> I wanted to create an agricultural enterprise, but my father had no money to set me up.

> I was thinking of becoming an engineer in a large private industry, but I graduated with a good rank and that put me in the corps of *ponts et chaussées*.

Table 5.4 does, however, pose the constantly recurring dilemma in the interpretation of data: do we say that "only" 50 percent

122

considered other careers, or "fully" 50 percent did not consider any career other than the administration? Neither statement would be wholly satisfactory. The interpretation becomes meaningful only when the data are placed in a larger context. Thus, for example, we have already explained the reasons for the large proportion of those who did not consider another career. Also, those who considered a liberal profession (law, medicine, teaching, engineering) or a military career did not ultimately see these professions as viable alternatives. The military and the colonial service did not appear as attractive as in the pre-World War II period, because the French empire was clearly heading toward its decline. As for the liberal professions, the length of time necessary to complete one's studies, the insecurity, and the extreme

TABLE 5.4

Careers Other Than Administration Considered (percent)

Law	4.9
Medicine	3.7
Military	7.4
Colonial service	6.2
Private enterprise	9.9
Teaching	11.1
Engineering	3.7
Journalism	1.2
Politics	1.2
None	50.7
Total	100.0

difficulties of upward mobility within these closely-knit professions led many to conclude that entry into the higher civil service provided them with security, prestige, and far quicker promotion possibilities. Even from a social point of view, the administration is more fluid and more open than are most other professions.[13] Again, it is necessary to see the "rigid stratification system" in the administration that Crozier and others have emphasized in a wider context: the stratification of the higher civil service is no

[13] For other professions, see Alain Girard, *La Réussite sociale* (Paris: Presses Universitaires de France, 1967).

more rigid—indeed it is undoubtedly less so than in other professions. This can be seen by the age distribution of those who reach the top of their professions. Graph 5.1, which compares the ages of men in directorial posts in the administration and the private

Graph 5.1 Age Distribution of Higher Civil Servants
and Upper Cadre of Private Sector

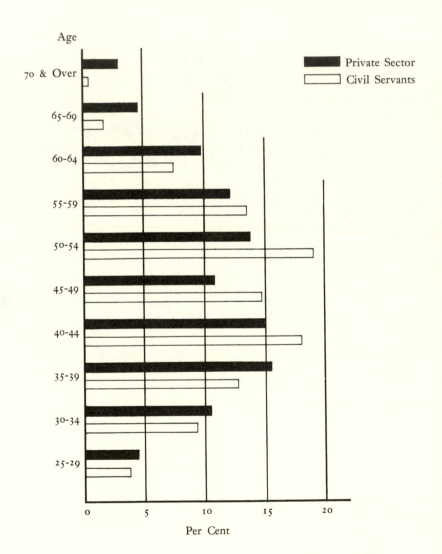

sector,[14] shows the relative youth of the higher civil servants, 65 percent of whom fall in the 40–60 age category as opposed to only 50 percent of the directors of the private sector. Other data show that the average age of members of ministerial cabinets, in 1968, was 42.6 years and was even lower for those cabinet members who belonged to the Grands Corps.[15] Pierre Lalumière has shown, moreover, that those who hold the most important posts in the administration—the civil servants in the Ministry of Finance—are extremely young, in both relative and absolute terms.[16] The average age of Directors of the central administration is approximately 50, which is relatively young compared to the Italian Directors General.[17]

The existence of a recruitment crisis into the higher civil service appears, then, to be a largely unsubstantiated phenomenon and born of the outsider's view of the bureaucratic state and the administrative career. For those faced with the task of choosing one career over another, the administration offers unique advantages, foremost among these being rapid promotion. Indeed, so extraordinary is this upward mobility in certain cases that it is not without its problems. A number of the Directors of the central administration, having reached the highest administrative post in their late thirties, face an uncertain future in their early forties. These Directors spoke candidly about this problem and were often eager to learn, through the interviewer, how some of their colleagues proposed to deal with it. One Director noted, for example, that at the age of forty-three, when it would be about time for him to move on to another post, he could not remain in

[14] The graph includes only the ages for the upper administrative cadres of the private sector and higher civil servants. Age data for other groups were not available. See Philippe d'Hugues and Michel Peslier, *Les Professions en France: évolution et perspectives* (Institut national d'études demographiques, Cahier no. 51, Paris: Presses Universitaires de France, 1969), pp. 325–329.

[15] J. Siwek-Pouydesseau, *Le Personnel de direction des ministères* (Paris: Armand Colin, 1969), p. 39.

[16] He notes that the average age of the Director of the Treasury before 1940 was 42, and even lower (38) in the period up to 1955. For the Director of Public Accounting the average age is 44, and was 38 in the period 1946–1953. For the Director of the Budget, perhaps the single most important administrative post in France, the average age is 38. *L'Inspection des finances* (Paris: Presses Universitaires de France, 1959), p. 141.

[17] See Alessandro Taradel, "La Burocrazia Italiana: Provenienca Collocazione dei Direttori Generali," *Tempi Moderni*, no. 13 (April–June 1963).

the administration without becoming "downwardly mobile." The alternatives, as he saw them, were a directorial post either in the semipublic sector or in the private sector.[18] Mme. Siwek-Pouydesseau's conclusion that the post of Director in the central administration is but one step in an upwardly mobile administrative career seems highly questionable, since neither returning to one's corps nor obtaining a post as an Inspector General nor, for that matter, opting for a more remunerative post in the private sector can be considered as moving "further up."[19] Certainly the Directors themselves did not view any of these posts as being "more interesting" or as constituting the apex of their careers. Indeed, the return to one's corps—particularly in the case of the Inspection des Finances and the Cour des Comptes—is resisted with the utmost force.[20]

The rapid promotion offered by the French administration applies, of course, only to that minority which already has more than a head start; that is, to those who are able to *begin* their careers as *hauts fonctionnaires*. Those whose backgrounds give them high aspirations but who for one reason or another are unable to obtain the required academic credentials inevitably suffer a considerable degree of frustration and may even be obliged to leave the country. France has traditionally had a relatively low emigration rate, but those who have emigrated have often come from the more privileged strata of society. This is because the son of a successful upper-middle-class businessman, professional, or higher civil servant who aspires to a similar status but who is unable to attain the necessary credentials recognizes from the outset that his aspirations will probably never be fulfilled. Those who entered the colonial administration before World War II, for example, were for the most part sons of middle- and upper-middle-class families who, lacking the required diplomas, would have been unable to achieve a high rank in the metropolitan administration. Indeed, of those who entered the corps of colonial administrators between 1929 and 1936 over one-third were sons

[18] Graph 5.1 shows how few higher civil servants fall in the age group of 60 or above, which is not the case for executives of the private sector. Indeed, because executives in the private sector tend to be relatively old, the Government has recently sought to pass a bill that would require their mandatory retirement when they reach the age of 65.

[19] Siwek-Pouydesseau, *Le Personnel de direction des ministères*, p. 88.

[20] This is explained in greater detail in Chapter x.

of higher civil servants. As William Cohen notes: "A colonial career . . . was as a rule a means of social and professional advancement, but at times it was a means of maintaining status. This was true for the sons of middle-class families who had failed to acquire the basic certificate of bourgeois status, the *baccalauréat*. Among those entering the Corps in its early years there were several sons of prefects, lawyers, and school teachers without a secondary school education."[21] To be sure, there were many advantages offered by a colonial career—adventure, power, better pay and living conditions—but it was seldom a question of a choice between the colonial and the metropolitan administration. The former was most often chosen when the latter was out of reach.

RELIGIOSITY AND THE ADMINISTRATIVE CAREER

In a recent study, two authors have attempted to establish a connection between religious practice and public service. The object of the book, which deals exclusively with the higher civil service, is, according to the authors, to present data showing the links existing today between the values of the higher civil service and Catholic values. Because this is an intriguing thesis, it is perhaps of interest to quote at some length the findings of Darbel and Schnapper.

It appears from our data that the number of regularly practicing Catholics is considerably higher in the higher civil service than in the upper classes as a whole—40 per cent of the civil servants declaring that they practiced regularly.

The analysis shows that the religious practice of the new civil servants of category A, that is, those who come from the middle and lower classes, and that of the civil servants who come from the upper classes, is always considerably greater than the religious practice for their classes of origin: 41.4 per cent of the civil servants from the lower classes and 33.8 per cent of those from the middle classes claim to practice regularly.

[21] William B. Cohen, "The Lure of Empire: Why Frenchmen Entered the Colonial Service," *Journal of Contemporary History*, IV, no. 1 (1969), 105. See also the same author's *Rulers of Empire: The French Colonial Service in Africa* (Palo Alto, California: The Hoover Institution Press, 1971), pp. 23–36.

Thus, the civil servants coming from the lower classes have attained the highest posts in the administrative hierarchy by an educational success that is atypical of their own milieu and by the effects of internal promotion, which supposes the appreciation of superiors and peers—therefore by an integration into the dominant values of the administrative milieu.[22]

In addition to religious practice as a determinant of religiosity, the authors of *Les Agents du système administratif* also use the size of family as an indicator. That the average size of a higher civil servant's family is larger than the national average as well as larger than the average for the private sector and the liberal professions is confirmed by all available data[23] (see Table 5.5).

TABLE 5.5

Size of Households of Directors of Central Administration, Contemporary Personalities, and Population

Number in Household	% of Directors[1]	% of Contemporary Personalities[2]	National Percentage[3]
7 and over	15.1	6.1	5.5
6	12.5	9.8	5.3
5	15.0	15.9	9.4
4	20.4	19.6	14.7
3	9.3	17.1	18.7
2	16.8	23.8	26.8
1	10.9	–	19.6
Total	100.0	100.0	100.0

[1] The group of Directors included in this table are those who held their posts in 1963. The choice of year was determined by the availability of data on the other groups.
[2] Girard, *La Réussite sociale in France*, p. 132. Girard's data include only number of children. It has been recalculated to reflect number in household.
[3] *Annuaire Statistique de la France*, 1963, Table III, p. xxiii.

The difference in the size of families between the elites and the population as a whole is somewhat greater than is reflected in Table 5.5, since the figures for the administrative elite and for the

22 Alain Darbel and Dominique Schnapper, *Les Agents du système administratif* (Paris: Mouton, 1969), pp. 94–95.
23 See Girard, *La Réussite sociale en France*, p. 134.

Contemporary Personalities include only parents and children, whereas the national figures, as they are given in the *Annuaire Statistique*, include, in addition to parents and children, boarders and other family members.

Having established the religious practice of the higher civil servants, Darbel and Schnapper proceed to link this variable to social origin and to the various corps to which the higher civil servants in their sample belong. I have summarized their data in Table 5.6, which shows a correlation between the level in the ad-

TABLE 5.6

Administrative Level, Social Origin, and Religious Practice

	High Social Origin %	Practicing Catholic %
Grands Corps	76.5	53.0
Administrative control corps	67.5	—
Technical corps	63.5	47.5
Regional services corps	50.0	41.0
Central administration corps	47.5	38.0

Source: Darbel and Schnapper, *Les Agents du systéme administratif*, pp. 102-103.

ministrative hierarchy and social origin on the one hand, and the degree of religiosity on the other. Thus the higher the social origin of a civil servant, the higher his status in the administrative hierarchy, and the more religious is he likely to be. The authors raise the interesting and intriguing question as to whether this correspondence between religious practice and belonging to a control corps is used by the administration—whether consciously or unconsciously is not indicated by the authors—for its own ends. In other words, the function of control is given to those whose moral indignation is likely to be most acute, because of their religiosity, when it comes to an infringement of the law.[24] This is mildly presented as a hypothesis and the authors do not attempt either to prove or disprove it.

It was noted earlier that a number of higher civil servants professed a hostility to the commercial world, going so far as to state: "I never wanted to deal with money," or "I entered the

[24] Darbel and Schnapper, *Les Agents du système administratif*, p. 103.

administration because I don't like to work for personal gain." It is also true that on almost every occasion that such an attitude was expressed, it was expressed by a Catholic.[25] But we found no correlation between disdain for pecuniary gain and religious practice—in fact, from our data it is difficult to establish a direct connection between religious practice and public service. Among those interviewed, 38.5 percent said that they did not practice at all and 23.5 percent said that they practiced very little, which often meant "agreeing to go with my wife to church once in a while." Darbel and Schnapper do more than merely link the degree of religiosity with public service: they maintain that there is a fundamental similarity in the values of both institutions, and they do not make light of the Protestantism-business, Catholicism-public service dichotomy. They note, for instance, the similarity to the "bourgeois'" integration into his job, which is linked to the demands of the church.[26] Annie Kriegel, among others, has made a similar argument with reference to membership in the Communist Party, suggesting that membership in the Party is much like belonging to a church.[27] In effect, there are few jobs in an industrial society that do not require the kind of regimentation described by Groethuysen. Nor are Darbel and Schnapper entirely consistent, for they themselves show the relative liberty enjoyed by a member of one of the more prestigious corps who does not have to live by a rigid timetable. They argue that this liberty is linked to the "ethos of the upper class."[28] But the ethos of the upper class is very different, as they well recognize, from the ethos of the bourgeoisie. If, then, belonging to one of the more prestigious corps endows a civil servant with "a liberty

[25] This is hardly surprising, since 84 percent of the respondents were of Catholic origin.

[26] The authors quote Groethuysen approvingly: "Imagine the bourgeois formed in accordance with the rules of the Church. He goes to bed and he rises at regular hours. He has his hours of work and of rest. . . . The spirit of his life is its regularity. . . . This bourgeois undoubtedly exists: he is the typical employee. The Church has contributed to forming a certain kind of 'bourgeoisie moyenne' and to filling the offices. An honest man, this bourgeois goes to mass every Sunday, just as he goes to his office every day of the week." Quoted in Darbel and Schnapper, *Les Agents du système administratif*, p. 96.

[27] Annie Kriegel, *Les Communistes français* (Paris: Seuil, 1969), pp. 117–128.

[28] Darbel and Schnapper, *Les Agents du système administratif*, p. 103.

symbolized by the absence of a schedule and, for the Grands Corps, the absence of an office,"[29] how does the "bourgeois ethos," or religiosity, explain the choice of an administrative career? In fact, a closer look at Table 5.5 might lead one to wonder why the number of practicing Catholics is not higher in a country that is almost totally Catholic. But one ought not to forget the aggressive anticlericalism that has characterized French official circles, particularly during the years of the Third Republic. In Georges Courteline's play, *Un Client sérieux*, a judge is ousted from his post because his enemies discover that his daughter had made her first communion. Given the anticlerical past, the number of practicing Catholics, as well as the general willingness of the officials to avow their religiousness should not be underestimated.

One cannot therefore totally deny the importance of the religious factor insofar as the choice of the administrative career and administrative behavior are concerned. It does not seem possible, however, in this case to grant this one factor the importance it has in, say, determining voting behavior,[30] where the religious factor has been shown empirically to be crucial. With regard to the administrative career, the religious factor has merely been assumed to play a determining role. The data presented by Darbel and Schnapper are important and original, but they do not allow for the generalizations that the authors draw from them. One reason for this is that no discussion of the choice of an administrative career can ignore the two factors that I have emphasized time and again: the educational system and the role of the State.

STATE EDUCATION AND THE RECRUITMENT OF ELITES

It has been said that the French educational system aims more "at selecting people for entering definite social strata than at training them for their future productive functions."[31] Perhaps it would be more accurate to say that the educational system

---

[29] *Ibid.*

[30] Mattei Dogan, "Political Cleavage and Social Stratification in France and Italy," in S. M. Lipset and S. Rokhan, *Party Systems and Voter Alignments* (New York: The Free Press, 1967), pp. 129–196.

[31] Michel Crozier, *The Bureaucratic Phenomenon* (Chicago: University of Chicago Press, 1964), p. 239.

131

trains people for certain strata, which may be occupational and/ or social. It has already been noted that the schools, and particularly the *grandes écoles*, have always seen as their primary aim the training of students to fulfill certain functions on behalf of the State. The role of the State in the French educational system has a clearly articulated philosophy, one that has been perhaps best expounded by Durkheim. In one of his classic essays on the sociology of education, Durkheim argued that in order for society to exist as a collective unit the State must have an important role in education. "If one attaches some value to the existence of society," he wrote, "education must assure, among the citizens, a sufficient community of ideas and of sentiments, without which any society is impossible, and in order that it may be able to produce this result, it is also necessary that education not be completely abandoned to the arbitrariness of private individuals."[32] Durkheim, like Napoleon, clearly equated a cohesive society with a strong State. How else was he able to write: "Since education is an essentially social function, the State cannot be indifferent to it. On the contrary, everything that pertains to education must in some degree be submitted to its influence. . . . There is no school which can claim the right to give, with full freedom, an antisocial education."[33]

The underlying philosophy of the role of the State in the educational system enables us to understand why the leading educational institutions of higher learning in France have, ever since their creation, had as their primary task the training of those destined to serve the State, whether as teachers, scientists, agronomists, or higher civil servants. An indissoluble link exists in France between State (elite) education and State service. The result of this link, insofar as the administration is concerned, is that the State is guaranteed an adequate and highly trained cadre of higher civil servants. With the possible exception of the Ecole des Hautes Etudes Commerciales, the institutions of higher learning do not train their students for service in the private sector, and it is fairly evident that the State has not been eager to do so.

This explains why to enter a *grande école* is to enter public service forthwith. ENA adhered to the tradition of its forerunners

[32] Emile Durkheim, *Sociology and Education* (Glencoe, Ill.: The Free Press, 1956), pp. 79–80.
[33] *Ibid.*, p. 80.

in that it was part of the civil service. Just as a *polytechnicien* is under the auspices of the military and supported by the Ministry of National Defense, and a *normalien* is a civil servant of the Ministry of National Education, so a student at ENA becomes a civil servant, and is paid as such, the moment he is admitted to the school. Upon completing the training program, not only is this civil servant obliged to serve the State for a certain number of years (if he chooses to resign he must reimburse the State for its outlay in educating him), but he becomes a member of a corps, a group that bears the unmistakable mark of distinction, and that crowns him with a title for the remainder of his career, if not his life. As Louis Armand observed in his critique of this system: "I wish that on completing secondary school adolescents spent a part of their time doing other things than solving the traditional arithmetic problems whose goal is to determine a precise grade on an examination. This always comes from the idea that studies are pursued so as to take examinations and *concours*, and to obtain at the termination of one's studies at X, at the Ecole Nationale d'Administration, or at the Ecole des Haute Etudes Commerciales, a title of 'Count' or 'Baron' that one will keep all one's life."[34]

These schools confer titles, in severely restricted numbers. Nor do any other means of obtaining these titles exist, for there is no lateral entry into such groups. One either obtains them early or not at all. In addition to conferring titles, the *grandes écoles*, as we noted earlier, are all oriented toward public service—there are no equivalent schools for the private sector. And because of the centralized nature of the French State, as well as the rapid upward occupational and social mobility that the administrative career offers, the administrative sector has been the one institution in France that has offered, among other things, the possibility of being at the "center of events." A number of higher civil servants remarked that industry was really too insignificant in France for them to have considered going into it. They were not

---

[34] Louis Armand, "Conversation sur l'avenir de l'administration," *Promotions*, no. 60 (1962), 697. One critic of the administration, himself a higher civil servant, notes that because of the rigid administrative structure certain boundaries are impossible to cross. "One is classified around the age of fifteen as 'literary' or as 'scientific.' And at the age of twenty, one is 'X,' 'E.N.A.,' or nothing for all one's life." René Mayer, *Féodalité ou démocratie?* (Paris: Arthaud, 1968), p. 23.

unwilling to acknowledge that the rise of large industrial enterprises is beginning to make available a viable alternative for the young, ambitious, and well-educated, who would previously have chosen without hesitation a public service career. One of the most influential technical civil servants (a graduate of *Polytechnique* and a nonpracticing Catholic) noted that a bright person always ended up in the administration because, having traditionally lacked respect for industrial development, the State has not encouraged, may have even discouraged, the creation of schools to train men for service in the private sector. Consequently, the choice of an administrative career in France must be seen in conjunction with the role of the State, the educational system, and the advantages inherent in this career—advantages that are not, contrary to folklore, widespread outside the administrative sector. For the most advantaged the administration has, heretofore at least, offered greater and more rapidly-attained glories than the private sector, including the liberal professions. Its stratification system has been more fluid and less rigid than that of industry, medicine, law, teaching, or the military. In other words, there are at times sound, objective reasons for choosing the administration as a career. There are also, to be sure, the subjective reasons. In this particular case, however, the subjective reasons—religiosity and the ecclesiastical ambiance of the administration—cannot, in the light of the data presented, be regarded as determining factors in the choice of an administrative career.

PART THREE

The Dynamics of the Central Administration

CHAPTER VI

The Minister and His Administration: Choice

*Le ministre n'a pas à choisir ses directeurs comme le prési-
dent ses ministres, mais qu'il n'hésite jamais à les changer
dès qu'apparaîtra un dissentiment d'idées, ou même une divergence tenace de caractère.*

—*Léon Blum*[1]

The relationship between ministers and higher civil servants in
France has always been portrayed as basically, and sometimes
irretrievably, antagonistic. Ministers have often complained that
the power of civil servants constituted, in Clemenceau's words,
"a danger because it is a power that is absolutely irresponsible,"[2]
while civil servants have maintained that ministers have tended
to make mere "factotums"[3] out of them. De Tocqueville noted the
tendency of the French parliament to become "less and less an
administrative and more and more a demagogic body."[4] This
trend, coupled with Napoleon's desire to create an administration
that would not be overdependent on politicians, has led, according to Luethy, to the paradox that "in France politics and the
state machine function in two watertight compartments."[5] And
a contemporary jurist observes that "there exists today a democratized political system whose jurisdictions have been reduced.
There also exists an administration closed unto itself, exhibiting
aristocratic tendencies, one whose powers have considerably increased."[6] It is commonplace to maintain today that the French

---

[1] Léon Blum, *La Réforme gouvernementale* (Paris: Grasset, 1936), p. 147.

[2] Georges Clemenceau, *Sur la démocratie* (Paris: Larousse, 1930), p. 85.

[3] Henri Chardon, *Les Travaux publics* (Paris: Perrin, 1904), p. 51.

[4] Alexis de Tocqueville, *The Old Regime and the French Revolution*
(New York: Doubleday Anchor, 1955), p. 59.

[5] Herbert Luethy, *France Against Herself* (New York: Meridian Books,
1954), p. 18.

[6] Charles Debbasch, *L'Administration au pouvoir: fonctionnaires et politiques sous la Vᵉ République* (Paris: Calmann-Lévy, 1969), p. 10.

137

bureaucracy "constitutes an island of resistance vis-à-vis the political milieu."[7]

The islands of resistance within the bureaucracy are symbolized by what have been referred to as the "Parisian Barons,"[8] the Directors of the central administration. These men are the heads of *directions*, or divisions, into which the French Ministry is divided. They occupy the highest posts in the administration and have no administrative superiors (save where there exists a Secretary General) within the ministry. The formal hierarchical divisions of a French ministry are shown in Diagram 6.1, which depicts no particular ministry but is, rather, a summary of the general lines of authority in French ministries. As will be seen, however, these formal hierarchical lines mask the fluid and uncertain responsibilities of one level to another. This is particularly the case at the apex. The diagram does, nevertheless, indicate the pivotal positions of the Directors in a French ministry. Nor are there many uncertainties in the responsibilities of the *Sous-Directeur* and of the *Chef de Bureau* to their Director.

CONSTRAINTS ON THE MINISTER'S CHOICE

The nomination of a Director is not based on or guaranteed by the *Statut Général des Fonctionnaires*. An appointment is made on the proposal of a minister, in the Council of Ministers. It is made official by a decree signed by the President of the Republic and countersigned by the Prime Minister and the minister who originally proposed the nomination. Nor need a minister's choice of a Director be limited to civil servants. In principle, he may choose whom he pleases either from within the civil service or from the private sector. This would seem to indicate that the minister has considerable freedom of choice in appointing the civil servants who occupy the highest posts in the ministry and with whom he has to cooperate in running it. In practice, however, his choice is circumscribed by a host of factors.

In the first place, upon taking office, the minister, like his British counterpart, finds an administration already in operation. Were he to seek to replace all or most of the Directors, he would probably meet with strong opposition from Matignon and the Elysée (the offices of the Prime Minister and the President). He

---

[7] *Ibid.*, p. 12.

[8] René Mayer, *Féodalité ou démocratie?* (Paris: Arthaud, 1968), p. 24.

138

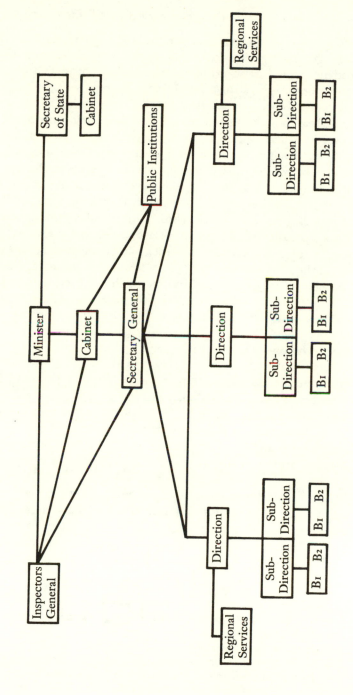

Diagram 6.1
Hierarchical Schema in a French Ministry

would also risk turning the entire ministry against him. He therefore generally accepts working with an administration that he had no great part in creating. It sometimes happens that ministers cannot, for personal or political reasons, work with certain Directors. In such a case they usually resort to an administrative reorganization that leaves vacant the posts they wish to fill. For example, when Giscard d'Estaing became Minister of Finance in 1963, he sought to remove a Director from the ministry with whom he had long been at loggerheads. Moreover the Minister, who intended to direct just about every aspect of the ministry's work himself, could not risk having his policies sabotaged by a higher civil servant, one of whose chief faults was, it appears, his strong personality and points of view. Giscard d'Estaing therefore fused two *directions* together and nominated his own man to fill the newly-created post. To take another example, when the Ministry of Labor and the Ministry of Public Health were joined together in 1966 to form the Ministry of Social Affairs,[9] the new minister, Jean-Marcel Jeanneney, took the opportunity of carrying out a veritable purge. He removed every Director and named men of his own choice in their places.

Second, although a minister may in theory nominate someone from outside the administration for the post of Director, he almost never does. The mobility between private and public sectors evident in the United States simply does not exist in France. What does exist is a one-way channel: from the public to the private sector, and never the other way. Moreover, civil servants look with great disfavor upon the appointment of a "foreigner" to an administrative post, as Table 6.1 shows.

The Fulton Commission strongly emphasized the need for and importance of bringing into the British Civil Service people with other than administrative backgrounds. The Commission urged that ministers make personal appointments of individuals who could contribute specialized knowledge and experience.[10] In

---

[9] With the formation of the Chaban-Delmas government in June 1969, the Ministry of Social Affairs was once again split into two ministries. In July 1972, with the formation of the Messmer government, it went back to being a single ministry.

[10] See the Fulton Commission's *The British Civil Service*, I (London: H.M.S.O., 1968), 44–45. In appointing a number of businessmen to high-level posts, Prime Minister Heath appears to have followed the advice of the Fulton Commission. See *The New York Times*, June 30, 1970.

France, such a practice is unlikely to occur. First, it recalls the era of patronage and political appointments of the higher civil servants. Also, these higher officials believe that the administration constitutes a world of its own, with particular mechanisms and traditions, and that an outsider would find it difficult to understand and to adapt to this world. They argue that "a man from the outside could not win the confidence of his subordinates." In other words, the "outsider" might pursue policies that did not have as their primary purpose the safeguarding of the particular institution's autonomy. To understand the mechanisms of an institution generally means to understand the interests of that institution—which are not necessarily linked to, and may

TABLE 6.1
Minister's Choice of Directors[1] (percent)

Minister should choose from outside administration	23.5
Minister should choose only from administration	56.8
Advantageous to choose from outside administration, but unworkable	19.8
Don't know	1.0
Total (N = 90)	100.0

[1] Question posed to Directors: Ought the minister's choice of his Directors to be extended to the private sector, or should it be confined only to higher civil servants?

even be in contradiction with, the function it is intended to perform. Even those civil servants who considered it advisable to bring men into the administration from the private sector usually added that it would not be practicable. The two reasons most often cited were the disparity in salaries, which would not make the civil service attractive to an executive in the private sector, and the outsider's lack of acquaintance with the rules and mechanisms of the administration, which would automatically disqualify him even if he were prepared to accept the lower salary and devote himself to public service. Finally, the civil servants believe that if a minister wishes to recruit outsiders he can easily do so by bringing them into his cabinet. We will examine in later chapters the important role that the ministerial cabinet has come to play in the French politico-administrative system, although some of the reasons for this may already be evident. The Directors, then, see themselves as the guardians of specialized knowledge about a world that is essentially *sui generis*. As one Director replied when asked whether it might be a good idea for the minister to appoint Directors from outside the administration, "The administration is a body and it rejects anything foreign to it."

The removal of a Director is also at the discretion of the minister and the Government, and the Conseil d'État recognizes that a Director may be removed for political reasons.[11] This apparent simplicity in removing and replacing a Director is counterbalanced, however, by practical difficulties. For one thing, it is generally considered to be very traumatic for a Director to be ousted from the highest administrative post. Also, the minister is obliged to find another post of adequate prestige for him, which often presents problems since prestigious sinecures are generally in short supply. What usually happens, therefore, in the case of an ineffectual Director whom the minister wishes to replace, is that the minister keeps the Director but appoints someone in his cabinet to do the requisite work. One *directeur de cabinet* noted that "this is a most unfortunate practice, but we have been obliged to do it." If, however, a Director is not ineffectual but, on the contrary, a strong personality who has his own policies that run, or might run, counter to those of the minister, then "one way or another," said this *directeur de cabinet*, "the minister will find a way to replace him."

Given that a minister's choice of his Directors is, for all practical purposes, limited to the civil service, we may ask whether his ability to choose from within the administration is as open as it may appear. In practice, the minister's choice of a Director is limited by or accommodated to the rivalries between the various corps. The technical and nontechnical corps are engaged in a never-ending battle to colonize sectors of the administration. First, there are *directions* that are strictly reserved for a particular corps, so that a minister's choice of a Director is more or less predetermined. In this category would fall such diverse and important *directions* as the *direction des mines* and the *direction des carburants* in the Ministry of Scientific Research and Industrial Development. The heads of these *directions* are always, and without question, chosen from the *corps des mines*. It would be difficult to imagine a minister seeking to turn his back on the "advice" of this corps and appointing someone from another corps.

[11] Victor Silvera, *La Fonction publique et ses problèmes* (Paris: Editions de l'Actualité Juridique, 1969), p. 562.

Similarly, the *direction des routes* and the *direction des ports maritimes et des voies navigables* are the province of the corps of civil engineers (*ingénieurs des ponts et chaussées*). In all these cases, a member of the corps has usually been groomed for the post by his corps and the minister has not far to look.

While in these technical *directions* there may be some technical justifications, in addition to the element of tradition, for choosing a civil servant from a particular corps to fill a certain post, in other cases a *direction* is monopolized by a corps for no other reason than "tradition," which may mean simply that the first Director named to the post at the time of its creation was a member of that corps. This is the case, for example, of the *direction de la sécurité sociale* in the Ministry of Public Health and Social Security, which the Conseil d'Etat considers its own because Pierre Laroque, the first Director of Social Security (and originator of the social security system in France) was a member of the Conseil d'Etat. It is important to note that were a minister to decide to appoint someone outside the Conseil d'Etat to this post it would not be the civil servants of the ministry who would protest—in fact, they resent the presence of an "outsider" in their ministry—but the Conseil d'Etat itself. This case illustrates how a corps not attached to a particular ministry maintains a hold over posts within the administration and circumscribes a minister's choice. How rapidly "traditions" are created can be seen from numerous other cases where a member of a corps is appointed for the first time to head a particular *direction* (the *direction* of civil aviation in the Ministry of Transport, the *direction* of local collectivities in the Ministry of Interior are cases in point) which the corps thereafter comes to consider its own. In many cases, however, the hold of a corps over a particular *direction*, while it may appear to circumscribe the choice of a minister, nevertheless suits his wishes. This is because having a member of one of the major corps on his staff adds to the prestige of the ministry and, ministers believe, increases their bargaining power within the politico-administrative system.[12]

In certain instances, a minister may be able to choose between two or three potential candidates who have followed similar

---

[12] This indicates a tacit acknowledgment of an informal network within the politico-administrative system. The operation of this network will be examined in greater detail in the following chapters.

careers, and who are generally regarded as being "in line" for a particular post. This is especially the case with the *directions nobles* (Budget, Tax, Treasury, Public Accounting, Economic Forecasting), the truly important and prestigious posts in the Ministry of Finance. Time and again the higher civil servants in this Ministry noted with pride: "I could tell you now who will be the Director of the Budget or the Director of the Treasury in ten years' time." Or, "I can tell you now who will be the Governor of the Bank of France in twenty years' time." In one instance, a higher civil servant in the Ministry of Finance knew that, no matter who the next minister would be, he would be chosen as the next Director of one of the most important *directions* in the Ministry. To bide his time, he took a post in one of the financial capitals of the world so as to consolidate the various contacts he would need in his next job. This suggests that one acquires a considerable degree of assurance and confidence as a result of belonging to a grand corps, for had this higher civil servant not belonged to the Inspection des Finances, he could have done no more than aspire to the post. But he was a member of the Inspection des Finances and possessed the necessary qualifications, so he was able to consider himself—and to be regarded by others—as the legitimate heir. Indeed, it was this Director who assured the author that he could name not only his successor, but all those who would be occupying the most important posts in the Ministry of Finance over the next ten years. Another Director in this Ministry, eager to make the same point, went so far as to document it by reeling off a list of posts and the names of those who would be filling them within the next decade and a half. For two of the posts, he admitted that he could not be certain whether x or y would be chosen. He was certain, however, that the choice had already been narrowed to these two candidates. Both, of course, were members of the Inspection des Finances.

On rare occasions, however, circumstances conspire to remove from the hands of a corps a post that the corps had grown accustomed to considering its own. In 1969, when Couve de Murville appointed Olivier Wormser, a diplomat, as Governor of the Bank of France, the Inspection des Finances felt it had lost what is perhaps the single most important financial post in France. All the more painful was this loss in view of the fact that a former Inspecteur des Finances had been responsible for it. Clearly, Couve de Murville had long before shifted his interests and attachments from his original corps (the Inspection des Finances) to the diplomatic corps—the appointment of Olivier Wormser left no doubt of this change in loyalties. But how did the Inspection des Finances justify its hold on the post? First, insofar as the post concerns the formulation of financial policy, the Inspection had reason to claim that one of its members was best able to occupy it. Second, and perhaps more important, was its invocation of tradition. The Inspection des Finances had long—at least since 1936 —considered the Governorship of the Bank of France one of its major conquests.[13] As we noted earlier in the case of the *direction de la sécurité sociale*, traditions are easily created; their strength is not directly related to their age, and they are not so easily changed. Consequently, in invoking "tradition" to justify the continuation of a particular practice, what is being invoked is a whole host of factors that have little to do with what happens to be the best solution at the moment. Rather, the "tradition" is fallen back on because it signifies that an equilibrium was, or has been, reached, that the distribution of power between sectors of the administration will be upset once again unless the "tradition" is observed, and that stability and order, while they may work in the interest of a particular group, are effectively serving the interests of the entire (administrative) community.

PROMOTION OF CIVIL SERVANTS AND THE MINISTER'S CHOICE

Having discussed the factors that circumscribe a minister's choice of the most important officials in his ministry—a choice that, theoretically, knows no bounds—we should now look at the factors that favor the promotion of certain officials over others. How does a higher civil servant become a Director in the French central administration? Table 6.2 shows that, according to these men themselves, the most important qualifications for becoming a Director are (1) belonging to a corps; (2) being professionally competent; and (3) having made a good number of contacts in one's previous post, which means, above all, having served in one or more ministerial cabinets. It is particularly important to note how closely linked are these qualifications: one is assumed to be professionally competent because one belongs to a corps, and one

[13] See Pierre Lalumière, *L'Inspection des Finances* (Paris: Presses Universitaires de France, 1959), pp. 154–157.

is more likely to belong to a ministerial cabinet if one belongs to a corps. Indeed, many of those who noted the importance of professional competence as a factor in a minister's choice added that such competence did not imply that the candidate was familiar with the problems with which he would be called upon to deal. Rather, because of his other qualifications, he could be trusted to acquire a quick grasp of those problems. The most important prerequisite for appointment to the post of Director is, therefore,

TABLE 6.2

Factors Influencing Nomination of Directors in the French Higher Civil Service (percent)

Factor	1st Choice	2nd Choice	3rd Choice
Seniority	1.2	2.5	1.2
Belonging to a corps	35.8	28.4	16.0
Political opinions	1.2	4.9	3.7
Professional capacity and familiarity with problems	54.3	17.3	8.6
Compatibility of personalities	2.5	2.5	4.9
Contacts established in earlier posts (ministerial cabinet)	2.5	33.3	40.7
Contacts established with political parties	–	–	1.2
Authority and prestige in ministry	2.5	8.6	17.3

membership in a corps from which flow numerous other advantages that may at times be confused with technical qualifications. But this applies not only to appointments to directorial posts; it also applies to promotion in the higher civil service in general. This is shown in Table 6.3, which indicates that, aside from hard work, which may mean no more than long hours at one's desk, the most important factors are membership in a corps and the backing of a superior. About the same proportion believed that original ideas were important ("not too original," was often added) as those who believed that it was important not to create problems for one's superior, whose support was so essential to promotion.

The importance of the data in Tables 6.2 and 6.3 resides in the fact that they are subjectively based, that is, they indicate how

TABLE 6.3

Factors Influencing Promotion in the French Higher Civil Service
(percent)

Factor	1st Choice	2nd Choice	3rd Choice
Seniority	4.9	7.4	2.5
Hard work	60.5	8.6	4.9
Initiative and original ideas	6.2	14.8	4.9
Extraprofessional activities	1.2	1.2	1.2
Not creating problems for superiors	1.2	8.6	14.8
Personal relations	—	2.5	4.9
Education	4.9	1.2	3.7
Chance	—	1.2	1.2
Membership in a corps	9.9	21.0	16.0
Support of superior	7.4	29.6	35.8

the higher civil servant himself perceives his career and his promotion prospects. The data do not, to be sure, tell us whether membership in a corps or service in a ministerial cabinet *are* in fact important factors in promotion and in appointment to the post of Director. This objective data is presented in Table 6.4, which bears out the higher civil servants' conception of advancement in the French administration system. The subjective and the objective data must be seen in conjunction with one another because the objective data do not, and often cannot, include certain crucial factors. A good example of this is the backing of one's superior (shown in Table 6.3) which, according to the higher civil servants, is indispensable for promotion. Another important factor not revealed by the objective data is the influence that a corps often exerts in securing a post for one of its members, and the influence it exerts in maintaining the post for other members. The objective data show the number of years it took to attain a particular post, the posts previously held, the age at the time of appointment, the posts held after leaving the post of Director, and the like. This is interesting and important data, and they have been attractively presented in J. Siwek-Pouydesseau's *Le Personnel de direction des ministères.*[14] Complete re-

[14] J. Siwek-Pouydesseau, *Le Personnel de direction des ministères* (Paris: Armand Colin, 1969), pp. 56–88.

TABLE 6.4

Promotion to the Post of Director, 1946-1969 (percent)

Membership in a corps	
Inspection des Finances	9.7
Conseil d'Etat	5.6
Cour des Comptes	2.3
Prefectoral Corps	11.0
Corps des Mines	2.7
Ponts et Chaussees	6.1
Colonial Corps	5.0
Service in Ministerial Cabinet	
Served in at least one cabinet	45.3
Served in two cabinets	9.0
Served in three or more cabinets	12.8
Service in Ministerial Cabinet after	
holding post of Director	3.6
Career confined to one ministry	81.3
Cabinet to Post of Director	
1 year or less	20.3
2 years	2.7
3 years	2.0
4 years	3.4
5 years	3.6

liance on this data, however, leads to the rather questionable conclusion that it is the minister who has the final word in the nomination of his Directors.[15] But we have already noted that the minister must, to a very considerable extent, adapt himself to a process of selection that takes place within the administration, a process that he may be able to influence, but which he cannot radically modify.

This is certainly the case, as was noted above, in the more important policy-making *directions* that are monopolized by certain corps. It is also the case, though to a lesser degree, in the *directions* that have a purely administrative function and that are not colonized by a corps. It is less the case in a *direction* where no corps has a particularly strong influence. The minister's choice, as our classification of *directions* indicates (Table 6.5), depends mostly on the influence of a corps in the ministry and in certain *directions*. Where the role of the corps is unimportant, the minister's choice is likely to be widest; where the role of the corps is important, regardless of the type of *direction*, the minister's

15 *Ibid.*, p. 33.

choice is liable to be most circumscribed. Our classification of *directions* may appear, and is to some extent, arbitrary. We have found, however, that previous classifications have been perhaps even more arbitrary because of their attempt to distinguish between two types of *directions*: administrative or technical, weak or strong, whether they have regional services or not. The chief difficulty in attempting to delineate the structure of the French central administration arises from the fact that there are great disparities in its organization. As Ridley and Blondel have noted:

TABLE 6.5

Classification of Directions *and Range of Minister's Choice of Directors*

Type of Direction	Role of Corps	Choice of Minister
Policy-making (strong)	Strong	Almost nonexistent
Policy-making (weak)	Strong	Very limited
Policy-making (weak)	Weak	Open
Administrative (strong)	Strong	Almost nonexistent
Administrative (weak)	Strong	Very limited
Administrative (weak)	Weak	Open
Newly created	None	Open

"Although the French have a reputation for logic and order, homogeneity of structure has never been a characteristic of their central administration. This is an odd contrast with the local government system where, originally at least, a fairly homogeneous pattern was imposed on very diverse areas."[16] Although our study is only incidentally concerned with the organization and structure of the French bureaucracy, it has nevertheless been essential to devise a classification of *directions* in order to gain a perspective on the minister's choice of his chief subordinates.

Within a single ministry there may exist *directions* of wholly unequal weight, depending not only on their function (policy-making or administrative) but on their organization as well. In the Ministry of Industrial Development and Scientific Research there are to be found strong policy-making and administrative *directions* (the *direction des mines* and the *direction des carburants*) which are tightly organized, autonomous, have well-trained civil servants supplied largely by the *corps des mines* and a free-flow-

[16] F. Ridley and J. Blondel, *Public Administration in France* (New York: Barnes and Noble, 1968), p. 58.

ing communication system between the various hierarchical levels within the *directions*. There also exist in this ministry weak administrative *directions* (the *direction des industries diverses et des textiles*) and weak policy-making ones (the *direction de la politique industrielle*), *directions* that are either poorly organized, poorly run, or poorly staffed, and so are unable to obtain the information necessary for exerting influence (as in the case of the former), or are created for the purpose of formulating policy without the necessary means and so cannot overcome the hostilities of other *directions* in the ministry (as in the case of the *direction de la politique industrielle*). In the Ministry of Finance are again to be found strong policy-making *directions* (the *direction du Budget*, the *direction du Trésor*, the *direction des impôts*), well staffed, well organized and hence autonomous, as well as weak administrative *directions* (*direction de la loterie nationale*), and strong administrative ones (*direction de la comptabilité publique*). In the Ministry of Social Affairs, generally regarded as a "low prestige" ministry, there coexist important policy-making *directions* (*direction de la santé publique*) that are weak, and others (the *direction des migrations*) that are strong.

The minister's choice is usually greatest in the administrative *directions* that do not fall into the hands of a corps: *directions* of Personnel, of General Administration, of Equipment, of Administrative and Social Services. These *directions* have purely intra-ministry responsibilities. The minister will almost always appoint someone who is familiar with the ministry, or someone who has held a similar post in another ministry; in other words, he will appoint someone with previous experience in large-scale management and personnel matters. It is not difficult to see why the major corps would have little interest in securing these posts for their members. For a post to be considered "significant" it must have policy-making and, hence, interministry responsibilities.

In certain technical ministries, where the task of a Director may also be largely administrative, such as managing the equipment and facilities of the ministry or managing the postal system, the minister's choice will be restricted because a corps will have a monopoly on these posts. It is interesting to note, for example, that when higher civil servants in the Ministry of Post and Telecommunications were asked about the desirability of ministers' bringing in someone from outside the administration to occupy the post of Director, they all responded in the same man-

150

ner, emphasizing that it was inconceivable for a minister to appoint someone from outside the ministry itself. Someone from "outside the administration" was so utterly inconceivable to the higher civil servants in this ministry that the question was misinterpreted on practically every occasion: to appoint a civil servant from outside "the house" would be a capital transgression; to appoint someone from the private sector would be an unpardonable sin. It is not insignificant that "outside the administration" was always interpreted as meaning "outside this ministry."

There have been instances of a civil servant from one ministry being appointed as Director in another ministry. For example, a sub-Director in the Ministry of Finance became a Director in the Ministry of Agriculture, and so did a member of the Conseil d'Etat. Both met with disdain and hostility. Their colleagues saw them as intruders who had some connection with the minister, while their subordinates saw themselves as being deprived of a "true" defender and representative. In general, life is made difficult for such Directors and often they are unable to survive the minister who nominated them. There are therefore important reasons for civil servants leading narrow careers within ministries and, in most cases, within particular *directions*. The nomination of a large number of persons to responsible posts in ministries to which they had no previous attachment whatsoever occurred after World War II, when a number of those who had played an active part in the Resistance were rewarded with important positions. Indeed, a few of those nominated to these posts continue to occupy them today. This practice has been criticized for supposedly making the administrative career, and particularly the diplomatic career, less attractive than it would otherwise have been, owing to the diminished promotion possibilities for the young civil servants.[17] Yet this was undoubtedly one of the rare instances that permitted the French civil service to alter, if only briefly, its upper-middle-class composition.

POLITICAL APPOINTMENTS IN THE ADMINISTRATION

It has been argued that the practice of political appointments, or the "open spoils system," as Philip Williams has called it,[18] was

[17] Wladimir D'Ormesson, "Grands Corps et Grands Commis–II; La Carrière diplomatique," *La Revue des Deux Mondes*, July 1, 1958, p. 66.
[18] Philip M. Williams, *Crisis and Compromise: Politics in the Fourth Republic* (New York: Doubleday Anchor, 1966), p. 359.

particularly flagrant under the Fourth Republic. One writer notes that the influence of political parties in the appointment of Directors was considerable under the Fourth Republic. "It is well known that under *Tripartisme*, the appointed Directors were quite closely linked to the minister's party—consequently, the SFIO, the MRP, and the Radical Party often shared among themselves the directorial posts in the administration."[19] Philip Williams notes also that political appointments to senior civil service posts were widespread under the Fourth Republic, and that such appointments "became systematic under *tripartisme* when the three government parties parcelled out the administration among them."[20] He maintains that with the ouster of the Communists from the government in 1947 "the open spoils system was checked, but politics could not be wholly excluded from appointments to policy-making posts."[21] It is difficult either to substantiate or to refute the degree to which such political appointments occurred. There are, however, indications that they were not nearly as widespread as Siwek-Pouydesseau and Williams claim. In the first place, the number of Directors who served under ministers of several parties far exceeded those who served only under the minister who nominated them, or under ministers of only one party: I draw on Mme. Siwek-Pouydesseau's own data to document this point. Her tabulations (Table 6.6) show that while there may have been wide variations in the stability of Directors in different ministries, the average is considerably greater than that of ministerial stability. Given that each ministerial change very often also entailed a party change, for wholesale political appointments to have occurred the average length of a Director's tenure would have had to be considerably less than it in fact was. For example, there were twenty-one party changeovers in the Ministry of Finance between 1944 and 1958. If each minister had in fact named his own Directors, the average length of a Director's tenure would have been approximately 0.7 years—that is, the same as the average length of each minister's tenure. Yet the average length of a Director's tenure in this ministry was actually 4.3 years. Similarly, there were seventeen party changeovers in the Ministry of Justice during the same period. Again, for each minister to have fired the appointees of his predecessor and named his own Directors would have meant that the average

[19] Siwek-Pouydesseau, *Le Personnel de direction des ministères*, p. 34.
[20] Williams, *Crisis and Compromise*, p. 359.
[21] *Ibid.*

length of a Director's tenure in this ministry could not have exceeded 0.8 years, whereas in fact it was four times as long.

Moreover, there were certain practical difficulties, partly emanating from the nature of the Fourth Republic's coalition governments, that made political firings and appointments unlikely. As was noted earlier, a Director is not appointed by a minister alone, and no appointment can be made that does not meet with

TABLE 6.6

Comparison of the Stability of Ministers and Directors of the Central Administration, 1944-1958 (expressed in years)

Ministry	Ministers	Directors
Health	0.7	4.3
Finance	0.8	4.3
Justice	0.8	3.3
Public Works	0.9	3.9
Labor	0.9	5.2
Construction	0.9	2.9
Agriculture	1.1	5.4
Industry	1.2	4.7
Education	1.2	5.0
Interior	1.2	2.8
Post and Telecommunications	1.3	5.1
Foreign Affairs	1.6	2.7
Average	1.1	4.1

Source: Siwek-Pouydesseau, *Le Personnel de direction des ministéres*, p. 73.

the approval of the Prime Minister and the President of the Republic. But since the President of the Republic and the Prime Minister did not necessarily belong to the same political party as a particular minister who wished to make wholesale changes of Directors, it is extremely unlikely that such changes were sanctioned, simply because those in power knew that the tables could be turned against them the next day.[22] Consequently, it is quite probable that political appointments were kept to a minimum not in spite of, but because of, the coalition nature of the Fourth Republic governments.

[22] Alfred Grosser also appears to take a view contrary to that of J. Siwek-Pouydesseau and Philip Williams, noting that even with regard to appointments to ministerial cabinets under the Fourth Republic, ministers often disregarded the party label of the civil servants. See his *La IVe République et sa politique extérieure* (Paris: Armand Colin, 1961), p. 56.

In fact, it could well be argued that political appointments—not necessarily pure patronage, but simply the congruence in political views between the minister and the Director—is less likely to occur under an unstable regime which is characterized by precarious coalitions, as was the Fourth Republic, than under a stable regime whose government is constituted by a cohesive political force that is not forced to share power. There is sufficient evidence to indicate that under the Fifth Republic both the Prime Minister's office and the staff of the President of the Republic have kept a scrutinizing eye on all appointments. This was unquestionably the case under the Premierships of Debré, Pompidou, and Couve de Murville. In one case, the nomination of a Director was held up in the Prime Minister's office for over a year. When Edgar Faure became Minister of Education in July 1968, he took a number of dramatic steps, first abolishing the post of Secretary General and then undertaking to reform the French educational system. Both moves were looked upon with various degrees of skepticism and hostility by orthodox Gaullists. When he nominated a civil servant in this ministry to the post of Director, the nomination was held up in the Prime Minister's office for over a year—the entire time that Couve de Murville was Prime Minister. This civil servant was thought by Matignon to have too close a relationship with the unions, and would thus be too sympathetic to them. Faure refused to withdraw his nomination and Couve de Murville refused to sign. All this time the civil servant in question was occupying the post as Acting Director, and he continued to occupy it for six months after Faure was ousted from the government. Finally Faure's successor, Olivier Guichard, an orthodox Gaullist, proposed this same man for the post of Director. The nomination was approved forthwith. There have been other known cases where Directors were forced out of their posts because their political views were known to be out of line with that of the Gaullist party. In fact, Mme. Siwek-Pouydesseau's calculations show that there were more changes of Directors between 1959 and 1966 than between 1951 and 1958.[23] This raises the question of the relationship between the regime of the Fifth Republic, or the Gaullist party, and the administration, a question that we will return to in Chapter XIII.

[23] Siwek-Pouydesseau, *Le Personnel de direction des ministères*, p. 75.

CHAPTER VII

The Minister and His Administration: Relationship

Non, Messieurs, le ministre ne peut plus être le maître de son ministère, ni en ce qui concerne le personnel, ni en ce qui concerne les affaires.

—*Henri Chardon*[1]

Il faut des ministres qui commandent.

—*Albin Chalandon, Former Minister of Equipment and Housing*

BUREAUCRATS AND POLITICIANS

It has often been argued that the bureaucrat and the politician represent two distinct species, each with his own approach to and perspectives on matters of national import. Weber, who most clearly defined the attributes of the two, did not view them as being in perpetual conflict or opposition to one another; rather, he saw the task of the bureaucrat as the indispensable complement to that of the politician. "According to his proper vocation," wrote Weber, "the genuine official . . . will not engage in politics. Rather, he should engage in impartial 'administration.' . . . Hence, he should not do precisely what the politician, the leader as well as his following, must always and necessarily do, namely, *fight*."[2] In his *Ideology and Utopia*, Karl Mannheim also attempted to define the specific qualities of the administrator, which he saw as characterized by a "military-bureaucratic mentality." This "mentality," according to Mannheim, has its own peculiar rationality, and it "constructs only closed static systems of thought."[3] "The

[1] *Le Pouvoir administratif* (Paris: Perrin, 1911), p. 187. This book is a collection of Chardon's addresses before a group of civil servants. Chardon himself was a member of the Conseil d'Etat.

[2] Max Weber, "Politics as a Vocation," in H. H. Gerth and C. Wright Mills, eds., *From Max Weber: Essays in Sociology* (New York: Oxford University Press, 1958), p. 95.

[3] Karl Mannheim, *Ideology and Utopia* (New York: Harcourt, Brace and World, 1936), p. 119.

attempt to hide all problems of politics under the cover of administration may be explained by the fact that the sphere of activity of the official exists only within the limit of laws already formulated."[4]

In the "ideal-type" system envisaged by Weber, the professional bureaucrat "is only a single cog in an ever-moving mechanism which prescribes to him an essentially fixed route of march. The official is entrusted with specialized tasks and normally the mechanism cannot be put into motion or arrested by him, but only from the very top."[5] The politician, by virtue of his distinct qualities and by virtue of being an elected official, thus prescribes what the official must carry out. In democratic systems it is the politician who is best suited to judge the needs of a society; the civil servant must then execute, without rendering personal judgment, the prescriptions of the elected official. Critical in this delimitation of the tasks of the two actors is the fact that the civil servant is appointed, whereas the politician is elected.[6]

If the Weberian schema is no more than an "ideal-type" that describes no particular system, it is also a *normative* prescription on which hinges, to a very considerable extent, the democratic process. In reality, it would of course be hard to find a political system where such a neat distribution of functions between politician and civil servant existed. The study of bureaucracy derives its importance, as Weber, Michels, and others have argued, from the possible undermining influences of bureaucracy on democracy.[7] Thus the relationship between higher civil servants and politicians raises the crucial question of the implementation of government policy and the influence of nonelected officials on that policy. This relationship differs from one society to another and the difference is partly owing, as I shall argue in this and the following chapters, to the actors' perception of their roles.

REPRESENTATIVE BUREAUCRACY

When Prime Minister Harold Wilson appointed the Fulton Commission, in 1966, to conduct "a fundamental and wide-ranging

---

[4] *Ibid.*, p. 118.

[5] Max Weber, "Bureaucracy," in Gerth and Mills, *From Max Weber: Essays in Sociology*, p. 228.

[6] Jean Meynaud, *Technocracy* (London: Faber and Faber, 1965), p. 117.

[7] See Seymour M. Lipset, *Political Man* (New York: Doubleday Anchor, 1963), pp. 9–12.

inquiry" into the Civil Service, he noted that "the Government's willingness to consider changes in the Civil Service does not imply any intention on its part to alter the basic relationship between Ministers and Civil Servants."[8] That the Government, and a Labor Government at that, could not envisage any modifications in the relationship between senior politicians and administrative officials testifies to the existence of a singular cooperation between the two groups. Both civil servants and politicians recognize that it is the former who bear the burden of the formulation and execution of policy. As Sisson has noted, "When a Minister announces in the House that he will *do* something he is rarely talking about the sort of thing that he himself *does*. . . . It is more usual to speak of what a Minister is *responsible for* than what he does."[9]

Whether one takes the view that the British higher civil servant's anonymity is what guarantees his impartiality, as Sisson argues, or whether one believes that "the view of the civil servant as a disinterested assembler of facts simply will not stand examination,"[10] one continually meets the assertion of the judicious and impartial predisposition of British higher civil servants. Kingsley, writing in the 1940's, has forcefully argued that the British civil servant is impartial not in any objective sense—a Labor government, he maintained, might be hampered by the civil service as it is now composed[11]—but in the sense that it is representative of the ruling class. It is a middle-class service serving a middle-class state. "The essence of responsibility is psychological rather than mechanical," wrote Kingsley. "It is to be sought in an identity of aim and point of view, in a common background of social prejudice, which leads the agent to act as though he were the principal."[12] The administration is truly responsible (and in this sense impartial) "when Ministers and Civil Servants share the same backgrounds and hold similar social views; when, in other words, the bureaucracy is representative."[13] One writer has noted that no bureaucracy is representative because the mid-

---

[8] Geoffrey K. Fry, "Some Weaknesses in the Fulton Report on the British Home Civil Service," *Political Studies*, XVII, no. 4 (1969), 484.

[9] C. H. Sisson, *The Spirit of British Administration* (London: Faber and Faber, 1959), p. 13.

[10] J. Donald Kingsley, *Representative Bureaucracy* (Yellow Springs, Ohio: Antioch Press, 1944), p. 275.

[11] *Ibid.*, p. 279.   [12] *Ibid.*, p. 282.   [13] *Ibid.*, p. 273.

157

dle class dominates the civil service in almost every country. This is indeed correct, as his data show.[14] However, as Kingsley makes clear, for a bureaucracy to be representative—hence, also for it to be responsible—it need be representative only of the body politic.

In France, as we have seen, the higher civil service is recruited, as are the political and other elites, from the higher social categories. How, then, does the theory of a representative bureaucracy help to explain the relationship between administrators and politicians? In the first place, it should be noted that this theory is based essentially on the classical Marxist argument that the bureaucracy is at the service of the bourgeois rulers.[15] To the extent that the theory seeks universal applicability based primarily on the social origin of the elites and to the exclusion of other factors, we are bound to conclude that it tells us very little. For if the theory of a representative bureaucracy implies, as it surely must, the cohesion of classes—based on a common social background, the commitment to "middle-class values," and a uniform mode of behavior of the members of this class—it ignores the divisions within classes, the adoption of values of a class other than one's own, and the role of the educational system in inculcating attitudes and modes of thought that are independent of one's social origin. In the case of France, the theory of a representative bureaucracy does not help us to understand the particular relationship that exists between the bureaucracy and the politicians, because it does not take into account a number of intervening historical variables: the historical development of the bureaucracy, the ideological heterogeneity of the political leaders, the development of the political parties, the importance of patronage in the recruitment of the administrative elite, the timing of the introduction of the merit system in recruitment—all of these factors have contributed to shaping the complex and shifting perception of roles which leads to complex and changing modes of behavior. Thus, the "mentality" of the official is far more elusive than has hitherto been recognized, and it can best be comprehended in terms of role theory, to which we will turn in Chapter IX.

In comparing the nature of executive government in Britain

[14] V. Subramaniam, "Representative Bureaucracy: A Reassessment," *The American Political Science Review*, LXI, no. 4 (1967), 1015–1017.

[15] Karl Marx, *The 18th Brumaire of Louis Bonaparte* (New York: International Publishers, 1963), p. 122.

and in the United States, Richard Neustadt observes that the British higher civil servant is "a man fulfilled, not frustrated."[16] This is the result of a mutual understanding, an "implicit bargain," between the civil servants and the ministers: they form what Neustadt calls "a Society for Mutual Benefit." The civil servants must be and are consulted by the ministers, who in turn do not interfere in recruitment and promotion matters and who protect the anonymity of their officials. "More important," writes Neustadt, "the politicians *lean* on their officials. They *expect* to be advised. Most important, they very often follow the advice that they receive."[17] This bargain has advantages for both sides. "It relieves the politicians of a difficult and chancy search for 'loyal' advisers and administrators. These are in place, ready to hand. And it relieves civil servants of concern for their security in terms both of profession and of person."[18]

The importance of appointing men with whom a minister can work was recognized long ago by Léon Blum, who was fully aware of the degree to which a minister's effectiveness was dependent on his own choice of civil servants. That is why someone like Blum could insist that a minister ought to replace a Director the moment it became apparent that they could not work together. Had Blum's advice been followed, it is quite possible that the structure and functioning of the French administrative system—at its apex, at any rate—would be very different. Having been deeply impressed by the relationship of the minister to his higher civil servants in Britain, Blum was vehemently opposed to any intermediary institution—the ministerial cabinet and the Secretary General—between the minister and the higher civil servants in his ministry. He was even opposed to the institution (no longer in existence) of a council of Directors that met periodically, because he feared that this would detract from the mutual confidence so necessary between the minister and each individual Director. As he wrote in his *La Réforme gouvernementale*: "I conceive of the minister's work with his Directors as being similar to that of the President with his colleagues, and I am opposed to a Council of Directors and to a Council of Ministers. . . . The consultation between a Director and a minister must

---

[16] Richard Neustadt, "White House and Whitehall," *The Public Interest*, II (1966), reprinted in Richard Rose, ed., *Policy-Making in Britain* (New York: The Free Press, 1969), p. 294.

[17] *Ibid.*, p. 294. Italics in original.   [18] *Ibid.*

be 'un travail en tête à tête,' with the *chef de cabinet* being the only witness."[19]

This proposal would be feasible only if the minister were able and willing to change the Directors in the ministry and place in their stead men in whom he had full confidence. The difficulties involved in this practice, if only because the administrative syndicalist movement was exerting greater pressures toward more rather than less security of tenure, led ministers to rely on their personal appointees who compose the ministerial cabinet, the institution which, as the following two chapters will show, has become crucial in the French administrative system.

Given that ministers do not appoint their own top administrative officials, it appears to follow that no strong bonds can be established between the minister and those officials whom he finds in place upon taking office. This is certainly the case in the United States where, though there exists no formal cabinet, a Secretary nevertheless gathers around him a team of advisers in whom he has complete trust. Also, our survey indicated that in the rare instances where a close relationship did exist between minister and Director, the Director had always been chosen by the minister. In every other case, a meeting between a minister and a Director takes place in the presence of the member of the minister's cabinet who is responsible for supervising the work of the Director's *direction*. But if the relationship between ministers and Directors is, in general, spasmodic and devoid of trust, this in no way answers the important question of the distribution of power between politicians and administrators. We have already attempted to view this question in light of the hypothesis concerning the representativeness of the bureaucracy and we concluded that, despite the existence of a representative bureaucracy —in Kingsley's sense of the term—in France, no harmonious relationship had developed between politicians and civil servants. Consequently, the theory of a representative bureaucracy, applicable as it may be to Britain, does not explain the distribution of power between politicians and the bureaucracy in France.

POLITICAL INSTABILITY AND ADMINISTRATIVE POWER

It is necessary now to turn to another hypothesis, which has been applied to France as often as the theory of a representative bu-

[19] Léon Blum, *La Réforme gouvernementale* (Paris: Grasset, 1936), pp. 145–146.

reaucracy has been applied to Britain: briefly, the hypothesis states that where there exists an unstable political system—i.e., frequent changes in governments—policy-making power will fall into the hands of the permanent bureaucracy.[20]

First, it is important to understand what is meant by governmental instability. To be sure, the recurring cabinet crises under the Third and Fourth Republics entailed constant changes of governments, the average life of a government being approximately eight months in both Republics. But these cabinet changes did not entail ministerial changes to the same degree; indeed, as Philip Williams has indicated for the Fourth Republic, there was a remarkable degree of ministerial continuity.[21] Moreover, Dogan and Campbell have shown that the same proportion of men tended to be reappointed to the new government after each cabinet crisis in both Britain and France.[22]

Since the governmental crises entailed constant reshuffles, even when the same men were appointed to the same ministries, let us define ministerial instability in a less strict sense. Let us consider the climate or atmosphere of instability which certainly affected the *expectations* of ministers. They were aware that the government they belonged to would sooner or later be toppled and, though they may have been certain of a position in the next government, they could not be certain of the same post. We must take account of this expectation of discontinuity or instability, since it appears to have entered into the relationship between ministers and civil servants. In short, we may say that ministerial instability was important because ministers and civil servants could not count on a long-term relationship.

One of the most persistent themes in writings on French poli-

[20] Herbert Luethy, *France Against Herself* (New York: Meridian Books, 1954), p. 14. See also Alfred Diamant, "The French Administrative System: The Republic Passes but the Administration Remains," in W. J. Siffin, ed., *Toward the Comparative Study of Public Administration* (Bloomington: Indiana University Press, 1959).

[21] Philip M. Williams, *Crisis and Compromise: Politics in the Fourth Republic* (New York: Doubleday Anchor, 1966), Appendix III, pp. 528–529. For the Third Republic, see A. Soulier, *L'Instabilité ministérielle sous la troisième République* (Paris: Recueil Sirey, 1939), and Jacques Ollé-Laprune, *La Stabilité des ministres sous la troisième République, 1879–1940* (Paris: Librairie Générale de Droit et de Jurisprudence, 1962).

[22] Mattei Dogan and Peter Campbell, "Le Personnel ministériel en France et en Grande Bretagne," *Revue française de science politique*, VII (April–June 1957), 340.

161

tics has been that ministerial instability shifted power from the politicians to the civil servants. The Directors of the central administration serving under the Fifth Republic appear to share this view,[23] although their answers cannot be taken as conclusive proof that power *was* in the hands of civil servants under the Fourth Republic. This is because the question posed called for a comparison between two distinct periods more than a decade apart, and the Directors interviewed were not, as many of them recognized, in a position to compare since they had not occupied the post of Director, or frequently any major administrative post, under the Fourth Republic.

Now, in what did the power of civil servants consist under the Fourth Republic? Was it in day-to-day affairs? Was it in the making of large, national policies? Finally, how was this "power" affected by the new regime that came into being in 1958?

Civil servants can be said to possess the same degree of influence in two respects under unstable and stable political regimes: power in carrying out day-to-day matters, and power in the application of decisions. Power in policy questions that orient a nation one way or another, however, cannot be regarded as the province of one force in a society whose institutions are largely differentiated. Philip Williams has written that "long-range policies had been the work of officials rather than politicians in the Third Republic as well as the Fourth. This situation was a by-product of ministerial instability; however undesirable in theory, it was preferable to having no long-range policies at all.[24] He sees the positive aspects of the Fourth Republic—economic expansion and European cooperation—as the work of civil servants who responded "to strong and deep desires of most (not all)

---

[23] Question posed to Directors: Ministerial instability under the Fourth Republic shifted policy-making powers from politicians to civil servants. Would you say that this is absolutely correct, quite correct, correct in certain cases, or not correct?

Reply	%
Absolutely correct	56.8
Quite correct	25.9
Correct in certain cases	8.6
Not correct	4.9
Don't know	3.7
Total (n=90)	100.0

[24] Williams, *Crisis and Compromise*, p. 365.

thinking Frenchmen," and who made these policies "more acceptable to politicians of different views because they were given
detailed form by civil servants rather than by one of themselves."[25]
Three objections must be raised to this widely accepted interpretation. First, Williams himself subscribes to the thesis
regarding "the influence of party politics on senior appointments,"
which, he says, "became systematic under *tripartisme* when the
three government parties parcelled out the administration between them."[26] If this was the case, then the influence which he
ascribes to the civil servants must surely have been negated as a
result of their having lost their neutral position. Second, it is difficult to maintain, and even more difficult to document, that those
policies that ultimately turned out to be positive were the responsibility of the civil servants, while all those that rocked the regime—the European Defense Community, colonial exploits, the
Algerian war—were the responsibility of politicians. Finally, this
thesis fails to take into account the profound divisions that exist
within the administration itself, divisions that render administrative coordination difficult and are hence one of the chief obstacles
to policy-formulation.[27]

Similar contradictions may be found in Lawrence Scheinman's
fine study of the formulation of atomic energy policy under the
Fourth Republic, in which he asserts that governmental weaknesses and ministerial instability deprive the executive and the
legislature of a strong voice in the formulation of and control
over policies, and consequently strengthen the hands of the administrators.[28] Scheinman defines as follows the central theme of
his study: "that atomic policy, both in its civil and military perspective, was molded, guided and developed by a small group of
persons operating through informal channels of communication
outside the mainstream of political activity. The formal policy-
making institutions, in other words, played a relatively minor,
and in the case of the Parliament, even a nebulous role in the

[25] *Ibid.*, p. 365–366.   [26] *Ibid.*, p. 359.

[27] Williams himself is not unaware of the rivalries between the various
administrations. See his fine discussion on this subject in *ibid.*, pp. 358–366.

[28] Lawrence Scheinman, *Atomic Energy Policy in France Under the
Fourth Republic* (Princeton: Princeton University Press, 1965). Scheinman
quotes Williams approvingly to the effect that ministerial instability "renders
the ministers impotent and therefore ineffective as representatives of the
deputies' will, leaving the bureaucracy as the principal source of policy
making" (p. 204).

formulation of atomic policy."[29] Who, then, shaped atomic policy? What groups constituted the "informal channels"? Scheinman maintains that "the small cadre of individuals which shaped atomic policy was drawn from administrative, executive, military and legislative sources in roughly that order of importance."[30] Clearly, then, atomic policy was not simply the work of a group of administrators working against the politicians. There were politicians involved in the formulation of this policy which, as Scheinman himself shows, could not have been carried through without their support. "The executive was not a source of atomic policy but a medium through which the crucial actors sought and gained support for their policies. Final authority, of course, rested with the responsible political authorities, and to the extent that their official imprimaturs were necessary for policy to be fully elaborated, they were essential elements in the policy-making process."[31]

In the light of this statement, how is it possible to argue that the study "lends support to the proposition that ministerial instability enhances the influence and policy-making role of administrative and technocratic services"?[32] My contention is that the policy-making process described by Scheinman and others is *not* a function of ministerial instability, that politicians and civil servants cannot be seen as two species in perpetual conflict, and that shifting alliances between the two are a common feature of the behavior of both groups.[33] How does the Fifth Republic differ from the Fourth? Has the stability of the regime increased the influence of ministers and of parliament? In effect, as I shall argue in Chapter XIII, what distinguishes the Fifth from the Fourth Republic is not so much the altered institutional arrangements in favor of the executive, nor the relative ministerial stability, as the existence of a majority party which dominates the executive, the legislature, and probably the bureaucracy. In other words, it becomes crucial to distinguish between governmental or ministerial stability and party stability. Administrative or ministerial stability has not varied very much between the Fourth and Fifth Re-

---

29 *Ibid.*, p. 203.   30 *Ibid.*   31 *Ibid.*, p. 210.
32 *Ibid.*, p. 211.

33 Chapter IX will elaborate on this argument. It will be seen that the behavior of civil servants may be independent of the type of regime in existence.

publics[34]—what has dramatically varied has been the party structure, so that there exists in France today a "party government," in Richard Rose's sense of the term.[35] If, then, the policy-making powers of the bureaucracy have changed under the Fifth Republic, this is not the consequence of ministerial and governmental stability—which is also to say that the power attributed to the bureaucracy under the Fourth Republic could not have derived solely from governmental instability. Indeed, Philip Williams himself has noted that it was frequently easier to get things done under a system that managed to adapt itself to continuous crises. Ministerial crises, he observes, performed very important functions; "they were not the futile aberrations they were generally supposed to be," for they did create constant motive forces of change.[36]

All this does not, however, imply that the altered institutional arrangements under the Fifth Republic—relative ministerial stability, impotence of parliament, incompatibility of ministerial and parliamentary duties—have not affected the relationship between ministers and civil servants. There is little doubt that this relationship has been affected, and a brief discussion of it is now in order if we are to be able to assess the degree of "administrative power" under both the Fourth and Fifth Republics.

MINISTERS AND CIVIL SERVANTS IN THE FOURTH AND FIFTH REPUBLICS

One of the most important factors that determines the nature of the minister's relationship to his higher civil servants is the possession of information, and this factor is intimately linked to, and affected by, the relative stability or instability of the minister's tenure. Information is generally a monopoly of the higher civil servants in the ministry, which can be eroded only if the minister *and* his cabinet remain in office for a sufficiently long time. Such power as the civil servants possess as a result of their hold on information is not so much power to initiate policies on their own

---

[34] The extent to which they have varied is shown in J. Siwek-Pouydesseau, *Le Personnel de direction des ministères* (Paris: Armand Colin, 1969), p. 73.

[35] Richard Rose, "The Variability of Party Government: A Theoretical and Empirical Critique," *Political Studies*, XVII (December 1969), 413–445.

[36] Williams, *Crisis and Compromise*, p. 457.

165

as power to facilitate or obstruct policies initiated by others. Under the Fourth Republic, the minister may have harbored a certain mistrust of his administration, but he was undoubtedly dependent upon it to a very considerable extent. Competence and expertise, which the minister could not acquire in his short tenure, were the primary reason for this dependence. Another reason was that the minister did not have the time to prepare major reforms, or, if he did prepare a reform, he did not have time to carry it through. Most important, perhaps, is the fact that he could not count on the support of the government. Often—the Ministry of Agriculture is an example—a minister wished to append his name to a reform, or to be associated with some novel undertaking, and he was therefore only too glad to append his name to a proposal made by his civil servants. It must be emphasized, however, that in such cases the minister did not sanction policies that were contrary to his wishes. If the minister had as his aim the desire to placate and to defend the small farmer, so did the civil servants in the ministry. In general, there was more of a concordance of aims between ministers and civil servants—particularly in ministries that handled entrenched interest—than has heretofore been recognized. A third reason for the minister's dependence on the civil servants was that he did not have sufficient time to win the confidence and respect of the services headed by the Directors in his ministry. In effect, he faced an organization where communication channels were blocked as a result of their being centralized in those occupying the highest administrative posts in the ministry.

This dependence of the minister on his administration created a situation in which the Directors saw themselves as "guiding" the minister. As one Fourth Republic Director put it, "the ministers were obliged to be very attentive to us." Nor could the members of the minister's cabinet obviate this dependency; they too had little time or expertise. It is not surprising, therefore, to find Directors who served under the Fourth Republic claiming to have established "good working relations with ministers of all parties." One Director even noted that his easiest relationship was with a communist minister.

Despite the wide influence that civil servants enjoyed over politicians, it was not necessarily the kind of influence that, as some writers have implied, was so wide-ranging that it included responsibility for major policy initiatives. Or, if the civil servants did have influence over major policies, such policies were carried out, or passed in parliament, with the aid of politicians. The civil servants' real power lay in obstruction. As one Director observed, "when a minister wanted something unfeasible done, we only had to say 'fine,' and chances were that we would hear no more of it." The minister, even if he remained in office longer than either he or his civil servants expected, could not follow up every idea that he proposed to them.

Civil servants possessed such a large degree of power to obstruct largely because of the functioning of the parliamentary regime. In addition to the lack of time for the minister to acquire the necessary expertise, there was the problem of the allocation of a minister's actual working hours under a parliamentary regime such as that of the Fourth Republic. The preoccupation of a minister under a parliamentary regime differs somewhat from that under a presidential or quasi-presidential regime, where, upon agreeing to become a member of the Government, the minister is constitutionally obliged to abandon his seat in the National Assembly. In the parliamentary regime of the Fourth Republic, a minister spent a large proportion of his time in parliament, and his electioneering activities consumed an equally large share. As a former minister has observed: "It is difficult to imagine today the hold that parliament had on the life of a minister of former Republics. . . . This almost permanent presence of parliament on the minister's horizon gave a special rhythm to his day and influenced the conduct of his affairs."[37] Under the Fourth Republic the parliamentary duties of the minister precluded his being able to immerse himself in the general affairs of the ministry or in its day-to-day management. The one important exception was that the minister took part in the ministry's work concerning his own constituency. This was true of most ministers under the Fourth Republic and it has been no less true under the Fifth Republic. All ministers seek, ultimately, to satisfy the demands of their constituents first.

It was not, therefore, simply the phenomenon of ministerial instability that appeared to give greater leeway to the higher civil servants and increase their influence over ministers. If anything, it was the combination of ministerial instability with the particular type of parliamentary regime that may have tended to orient

[37] Bernard Chenot, *Etre ministre* (Paris: Plon, 1967), pp. 45–46.

the minister more toward answering questions in parliament and toward looking after his constituents' demands than toward securing control over the conduct of his ministry's affairs.

Has the semipresidential system of the Fifth Republic and the stability of the executive affected in any way the influence of civil servants over the minister? It is undoubtedly true that the decline in parliamentary activity has released the minister from what had previously been his most time-consuming function. He is, it is argued, better able to allocate his time as he pleases. A former minister of General de Gaulle notes that the minister "is master of his time, far more than previously. He scarcely goes to Parliament, and when he does go it is only to defend his budget and his projects, or to listen to a bit of eloquence from the Prime Minister. Since 1962, he no longer frequents the Senate. It is even recommended to him to show himself there only rarely. His appointments are well spaced and his agenda is more human. He is able to work, take some vacations, limit his official travels, when he is not undergoing the servitude of elections."[38]

This newly gained freedom from the shackles of parliament generally means that the minister is able to immerse himself in the "dossiers." It also follows that the members of his cabinet are able to follow closely the work of the ministry. This has meant that the monopoly on information and expertise enjoyed by the higher civil servants in the ministry has been, to some extent, compromised. According to Chenot, "The stability of the political system, the competence of the cabinets, give him [the minister] the means, more than previously, to impose his will on his services. And this is indeed the essence of his role."[39]

The Directors interviewed take the position that ministerial stability has in fact reduced their influence in comparison with that of the Directors who served under the Fourth Republic. Over half of them gave as the reason the fact that ministers and the members of their cabinets have become as competent as the Directors. The expertise of members of a ministerial cabinet results, in part, from the longer tenure in office that the minister enjoys. Information flows more freely between the administration and the cabinet—a fact that, as we shall see, Directors resent—because the cabinets are able to obtain necessary information directly from the Directors' subordinates. Even more important

---

[38] *Ibid.*, pp. 48–49.   [39] *Ibid.*, p. 67.

has been the fact that the governments of the Fifth Republic have been party governments, which has made for greater coordination, through the ministerial cabinets, in the formulation of policies.

As important as the actual length of ministerial tenure is the expectation of relatively long tenure. The fact that a minister expects to remain in his post and that the Directors expect the minister to remain more than a few months affects the attitude that the minister and the Directors adopt toward one another. As one Director put it, "It is very difficult to hide something from a minister who expects to stay. When he proposes a project we know that he is likely to follow it up, either by himself, if it's something to which he is particularly attached, or his cabinet will keep after us." Under the Third and Fourth Republics, as we noted earlier, governmental instability was not as traumatic for ministers as is often thought, simply because a minister could usually be fairly certain that a place was awaiting him in the next government. But what counted, in the relation between minister and civil servants, was the *expectation* that the minister would depart before very long.

If ministers are now freer to roam their ministries, if their cabinets keep a close watch on the activities of the administrators, and if the higher civil servants are more obliged to impart information than previously, has this meant that a minister is now more able to impose his will on the higher civil servants?

In day-to-day affairs, as in the application of decisions, civil servants have tended to remain their own masters despite the fact that ministers have more time to devote to the work of their ministry than was the case under the Fourth Republic. This extra time is not, and probably cannot be, devoted to administrative supervision. Also, it should be noted that while the minister is no longer a deputy, he is by no means as free from politicking as this would suggest. He is obliged to maintain and nurture his contacts in his local constituency, whether as mayor, as general councillor, or as a future candidate in legislative elections. He must be as attentive to his constituency as he would be as a deputy—probably more so, because he must avoid giving the impression of having abandoned his electors for a ministerial post. When running in elections later on, he will invoke what he accomplished for his constituents while he held a ministerial post. Most important, perhaps, is the fact that as minister he is able to do for his con-

169

stituents far more than if he were a deputy or deputy-mayor. As former Prime Minister Chaban-Delmas, who was Mayor of Bordeaux at the same time, remarked in an interview, "When all important decisions for cities are taken in Paris, the cities must have as mayor a man who can obtain in the ministries in Paris the decisions that command their destiny in all fields." And he was quite willing to acknowledge that "the State gives Bordeaux what it needs and . . . can legitimately claim." The reason for this happy situation was humorously—and significantly—expressed thus by the Prime Minister and Mayor of Bordeaux: "The Mayor will write to the Premier. I hope the letter gets there."[40] This suggests that the minister is by no means as free as the constitution intended him to be when it stipulated that the ministerial post was incompatible with that of the legislator.

To be sure, his cabinet, part of which is concerned solely with his local constituency, seeks to keep abreast of the ministry's activities and to keep the minister informed. But it too, as we shall see, is overburdened with tasks that have little to do with supervision. This would seem to indicate that the French bureaucracy remains as impervious to control as it always was. This, however, is not entirely the case, because political control over the bureaucracy has changed under the Fifth Republic in one very important respect: when a minister has been determined to push through a reform opposed by his civil servants he has usually been able to win, though not without conflict and even crises. The chief weapon in the minister's arsenal is the backing of his government, without which his projects cannot be implemented. Clearly, this backing is more likely to be forthcoming in a party government than in a coalition of the type that existed under the Fourth Republic. Two examples will illustrate this point.

INITIATION AND IMPLEMENTATION OF REFORM:
TWO CASES

As Minister of Agriculture (1961–1966), Edgard Pisani sought to undertake a far-reaching administrative reform of that ministry, which would clearly affect various entrenched interests within it. Pisani believed, however, that without a major reform the ministry would be incapable of dealing with the enormous prob-

[40] Henry Ginger, "France's Premier is Bordeaux's Mayor, and Vice Versa," *The New York Times*, July 30, 1970.

lems that would confront French agriculture and rural society in the future. He saw the ministry, as it was then constituted, as large and rigidly organized, with no lines of communication between the various sectors. It was, he insisted, composed of fiefdoms that looked toward their own selfish interests rather than toward rational agricultural policies. The chief culprits of this compartmentalization, he maintained, were the numerous corps that existed within the ministry. This in itself was sufficient to make the minister suspect in the eyes of the civil servants. But Pisani was also a type of minister that the Ministry of Agriculture had scarcely ever known before. He refused to cater to or abide by the traditions of the ministry; doing so had always entailed the defense of the small farmer and, consequently, deference to the policies of the ministry's officials. He intended to become head of the Ministry of Agriculture rather than the Ministry of *Agriculteurs*, as it had come to be known under the Third and Fourth Republics.

Pisani met with strong opposition from the corps when he sought to combine certain of them in order to be able to integrate policies without the traditional divisiveness of the corps. Each corps was determined to preserve its own independence, to guard its monopoly over its own domain and to defend the interests of its members. Fusion posed the greatest threat to autonomy. Yet the existence of numerous corps within the ministry was, as Pisani recognized all too well, an obstacle to rational policy-formulation, since the interests of the corps always took precedence over the feasibility or suitability of a particular policy. As soon as he became Minister of Agriculture, Pisani proposed to regroup the ministry's numerous *directions* into three large *directions* which were to conform to the motto he had established for the ministry: *l'homme, l'espace, le produit*. In order to insure that the problem of compartmentalization would not arise again, he proposed to create the post of Secretary General,[41] whose function would be to coordinate the activities of the three *directions*. This project did not materialize, principally because all the corps were firmly opposed to the creation of the post of Secretary General, and the two chief corps—Eaux et Forêts and Génie Rural—were unlikely to tolerate the creation of a *direction*

[41] The only time that this post had existed in the Ministry of Agriculture was under the Vichy government, 1940–1944.

171

d'espace, which would have entailed something approaching the disappearance of both of them.[42]

After finding that such a reform would elicit little sympathy with any of the ministry's groups or indeed with the government, Pisani presented two alternative projects to Matignon. The reform that was accepted by the Interministerial Committee and finally put into effect was only slightly less far-reaching than that originally proposed: it entailed a reorganization of the ministry as well as the fusion of two corps.[43] The opposition of the corps was less serious this time because they were divided among themselves. As a student of Pisani's reform summed it up: "Each corps therefore adopted a distinctly particularist position in accordance with its own interests. Even when certain attempts were made to coordinate the actions of the different corps, they did not give tangible results. The position of each corps was not affected in the same manner by the measures prescribed in the reform. Not only were the interests of the corps not identical, but they were often contradictory. Instead of joining forces against the reform, the corps were fighting each other."[44]

Despite the vigorous opposition of the ministry's civil servants, Pisani succeeded in his aims, partly because of dogged persistence and partly because of his particular political and administrative skills, which enabled him to win the confidence of at least some of the higher civil servants in the ministry. But perhaps the most important factor was the backing he received from Matignon and the Elysée. A number of higher civil servants in the Ministry of Agriculture, some of whom praised and some of whom criticized Pisani's methods of work and skills, noted that he could not have succeeded in carrying out his reform had he not had the support of the government. In fact, the reform was announced by Pisani only after it had been sanctioned by Matignon. Had Pisani not enjoyed the backing of the government, there is little doubt that he would have been forced to drop his program.

It is not unimportant that Pisani showed certain unique qualities as a minister during his five years as Minister of Agriculture. He managed to avoid, to a very large extent, pitting the members of his cabinet against the Directors. He attempted to make the

---

[42] Pierre Blanc-Gonnet, *La Réforme des services extérieurs du ministère de l'agriculture* (Paris: Editions Cujas, 1969), p. 63.

[43] For an analysis of the reform that was eventually adopted, see *ibid.*

[44] *Ibid.*, p. 89.

formulation of policy a cooperative venture in which the cabinet and the Directors were associated.[45] Nor did most Directors regard the cabinet as a barrier separating them from the minister, since they were able to keep direct contact with Pisani. Most civil servants who worked under him in the Ministry of Agriculture as well as those in other ministries regarded his working methods as unique and worthy of emulation by other ministers. Despite his determination to do away with what were regarded as sacred traditions in the Ministry of Agriculture, Pisani did not regard his administration as an enemy from the start—as a former prefect, he possessed a remarkable sensitivity to the mechanisms of the French administrative system.

A more traumatic case was the long-drawn-out battle between Albin Chalandon, Minister of Equipment and Housing (1967-1972), and the higher civil servants in this ministry, which is the province of one of the most powerful and prestigious corps in France—the *corps des ingénieurs des ponts et chaussées* (the corps of civil engineers). Chalandon, an Inspecteur des Finances, a former banker and Secretary General of the UDR, took the view that "France is stifled by an excessive hold of the State,"[46] and that a shift in power from the State to the private sector is highly desirable. His task as minister, he believed, was not to defend his administration, but to defend the country against the administration.[47] In 1967 he became Minister of Equipment and Housing, a ministry that came into being in 1966 as a result of the fusion of the Ministry of Public Works and the Ministry of Construction.

Having entered the government with considerable experience in banking and finance, Chalandon was immediately suspect in the eyes of the civil servants in the Ministry of Equipment and Housing because it was supposed that he came to his office with preconceived ideas. A crucial factor that undoubtedly strengthened his resolve to wage an unrelenting battle with his higher civil servants was the rebuff that he received on two occasions

[45] This information about Pisani's working methods derives from interviews with members of his cabinet and with Directors who served under him in the Ministry of Agriculture and in the Ministry of Equipment and Housing. A slightly different picture of Pisani is given by Blanc-Gonnet in *ibid.*, pp. 61 and 90-91.

[46] Quoted in *L'Express*, 29 September–5 October 1969, p. 62.

[47] For Chalandon's views on this, see his article, "Comment je conçois le rôle de L'Etat," *Preuves*, 2ème trimestre (1970), and his exchange with Michel Rocard in *L'Expansion*, XXVIII (March 1970).

173

when he attempted, in the first months of his ministership, to appoint two Directors of his own choice.[48] He noted from these incidents that the administration possessed power and responsibility without sanctions, since the tenure of civil servants was not related to their efficacy, that it was therefore basically conservative, that it was concerned solely with its own interests, and that it had a privileged position because it escaped political control. He concluded that the administration must be controlled and that civil servants should be subject to greater sanctions, as in the private sector. And in order for this to occur "it is necessary to have ministers who command."[49] Unlike Pisani, therefore, Chalandon came to regard his administration as an enemy, and came to rely solely on his cabinet for the formulation and execution of policies. This was almost inevitable, since his first battle was not on behalf of a particular national policy but was directed essentially against his own administration or, rather, against the corps of civil engineers. He sought to change the method by which departmental directors and regional service chiefs were nominated. He objected to the practice of these posts being allocated on the basis of one's rank and seniority in the corps of civil engineers. Above all, he wanted ministers to be liberated from the "administrative totalitarianism" which always threatens, as he put it, to paralyze *political* power.[50] If a minister is denied the power to name his own senior officials, insisted Chalandon, he cannot command. He must, unlike his counterpart in the private sector, be constantly attempting to convince and persuade his subordinates, which ultimately means that his projects must be ratified by his subordinates.

The corps of *ponts et chaussées* decided to fight against Chalandon's reforms. A special meeting of the corps was convened to attack Chalandon's proposed reform of naming civil servants who did not belong to the corps of civil engineers to posts hitherto strictly reserved for members of this corps. The corps went so far as to attempt to challenge the legality of this change, and even considered requesting an audience with the President of the Republic.

The furor aroused by the proposed reform was due to the fact that Chalandon was seriously threatening to weaken the power of

[48] Michel Boyer, "M. Albin Chalandon s'en prend au corps des ponts et chaussées," *Le Monde*, 2 May 1970.
[49] *Ibid*.   [50] *Ibid*.

the corps of civil engineers which, after all, had its own battles with other corps. But Chalandon did not stop there. Desiring to make the State administration resemble the private sector, he proposed to remedy the highly unsatisfactory highway-building policies. Here again, he appeared to be questioning the very *raison d'être* of his ministry and of the corps of civil engineers, since he sought to remove the building of highways from the State and turn it over to the private sector. He believed that through this transfer of responsibilities highways would be built more quickly, more efficiently, and more economically. The project appeared revolutionary in the eyes of the entire French administration, and it naturally became suspect. Once the State began divesting itself of some of its responsibilities—and hence its powers—many civil servants asked, where would it stop? Would this not turn into a process with a momentum of its own? It was the corps of civil engineers that was once more most severely threatened by this reform, since it involved a loss of control over a large and important domain that had traditionally been under their jurisdiction. Why, a number of members of the corps wondered, would there any longer be a need for a *direction des routes*—one of the most prestigious *directions* in the French administration—if the State was no longer to have a monopoly on road and highway construction? For Chalandon, it was principally a question of efficiency; for the corps of civil engineers, it involved a loss of power and prestige vis-à-vis the other corps, and constituted a challenge to its very existence.

The conflict between Chalandon and the corps of civil engineers was one of the more serious conflicts between a minister and his administration in France, and the fact that the battle was fought more or less publicly testifies to the gravity of the situation. This long battle was rendered more acute by several factors. First, unlike Pisani, Chalandon had from the start a profound mistrust of his administration, a mistrust that had its origins in Chalandon's own particular philosophy which tended to oppose statism and liberalism. He was singularly unimpressed by arguments regarding the possible adverse consequences of a shift in power from the State to the private sector. Since he believed that the State "stifled" the society, he did not subscribe to the view that the society, or the private sector, with its competitive aspects—"power with sanctions," as Chalandon himself characterized it—would stifle the State.

Second, the corps of civil engineers appeared to be challenged at the very moment that it was most vulnerable. It had recently been undergoing what might crudely be called an "identity crisis," as a result of challenges by other corps which had been encroaching on its various domains. Of particular importance was its declining position in ministerial cabinets, which were becoming almost totally monopolized by graduates of the Ecole Nationale d'Administration. Chalandon's attacks came therefore at a moment when the corps was beginning to recoup its position by its newly acquired hold on urban development.

A third reason that contributed to making the conflict particularly acute was the fact that this ministry had scarcely ever encountered such a challenge from a minister. For one thing, the ministry had experienced as frequent a turnover in ministers under the Fifth Republic as it had under the Fourth. For another, the corps of civil engineers had always considered itself as practically unchallengeable, being the oldest of the corps and one with deep roots in a number of sectors. It was thus inclined to see itself as guiding ministers, rather than being guided by them. In discussing civil servants' perception of the role of a minister, we shall see how widespread is the view that ministers are in need of guidance.

Finally, the minister was strongly backed by the Prime Minister and, what was undoubtedly decisive, by the Ministry of Finance. The Prime Minister was convinced of the need for more roads and highways and the Ministry of Finance was convinced of its inability to provide the necessary funds. Consequently, the minister was in a strong position to challenge his administration.

All this notwithstanding, it is important to emphasize that the *original* administrative reorganization—the fusion of the Ministry of Public Works and the Ministry of Construction—had itself been a major reform initiated by Pisani, the first minister of Equipment and Housing, with the aid of the corps of *ponts et chaussées*. Without the help of that corps it is doubtful whether Pisani's attempts to achieve integrated public transportation and urban and housing policies would have been attained. And it was only because of the full backing of the corps of *ponts et chaussées* that de Gaulle sanctioned Pisani's project.[51] This ap-

[51] Jean-Claude Thoenig and Erhard Friedberg, *La Création des directions départementales de l'équipement: phénomènes de corps et réforme administrative* (Paris: C.N.R.S., 1970). According to Thoenig and Friedberg, the decisive moment for the initiation of the reform came when de Gaulle sanctioned Pisani's plans.

pears to have been, however, no more than a marriage of convenience between Pisani and the corps, a marriage that would have soon ended even if Pisani had remained as Minister. As Thoenig and Friedberg have noted in their study of the origins and implications of this reform, the alliance between Pisani and the corps was merely tactical. "The objectives sought by Pisani and the corps of *ponts et chaussées* were fundamentally different. If the engineers of *ponts et chausées* rallied to the minister, they did so not so much because they shared his political and philosophical beliefs but because they hoped to accomplish their own objectives. To be sure, basically and in the context of the intellectual effervescence of the beginning of the reform, the ideas of the one could scarcely be differentiated from the ideas of the other. But, in the final analysis, the young *ingénieurs des ponts* took part in the minister's work for totally other than political motives."[52]

CONCLUSION

The two examples given in the previous section of conflicts between ministers and their higher civil servants suggest that even under a governmental system of ministerial stability, there is not likely to be established in France the mutual trust and confidence that exists between ministers and their civil servants in Britain. We have already seen that neither the theory of representative bureaucracy nor the popular theory of institutional changes between the Fourth and Fifth Republics accounts for the persistent conflicts between the minister and his senior officials. To be sure, institutional changes and ministerial stability do have a role that may at times be decisive insofar as long-range policies are concerned. Thus a minister like Mandel, who attempted to reform the entire Ministry of Post and Telecommunications in the Third Republic, had to abandon his plans when he lost his post after six months.[53] The same fate would undoubtedly have befallen Pisani and Chalandon had they not been certain of being able to remain in office long enough to accomplish their reforms. On the other hand, while ministerial instability may not allow for long-range planning, it does allow for quick, surgical reforms, some of which fail for reasons that have little to do with the process of policy formulation, such as Edgar Faure's proposed tax reform in 1955. Some succeed and are not without far-reaching

[52] *Ibid.*, p. 20.   [53] Chenot, *Etre ministre*, p. 56.

consequences, such as Antoine Pinay's economic policy of stabilization which *was* implemented against the advice of his higher civil servants, all of whom informed the minister of their opposition. Pinay, it is reported, invited all his Directors to submit their resignations, if they wished to do so. No Director resigned and Pinay's policy was carried out. Undoubtedly the institutionalization of crises, as Philip Williams has referred to the governmental system of the Fourth Republic, allows for rapid reforms because of the constant state of flux of relationships and policies. It is not surprising, therefore, that many of the more important reforms carried out in the Fourth Republic were, as Williams has noted, undertaken as soon as the ministers had taken office. Clearly, such a system allows for little long-range planning by any single minister, but it also has the advantage of not permitting relationships among the higher civil servants and ministers to settle at any given level. As Williams observed, "Naturally some politicians saw—or made—in them [cabinet crises] opportunities to advance their careers. But in doing so they had to attach their fortunes to a problem of public policy, and might even contribute to its solution."[54]

If certain ministers under the Fifth Republic have been able to overcome the opposition of civil servants and push through far-reaching, if at times debatable, reforms, this has been, as I have indicated, only partly because of their relatively long stay in office. Far more important has been the existence of cohesive governments that could not collapse as a result of disagreements on some particular project. Once a project had received the approval of the Elysée, it became government policy. Thus Pisani's reforms in the Ministry of Agriculture, as well as his reforms concerning the rationalization of urban policies, were initiated only after they had received the approval of Matignon and the Elysée. In the latter case Pisani received General de Gaulle's personal approval. With regard to Chalandon's reforms, the backing of the Prime Minister, which in part depended on the backing of the Ministry of Finance, allowed Chalandon to launch an attack on the corps of *ponts et chaussées*. The potential of the corps for obstruction was to a large extent preempted, since Chalandon's projects now became government policy.

No two ministers could have been more different in most respects than Pisani and Chalandon: the former determined but

---

[54] Williams, *Crisis and Compromise*, p. 457.

tactful, impatient with and yet sensitive to the administrative "rules of the game"; the latter determined but brusque, and totally impatient with and unsympathetic toward the administrative machine. Chalandon's principal aim was to make the administration "cost-efficient" and to insure that each time political power confronted administrative power, the former would win.[55] But despite the differences in their approach to the administration, neither Pisani nor Chalandon could have achieved their aims if they had not shared one thing in common: the backing of a relatively cohesive executive controlled by a dominant political party.

We have discussed in some detail the relationship between ministers and higher civil servants, but it nevertheless should be emphasized that such a relationship provides only a limited framework for examining the bureaucracy's power in a political system. A bureaucracy is composed not merely, as is generally supposed and as I may have inadvertently implied, of a few higher civil servants in the central administration in Paris. It is also composed of the platoons that represent them in the provinces. To understand, therefore, the role of the bureaucracy in the French political system it would also be necessary to understand the relationship of local officials—particularly prefects, mayors, and the regional representatives of the central administration—to the central authorities. It would be important to know, for example, how this relationship has changed, if at all, under the Fifth Republic, because administrative power involves the prefects and the regional civil servants as much as it does the Directors of the central administration. It has been customary, and not very helpful, in the literature on French politics to speak of the bureaucracy as being either responsive or unresponsive to the political authorities, without taking into account the different and sometimes largely autonomous segments of the bureaucracy, which vary in responsiveness and in autonomy. Does the responsiveness and autonomy of different segments of the bureaucracy differ with various regimes? Do some segments remain unaffected by what goes on "up there in the capital?" Unless local officials, hitherto assumed to be merely obedient subordinates of the cen-

---

[55] It should be pointed out that Chalandon was subsequently to become less favorably disposed toward the private sector. Some months before his ouster from the government, in July 1972, he declared: "Urbanism must be regarded as a public service." *Le Monde*, 8 July 1972.

tral authorities, are considered in discussions on the "power of the bureaucracy," only a partial picture of the role of the bureaucracy is likely to result.[56]

I have tried to suggest in this chapter that superficial generalizations, such as those having to do with the stability or instability of ministers and with the representativity of the bureaucracy, do not help to explain the complicated relationship that exists between ministers and civil servants. This relationship is rendered the more complex by the fact that civil servants are by no means a unified block; some, indeed, have more in common with their ministers than with their colleagues. The application of role theory will give us some understanding as to the widely divergent outlooks and role perceptions of ministers and civil servants. It is important to note now, and it will be emphasized again in subsequent chapters, that the divergent outlooks do not emanate from the traditional distinction between administrators and politicians. Indeed, we reject the view that there are two distinct species, and we shall show in our discussion of the ministerial cabinets—almost all of whose members are higher civil servants— that it is possible, under certain circumstances, for civil servants to adopt outlooks that are indistinguishable from those of their ministers.

Since service in a ministerial cabinet is an important stepping-stone to the post of Director (it is, as we have seen, largely the same civil servants who serve as cabinet members and as senior officials in ministries), we have an ideal opportunity for studying the role perceptions of higher civil servants in different posts within the politico-administrative hierarchy. In view of the fact that the ministerial cabinet has assumed a paramount role in the French politico-administrative system, the following two chapters will be devoted to an analysis of its rationale and functions, to the conflicts it engenders within the central administration, and to its impact on the role perceptions of higher civil servants.

[56] The relationship between the local and the central authorities has not received much attention in the literature on the French administration. That even within a single ministry there are wide variations in the type of relationship established can be seen from a study of the regional services of three *directions* of the Ministry of Finance. See Pierre Grémion and François D'Arcy, *Les Services extérieurs du ministère de l'économie et des finances dans le système de décision départemental* (Paris: C.N.R.S., 1969).

CHAPTER VIII

The Ministerial Cabinet

Ces hommes qui nous gouvernent[1]

THE CABINET OF "MONSIEUR LE MINISTRE"

It has long been a tradition in France for each minister to surround himself with a staff that forms what is known as the ministerial cabinet—"le cabinet de M. le Ministre," which should not be confused with the term used to designate the members of the government. Indeed, in France the members of the government —the ministers—are grouped not into a cabinet, as is the case in Britain and in the United States, but into the Council of Ministers. Consequently the term "cabinet," as it is used throughout this book, refers to the minister's associates and not to the members of the government.

In its organization, personnel, and responsibilities the cabinet is a peculiarly French institution. To be sure, ministers in every country, regardless of the form of government, have close associates and advisers. But rare has been the case where an institution has been created for this purpose, an institution whose functions have developed over the past century and a half depending on political and administrative mores, as well as on the needs of particular ministers. The ministerial cabinets in France also illustrate the degree to which higher civil servants occupy, indeed almost monopolize, the highest political and administrative posts.

It would be difficult to delineate with any precision the nature of the modifications that the cabinet has undergone, and still more difficult to trace the effects on it of different regimes. No historical or political study of the cabinet as yet exists. The argument has been advanced, notably by Jean-Louis Seurin, the author of the only comprehensive—now slightly dated—study of the institution,

[1] P. Hymann and J. M. Carzou, "Les Directeurs de cabinet: Ces hommes qui nous gouvernent," *Entreprise*, no. 647, 3 February 1968.

181

that the cabinets of the beginning of the nineteenth century were essentially identical in character to those of today and fulfilled analogous functions. Although he acknowledges that parliamentary regimes, starting with that of the Restoration, encouraged the development of the cabinet, Seurin nonetheless concludes that "its fundamental character has not been modified."[2] Given, however, the haphazard nature of the development of the cabinet as well as the impact of administrative changes, it would seem difficult to sustain the argument that it has undergone no major changes. In the first place, the cabinet "is one of the few almost totally customary, in contrast to statutory, institutions in France."[3] Second, it could well be argued that, because it has been the instrument of individual ministers and because it is based on no statute resembling that of any corps in France, the cabinet has been considerably transformed in character over the past one hundred and fifty years. The lack of a statute or of effective regulations has meant that all sorts of abuses could arise, foremost among which has been advancement within the administrative hierarchy resulting from service in a minister's cabinet rather than from prior administrative experience. It was not until the Finance Law of 13 July 1911 that this practice was rendered illegal.[4]

An analysis of the role of the cabinet in the politico-administrative system becomes all the more important in view of the crucial role that this body has come to play in the French administration, as well as the conflicts it engenders. We will turn to an analysis of this triangular relationship—minister, cabinet members, and Directors—in the next chapter. But first we should look into the justifications for the institution of the cabinet and into its organization.

[2] Jean-Louis Seurin, "Les cabinets ministériels," *Revue du Droit Publique et de la Science Politique*, no. 6 (November–December 1956), 1210.

[3] A. Dutheillet De Lamothe, "Ministerial Cabinets in France," *Public Administration*, XLIII (Winter 1965), 372.

[4] A further abuse was the swelling of a cabinet to any size that the minister thought would be adequate for rendering political favors. This was rendered illegal by the Poincaré Decree of 13 February 1912, and the decrees of 28 July 1948 and 21 August 1951 which limited the size of ministerial cabinets to ten members. There have, however, always been ways to circumvent this limitation which, as we shall see, is less adhered to today than ever before.

182

Purpose of the Cabinet: Two Views

An examination of the literature on the cabinet reveals that two basic arguments have been used to explain or justify its existence: first, the need for a political institution to counterbalance, or complement, the work of the administration; second, the unstable nature of French politics obliged ministers to create a counterweight to the permanent administration. Let us examine both these arguments.

The distinction between politics and administration corresponds neatly to the distinction between formulation (the domain of politics) and execution (the domain of administration). This dichotomy, which forms the basis of the study of public law in France and which permeates the writings of politicians and scholars alike,[5] is crucial not only for understanding the justifications underlying the existence of an institution like the cabinet, but also for understanding the behavior of French higher civil servants. It is crucial, as we shall see, not because it is an accurate description of reality but, on the contrary, because it constitutes a rather gross oversimplification of the actual state of things.

Most writers on the subject have maintained that at the time when the cabinet consisted of a coterie of the minister's political appointees who concerned themselves solely with matters external to the ministry, a neat division of labor existed between the functions of the higher civil servants in the ministry and the functions of the cabinet. The classical age for this felicitous state of affairs is believed to have been the Third Republic (and, to a slightly lesser extent, according to some writers, the Fourth Republic), the argument being that under the Third Republic the task of the minister was more political than administrative. This helps to explain, or so it is argued, why the cabinet members were chosen on the basis of their personal and political loyalty to the minister. In those distant times, writes a former high-ranking diplomat, their role was simple: "The cabinet was the intermediary between the minister, his services, and the parliament,

[5] See Michel Debré's *La Mort de l'Etat républicain* (Paris: Gallimard, 1947); *La République et son pouvoir* (Paris: Nagel, 1950); *Au Service de la nation* (Paris: Stock, 1963); and Robert Catherine, *Le Fonctionnaire français* (Paris: Albin Michel, 1961).

183

and it acted as the minister's personal secretariat. It intervened not at all, or very little, in the work of the administration."[6]

This idealized view of the separation of functions between the cabinet and the higher civil servants is shared by most contemporary writers.[7] Yet their retrospective view is hardly an accurate one, for it is belied by all available evidence about the working of the cabinet under the Third Republic. The cabinet has always engendered serious conflicts within the politico-administrative system because its members and the higher civil servants in the ministries (the Directors) have been constrained to share functions. This conflict has been denied, now on the basis of the neat separation of political and administrative functions, now (for the Fifth Republic) on the basis of a shared "technical" approach to the solution of problems.[8] Neither the conflict between cabinet and Directors, nor the causes of it, have ever received serious analysis. Current literature on the French administration, or on the cabinet, does not even begin to suggest the importance of this conflict. Indeed, it attempts to deny its existence.

An examination of the functioning of the cabinet under the Third Republic reveals that there was more tension than co-operation between members of ministerial cabinets and Directors. The cabinets were referred to within the administration, as Chardon, a member of the Conseil d'Etat in the Third Republic, informs us, as the "octopi," and as "the ulcer of the Third Republic."[9] They were criticized for attempting to delve too deeply into the administrative work of the ministry, conceiving of their task as "faire marcher les bureaux." They were also criticized for being far too large.[10] As Robert de Jouvenel humorously expressed it: "The members of the cabinet, 'the guests of the *patron*,' roam

[6] René Massigli, *Sur Quelques maladies de l'Etat* (Paris: Plon, 1958), p. 42.

[7] Siwek-Pouydesseau, *Le Personnel de direction des ministères* (Paris: Armand Colin, 1969), p. 119; Dutheillet de Lamothe, "Ministerial Cabinets in France," p. 77; Roger Léonard," La Haute administration et ses problèmes," *Revue des Deux Mondes*, April 1, 1959, p. 395; and Robert Catherine, *Le Fonctionnaire français*, p. 300.

[8] Victor Silvera, "De Quelques réflexions sur certains aspects de la stabilité gouvernementale et de l'exercice de l'action administrative sous la Vᵉ République," *Actualité Juridique*, xxiii (February 1967), 81.

[9] Henri Chardon, *L'Administration de la France: les fonctionnaires* (Paris: Perrin, 1908), p. 129.

[10] Henri Chardon, *Les Travaux publics* (Paris: Perrin, 1904), p. 35. See also H. Noël, *Les Ministères* (Paris: Berger-Levrault, 1911), p. 92.

the factory. They look at everything with curiosity: here they get behind a wheel; there they replace a lever. The professionals follow them with ironic eyes and a little anxiety. . . . They [the members of the cabinet] are no longer content to touch everything; they begin wanting to reform certain things. The professionals get all upset. They no longer answer their questions and they protest their incursions. They ask them kindly to tend to their own business."[11]

De Jouvenel has here described splendidly not only the tension between the "guests of the *patron*" and the "professionals," but also the remarkable self-assurance of the members of the ministerial cabinet, which emanates from the posts they occupy and about which more will be said in the next chapter. The case against the cabinets of the Third Republic was expressed very forcefully, at the beginning of this century, in an official report on the budget of the Ministry of Foreign Affairs. The author of the report, M. Pressensé, might very easily have been describing the situation that exists in our own day when he stated:

The question of ministerial cabinets, of their unreasonable and constant growth, of the excessive role played in the most delicate matters by an improvised *état-major*, above all, of the manner in which ministerial gratitude is paid at the expense of the State and with disregard for the rights of ordinary civil servants whose positions place them far from the sun's rays must, sooner or later, be posed and resolved by Parliament. I would readily invoke, in this regard, the celebrated remark, pertaining to another matter, made by Burke: There is here a large and growing abuse which must be diminished. This regrettable state of affairs, which has only been aggravated under the Republic, tends to create in a fully democratic State a privileged nursery, a hothouse for the premature flowering of the young men of the State.[12]

It is evident that the golden age of the separation of administrative and political functions that Massigli and others have seen in the Third Republic never really existed. Furthermore, the criticisms directed at the cabinets—their growth and their intrusion into the work of the ministries—are, as we shall see, made with

[11] Robert de Jouvenel, *La République des camarades* (Paris: Grasset, 1914), pp. 109–110.
[12] Quoted in Chardon, *L'Administration de la France*, pp. 129–130.

185

as much frequency and force today as they were under the Third Republic.

In addition to the distinction between the domains of politics and administration, it has been argued that the institution of the cabinet is further justified by the unstable nature of French politics. The minister—that ephemeral being—is obliged to create a counterforce to the administration, that permanent and immovable institution. "It is this flagrant contrast," writes Seurin, "between the permanence of the bureaus [administration] and ministerial instability that furnishes the *raison d'être* of the ministerial cabinet."[13] And a Fourth Republic minister has stated that, in addition to the personal qualities of a minister, "it is his cabinet which, to a large extent, will contribute to his success or will precipitate his downfall."[14] This attitude takes for granted the mutual mistrust between the minister and the administrators in his ministry. In order to be able to carry out his tasks, as well as in his need for the "incessant surveillance of the administration,"[15] the minister, it is argued, needs to be aided; not, however, by the civil servants in the ministry, for that would be tantamount to "confining the task of supervision to the supervised,"[16] but by a group whose loyalty to the minister is incontestable.

There is little basis for close collaboration or mutual confidence, so the argument runs, between politicians playing the game of musical chairs and administrators divorced from political chicanery who carry the burden of running the State. It is no wonder that the cabinet finds its *raison d'être* in this situation and that the minister "needs a team to help him govern his administration."[17] How can the minister face those serious administrators who disapprove of everything he does? "Naturally," wrote de Jouvenel, "the minister feels far more at ease with his cabinet, who at least don't overwhelm him with their professional competence."[18] De Jouvenel was writing of the Third Republic, as was Massigli almost half a century later, when he expressed his

---

13 Seurin, "Les cabinets ministériels," p. 1210.

14 André Morice, "Le Ministre et l'administration," *Promotions*, no. 28 (1954), 17.

15 Chardon, *L'Administration de la France*, p. 127.

16 *Ibid.*

17 Heymann and Carzou, "Les Directeurs de cabinets: Ces hommes qui nous gouvernent," p. 51.

18 De Jouvenel, *La République des camarades*, p. 104.

admiration for the manner in which this institution functioned "in those distant times," and observed that the minister's need for a cabinet was "all the more necessary in view of the fact that the governments, one after the other, were collapsing more quickly. . . . The ministers of a few weeks who lack not only parliamentary experience and the experience of holding power, but often any experience whatsoever, have the impression—are they completely mistaken?—that they are not highly regarded by the Directors who know their business."[19] But rather than arguing that such a system contrived to replicate itself under the Fourth Republic when Massigli himself was a high-ranking official at the Quai d'Orsay, he sees a sharp difference in the role of the cabinet between the Third and Fourth Republics: "For the conception of the cabinet as a liaison between the minister and parliament has therefore been substituted the notion of a cabinet which is at once the brain of the minister and, with regard to the administration, the eyes of the master. A study group on the one hand, a means of supervising on the other."[20]

The argument that the cabinet of the Third Republic was merely a "political" institution that did not concern itself with "administration" is not a convincing one, Massigli's reasons notwithstanding. As we have seen, the cabinet of the Third Republic was subjected to strong criticism by contemporaries for "meddling" in the work of the administration. In other words, the theoretical distinction between the realms of politics and administration was not, and could not be, observed in practice. As for the assertion that the cabinet found its *raison d'être* in ministerial instability, it too is seriously open to question. Assuming, for the sake of argument, that the growing importance of the cabinet was, if not a creation of, then a response to the chronic instability of French politics, what would be the expected effect of the relative ministerial stability of the Fifth Republic? Has the cabinet declined in importance? Have ministers been able to work more closely, as Léon Blum had hoped, with their Directors? Our survey revealed that the role of the cabinet has, if anything, grown in importance under the Fifth Republic. A former minister of General de Gaulle has described the cabinet as "a tower overlooking the entire administration of a ministry."[21] And

[19] Massigli, *Sur quelques maladies de l'Etat*, p. 25.
[20] *Ibid.*
[21] Chenot, *Etre ministre* (Paris: Plon, 1967), p. 58.

in the first meeting of the Council of Ministers held after the formation of the Couve de Murville government in July 1968, General de Gaulle, a man not known to have been much concerned with administrative matters, advised his ministers to have smaller cabinets and to work more closely with their Directors than with their cabinets. For the President of the Republic to have been aware of, and to have considered it necessary to remark on the dissatisfactions of the Directors, clearly reveals that serious tensions were evident.

From the "ulcer of the Third Republic," the cabinet became the "saint of saints of French political life" in the Fourth Republic,[22] and the control tower of ministries in the Fifth. What, then, is the effect of different regimes on the functioning of administrative institutions? In the following chapter it will be seen that the influence of regimes is by no means as great as it has been thought to be, and that the relationship between institutions depends on the perception of their roles by the actors, which is, to a very considerable extent, independent of the nature of the regime. But before we turn to an examination of the role of the cabinet in the French administrative system, it is necessary to look briefly at its composition and organization.

Composition and Organization of the Cabinet

It is often difficult to know the exact number of members that a minister brings into his cabinet, for in addition to the official appointments that are published in the *Journal Officiel*, there are also what are known as *officieux* members, who have similar functions and receive the same remuneration.[23] What distinguishes the *officieux* members from the official ones is that the nomination of the former does not appear on the official list. This permits the minister to adhere, as far as the record is concerned, to the law that regulates the number of men he is permitted to

[22] "Les Saints des saints de la vie politique française," *Réalités*, no. 145 (February 1958), 30–33.

[23] Cabinet members do not receive salaries. They only receive supplements (approximately $100–$200 a month) to the salaries that they draw from their corps or administration of origin. Thus a member of the Prefectoral corps or the Inspection des Finances on leave to serve in a minister's cabinet continues to be paid by his corps. Since ministers do not receive budgetary allocations from which to pay their cabinet members, it is not surprising that they should call on the service of civil servants.

bring into his cabinet. This practice appears now to be widely accepted, since no attempt has been made in recent years to compel ministers to adhere strictly to the legal maximum of ten. Moreover, since a minister does not have to pay his cabinet, it also means that he can have virtually as many members as he deems necessary. For example, Edgar Faure's cabinet at the Ministry of Education in 1968–1969 is reported to have numbered between fifty and eighty. While this is probably the largest cabinet to have existed under the Fifth Republic, one source has it that some cabinets in the Fourth Republic numbered between 100 and 200.[24] There is, of course, no way of verifying whether such large cabinets existed under the Fourth Republic, but it does seem improbable. In the first place, there is simply no way of accommodating such a large number of people in the quarters allocated to the minister and his cabinet. Second, if such a large cabinet did exist, it seems fairly clear that most of the members did no more than attach to their person the title of "membre de cabinet du Ministre," which would have enabled them to run political errands for the minister—in his party and his local constituency. The free dispensation of the status "membre de cabinet du Ministre" is a rather innocuous way of rendering favors and paying political debts, but the bulk of the members in such grossly oversized cabinets had no function whatever in the ministry. This was true even of Edgar Faure's cabinet in the Ministry of Education. Many of the higher civil servants in this ministry who were severely critical of Faure's large cabinet conceded that the idiosyncratic manner in which Faure composed his cabinets only testified to his political acumen: his hallmark was to do favors for friends and enemies alike.

In my interviews with members of ministerial cabinets, I found that there was no attempt to hide the number of members. Indeed, I was able to procure without difficulty the rosters of several cabinets, which listed the name and function of each member. In only one cabinet was the name followed by the notation *officiel* or *officieux*, which indicated nothing more than that the names of the former appeared on all official lists and those of the latter did not. The *officiels* members were not hierarchically superior to the *officieux* and did not have greater responsibilities.

---

[24] B. Gournay, J.-F. Kesler and J. Siwek-Pouydesseau, *Administrations publiques* (Paris: Presses Universitaires de France, 1967), p. 243. See also Siwek-Pouydesseau, *Le Personnel de direction des ministères*, p. 23.

From these lists I concluded that a minister's cabinet varies from ten to thirty, depending on the minister and the ministry. Some—like Finance—will have fairly large cabinets irrespective of who happens to be minister. In others—Foreign Affairs, Industry, Agriculture—the cabinets vary from one minister to another. When Couve de Murville was Minister of Foreign Affairs his cabinet at one point contained only three or four persons. The Secretary General's office played, effectively, the cabinet's role. This is partly the case today, though Schumann's cabinet, for example, consisted, as his cabinets have always done, of ten.

If cabinets are relatively small as institutions, there nevertheless exists a hierarchical pattern in their organization (Diagram 8.1). A cabinet is always headed by a *directeur de cabinet*, who

Diagram 8.1
Hierarchical Schema of a Ministerial Cabinet

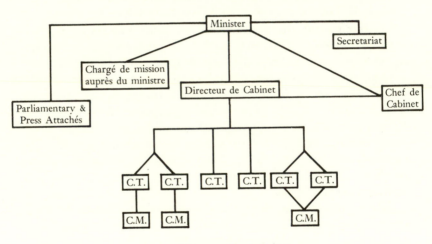

C.T.—conseiller technique
C.M.—chargé de mission

is the key man, after the minister, in the ministry. Because he is endowed with the authority of the minister, conflict is rare between him and the Directors. His stature as a "sous-ministre" may, as will be seen, sometimes be challenged when there is a Secretary General in the ministry. But this post now exists in only two ministries, so the *directeur de cabinet* can generally be regarded as the "sous-ministre" insofar as his relations with the members of the cabinet and the civil servants in the ministry are concerned. This authority stems in large part from his powers of signature, which the minister delegates to him. His tasks are many, but they consist essentially in separating the specific responsibilities of the ministry from the general policies of the government, insuring that the minister's policies are carried out by the services in the ministry, insuring the coordination of the ministry's *directions*, supervising the work of the cabinet, arbitrating conflicts among the *directions* and between the *directions* and the cabinet and, finally, receiving individuals and groups on behalf of the minister. On rare occasions the *directeur de cabinet* may himself be responsible for a particular sector in the ministry, in much the same way as a *conseiller technique* is. One *directeur de cabinet* is currently a Director in the ministry also. He held the latter post before becoming *directeur de cabinet* and decided not to abandon it.[25] In addition to all these functions, the *directeur de cabinet* acts as the minister's closest adviser.

In recent years there has also been created in some cabinets the post of *chargé de mission auprès du ministre*.[26] This may be either a part-time or a full-time position, but it is always occupied by a trusted confidant of the minister. When it is a part-time position, the holder of this post generally undertakes specific—often sensitive—tasks on behalf of the minister. For example, Pierre Racine, currently Director of the Ecole Nationale d'Administration, was Michel Debré's *directeur de cabinet* when Debré was Prime Minister from 1959 to 1962. When Debré became Minister of Finance in 1966 and Minister of Foreign Affairs in 1968, Racine occupied the post of *chargé de mission auprès du ministre*, a post that in this case was full-time and entailed responsibility for a specific sector of the ministry. To avoid possible conflicts between the *chargé de mission auprès du ministre* and the *directeur de cabinet*, the former is always considered to be *outside* the hierarchy of the cabinet. In the official published lists of the cabinets, the *chargé de mission auprès du ministre* is sometimes listed above and sometimes below the *directeur de cabinet*, but not

[25] This official conceded that "this is not a situation that can last very long" simply because of the work load involved.

[26] This post should not be confused with that of *chargé de mission*, identified as "C.M." in Diagram 8.1.

much importance should be attached to this ranking since no minister can afford the slightest conflict between his two closest associates.

A cabinet always includes a *chef de cabinet*, who under the Third Republic was the equivalent of today's *directeur de cabinet*. But the rank of the *chef de cabinet* in the hierarchy today varies according to his relationship to the minister.[27] Sometimes he is a personal friend and associate of long standing and is therefore given wide responsibilities, such as handling all of the minister's political mail, coordinating press and parliamentary activities, and being primarily responsible for looking after the minister's personal political affairs, which include maintaining contacts with local officials, constituents, and the minister's political party. In one ministry where the minister was an important figure in a political party, these tasks were shared with another person in the cabinet. In another, where the *chef de cabinet* was not previously known to the minister, he had the minor functions of arranging the details of the minister's trips, seeing to decorations and nominations for honors, and answering the less sensitive political mail.

It has always been argued that a ministerial cabinet is divided into political and technical elements.[28] The former is supposed to consist of the *directeur de cabinet*, the *chargé de mission auprès du ministre*, the *chef de cabinet*, and the parliamentary and press attachés who were found more frequently in Third and Fourth Republic cabinets. The latter is thought to consist of the *conseillers techniques* and *chargés de mission*, the intermediaries between the minister and the administration. Because their task is confined ostensibly to the ministry, they are said to fulfill "technical" functions. Such a distinction between political and technical functions owes more to theory than to practice, and is, for the most part, based on a narrow and outdated distinction between two domains that are daily becoming less distinguishable. Although the *conseillers techniques* and the *chargés de mission*—the former are hierarchically superior to the latter—see their role as basically a technical one, they acknowledge that they cannot be "pure technicians" since a political awareness is indispensable

---

[27] See Robert Buron, *Le Plus beau des métiers* (Paris: Plon, 1963), p. 184.
[28] *Ibid.*, p. 187. See also Siwek-Pouydesseau, *Le Personnel de direction des ministères*, pp. 96–101; and Marie-Christine Kessler, *Le Conseil d'Etat* (Paris: Armand Colin, 1969), p. 242.

to carrying out their technical tasks. Unlike the Directors of the central administration, they see their tasks, as will be seen in the next chapter, as being at once administrative and political.

The *conseillers techniques* are the chief links between the minister and the *directions*. Being solely responsible to the minister they do not, except under certain circumstances (which will be discussed in Chapter IX) represent the *directions* vis-à-vis the minister. The types of liaisons established between the cabinet and the *directions* generally follow one of two patterns. They may be either vertical or horizontal. The vertical type of relationship (Diagram 8.2) is clearly the simpler one, since each *conseiller technique* has a specific responsibility with regard to one *direction*.

Diagram 8.2
Cabinet and *Directions*: Vertical Relationship

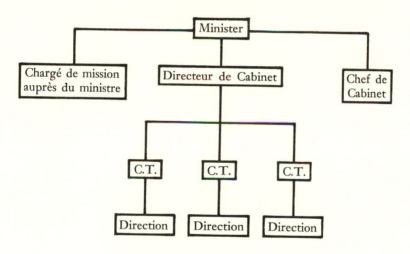

C.T.—conseiller technique

His functions do not cut across *directions*. In the horizontal type of relationship (Diagram 8.3), the web of relationships becomes considerably more complex, since the responsibilities of the *conseillers techniques* are allocated on the basis of problems or tasks that fall within the ministry's purview. Consequently, the tasks of a *conseiller technique* may cut across two or more *directions*, so that a Director will have to be constantly in contact with and responsive not to one cabinet member, as is the case in the vertical type of relationship, but to several. Conflicts between cabinet members and Directors are generally more acute in a horizontal relationship than in a vertical, and always occur between the *conseillers techniques* and the Directors. When we add to this web of relationships the responsibilities that all cabinets have for the coordination of policies, it becomes clear that in addition to their specific tasks as intermediaries within the ministry, the cabinet members are also obliged to cultivate links

Diagram 8.3
Cabinet and *Directions*: Horizontal Relationship

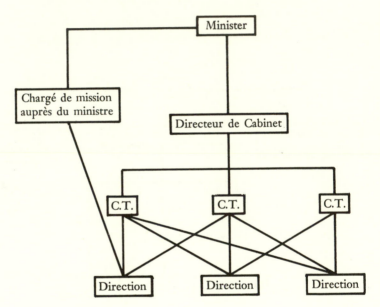

C.T.—conseiller technique

with their counterparts in other ministries. Consequently, the *conseillers techniques* maintain at all times two sets of relationships, one internal and one external (Diagram 8.4). The relationships internal to the ministry may cut across several *directions*, while the external relationships may cut across ministries as well as other public or parapublic institutions. Table 8.1 (at the end of this chapter) shows the organization of an actual cabinet where relationships are more or less based on the vertical princi-

194

ple (Diagram 8.2). Table 8.2 (at the end of this chapter) shows the organization of a cabinet where relationships are based on the horizontal principle (Diagram 8.3). The external relationships of this cabinet are also indicated, and it can be seen that for every internal relationship there is one or more external relationships, necessitated by the need for the coordination of policies.

FORMAL STRUCTURES AND INFORMAL RELATIONS

The preceding discussion of the organization of the cabinet and the relationship of its members to the administration has been seen in a rather formal context. Although Crozier has suggested

Diagram 8.4
Internal and External Relationships of a Cabinet

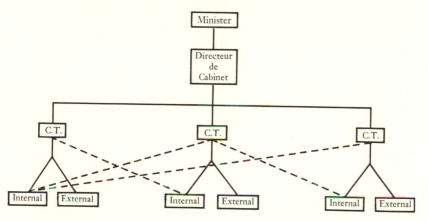

C.T.—conseiller technique

that "formal structure and informal relationships should not be opposed [because] they interpenetrate and complete each other,"[29] we should bear in mind that this may be true only for certain levels of an organization's hierarchy. Unlike the levels of the two organizations Crozier studied, the apex of the French administrative pyramid is one in which the *formal* hierarchical power relations are not strictly defined, so that the informal relationships between the various levels are characterized by

[29] Michel Crozier, *The Bureaucratic Phenomenon* (Chicago: The University of Chicago Press, 1964), p. 164.

extreme conflicts and tensions. For example, and here we are leaping slightly ahead of our analysis, Diagram 9.1 (p. 217), shows, as does Diagram 8.1, the hierarchical structure of the French ministry. The dotted lines in Diagram 9.1 indicate, however, the uncertainties involved in a multitude of hierarchical arrangements. To be sure, these uncertainties are generally as important as Diagram 9.1 indicates only where there exists a Secretary General in a ministry. But even where there is no Secretary General, there remains a considerable fluidity in the hierarchical relationships. This is one of the more important factors that make Crozier's analysis of the lower levels of the French bureaucracy not wholly applicable to the higher level, for his analysis is predicated on a rigid hierarchical arrangement sanctioned by rules and regulations. In the case of the higher echelons of the French bureaucracy there are often no regulations to indicate the degree of subordination of one level to another. Is the Director or Sub-Director more responsible or answerable to the *directeur de cabinet* or to the Secretary General? What of the relationship between the *directeur de cabinet* and the Secretary General? Are the *conseillers techniques* the superiors, the equals or the subordinates of the Secretary General? Are the regional services directly responsible to their *directions* in the central administration or to the cabinet? Clearly, this type of hierarchical arrangement does not fit Crozier's analysis of the French bureaucracy "where nearly everything is predictable."[30] Indeed, at the level of the bureaucracy with which we are dealing, few things are predictable.

Crozier, however, does take account of power vacuums that exist despite determined efforts to eliminate them. He writes that "since it is impossible, whatever the effort, to eliminate all sources of uncertainty within an organization by multiplying impersonal rules and developing centralization, a few areas of uncertainty will remain. Around these areas, parallel power relationships will develop, with the concomitant phenomena of dependencies and conflict."[31] The cabinet does in many ways appear to fit Crozier's description of a parallel power. In fact, it has been called by some of its critics in the administration a "parallel hierarchy," in the sense that it duplicates the work of the *directions*. But the need for this type of institution that is superimposed on the hier-

---

[30] *Ibid.*, p. 192.　　　　[31] *Ibid.*

archical pyramid is not so much the result of an uncertainty in the sphere of power—for the cabinet itself contributes heavily to this uncertainty—as a necessary consequence of divergent role perceptions which make communications between the minister and his officials in the ministry difficult, at best. It must be emphasized that this is very different from saying that communications are made difficult by an abhorrence of face-to-face relations—we could find little evidence of this at the apex of the administrative pyramid. In fact, even the delimitation of a *group* at this level of the bureaucracy presents certain difficulties, for the Directors of a ministry do not constitute even a loosely-knit group and the members of a cabinet do not, as we shall see, act as a group. Crozier's study does not distinguish between the *dirigés* and the *dirigeants*, and so tends to impute a type of behavior to the latter based on observations regarding the former.

TABLE 8.1

Organization of Actual Cabinet: Vertical Type

Name of Official[1]	Domain of Competence	Corresponding Direction
Directeur de Cabinet		
Conseiller Technique	Liaison with the Secretariat of State (same ministry), population, demography, medical research, pharmacy	Cabinet of Secretary of State; *Direction* of Family, Old Age, and Social Action; *Direction* of Population and Migration; INSERM; INED; Service of Pharmacy
Conseiller Technique	Financial matters	*Direction* of General Administration, Personnel and Budget
Conseiller Technique	Relations with the press; foreign relations; speech writing for Minister	Press office; Division of International Relations
Chef de Cabinet	Minister's mail; "Interventions"; functioning of Cabinet	Bureau of the Cabinet; Bureau of Public Relations
Conseiller Technique	Liaison with the Secretariat of State; relations with unions and the *patronat*	Cabinet of Secretary of State; *Direction* of Labor and Employment
Conseiller Technique	Public health; regulation and control of institutions	*Direction* of Public Health; Service of Health Institutions
Conseiller Technique	Plan; equipments; economic studies	*Direction* of Social Equipment; Service of Studies and Forecasts
Conseiller Technique	Legislation, regulation, statutes, administrative organization of ministry and of regional services	*Direction* of General Administration; Personnel and Budget; Inspectorate General of Social Affairs
Conseiller Technique	Hospital-University matters, medical profession	*Direction* of Public Health; Service of Health Institutions
Conseiller Technique	Medical insurance; Old Age, Family Allowances	*Direction* of Family, Old Age and Sociage Action; *Direction* of Medical Insurance and Social Security
Parliamentary Attaché	Parliamentary mail, relations with Parliament	

[1] Since the information contained in this table (as in Table 8.2) is derived from an actual cabinet, the names of the officials have been omitted.

TABLE 8.2
Organization of Actual Cabinet: Horizontal Type

Name of Official	Technical Competence	Internal Liaisons	External Liaisons
Directeur de Cabinet			
Directeur adjoint	Political affairs; political aspects of all matters	*Direction* of Political Affairs	Presidency of the Republic; Prime Minister
Conseiller Technique	Economic affairs (in conjunction with Messrs.—); for European negotiations; for aid to developing countries; for financial aspects	*Direction* of Economic and Financial Affairs	Ministries: —Agriculture —Finance —Industry —Transport —Labor —Nat'l. Defense (industrial affairs) —SGCI (with Mr.—).
Conseiller Technique	Political affairs (to assist Director adjoint); Minister's speeches; press and information	*Direction* of Services of Press, Information and Documentation; *Direction* of United Nations; *Direction* of Diplomatic Archives; Cabinet of Sec'y. of State (same ministry)	Interministerial Committee for Information; Government spokesman
Chef de Cabinet	General problems of the ministry; Cabinet matters; Minister's personal affairs and Minister's mail; problems of national defense (other than industrial)	General services; diplomatic correspondence, codes	Ministry of Interior; Ministry of Nat'l. Defense (for matters other than industrial)
Conseiller Technique	French relations with developing countries (in conjunction with Mr.— for economic aspects and with Mr.— for cultural, scientific and technical aspects)	*Directions:* —of African & Madagascan Affairs —of Aid to Developing Francophone States —of Service of Cultural Cooperation with Francophone states —Cabinet of Sec'y. of State (same ministry)	Secretariat General for African and Madagascan Affairs

TABLE 8.2 (continued)

Name of Official	Technical Competence	Internal Liaisons	External Liaisons
Chef adjoint de Cabinet	Foreign officials seeking audience with Minister; preparation of visits in France of heads of State and Foreign Ministries; protocol matters	Protocol	All ministries (for visits of foreign officials)
Conseiller Technique	Legal, administrative and organizational questions; matters pertaining to repatriated persons; dossiers of Council Ministers	*Directions:* —of Administrative Conventions and Consular Affairs —of Personnel and General Administration (except financial questions) —of Legal Affairs —of Inspection of Diplomatic Posts	Secretariat General of Government; Conseil d'Etat; Civil Service
Conseiller Technique	Cultural, scientific, and technical policy (in conjunction with Mr._ for technical and cultural assistance to developing countries and with Messrs._ for questions of industrial technology)	*Direction* of Cultural, Scientific, and Technical Relations	Ministries: —Education —Cultural Affairs —Public Health —Industrial Development and Scientific Research
Conseiller Technique	International financial questions; questions of social security; budget of Ministry.	*Direction* of Personnel and of Gen'l. Administration; *Direction* of Administrative Conventions (for social security matters)	Ministry of Finance; Ministry of Public Health
Parliamentary Attaché	Minister's parliamentary mail; Minister's appearance before commissions; National Assembly agenda; oral and written questions; parliamentary missions abroad.		Ministry for Parliamentary Relations; Secretariat of Parliamen. Commissions

The Cabinet and the Administration: Political and Administrative Roles in the Higher Civil Service

L'envahissement systématique du cabinet par les bureaux serait tout aussi fâcheux que celui des bureaux par le cabinet. Les deux organismes doivent être en contact permanent. Mais les deux personnels doivent, en principe, demeurer distinct; les deux rôles, nettement différents et présentant l'un et l'autre une utilité particulière, ne doivent à aucun prix se trouver confondus.

—*Henry Noëll*[1]

If some of those cabinet members would just take time out to stop and ask themselves "What would I want if I were President?", they wouldn't give him all the trouble he's been having.

—*Aide to President Eisenhower*[2]

CABINET MEMBERS AND DIRECTORS: INTERCHANGEABLE PERSONNEL

It has been remarked of the British civil servant that his chief merits emanate from his nonentity. His nonentity insures his loyalty to politicians, as well as his practical and impersonal approach to problems. In France and other continental countries, it is argued, "a certain distrust of the 'selfless administrator' is . . . openly written into the administrative system." This is evidenced by the fact that "the French Ministry is, in effect, divided into two interacting parts, a large neutral part and a small part of high political voltage."[3] The "neutral part" is made up of the

[1] Henry Noëll, *Les Ministères* (Paris: Berger-Levrault, 1911), p. 98.
[2] Cited in Richard E. Neustadt, *Presidential Power* (New York: The New American Library, 1964), p. 48.
[3] C. H. Sisson, *The Spirit of British Administration* (London: Faber and Faber, 1959), p. 10.

201

services within the ministry and the small political part—the minister's "dynamite,"[4] as Sisson refers to it—is the cabinet. Noting how alien this form of organization is to the British way of doing things, Sisson writes: "In our complicated society there are and are going to be a lot of officials, and the only question is whether anything is to be gained by making within their ranks a distinction between those the Minister has to put up with and those he can really trust. It need hardly be said that such a distinction would cause a decline of confidence as between Ministers and officials, and would produce serious faults in the transmission within the service."[5]

Sisson, whose book is an interesting defense of the British civil service against its detractors,[6] and who speaks of "the mind of the administrator," is correct in pinpointing certain administrative conflicts in France that may have a detrimental effect on the formulation and execution of policy. He seems to be unaware, however, that there is no meaningful distinction between what he calls the minister's "wandering hangers-on" and the "permanent administration."[7] They are the same people; they merely alternate positions and, hence, roles. The French civil servant's ability to assume seemingly incompatible roles constitutes the theme of this chapter.

The ministerial cabinets have come more and more to be composed of civil servants—in fact, they have recently been referred to as "a domain reserved for the civil servants."[8] A glance at Table 9.1 is sufficient to indicate this near-monopoly, and it is equally evident that the Grands Corps have the largest representation.[9] (Nevertheless, although no equivalent data are available for the Third Republic, the number of civil servants who

---

[4] *Ibid.,* p. 111. [5] *Ibid.,* p. 145.

[6] For a British view that, unlike Sisson's, admires the European system of administration and finds much to criticize about the British civil service, see Brian Chapman's *British Government Observed: Some European Reflections* (London: George Allen and Unwin, 1963).

[7] Sisson, *The Spirit of British Administration*, pp. 110–111.

[8] Charles Debbasch, *L'Administration au pouvoir: fonctionnaires et politiques sous la Vᵉ république* (Paris: Calmann-Lévy, 1969), p. 59.

[9] The role of the Grands Corps in ministerial cabinets is treated in Chapter x. See also, B. Gournay, J.-F. Kesler, and J. Siwek-Poydesseau, *Administrations Publiques* (Paris: Presses Universitaires de France, 1967), p. 245; and J. Siwek-Poydesseau, *Le Personnel de direction des ministères* (Paris: Armand Colin, 1969), p. 46.

TABLE 9.1

Professional Background of Cabinet Personnel, 1970

Ministry	I.F.[1]	C.C.[2]	C.E.[3]	Admin. Civils	Dipl. Corps	Pref. Corps	Ponts et Chaussees	Corps des Mines	Other Civil Service	Army	Justice	Academic	Non-Civil Service	Prof. Unknown	Total
Prime Minister	3	–	2	2	5	4	1	1	6	1	2	–	1	1	29
Defense	2	1	1	1	1	1	–	–	–	1	–	–	–	–	8
Culture	–	1	1	1	–	2	–	–	1	1	1	–	1	2	11
Relations with Parliament	–	–	1	–	3	2	–	–	–	–	–	2	–	–	7
Justice	–	–	1	1	–	–	1	–	1	–	5	–	–	2	10
Foreign Affairs	1	1	1	1	–	1	1	–	1	–	5	–	1	1	12
Interior	–	1	1	3	2	4	1	1	4	–	–	1	1	–	11
Finance	5	–	4	4	1	1	–	–	2	–	1	–	1	–	16
Education	–	2	2	2	–	1	–	1	3	–	–	1	–	–	12
Industrial Development	1	1	1	1	1	2	1	1	3	–	–	1	–	–	12
Equipment & Housing	1	–	1	1	–	1	1	2	2	–	–	–	–	1	11
P.T.T.	1	1	–	1	–	2	3	–	6	–	–	–	2	–	9
Agriculture	1	–	2	1	–	1	–	1	6	–	–	–	–	–	9
Transport	–	–	–	1	–	2	1	4	4	1	–	–	–	1	10
Labor & Employment	1	1	1	1	–	1	1	1	4	1	–	–	–	–	10
Public Health	1	2	–	–	–	2	–	–	3	–	–	–	–	–	9
Veterans	1	–	1	1	–	1	–	–	1	–	1	–	2	2	10
Total	18	8	13	21	8	28	10	12	38	3	10	5	6	12	192

[1] Inspection des Finances. [2] Cour des Comptes [3] Conseil d'Etat

served in earlier ministerial cabinets should not be underestimated.)[10] Some have seen in the civil-servant monopoly of the cabinets under the Fifth Republic the "conquest of power by the civil servants."[11] It has therefore been argued that the homogeneity in their backgrounds and training mitigates conflict between the cabinet and the Directors, and such conflict has also been reduced, it is often maintained, by the practice, under the Fifth Republic, of appointing as ministers men with civil service backgrounds. To suggest, however, that in the formulation of policy there has come to exist something approaching complicity between ministers, their cabinet members, and the higher officials in ministries is to ascribe to the French administrative system a remarkable degree of coherence, and to lay what may be undue stress on the backgrounds of these men.

In our survey of the Directors of the central administration a marked hostility to the institution of the cabinet emerged, a hostility that evidenced a persistent rift at the apex of the French administrative system. The cabinet was accused by the Directors of having become a screen between the administration and the minister; of being a parallel hierarchy; of trying to take over the functions of the Directors; and of fulfilling the desire of some ministers to "divide and rule and, like Catherine de Medici, create functions." It was accused of short-circuiting the Directors not only vis-à-vis the minister (the most general complaint), but vis-à-vis their own services, thus undermining the authority and prestige of the Directors. "The Director must have more leeway," said one Director who had himself previously been a *directeur de cabinet*, "and he must be permitted to take more decisions on his

---

[10] That civil servants, and particularly members of the Grands Corps, played important roles in cabinets of the Third and Fourth Republics can be seen from a number of studies. For the Fourth Republic, see Jean-Louis Seurin, "Les Cabinets ministériels," *Revue de Droit Publique et de la Science Politique*, no. 6 (November–December 1956), 1293. For the Third Republic, see Pierre Lalumière, *L'Inspection des finances* (Paris: Presses Universitaires de France, 1959), p. 168; Marie-Christine Kessler, *Le Conseil d'Etat* (Paris: Armand Colin, 1968), p. 235; Siwek-Pouydesseau, *Le Personnel de direction des ministères*, pp. 49–53.

[11] Debbasch, *L'Administration au pouvoir*, p. 59. See also Jacques Mandrin, *L'Enarchie, ou les mandarins de la société bourgeoise* (Paris: La Table Ronde de Combat, 1967), p. 100; Jean Meynaud, *Technocracy* (London: Faber and Faber, 1965), p. 87; and Pierre Avril, *Le Gouvernement de la France* (Paris: Editions Universitaires, 1969), pp. 139–154.

own without first having to go to the cabinet." Another Director noted that "civil servants from regional services who would normally call their Directors now call the cabinet instead. Often, they feel more answerable to the cabinet than to their real superiors in Paris." Finally, the cabinet was accused of hampering the Directors' initiative in introducing reforms. "There is a tendency for Directors to be treated like children. The effect of this is to encourage them to shirk responsibility and discourage them from initiating reforms." Another Director made the same point by way of a rhetorical question: "Why is it that it is no longer possible to have a Director like Pierre Laroque [the originator of the social security system in France]?" The Directors' view of, and hostility toward, the ministerial cabinet can be seen from Tables 9.2 and 9.3: the Directors find themselves constantly short-circuited and regard the cabinets as more of a hindrance than a help. Indeed, of all the topics covered in the lengthy interviews with the Directors, none elicited such vigorous responses as their conflicts with the ministerial cabinet.

The seriousness of this conflict has not hitherto been sufficiently recognized. In the only study available of Directors and minis-

TABLE 9.2

Director's View of Cabinet[1] *(percent)*

1. Brain of minister which short-circuits the administration	79.0
2. Neither brain nor short-circuit	11.1
3. General tendency to short-circuit, but not in this ministry	4.9
4. Brain of minister, but does not short-circuit administration	2.5
5. Don't know	2.4
Total (N = 90)	100.0

[1] Question: An *Ambassadeur de France* has written that under the Third Republic the ministerial cabinet was only a means of liaison between the minister and his administration and the minister and parliament; the cabinet, according to him, hardly intervened in the work of the administration. Since the Liberation, however, the cabinet has become, according to this ambassador, the minister's brain and, with regard to the administration, the minister's eyes, which short-circuits the administration. Do you find this description accurate?

205

terial cabinets the author suggests that while there may exist a certain amount of distrust, conflicts are mitigated when the Director has himself previously served in a ministerial cabinet.[12] This appears, *prima facie*, only logical since such a Director could be expected to appreciate the complexities, and hence avoid the conflicts, that inhere in this relationship. The facts, how-

TABLE 9.3

Cabinet: Screen or Intermediary?[1] (percent)

1. A screen between minister and directors		60.5
2. A useful intermediary		32.1
3. Depends on ministry		6.2
4. Don't know		1.2
Total	(N = 90)	100.0

[1] Question: Would you say that the cabinet has become a screen between the minister and the administration, or would you consider it as a useful intermediary.

ever, indicate otherwise: the tensions between cabinet members and Directors are almost never lessened as a result of a Director's having previously served in a ministerial cabinet. The question, then, is: why does such a conflict exist between Directors and cabinet members when over half of the Directors have belonged to one, and frequently more, ministerial cabinets?

THE BUREAUCRATIC MENTALITY

In a remarkable analysis of the concept of social roles, Ralf Dahrendorf discusses what he calls the "vexation of *homo sociologicus.*"[13] This vexation, or the "vexatious fact of society," as Dahrendorf also refers to it, is the result not simply of an enduring conflict between roles that are predetermined for man and those that leave him a certain degree of choice, but also of the number of roles that man is called upon to assume. "Every position carries with it certain expected modes of behaviour; every

[12] Siwek-Pouydesseau, *Le Personnel de direction des ministères*, p. 122.

[13] Ralf Dahrendorf, *Essays in the Theory of Society* (Stanford: Stanford University Press, 1968), p. 32.

position a person occupies requires him to do certain things and exhibit certain characteristics. To every social position there belongs a social role."[14] It is in terms of *positions* and *roles* that, according to Dahrendorf, "we describe *homo sociologicus*, sociological man, the basic unit of sociological analysis."[15] Man has to accept the requirements imposed by society and, in order to act upon these requirements, he has to internalize them: "Position allocation and role internalization are complementary."[16]

Now this is man in society at large. What of man in a more circumscribed sphere of activity, such as that of a bureaucratic organization? The need for man to assume a number of roles that appear at odds with one another—head of a family, employee, member of a club or a church—is a common enough concept in sociological theory. Yet it is very meaningful when applied to the various tensions and complexities of a single occupational role. Crozier has suggested in *The Bureaucratic Phenomenon* that there exist a "set of roles" corresponding to the hierarchical arrangements within an organization.[17] Like Dahrendorf, Crozier notes the multiplicity of roles that man assumes in his daily life and suggests that this is what is in fact responsible for rendering the organization less oppressive than it used to be.[18] Positing as he does a cultural explanation of bureaucracy, Crozier is driven to conclusions that seek out uniform modes of behavior irrespective of positions and roles. In other words, he does not examine the implications of "role sets" that correspond to various levels of an organization's hierarchy, "the complement of role-relationships in which persons are involved by virtue of occupying a particular social status."[19] Following the analyses of Dahrendorf, Crozier, and Merton, I should like to raise the question of whether one or more roles can be subsumed, or internalized, within a single occupational role. We are interested here in the role, or more precisely in the role perception, of higher civil servants. Does the civil servant perceive his role in a uniform manner that is largely dictated by his socialization experience—education, training, and social background—or is he capable of internalizing other roles,

---

[14] *Ibid.*, p. 35.   [15] *Ibid.*   [16] *Ibid.*, p. 56.

[17] Michel Crozier, *The Bureaucratic Phenomenon* (Chicago: University of Chicago Press, 1964), p. 202.

[18] *Ibid.*, p. 185.

[19] Robert K. Merton, "'The Role-Set: Problems in Sociological Theory," *The British Journal of Sociology*, VIII, no. 2 (1957), 110.

roles that may in fact contradict the ethos of his socialization experience? The question derives its importance from the fact that it relates to the "mind" or "mentality" of civil servants and, as a consequence, to their mode of behavior.

In his *The Spirit of British Administration*, Sisson argues that it is possible to speak of "the mind of the administrator." This "mind," however, is grounded not in universal principles of administration but, on the contrary, in peculiarly national elements. "A comparison of one national administration with another," he writes, "inevitably involves much more than a confrontation of techniques. It involves a confrontation of cultures."[20] Karl Mannheim goes still further and maintains that all administrators exhibit the same characteristics and react in similar fashion to the problems with which they are called upon to deal; he argues that there is such a thing as a universal bureaucratic mentality. He is, as is clear from his writings, profoundly influenced by the example of the Prussian bureaucracy: from that one example he draws his universalistic conclusion. "Every bureaucracy, therefore, in accord with the peculiar emphasis on its own position, tends to generalize its own experience and to overlook the fact that the realm of administration and of smoothly functioning order represents only a part of the total political reality. Bureaucratic thought does not deny the possibility of a science of politics, but regards it as identical with the science of administration."[21]

That there exists a universal "bureaucratic mentality" seems highly questionable in the light of what we know about the significance of cultural, political, and institutional peculiarities and their effect on the organization and functioning of institutions.[22] Moreover, even within a particular society it seems difficult to maintain that civil servants share a uniform and unvarying approach to problems, methods of work, attitudes, and perception of roles. There is, first, a profound divergence in all these aspects between higher and lower civil servants,[23] the importance

[20] Sisson, *The Spirit of British Administration*, p. 119.

[21] Karl Mannheim, *Ideology and Utopia* (New York: Harcourt, Brace and World, 1936), p. 119.

[22] See Crozier, *The Bureaucratic Phenomenon*; Sisson, *The Spirit of British Administration*; and Ralf Dahrendorf, *Society and Democracy in Germany* (New York: Doubleday, 1967).

[23] One example will suffice to illustrate this point. In July 1963 the French Government passed a law regulating the right of public employees to

of which is not sufficiently recognized in *The Bureaucratic Phenomenon*. A second divergence exists between groups, or corps, within the administration (civil servants in the provinces versus those in the central administration; technical versus other corps).[24] A third divergence in outlook, and one that has not hitherto been recognized, results from the variations in the perception of various roles by the same individual. It is the phenomenon of shifting perceptions of role that sometimes bear the marks of a "bureaucratic mentality," and sometimes appear to contradict this mentality, that we are here concerned with. It will be seen that the fundamental perception of their roles by civil servants varies according to the positions they occupy in the politico-administrative hierarchy, positions that call for basically different approaches to their work. The application of role theory will help to clarify the complex problem of the "bureaucratic mind" and will enable us to analyse the serious conflict between higher civil servants.

BASES OF CONFLICT BETWEEN DIRECTORS AND CABINET

A higher civil servant's view of his role will vary according to the degree to which he feels he possesses influence or lacks it—not influence in an absolute sense, but influence commensurate with his hierarchical position. The Directors and the cabinet members have markedly divergent views as to what ought to be their own degree of authority. Most of the Directors are part of the apparatus of the ministry which the minister finds upon taking office.

---

strike. The unions, who were now required to give five days' notice before a scheduled strike, argued that the Government was aiming to limit the unions' right to strike. The Government, on the other hand, maintained throughout the long and bitter debates that it was merely attempting to put some order into the hitherto chaotic and ill-defined conditions pertaining to the rights of public employees to strike. It claimed that it did not restrict, nor did it have the intention of restricting, the right to strike. In our survey of the Directors of the central administration it was found that the Directors almost unanimously believed that the Government *did* attempt to limit the right of public employees to strike and, as the answers to the follow-up question revealed, that the right to strike of the State's employees *should* be totally restricted.

[24] See Bernard Gournay, "Un Groupe dirigeant de la société française: les grands fonctionnaires," *Revue française de science politique*, XIV, no. 1 (1964), 217-222.

The members of the cabinet are handpicked by him. This is in itself a significant factor which affects the degree of influence that Directors and cabinet members are able to exert on the minister, since the minister has an understandable tendency to rely on those whom he himself has placed in pivotal positions, rather than on officials who may have been picked by his predecessor (perhaps a political opponent). Ministers fear the dispersion of their power when it is placed in the hands of officials over whom they may feel they have little control. The very organization of the cabinet, which makes *conseillers techniques* responsible for specific matters of the ministry, suggests that ministers fear losing their grip over their departments. One former minister remarked that a minister always takes a risk if he leaves decisions in the hands of men who owe him no loyalty instead of leaning heavily on those whom he himself picks. "It is always important for ministers to have strong cabinets," he said, "because they need people they can trust in order to get things done."

Moreover, neither the Directors of the central administration as a whole nor the Directors within a particular ministry constitute in any sense a cohesive group. Each Director is head of a *direction*, or as the Directors themselves prefer to refer to it, an "administration," and each faces the minister and the cabinet alone. Nor do the members of the cabinet act collectively. But this does not, as in the case of the Directors, who are more rivals than co-workers, detract from their power, since each cabinet member acts in the name of the minister. The charge that the members of the cabinet see themselves as "nous le ministre" is not entirely without basis in theory or in fact for, as Seurin has noted, each member of the cabinet acts individually with the authority of the minister.[25] As one cabinet member put it, "The cabinet does not exist; each cabinet member acts on behalf of the minister and in the minister's name." It must also be noted that the power of cabinet members derives in large part from an incontestable vagueness as to the basis of their authority when it comes to certain questions, for it is not always evident that when they act they are doing so on behalf of the minister. This vagueness is a key to the cabinet's power, for it allows its members to range far and wide into the work of the Directors. It also, as we shall see, contrasts markedly with the Directors' desire for a narrowly defined sphere of activity. But the ill-defined source of the cabi-

[25] Seurin, "Les cabinets ministériels," p. 1285.

net's power also serves an important purpose for the minister. If conflict between a Director and a cabinet member becomes particularly acute, the minister may be able to moderate it by claiming that the cabinet official has overstepped the bounds of his authority.

Nevertheless, the cabinet cannot be regarded as an institution possessing institutional interests of its own upon which it acts. Its interests are those of the minister, which also means that it is deeply concerned with the general policies of the government of the day. One of its chief tasks is not only to incorporate the minister's own policies within the framework of the government's policies, but also to separate from the government's policies what belongs specifically to the minister. The Director, on the other hand, is little concerned with overall governmental actions. He has to supervise and protect an administration made cumbersome by a plethora of traditions and regulations.

Still another reason why conflicts arise between Directors and ministerial cabinet members is that for the latter there does not exist the gap between authority and influence with which many Directors have to live. All Directors have a certain degree of authority simply by virtue of the position they occupy in the administrative hierarchy. But their influence does not always correspond to this authority. When one Director spoke at length of what he called "la bataille des articulations" as being one of the central preoccupations of a Director, he was referring to the critical importance, for a Director, of bridging the gap between authority and influence. Whether a Director chooses to be what this one called a "petit commis" or whether he chooses to be a "grand commis" depends on his ability to conduct his "bataille des articulations." It is the duty of each Director, according to this civil servant, to establish his relationship with the cabinet in a manner designed to insure his maximum influence. The Director must regard this effort as a constant "battle" because for members of ministerial cabinets authority and influence go hand in hand, and excessive influence on the part of the cabinet detracts from the influence of the Directors. In reality there are few cases where the cabinet is uniformly strong and the Directors uniformly weak: usually each Director in a ministry establishes his own type of relationship with his liaison in the cabinet.

From the Director's point of view, to establish a suitable relationship is, in effect, to maintain control over the flow of informa-

211

tion. This is a critical factor in the relationship. Information is generally a monopoly of the higher civil servants in the ministry, but it begins to be eroded if a minister and his cabinet serve for a considerable time. The cabinet becomes as competent to deal with the tasks of the ministry as are its officials. Now, there are cases where the Directors will guard their freedom of action by appearing to maintain the flow of information from their services to the cabinet but in fact allowing only partial information to filter through. This occurs in certain extremely technical domains where a Director may do as he pleases, provided he sells, in simple language, his projects to the cabinet. Why then does the minister not take into his cabinet a technician with a training and background similar to that of the Director? This is a question that we shall return to in the next chapter, but suffice it to say here that ministers do not normally appoint to their cabinets members of the corps with which the ministry is identified because they fear the creation of what might be called split-loyalty cabinets. A member of the ministry's corps in the cabinet would have an undeniable loyalty to the Director he was supposed to supervise, since his promotion would ultimately depend not only on the minister he was serving but even more on the Director to whom he had been—and might again be—subordinate (see Chapter x).

The cabinet's influence derives to an important degree from its ability to undertake functions that Directors cannot—nor do they desire to—assume. Foremost among these is the coordination of activities within and between ministries.

The central administration in France is by no means a rationally or coherently organized entity, the proverbial French penchant for rationality notwithstanding. Ministries are created, joined together, abolished, only to reappear in their original form some years later. This means that services are constantly transferred from one ministry to another, for a ministry disappears only in name—all its functions remain intact. The result is that jurisdiction over a particular domain tends to become dispersed. Crozier has suggested that Americans don't mind creating two or three competing agencies to deal with a particular problem, whereas the French have a very definite dislike of such a situation.[26] This may well be correct, but the interesting fact is that, despite the fear of dispersed powers, the dispersion of power is

[26] Crozier, *The Bureaucratic Phenomenon*, p. 253.

a distinctive feature of the central administration in France. There is scarcely a question that can be settled within a single *direction* or in a single ministry: jurisdiction is widely distributed and often without the least concession to rationality.

The dispersion of administrative jurisdiction gives rise to the problem of the never-ending "bataille des compétences," as it is commonly referred to in the French administration. This battle involves not only interministerial jurisdictional squabbles, but also intraministerial conflicts. I once heard two Directors in the same ministry engage in a heated discussion over a sentence that threatened to shift an element of control over a minor domain from one *direction* to another. The discussion, not surprisingly, did not lead to a resolution of the problem, and an agreement was reached to let the *directeur de cabinet* or the minister arbitrate. After the exchange, one of the Directors confided that the matter would be resolved rapidly because of its relative insignificance. The discussion had become somewhat tense, he observed, because "I thought he was trying to knife me in the back," that is, to assume for his own *direction* that which properly belonged to the other.

Such "batailles des compétences" indicate, first, the Directors' conception of power. Power, for them, is strictly definable; it does not emerge from complex relationships. It is to be located, as the quarrel between the two Directors suggested, in the list of jurisdictions. That there is no necessary connection between the legally defined jurisdictions of a *direction* and the influence that a Director actually exerts is not evident to most of the Directors. There is no fear of face-to-face relations or of a restrictive equality within a peer group, which Crozier found to be the case in his study of low-level civil servants. Indeed, at upper levels of the bureaucracy face-to-face relations are often aggressively sought and, as indicated earlier, the Directors within a ministry do not constitute, in any sense, a group. Instead, there is among them a profound urge to delimit a sphere of activity without engaging in the interactions that necessarily call for "power relations." In some instances the desire clearly to define a sphere of activity leads to imperialistic tendencies, in others to a rather narrow delimitation of jurisdictions. In the case of cabinet members, there is no attempt to define or circumscribe jurisdictions. In fact, there is an attempt to keep intact that vagueness in relationships and jurisdictions that we described earlier.

213

Because the Directors seek a strict delimitation of their jurisdictions in fact as well as in principle, the problem of the coordination of activities poses a number of difficulties. When, as very often happens, a particular problem does not neatly fit into anyone's list of jurisdictions a squabble commences, one that may involve several *directions* within a ministry or several ministries. Given the conception that the Directors have of their function and of the nature of power, they are unable to resolve these conflicts themselves. Who, then, is to assume the responsibility for coordinating the activities within and between ministries but a group operating within a framework that encompasses the overall policies of the minister and those of the government, that shoulders no responsibilities or burdens equivalent to those of the Directors, has no traditions to safeguard, has no perpetual enemies who may be nibbling away at its powers—above all, a group that sees its power and influence not as statically defined but as the result of complex maneuvres and interactions? Because the cabinet's power and influence depend to a great extent on its coordinating function, it is important to digress briefly in order to examine the role of the Secretary General.

THE SECRETARY GENERAL

It has often been suggested that a Secretary General in each ministry would more than adequately fulfill the task of coordination within the ministry. That, in fact, has generally been the function of a Secretary General in the ministries where the post has existed. There remain, however, but two ministries—Foreign Affairs and Post, Telegraph and Telecommunications (P.T.T.)—where it exists today. The post of Secretary General has been created and suppressed on and off in a number of ministries, and it is not difficult to understand why ministers have a particular mistrust of this position. As Léon Blum wrote, the post of "Secretary General, which was proposed, which has been created, and which currently exists in England, presents the disadvantage of placing near the ephemeral ministers a permanent head of the administration who will usurp all authority from weak ministers and who will find himself in an almost unavoidable conflict with strong ministers."[27]

[27] Léon Blum, *Le Réforme gouvernementale* (Paris: Grasset, 1936), p. 142.

Although Blum was referring to the post of Secretary General under a system of ministerial instability, the danger of a Secretary General establishing a power base is a very real one even in a system of ministerial stability. Nor is a clash likely to arise simply between a weak minister and a powerful Secretary General, for a weak minister often has a strong cabinet which is likely to come into conflict with the Secretary General.

In July 1968, when Edgar Faure became Minister of National Education in Couve de Murville's government, one of his first acts was to abolish the post of Secretary General in that ministry. The post had been held for a number of years by a strong-minded member of the Conseil d'Etat, and Faure did not wish to have his authority challenged or risk having his reforms sabotaged by intraministerial squabbles.[28] It had become abundantly clear that very little work of a serious nature was being done in the ministry under Faure's two predecessors, Christian Fouchet and Alain Peyrefitte. This was undoubtedly owing in part, as has been argued, to the lack of imagination of these ministers. It was clear, nevertheless, that no serious reforms could be undertaken when the minister was pitted against the Secretary General, the cabinet against the Secretary General, the cabinet against the Directors, and the Directors against the Secretary General. In fact, for the year preceding the student outbreaks of May 1968 the Ministry of National Education was utterly paralyzed by a situation that had deteriorated from an internecine war to one in which those responsible for running the ministry were, as one Director in this ministry put it, scarcely on speaking terms. The communication process within the ministry had completely broken down when the student uprisings occurred.

This untenable situation does not necessarily imply that all the ministry's problems emanated from the Secretary General. It does, nonetheless, indicate that a power struggle becomes more likely, perhaps inevitable, where there are two or three heads in a ministry (the minister, his cabinet director, and the Secretary General). The power struggle may be between the minister and the Secretary General or between the *directeur de cabinet* and the Secretary General. In any case, the struggle relegates the Directors to positions of little importance and the ministry grinds

[28] In his inimitable manner, Faure explained his action thus: "I have been told that Monsieur Laurent is irreplaceable; therefore I will not replace him!"

215

to a halt. Often, it should be noted, such serious conflicts within a ministry can place the Directors in a favorable position, since they are able to play one superior against another. But the higher civil servants in the Ministry of Education were prepared to recognize that whatever the immediate advantages of such internecine conflict, no reforms could be formulated, let alone undertaken. How complex the hierarchical arrangements become in a ministry when there exists a Secretary General can be seen from Diagram 9.1. The dotted lines indicate the uncertainties involved in the hierarchical arrangements. It is important to observe that these uncertainties are lessened where there is no Secretary General, but they do not entirely disappear.

In the Ministry of Finance, as in the Ministry of Agriculture, the post of Secretary General was created briefly under Vichy and abolished at the Liberation. It was never again to appear. It is now all but inconceivable for the post to be re-created in this ministry, not simply because it is associated with Vichy, but because, as most officials in the ministry affirmed, the higher civil servants would hardly tolerate a situation in which one of them would reign over his colleagues. While acknowledging that a Secretary General would obviate the need for a cabinet, Dominique Leca, an Inspecteur des Finances and a former high-ranking official in the Ministry of Finance, maintains that "experience has shown that such a substitution [the Secretary General for the cabinet] can never work. The Directors [of the Ministry of Finance] strongly resent the permanent insertion of a higher screen between them and their successive political superiors."[29] The cabinet director is acceptable to the Directors in this ministry even though he is almost always a higher civil servant from the ministry itself—i.e., a colleague of the Directors. The reason for this is twofold: first, the *directeur de cabinet*'s power and authority emanate from the minister and are in no way independent of him, since each minister appoints his own *directeur de cabinet*. This was not the case with the Secretary General, who survived ministers. Second, the *directeur de cabinet*'s task, unlike that of the Secretary General, goes beyond the mere coordination of the *directions*' activities. In day-to-day affairs, the Directors of the Ministry of Finance enjoy a degree of autonomy not known in most ministries. This leeway might be curtailed if a Secretary

[29] Dominique Leca, *Du Ministre des finances* (Paris: Plon, 1966), p. 20.

Diagram 9.1
Fluidity in Hierarchical Relationships
in the French Administrative System

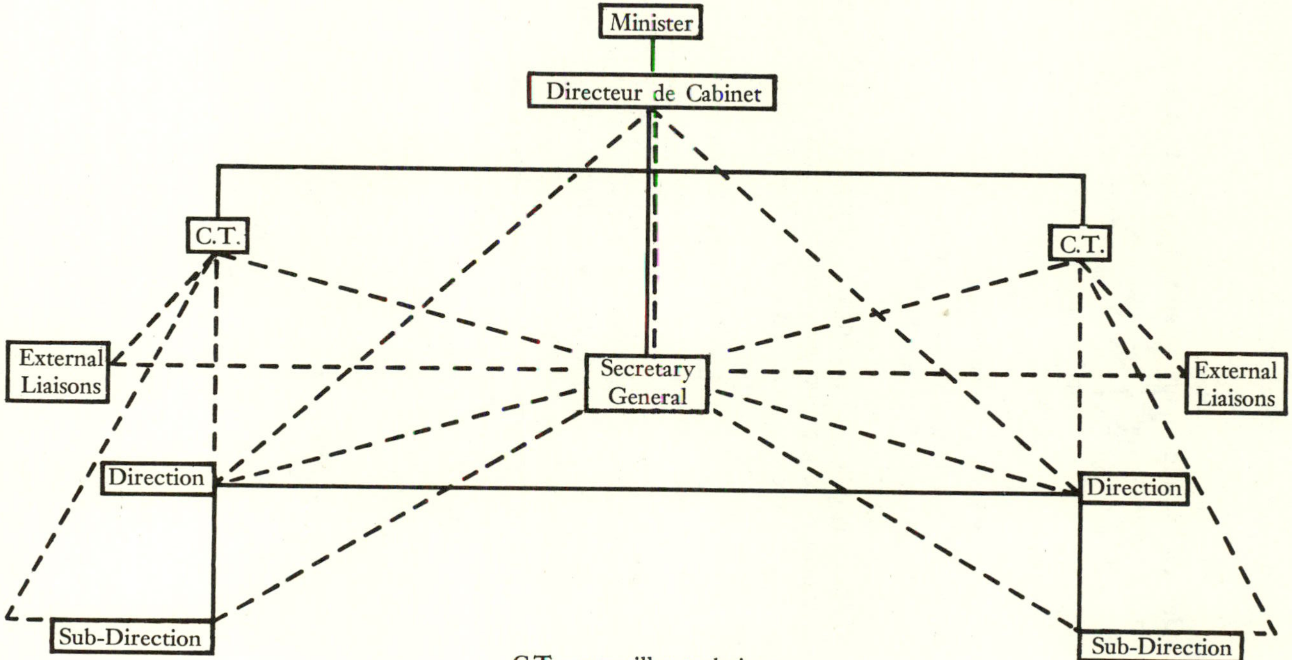

C.T.—conseiller technique

General were appointed, for his primary task would be to coordinate and supervise the activities of the Directors. The cabinet—as the majority of cabinet members in all the other ministries also indicated—would be unalterably opposed to a Secretary General placed between them and the Directors. Nor is it conceivable that a Minister of Finance would permit his powers to be threatened by a civil servant occupying a crucial position, and a man whom he had not appointed. This was precisely the dilemma confronting Edgar Faure when he became Minister of Education in 1968. As Leca has observed with regard to the Ministry of Finance: "The minister can never consider as an emanation of his person someone whom he finds in place when he arrives at the ministry and who will survive him when he departs. As a result of this mutual lack of confidence, no matter who the men are, the intermediary institution perishes and always ends up by disappearing for the simple reason that no one desires its existence. On the contrary, by its ephemeral and mixed nature, the cabinet is accorded the possibility of fulfilling, without causing umbrage to anyone, the difficult task of coordination."[30]

It appears unlikely that the post of Secretary General will be re-created in some ministries or created anew in others. In the first place, the post tends to complicate administrative relations. Second, it evidences a centralizing tendency without producing concomitant rationalization in organization or in the formulation of policies.[31] Third, the post is strongly disliked by ministers. In effect, the functions of the minister's cabinet cannot be easily separated from those of the Secretary General, so that a certain degree of conflict is inherent in the existence of both.[32] In the case of the Ministry of Foreign Affairs there is undoubtedly a tendency for duplication of work by the Secretary General and the cabinet. Under the Fifth Republic, however, conflict between the Secretary General and the cabinet has, by and large, been avoided. Couve de Murville, who was Minister of Foreign Affairs

[30] *Ibid.*, p. 21.

[31] As the authors of a previously cited work have observed: "Contributing in theory to coherent decision-making and to the execution of decisions, centralization, in effect, reveals itself as a generator of compartmentalization, isolation and duplication of work." C. Alphandery, et al., *Pour nationaliser l'Etat* (Paris: Seuil, 1968), p. 44.

[32] This is precisely why Léon Blum suggested in his *La Réforme gouvernementale* that the post of Secretary General be amalgamated with the cabinet.

from 1958 to 1968, chose to have small cabinets and relied heavily on the Secretary General. Maurice Schumann, who was Minister until March 1973, also tended to work closely with the Secretary General, undoubtedly because the conduct of foreign policy is now incontestably the domain of the President of the Republic, so that a cabinet to supervise the Directors is not necessary.[33] Also, the administration of this ministry is scattered around the world and the Quai d'Orsay employs only a skeleton staff. In most ministries, however, in the absence of a Secretary General the task of coordination among *directions* and ministries falls to the cabinet.

POLITICS AND ADMINISTRATION

The great divide between the world of administration and that of politics has retained its strong appeal for scholars as well as for the actors involved. Institutions are generally classified as belonging to one or the other of these domains, and no institution has been able to escape this categorization. André Siegfried, for example, saw even the mayor of a large town as a mere administrator and believed that the mayoral function was incompatible with the holding of a seat in the National Assembly.[34] The view that local politics is no more than local administration is widely held; it emanates from the assumption that "the powers of the territorial units are purely administrative, limited to the implementation of the laws voted at the center. . . ."[35] This theoretical distinction between politics and administration has tended to complement the apolitical stance of key administrators in France at both the local and national levels. The French mayor proclaims that he does not engage in politics and that his functions are administrative in nature,[36] and the higher civil servant states that his task, like the mayor's, is strictly nonpolitical. Few of the Di-

---

[33] It is interesting to note that Schumann's cabinet contained the same members that he had with him at the Ministry of Social Affairs from 1967 to 1968. Yet, whereas the cabinet was given the authority to practically run the Ministry of Social Affairs, it had a relatively secondary function in the Ministry of Foreign Affairs.

[34] André Siegfried, *De la IIIème à la IVème République* (Paris: Grasset, 1956), p. 245.

[35] Stanley Hoffmann, "The Areal Division of Powers in the Writings of French Political Thinkers," in Arthur Mass, ed., *Area and Power: A Theory of Local Government* (Glencoe, Ill.: The Free Press, 1959), p. 139.

[36] Mark Kesselman, *The Ambiguous Consensus* (New York: Alfred A. Knopf, 1967), pp. 136–149.

rectors interviewed, however, would agree with Siegfried as to the apolitical nature of the functions of the mayor of a large town. While they, too, believed (Table 9.4) that the mayor's functions were apolitical, they almost all agreed that he exercised a function that was undeniably political. It should be noted, of course, that the belief that politics takes place in France *only* at the national level, and even then only in a number of specified institutions, is not without legal sanction. Civil servants are permitted to be elected as Municipal Councillors, General Councillors, or Mayors, though not in the *département* in which they are serving

TABLE 9.4

Compatibility of Civil Service Post With Other Functions, According to Directors[1] (percent)

Function	Yes	No
Member of political club	46.9	45.7
General councillor	65.4	28.4
Municipal councillor	84.0	9.9
Mayor	77.8	16.0
Member of political party	45.7	48.1

[1] Question: Do you think that one can be a higher civil servant at the same time as being a member of a political club, a general councillor, a municipal councillor, a mayor, or a member of a political party?

as representatives of a ministry. A number of Directors interviewed were at the same time mayors of small towns, and when asked whether being a mayor did not entail a certain amount of political activity, they generally replied that being mayor, especially of a small commune, involved minor administrative tasks. One Director noted, in a vein strikingly similar to that of the Prime Minister cited earlier, "the commune is flattered to have as mayor a higher civil servant who can get things done for them in Paris."

In the case of the central administration, there is again an important distinction made between the domains of politics and administration, one that has continually been reinforced by scholars. Even today a prominent specialist on the French administration can state that "the cabinet is 'politique,' the services are 'technique.' "[37] Echoing this approach, an English textbook on French public administration states that the primary function of the cabinet "is to bridge the gap between the world of politics and the world of administration."[38] And Henry Ehrmann writes that "at the ministerial level, the cabinets form a link between politics and administration and the outer environment, the latter comprising organized interests as well as other administrations."[39] None of these writers considers the crucial question of what, at the highest administrative level, distinguishes politics and administration. The assumption that one institution constitutes a "link" between two domains necessarily takes for granted what in fact needs to be proven: namely, that there *are* two domains.

Thus, to maintain that the administration is "technique" and the cabinet "politique" is to establish a priori that there exist two separate domains having distinct personnel and distinct, recognizable functions. This is more of a normative or prescriptive viewpoint than a descriptive one. In treating this question, Demartial noted in 1911: "What is a civil servant? He is a citizen called to serve the State, a moral being who survives the transformations and the battles of [political] parties. What is a political person? He is a citizen elected to serve a party. The same man cannot honestly fill both roles at the same time, because he then becomes not a political civil servant, but a civil servant who traffics in politics. . . ."[40] This is a view that ignores the problem of overlapping functions and the interchangeability of personnel. Most remarkable, perhaps, has been its staying power, for it appears to be as accepted today as it was in the nineteenth century. One reason for this is that it has always been used to explain the purity of the administration. Typifying this view is a recent study of the Conseil d'Etat in which the author, while admitting that it is scarcely possible to separate the technical and political spheres when the latter is conceived of as "collaboration" with a

[37] Robert Catherine, *Le Fonctionnaire français* (Paris: Albin Michel, 1961), p. 300.

[38] F. Ridley and J. Blondel, *Public Administration in France* (New York: Barnes and Noble, 1965), p. 65.

[39] Henry Ehrmann, *Politics in France* (Boston: Little, Brown, 1968), p. 263.

[40] G. Demartial, *Le Personnel des ministères* (Paris: Berger-Levrault, 1911), p. 28.

221

minister, nevertheless writes: "The facts seem to prove that, except for exceptional periods when the notions of politics and administration clash, a distinction between the two is possible. There exists in ministerial cabinets a division of labor and a distinction in preoccupations which prove that the role of the higher civil servants is essentially technical."[41]

This represents a reiteration of the traditionally accepted view that civil servants, regardless of the posts they hold in the politico-administrative system, always play technical roles. Yet it is precisely the close relationship, indeed the inseparability of politics and administraton, that is at the heart of the conflict between the cabinet and the Directors. We must turn to an examination of the respective role perceptions of cabinet members and Directors if we are to understand this particular conflict and gain a greater understanding of the bureaucratic "mentality."

ROLE PERCEPTIONS AND ROLE CONFLICTS

The conflict between cabinet members and Directors manifests two diametrically opposed role perceptions: for the Directors, politics and administration are distinct domains that only infrequently come into contact with one another, and which, in any case, ought always to remain strictly separated. For the cabinet members, the two domains cannot be separated at the highest levels of the administrative system, where decisions are prepared for and alternatives submitted to the minister. In other words, the members of ministerial cabinets have a view of their role that does not accord with Kessler's interpretation.[42]

In her *Le Personnel de direction des ministères*, J. Siwek-Pouydesseau touches on the relationship between politics and administration, and tells us that Directors make no distinction between technical and political functions.[43] Were that in fact the case, the

---

[41] Kessler, *Le Conseil d'Etat*, p. 242.

[42] This is undoubtedly due to the fact that Mme. Kessler's conclusions are based on interviews with members of the Conseil d'Etat who were serving in the Conseil at the time they were interviewed, so that they were expressing opinions concerning the role of the civil servant in general. My own data, on the other hand, are based on interviews with Directors and cabinet members exercising their functions at the time of the interview. Both were therefore answering questions concerning their current functions and their perceptions of their current roles.

[43] P. 122.

crucial divergence in role perception between Directors and cabinet members would disappear. Our survey revealed the very opposite: Directors were at pains to distinguish between what they regarded as two distinct domains. Tables 9.5 and 9.6 show that while cabinet members accept the political and administrative aspects of their tasks, Directors prefer to think of their work as being more or less purely administrative. Despite the fact that an equal proportion of Directors think that it is or is not inevitable that civil servants should today occupy political posts, only 10 percent affirmed that the problems being treated by the politi-

TABLE 9.5

Politics and Administration: Inevitability and Desirability of Link, According to Directors[1] (percent)

Inevitable		46.9
Not inevitable		46.3
Don't know		6.8
Total	(N = 90)	100.0
Desirable		30.9
Not desirable		65.4
Don't know		3.7
Total	(N = 90)	100.0

[1] Question: Many higher civil servants and former graduates of ENA occupy today posts in the Council of Ministers and other purely political posts. Would you say that this phenomenon is inevitable or not, desirable or not?

TABLE 9.6

Administrative and Political Functions of Cabinet, According to Cabinet Members[1] (percent)

Administrative		11.1
Political		23.4
Both		65.5
Total	(N = 44)	100.0

[1] Question: Would you say that your function as a cabinet member is administrative, political, or both?

cians and the civil servant "are the same." Twenty-six percent noted that ENA has had a tendency to stimulate the ambition of its graduates, "who all want to become ministers," and 30 percent blamed de Gaulle for having started the process of effacing the important distinction between politics and administration by taking civil servants into his government. The cabinet members did not accept this analysis because, to them, the functions of a higher civil servant, insofar as these functions touch upon government policy, are inevitably at once administrative and political.

This divergence of views is well illustrated by the opinion of the Directors with respect to the function of the cabinet: "to look after the political aspects of our technical proposals." Why should Directors adopt such a view, which one would expect to find only in textbooks on administrative law? It persists, it might be suggested, because the Directors wish to create a division of labor based on a theoretical distinction of functions which, although it is belied by their daily tasks, will protect them against intruders seeking to infringe their autonomy. To acknowledge that their role is as much political as the cabinet's is administrative would be, in their eyes, to endanger their independence: information would then have to flow freely, coordination would no longer be foreign to them, and overlapping functions would be accepted as a necessary part of their work, all of which would mean that their administrations would become "infiltrated" and would be constantly vulnerable. The interpenetration of the domains of politics and administration implies above all a recognition of vague boundaries between functions, which all administrators resent. That, after all, is what the famous "bataille des compétences" is all about. As Crozier has very justly noted: "French higher civil servants have a sort of panicky fear of possible overlapping," so that "they spend much of their time trying to avoid possible overlapping. They are motivated by their conception of authority as an absolute that cannot be shared, discussed or compromised. If they prefer restraint to imperialism, this is not for cooperative purposes, but for the preservation of the integrity of the organization's power."[44]

The profound hostility that Directors feel toward the cabinet does not, oddly enough, lead them to regard it as a useless institution. Indeed, they think it more indispensable for themselves than for the minister (Table 9.7). Yet, as Table 9.8 shows, it is in-

[44] Crozier, *The Bureaucratic Phenomenon*, p. 254.

dispensable because "we can throw anything that smells of politics onto the cabinet." The significance of this cannot be exaggerated. It implies an unwillingness to become wholly involved in the decisions of the minister, as well as a desire to safeguard the Directors' autonomy vis-à-vis the minister. It was often the strongest critics of the cabinet who said: "The cabinet is indispensable because it guarantees the stability of the Directors. If there were no cabinet, each minister would have to change the Directors when he came in." For the cabinet, this is sufficient evidence of what they call the Directors' *politique du parapluie*: when a Director does not wish to treat a particular matter, see

TABLE 9.7

Indispensability of Cabinet, According to Directors[1]

Indispensability of Cabinet	For Minister %	For Directors %
Cabinet is indispensable	29.6	34.6
Useful, if small	18.5	17.3
Not indispensable	50.6	46.9
Don't know	1.2	1.2
Total	100.0	100.0

[1] Question: France is one of the rare countries in which there exist ministerial cabinets. Do you think that ministerial cabinets are indispensable from the point of view of the minister and of the directors?

TABLE 9.8

Utility of Cabinet for Administration, According to Directors[1]

Function	%
Coordinating body	12.3
Interministerial work	9.9
Depoliticizes work of directors	44.4
Facilitates contact with minister	11.1
Others	24.3
Total	100.0

[1] The information contained in this table derives from answers to the question posed in Table 9.7. These answers were later coded.

a particular deputy or interest group, he opens the umbrella (i.e., the cabinet) in order to protect himself.[45] He hands over to the cabinet what ought to be his own responsibility, which means, according to the cabinet members, that "we come to rely more and more on ourselves for carrying out the essential tasks of the ministry."

The view that officials in the cabinets have of their role as civil servants is totally at odds with the view that Directors have of theirs. Cabinet members, as we have noted, make no distinction between administration and politics. They acknowledge that while they may be essentially technicians, their function by no means lacks political aspects. Their task is that of preparing decisions for the minister, which means "in addition to being concise, also being aware of the alternatives *and* of their political implications." The Directors, as cabinet members see them, want no part of this political awareness. As one cabinet member noted, "The Directors want to have the image of a 'pure administration' that doesn't get involved in politics. But that is not what the minister needs. What he needs is a team that links the so-called 'pure administration' (which is an absolute myth) and politics." This official went on to emphasize that "every aspect of the Directors' work has a political element. Theirs is not, nor can it be, a purely administrative task. They do not want to recognize that they play a political role. It's the 'pure administration' image that they want to guard."

Other members of the cabinets put the blame on the nature of the French administrative system. One sub-prefect serving in a cabinet noted that "the Directors are not in a position to feel the political implications of their actions, whereas we live in a political milieu. What is also important is that the cabinet accompanies decisions with press releases, publicity, etc., to make them acceptable. The Directors—and the stronger they are, the more likely for it to happen—have a tendency to dictate, which is incompatible with a truly political function." The Directors are thus seen as daily engaging in politics without accepting the responsibilities that politics entails; in fact, they are seen by cabinet members as engaging in politics only where their own interests are concerned.

[45] For an analysis of "umbrella politics" in the French administration, see Henri Deroche, *Les Mythes administratives* (Paris: Presses Universitaires de France, 1966), pp. 90–94.

The critical difference in role perception between Directors and cabinet members is best evidenced by the way they view their roles in relation to that of the minister. The cabinet members see no divergence between their role and that of the minister. Our survey revealed that they see their primary task as that of keeping abreast of the workings of the ministry and keeping the minister informed of the ministry's activities. That this is what the minister expects was more than adequately documented by the instructions issued by a *directeur de cabinet* to the members of the cabinet he headed, immediately after the minister took office. He listed the three essential tasks of the cabinet as follows:

1. Keep a dossier for the minister on all of the ministry's concerns;
2. Keep the minister informed on the functioning of the ministry;
3. Maintain the liaison of the ministry with the Secretariat General of the Presidency of the Republic, the cabinets of other ministers and the Assemblies.

It is not difficult to see how deeply involved in the Directors' work the cabinet members have to be in order to perform these functions. But it is equally necessary that they embrace the minister's outlooks and interests and, to the extent that they do so, they come into conflict with the Directors.

The Directors, for their part, laid particular stress on what they regarded as a fundamental divergence of preoccupations between them and the minister. As far as they are concerned, the essential task of a minister is "to fight for his ministry." It is to obtain funds. He ought to hear the needs of the ministry from his Directors and act as the ministry's representative or lawyer in the Council of Ministers and vis-à-vis the Ministry of Finance. He has no expertise and, therefore, he cannot initiate reforms. Directors believe that if ministers come into office with ideas, these ideas are likely to be unworkable at best, and utopian at worst. More often than not, however, Directors take the view that ministers come to their office without ideas and that it is their essential task to guide him. This is best illustrated in the Directors' response to the following question: "It has been said that when a minister comes into a ministry he sometimes has precise programs which are more or less unrealistic, perhaps even utopian, and that it is the higher civil servants that render these programs more realistic. Would you say that this is an accurate statement?" Although a substantial number of Directors prefaced their reply with the statement "Ministers never have ideas," 92 percent said that the statement was absolutely correct. The same question was posed to members of ministerial cabinets, over 90 percent of whom disagreed with the statement. They contended that the minister's ideas are generally thwarted by the Directors under the guise of making them more "realistic."

As a result of this particular role perception of the Directors, a wide gulf is created between the views that they and the ministers have of their respective roles. Ministers view their role as essentially that of carrying out their own and the government's policies, for which they alone are responsible. They see the civil servants as being there to execute the minister's policies. When ministers seek to act upon this view, that is, when they see themselves as guiding their civil servants, a conflict is likely to ensue because they pose a challenge to the civil servants' image of their role. This is precisely what occurred in the Chalandon case described earlier. As a former minister has noted, "The exchange of conflicting ideas between Minister and Director is excellent, but the last word must be the Minister's. A Director is not worthy of his title unless he is as zealous in the application of a decision by the Minister with which he does not agree as he would be if his own solution had triumphed."[46] The Director, on the other hand, views himself as the guardian of technical or specialized knowledge which he imparts to the minister and without which the minister cannot carry out his tasks. A former minister once observed: "In my first post as Secretary of State, I was struck by the attitude of men who, in front of the newly arrived [Secretary] made it only too clear that after the minister had come and gone 'they' would remain in their places."[47] This ex-minister recounts an incident that took place while he was in office: an "important man" (a Director) was astounded when the minister, after having given serious study to a project, refused to sign the necessary document submitted to him by the Director. After an argument, the Director said: "But the signature of a minister is only a formality."[48] Bernard Chenot, a former minister of the

[46] André Morice, "Le Ministre et l'administration," *Promotions*, no. 28 (1954), 17.
[47] *Ibid.*   [48] *Ibid.*, p. 18.

Fifth Republic, also observes the tendency of Directors to regard the minister as a signing machine or rubber stamp. "In the morning," he writes, "the minister would receive the members of the cabinet while the ministry's Directors cooled their heels outside the door, waiting not to discuss a problem—there was no time for that—but to snatch a signature."[49] That the Directors see themselves as responsible for setting policies and guidelines can be seen from Table 9.9, which shows that they attach the greatest importance to "establishing norms and general guidelines"—pre-

TABLE 9.9

Importance Attached to Various Administrative Functions by Directors

Function	1st Choice %	2nd Choice %	3rd Choice %	Total %
Giving orders	12.3	2.5	8.6	23.4
Ratifying or supervising decisions of others	7.4	16.0	6.2	29.6
Explaining decisions already taken	3.7	7.4	4.9	16.0
Studying technical propositions	4.9	14.8	17.3	37.0
Obtaining information on the activities of your ministry	1.2	1.2	4.9	7.3
Resolving conflicts involving personal relations of subordinates	4.9	–	1.2	6.1
Working on long-term projects and plans	27.2	18.5	11.1	56.8
Establishing norms and general guidelines	28.4	28.4	8.6	65.4
Obtaining information on matters of direct concern from other ministries	1.2	–	13.6	14.8
Explaining decisions to be taken[1]	3.7	6.2	11.1	21.0

[1] This was not a precoded choice.

cisely what the minister considers to be his own prerogative. They also attach great importance to "working on long-term projects and plans," which the minister and the cabinet consider to lie within their domain. It should be noted that although the Directors saw long-range planning as one of their most important tasks, they did not hesitate to observe that "there is little or no time for this."

The members of ministerial cabinets regard the attempts of

[49] Bernard Chenot, *Etre ministre* (Paris: Plon, 1967), pp. 46–47.

Directors to render the minister's ideas more "realistic" as an attempt to put a brake on the minister's desire for reform. They contend that reforms never originate in the services, which they see as being conservative and shackled by tradition. "The *directions*," said one cabinet member, "are conservative by their very nature. They do not take a *general view* of things. They see their own point of view only; so it is only the cabinet that can have a general view, which makes it automatically more free and less conservative." Another cabinet member noted that "the *directions* are ministries in themselves. They have their rivalries, ideas, traditions. It is not out of this that you construct economic policy or a housing policy." The cabinet sees itself as the instigator of reforms and the *directions* as the agents responsible for the execution of these reforms. The Directors see themselves as responsible for both formulation and execution. Consequently, the functions of the two come to overlap. Nor is this overlap confined to the formulation of policy. It can also be found in its execution, as when cabinet members, following up on a particular project, go directly to those in the hierarchy who are responsible for it without first going "through the channels," i.e., through the Directors. This kind of behavior, as the members of the cabinets recognized, might be termed precipitous or overzealous. They always justified it, however, on the ground that it was necessary to insure that the minister's policies were being properly carried out. Sisson, in writing of those who surround the British minister, might very well have been writing of the reasons offered by the French ministerial cabinets for their deep involvement in the ministry's work: "Near the centre, that is to say, near the Minister, there is a group of officials, now usually fairly numerous, who, whatever the subject of their particular work, may be said to specialize in the awareness of ministerial responsibility. . . . In the work they have to do, the members of this group are nearer to his point of view than are the officials who are further from the Minister either geographically or, wherever they may be stationed, in the nature of their concerns."[50] Sisson, of course, would not equate this group to the French cabinet, if only because it comprises, according to him, approximately the entire Administrative Class of the British civil service. Nevertheless, this does indicate the need for a minister to have around him officials who

[50] Sisson, *The Spirit of British Administration*, pp. 13–14.

adopt his own perspectives, which the Directors in French ministries are loath to do.

The importance that the Directors attach to defining a role that is different from, if not diametrically opposed to, that of the minister and the cabinet is illustrated in the answers to two questions: whether the Directors thought a minister ought to be a politician or someone with an administrative training or background, and which of the two it was easier to work with. There was little question that in both cases the politician was preferred. The reasons given document our analysis further. They almost always had to do with "each having his role," or "one brings to the other what the other lacks," or "each operates within a different domain." What these answers have in common is best summarized in a phrase that was repeated again and again: "The politician does not enter into details." As a higher civil servant noted long ago: "The minister cannot be master of the affairs of his ministry. . . . The minister himself staggers beneath the load and he pleads to be relieved of many matters for which he cannot really assume responsibility and of which he does not even have the time to acquire the most superficial knowledge."[51] Here again can be noted the Directors' desire to aid or guide the minister: this is their view of their role. When a minister, therefore, seeks to guide his administration, a serious conflict ensues. Indeed, this is precisely why Chalandon's battles with his administrators proved so serious: the minister was upsetting the cardinal element in the self-perception of his officials. Instead of guiding, they were being guided.

The belief that the politician ought not to enter into the details of the work of the Directors reflects a significant self-definition of the civil servant's role: a technician with a monopoly over a domain. A politician either does not infringe upon this monopoly because of his other, more enduring interests, or he cannot because of lack of competence. A minister who shares the Directors' own background, that is, one who is technically competent, would be all too likely to desire to infringe on the technical domain of the Director. We observed in our survey that certain ministers with a technical background had a reputation for tending to immerse themselves in the details of the work of the ministry. One Director compared his present minister (a politician)

---

[51] Henri Chardon, *Le Pouvoir administratif* (Paris: Perrin, 1911), p. 190.

with his former minister (a law professor), noting that with the politician he was given a general framework within which to work. How he accomplished his task was entirely up to him. With the technician, on the other hand, "it was not possible to make out a simple decree without his noting that 'you ought to check this or that because I seem to remember reading in *Le Monde* four or five years ago that a similar decree had appeared.' His nose was dug so deeply in the work of the ministry that the Directors had almost no leeway." The case of Giscard d'Estaing was frequently cited by civil servants in the Ministry of Finance. Giscard d'Estaing was successively a high civil servant in the Ministry of Finance, Deputy-Minister of Finance, and then Minister of Finance from 1962 to 1966.[52] In explaining how difficult it was to work with him, every higher civil servant who had had this experience pointed to his all-embracing knowledge of the Ministry's work. The "pure" politician, on the other hand, is thought to be too concerned with general orientations, with day-to-day politics, with party policies, and with his local politics, to delve into the details.

For the members of cabinets, there was no clear preference for one type of minister over another. It is significant, however, that they did not emphasize two distinct roles, as we noted in the case of the Directors. Just as they regard technical expertise as an indispensable element of their work, so they regard contact with politicians, interest groups, the press, as also an integral part. With regard to Deputies, as will be seen in greater detail in Chapter XI, our survey showed that the Directors tended to avoid such contacts, considering them to be too "political" and to fall within the domain of the cabinet.

Still another key divergence in role perception that sets the Directors against the minister and the members of his cabinet concerns the Directors' view of their respective constituencies. For the Directors, a minister is first and foremost a politician. This means that his interests are always segmental, whether they concern the interests of his party, his local constituency, or even, for that matter, his ministry.[53] They are never the general interest. The Directors see themselves, on the other hand, as the

---

[52] He was reappointed Minister of Finance in the Chaban-Delmas Government in July 1969, and in the Messmer Government in July 1972.

[53] See Brian Chapman, *The Profession of Government* (London: Unwin University Books, 1959), pp. 273–280.

guardians of the general interest.[54] This sets them apart from the minister. It defines for them a role that the minister cannot claim, if only because he belongs to a political party and a government. As Chardon, addressing a group of civil servants at the turn of the century, noted:

> But what is a minister? Can he be the most impartial of men, the one who is far above all political contingencies? I have a profound admiration for the talent of a large number of our ministers. But, on the whole, a minister is the representative of a political party and not always of the political party that he belonged to yesterday (loud applause). He is the representative of a political party who succeeds the representative of another political party, because the cabinets are made and unmade precisely by the game of these conflicting politics. But, in that case, are all the civil servants of a ministry to be punished by today's minister for having devotedly served his predecessor?[55]

Ministers thus do not, and cannot, be concerned with the general interest in the way that Directors claim to be. Yet, as we noted above, one of the chief causes for the conflict between Directors and cabinet members is that the latter see the Directors as confusing the general interest with the interests of their own *directions*. Indeed, the cabinet members claim that, because they bear no responsibility for a particular administration and because they are free from all matters that constantly preoccupy a Director— management of an organization, personnel problems, jurisdictional battles, and so on—they are more truly the representatives of the general interest. That some civil servants should claim to be guardians of the general interest as against others testifies not only to the ambiguity of the term but also to the diversity of role perceptions that exist within the higher civil service.

CONCLUSION: THE IMPORTANCE OF POLITICAL COGNIZANCE

This chapter has attempted to show how dangerous it is to speak of an administrative "mind" or "mentality," even when civil servants have shared a common socialization experience. We

[54] The Directors' view of and attachment to the concept of the general interest is discussed in detail in Chapters XI and XII.

[55] Chardon, *Le Pouvoir administratif*, p. 189.

have seen the relative ease with which a civil servant's loyalties can shift from one organization to another. Thus, when those in a cabinet become Directors they adopt a view totally at odds with the view they held while in the cabinet. Nor are they always unaware of this sharp change in roles and outlooks. One Director in the Ministry of Finance talked freely of the time when he had been the second highest-ranking official in a minister's cabinet. With the aid of five assistants, he had insisted on practically taking over the work of the entire *direction* for which he was ostensibly the liaison man. When asked how he reacted, now that he was on the other side of the fence, to an encroaching official in the cabinet, he replied: "I make sure that that doesn't happen. It is important, in order to accomplish anything, to act always only in the interest of your administration." Another Director in a different ministry observed that when he was *directeur de cabinet* in this ministry "everything had to go through me before it reached the minister." He noted that this was partly because the minister wanted it this way and partly because "it was the only way of seeing that the minister's wishes and policies were carried out." Now that he had become a Director in the ministry, however, he found himself constrained by the "growing importance of the cabinet, which wants to concern itself with everything." Evidently a civil servant's interests change with the position he occupies in the politico-administrative hierarchy, and his perception of his role changes too.

To be sure, I have emphasized a particularly acute conflict at the apex of the French administrative system and I have not discussed those other factors that tend to unite civil servants. Nor have I yet discussed the important role of the Grands Corps in ministerial cabinets and in administrative posts proper, an analysis of which will shed considerable light on one of the keys to the French administrative system.[56] But the "shared experience" that is supposed to lead to the common outlook and mode of behavior of civil servants has been readily invoked without ever having been subjected to serious analysis. The mode of behavior of civil servants has been assumed to emanate from a common social origin and training. Just what this background and training inculcate has never been analyzed. It may well be that they inculcate something approaching a remarkable ability to

[56] For a discussion of both these questions see Chapter x.

assume seemingly incompatible roles. Nevertheless, the changing roles and role perceptions of higher civil servants with which we have dealt in this chapter suggest that there is a considerable degree of functional autonomy which influences their behavior. If the behavior of civil servants is in large measure defined by the function performed this also means that it is largely independent of social origins. The shifting perception of role was not influenced by social background—it was influenced more by the position of the official in the administrative hierarchy.

The changes in role perception also help explain the minister's need for a cabinet which shares his own outlook. Insofar as the Directors seek a role that differs from their minister's, it follows that the minister is constrained to rely upon other officials to formulate and, to a considerable extent, supervise the execution of his policies. The Directors, as we have observed, have definite interests of their own. As Neustadt has noted, describing the problems that an American President faces in this regard: "Most men who share in governing have interests of their own beyond the realm of policy *objectives*. The sponsorship of policy, the form it takes, the conduct of it, and the credit for it separate their interest from the President's despite agreement on the end in view."[57] In Britain, the close relationship between ministers and their senior officials is owing not so much to the fact that they share a common background, as Kingsley and others have argued, as to the acceptance of a political role by the officials.[58] Neustadt has pinpointed this crucial fact in a rather casual observation. He notes that the senior official, the Permanent Secretary, "knows far more of what it feels like to perform as a politician than his opposite number, the department's minister, can ever hope to fathom in reverse."[59] The Directors in French minis-

[57] Neustadt, *Presidential Power*, p. 54.

[58] One student of British administration notes in a recent study that in the early part of the nineteenth century "the social standing of civil servants was . . . an important factor in their relations with ministers. If it was inferior, it was likely to curtail their influence. If it was equal, easy cooperation was facilitated." While he subscribes to the theory of representative bureaucracy, this author also notes that in Taylor's famous book, *The Statesman* (1836), "statesmanship was a career embracing politics and administration." See Henry Parris, *Constitutional Bureaucracy* (London: George Allen and Unwin, 1969), pp. 146, 148.

[59] Richard Neustadt, "White House and Whitehall," in Richard Rose, ed., *Policy-Making in Britain* (New York: The Free Press, 1969), p. 295.

tries, on the other hand, do not know and do not *wish* to know "what it feels like to perform as a politician." This is shown in their perception of their roles and in their everyday relations with ministers. In attempting to dissuade ministers from undertaking certain policies, they tend to categorize the arguments they employ into "political" and "technical." The argument most frequently used to deter the minister from pursuing a policy which the Directors oppose has to do with cost (Table 9.10).

TABLE 9.10

Arguments Used by Directors to Influence Ministers[1]

Argument	1st Choice %	2nd Choice %
Lack of qualified personnel	1.2	7.4
Technical difficulties	16.0	29.6
Cost of program	56.8	8.6
Legal implications	2.5	9.9
Parliamentary opposition	7.4	3.7
Interest-group opposition	4.9	4.3

[1] Question: What are the two arguments that you consider the most important for convincing a minister to abandon a particular program?

There is some evidence to indicate that ministers have frequently been too much impressed by a Director's assertion that "the Ministry of Finance will not go for it." Where a minister has not shown himself susceptible to this argument, civil servants have not hesitated to conspire with officials in the Finance ministry to insure that the money would not be forthcoming. But the importance of the argument regarding cost lies in the fact that, as one Director put it, "it is a technical argument, and mine is a purely technical post." In effect, 38 percent of the Directors noted that they could not use arguments having to do with parliamentary opposition or with interest group opposition because —and the phrase was repeated over and over again—"this is not for us to bring to the attention of the minister." Although there is no empirical data for the British higher civil service, it seems unlikely, at least from all the evidence available, that the minister's closest officials categorize into "political" and "nonpolitical" the arguments they employ when advising their minister.

In France, the members of ministerial cabinets noted that because Directors tend to present incomplete pictures when presenting the minister with proposals, the cabinet's incursion into and duplication of the Directors' work inevitably increased. One cabinet member observed that when Directors prepare decisions for the minister it is invariably necessary for the cabinet to send the dossier back to the *directions*. "The dossier is usually too long and ponderous and it often ignores the minister's desires. Consequently, we either have to send it back or re-do it ourselves." Another cabinet member pointed out that "the cabinet, unlike the Directors, has to look at things only from the point of view of the minister. This means taking into account both technical and political factors that enter into a decision." It should, however, be pointed out that cabinet members often encourage (while at the same time decrying) the Directors' desire to be concerned solely with "technical" matters. Thus, for example, cabinet members accept contact with deputies as part of their normal duty, but consider it part of the Directors' task to avoid such contact. This view is evidenced in the following statements:

It's absolutely normal that Directors don't have contact with Deputies. That is how it should be. They shouldn't meddle in politics. Also, the minister does not accept that the deputy goes directly to the services and short-circuits the cabinet.

The little contact between Directors and Deputies is a good thing. The cabinet is there for the contact with parliamentarians.

Here it is part of my job [having contact with Deputies]. I don't mind seeing them. If I were back in my *direction*, I wouldn't want to see them. It's a question of hierarchy and therefore they have to go to the cabinet. It's also a question of roles and custom.

The external contacts should always be the job of the cabinet. Otherwise the *directions*, as is the case of the Ministry of Agriculture, come to be the lawyers for particular groups.

Cabinet members thus sharply differentiate between their own role and that of the Directors. This too constitutes a definition of a role—and a weapon: it allows them to see themselves as more concerned with the minister's responsibilities than are the Directors, and it allows them to assume the important contacts of the ministry with the outside world, particularly with politicians. There is, then, in certain domains at least, a mutual recognition of roles among the Directors and the cabinet. But this recognition does not negate the existence of overlapping functions—hence the conflicts that we have discussed in this chapter.

CHAPTER X

The Administrative Super-Elite: Les Grands Corps de l'Etat

. . . L'Aministration représentée par "les grands corps" exerce une action parfois peu apparente, mais réelle. Elle est l'Etat.

—*Michel Debré*[1]

The point of departure for the incessant and unrelenting attacks against the French administration that daily pour off the presses in France is that this institution operates within a world of its own, a world composed of approximately 1,200 warring fiefdoms or corps.[2] The authors of *Pour nationaliser l'Etat* observed that, because of this rigid compartmentalization, the excessive centralization from which the French nation suffers has not even the one advantage that centralization, with all its disadvantages, might have been able to offer: namely, assuring coherence in the policy-making of the authorities.[3] To their admirers, the Grands Corps symbolize all that is laudable about the French State—the dedication, excellence, and impartiality of its chief servants.[4] For their detractors, they symbolize the ad-

---

[1] Michel Debré, *Ces Princes qui nous gouvernent* (Paris: Plon, 1957), p. 9.

[2] René Mayer, *Féodalité ou démocratie?* (Paris: Arthaud, 1968), p. 23.

[3] C. Alphandery et al., *Pour nationaliser l'Etat* (Paris: Seuil, 1968), p. 12.

[4] For a view of the Grands Corps that borders on eulogy, see the following series of articles that appeared in *La Revue des deux mondes*: Roland Maspetiol, "Grands Corps et Grands Commis—I. Le Conseil d'Etat," June 15, 1958; Wladimir D'Ormesson, "Grands Corps et Grands Commis—II. La carrière diplomatique," July 1, 1958; Henri Deroy, "Grands Corps et Grands Commis—III. L'Inspection des finances," August 1, 1958; Paul Loppin, "Grands Corps et Grands Commis—IV. La Magistrature," September 1, 1958; Pierre Escoube, "Grands Corps et Grands Commis—V. La Cour des comptes," October 1, 1958; Louis Armand, "Grands Corps et Grands Commis: Les Corps d'ingénieurs," November 15, 1958; and Emile Pelletier,

ministration's centralized, compartmentalized, oligarchic, and undemocratic character.[5]

The study of the Grands Corps, as of the higher civil service in general, has thus far been largely confined to the realms of jurisprudence and polemics. This chapter belongs to neither of these venerable categories. It is concerned with the role of the Grands Corps in the French State apparatus, and it seeks to examine: (1) the positions that the members of the Grands Corps occupy within the politico-administrative hierarchy; (2) the implications for the administrative system of the ubiquity of members of the Grands Corps in the State bureaucracy; and (3) the degree to which the administrative and political roles of these higher civil servants overlap. Underlying these questions is the further, and no less important question: are these corps, as Crozier has suggested, agents of change within the French bureaucracy, or are they an integral part of a system that is resistant to change?

The members of the Grands Corps also occupy posts outside the politico-administrative system proper—in the nationalized industries, in semipublic institutions, and in the private sector. Since these posts, however, impinge only in an intermittent and circumscribed manner on the politico-administrative sector, I shall not be concerned with them here. The primary focus in this chapter will be on the extent to which the tasks of the members of the Grands Corps have a direct bearing on the functioning of the French bureaucracy. Although there is no strict definition of the Grands Corps, included in this category are generally the major technical corps (*mines, ponts et chaussées, eaux et forêts*) and the major nontechnical corps. Although references will be made to the technical corps, our emphasis will be on the nontechnical ones: the Conseil d'Etat, the Inspection des Finances, the Cour des Comptes, and to a lesser extent the Prefectoral corps.

"Grands Corps et Grands Commis: Le Corps Préfectoral," December 1, 1958.

[5] As one writer has noted: "The principal disadvantage peculiar to the French bureaucracy resides in the problem of *hautes castes*, that is to say, in the Grands Corps de l'Etat." Octave Gelinier, *Le Secret des structures compétitives* (Paris: Editions Hommes et Techniques, 1966), p. 103.

THE PRINCIPLE OF *Détachement*

"From the nineteenth century to the second half of the twentieth," wrote a member of the Conseil d'Etat in 1953, "one thing at least has remained unchanged: the power of the 'grands corps de l'Etat.' . . . The core of the administrative oligarchy is constituted by the Inspection des Finances, the Conseil d'Etat, the Cour des Comptes, the Diplomatic corps and also, to a lesser extent, by the technical corps recruited by X [Ecole Polytechnique]. We must insist on the first three and particularly on the Inspection des Finances, which has the preponderant voice in the economic sphere."[6] The power of the Grands Corps has always been regarded as a given, as something that was so evident as not to require analysis. But any examination of the role of the Grands Corps must begin with a fundamental distinction between the roles that the corps play on their own behalf and those they play in diverse areas of French politics and administration.

Each corps has its own jurisdictions, and has a particular sphere of activity. For example, that of the Inspection des Finances consists of the verification of the State's finances and expenditures; that of the Conseil d'Etat consists of its dual role as advisor to the government and as an administrative court; and that of the Cour des Comptes in its role as a court that verifies all public accounts. In performing these tasks the corps are fiercely independent institutions: they have their own statutes, by which all members are bound, and they are subject to little interference by the State. They have thus come to be regarded as being at once an integral part of the State apparatus and the State's means of checking its own excesses. It has even been suggested that the corps should be regarded and analyzed as pressure groups, since, as two Spanish authors have noted with regard to the corps that exist in the Spanish administration, "Every interest group which attempts to obtain from the public authorities decisions that favor its members is . . . a pressure group. In this sense, the term 'pressure group'— without attributing any pejorative connotations to it—can be applied to the civil service corps."[7]

[6] Charles Brindillac, "Les hauts fonctionnaires et le capitalisme," *Esprit*, XXI, no. 6 (1953), 863.

[7] A. De La Oliva De Castro and Alberto Reñón, "Los Cuerpos de Funcionarios," in *Anales de Moral, Social y Economica, Sociología de la Administración Pública Española* (Madrid: Raycar, 1968), p. 106.

Independently of the institutional role of the Grands Corps, the members of these corps perform tasks that transcend the spheres of activity of their respective corps. They occupy, as we shall see, critical posts in the politico-administrative sphere, and thus come to play a decisive role in the administrative system. These "influential princes," as Debré called them over a decade ago, occupy the key positions in the administration. The prestige of the Grands Corps has usually derived from the wide jurisdictions with which they were endowed at the time of their creation. Today, however, their power and prestige owe perhaps more to the functions that their members perform and the posts they hold *outside* their corps and within the State apparatus than to those within the corps itself. Our primary interest here, then, is not with the functions and jurisdictions of the corps *qua* corps. It is, rather, with the role that these corps play within the French administrative system.

The first thing to note about the Grands Corps is that the posts their members hold in the administrative and para-administrative sectors gives these men a significant role in the day-to-day conduct of the nation's affairs. At the time of the creation of the Grands Corps, when Napoleon laid down the guiding principles and established the basic structures of the French administration, certain important functions had to be carried out on behalf of the State. The creation of a corps was thus intended to provide high-quality recruits—an elite—to carry out these tasks. The *Corps des mines*, for example, the most prestigious technical corps in France, was created and grew in importance at a time when mines were responsible for providing the nation with its chief source of energy. Today, of course, the chief source of energy is no longer the mines; yet the power and prestige of the *Corps des mines* has in no way diminished. Those graduating at the top of their class in the Ecole Polytechnique continue to elect to go into the *Corps des mines*. It goes without saying that few *polytechniciens* approach a mine in the second half of the twentieth century. But the career opportunities and rapid promotion within the corps itself, within the administration, or even outside it that the *Corps des mines* offers its recruits, and its diversification into domains that transcend its limited, albeit important, jurisdictions, continue to attract the top graduates of the leading scientific institution of higher learning in France. To a greater or lesser extent the other Grands Corps have likewise been able to maintain the closely guarded autonomy of their own jurisdictions, and at the same time to invade diverse sectors of the administration. This is what the authors of a semi-official publication of the Ministry of Finance meant, when they noted with regard to the Inspection des Finances: "All in all, the Inspection has evolved by remaining itself."[8] This imperialistic nature of the Grands Corps is, as we shall see, a natural consequence of the wide dispersion of focal points of decision-making within a centralized system. There is no necessary contradiction between the diffusion of decision-making powers and centralization, a situation that has even been referred to as "authoritarian anarchy."[9]

The second factor that should be noted about the Grands Corps is that entry into them is recognized as a necessary, frequently indispensable *tremplin*, or springboard, to the highest administrative posts. "Doubtless they all [the new recruits into the Inspection des Finances] hope to see themselves charged as quickly as possible with important responsibilities in ministerial cabinets or in the important *directions* of the central administration. Frequent consultation of the Inspection des Finances yearbook persuades them that in entering [the Inspection] they augment their chances for the career of their dreams."[10] The top graduates of the Ecole Nationale d'Administration always choose to enter one of the three major corps—the Inspection des Finances, the Conseil d'Etat, or the Cour des Comptes—not because of the inherent interest of the work of these corps, but because of the career opportunities open to them once they belong to the Grands Corps. The Inspection des Finances, for example, recognizes and accepts the ambiguous attachment of its members "to an institution into whose ranks they dearly desired to enter and from which they just as dearly desired to depart as quickly as possible."[11] As another writer put it: "To be certain of a brilliant career in the Inspection, it is important to enter the

[8] F.-L. Closon and J. Filippi, *L'Economie et les finances* (Paris: Presses Universitaires de France, 1968), p. 106.

[9] See Julien Cheverny, *Ces princes que l'on gouverne: Essai sur l'anarchie autoritaire* (Paris: Juillard, 1966); and "Le Mode autoritaire de l'anarchie," *Esprit*, Special Number (January 1970), 56–68.

[10] Closon and Filippi, *L'Economie et les finances*, p. 105.

[11] *Ibid.*, p. 106.

Inspection, but it is even more important—and more urgent—to leave it."[12] What permits the members of the Grands Corps to belong to a corps but render little service to it is the principle of *détachement*, which is a leave of absence granted by the corps to a member serving in an administrative or para-administrative institution. It is not surprising, therefore, that a corps like the Inspection des Finances has been seen as "a veritable school of the higher civil service."[13]

The corps themselves have come to see that one of their important tasks is to secure important posts for their members, as is evident from the pride they take in "lending" their members to other administrations. "The Inspection Générale des Finances," notes the semi-official publication quoted earlier, "is far from being a corps closed unto itself: well before the general principle was established, it made 'mobility' its tradition. It facilitated the departure of its members to administrative posts. It has always desired that some of them return to offer their services to the corps after a . . . leave. But it must be admitted that this happens all too rarely."[14] A member of the Conseil d'Etat has also noted the importance of the principle of *détachement*, for the corps as well as for the administration in general. "The principle of these external functions," he writes, "merits complete approval. In enriching the experience of its members, the practice is as advantageous for the administration as it is for the Conseil [d'Etat]."[15] Yet despite the avowed merits of *détachement*, it was recently felt that it had been too often abused: members would request a leave, having rendered scarcely any service to the Conseil. A decree of July 30, 1963, therefore imposed certain limitations on the *détachement* of members of the Conseil d'Etat. The Commission set up to propose reforms maintained that there was a need to insure "a minimum of fidelity" of the members of the Conseil d'Etat to their corps.[16]

[12] Pierre Escoube, *Les Grands Corps de l'Etat* (Paris: Presses Universitaires de France, 1971), p. 69.

[13] Pierre Lalumière, *L'Inspection des finances* (Paris: Presses Universitaires de France, 1959), p. 121.

[14] Closon and Filippi, *L'Economie et les finances*, p. 113.

[15] Roland Maspetiol, "Grands Corps et Grands Commis—1. Le Conseil d'Etat," *La Revue des deux mondes*, June 15, 1958, p. 648.

[16] See Marie-Christine Kessler, *Le Conseil d'Etat* (Paris: Armand Colin, 1968), p. 172.

The extent of leave-taking from the Grands Corps can be seen from Tables 10.1 and 10.2. In the Conseil d'Etat, approximately one-third of the members are *détachés* at any given time. Those taking a leave in order to perform other functions are neither the oldest members (the *Conseillers d'Etat*) whose administrative

TABLE 10.1

Détachement *from the Conseil d'Etat, 1970*

Position in Corps	Total No. of Members	Working in Corps	Détaché	En disponsi-bilité[1]
Conseiller d'Etat	81	64	13	4
Maître de Requêtes	113	70	40	3
Auditeur	35	28	7	0
Total	229	162	60	7

[1] On leave from corps under (juridically) different conditions from *détachement*.

TABLE 10.2

Détachement *from the Inspection des Finances, 1970*

| Total No. of Members | Cadres[1] | | Détaché | En Dispon-sibilité[2] | Hors cadres[2] | Re-signed | Re-tired |
	Not Integrated in Corps	Integrated in Corps					
364	96	53	114	38	8	66	42
	149						

[1] All members classified in the *Annuaire* of the Inspection des Finances as integrated within the corps. Only those in the right-hand column, however, are really engaged in activities on behalf of the corps.

[2] On leave from corps under (juridically) different conditions from *détachement*.

or political careers are generally behind them, nor the youngest (the *Auditeurs*), who are recruited upon graduation from the Ecole Nationale d'Administration. They are the *Maîtres de Requêtes*, who have rendered some service to the Conseil, are not old enough to be named *Conseillers d'Etat*, and are either pursuing careers in the administration or have taken a temporary leave to serve in, for example, a ministerial cabinet. As for the Inspection des Finances, only one-quarter of the members of this corps are to be found working within the corps at any time. According to the Yearbook of the Inspection des Finances, on which our calculation is based, the figure is considerably higher (almost double), but this owes more to the method of classification that the Inspection uses than to the actual state of things. Thus, for example, all those members of the Inspection des Finances who serve in ministerial cabinets are listed as "cadres" (Table 10.2, column 2), a classification that also includes all those who are actually working in the corps of the Inspection. My own calculation is based on a different classification: I have separated those who are actually carrying out tasks within the Inspection and those who are not. The main reason for the Inspection's classification is that it considers all those who draw their salaries from the Inspection, whether they are working in the corps or, strictly speaking, *détachés*, as being integrated within the corps. The largest group affected by this type of classification, which serves to distort considerably (i.e., underestimate) the extent of *détachement*, includes those who serve in ministerial cabinets. Since ministers have very limited budgets, all members of their cabinets who are civil servants are paid by their corps of origin. The corps "lend" these members and hence do not classify them as *détachés*.

The corps defend the principle of *détachement* on the ground that it permits their members to exploit their capacities to the full, as well as giving the French nation the benefit of these capacities. It must be noted, however, that without the possibilities of *détachement*, that is, without the vast career opportunities that membership in the Grands Corps entails,[17] the corps would probably not be able to attract, as they do now, the cream of the higher civil service. Indeed, after initial service in a corps, a successful civil servant does not normally return to it. Going back to the bosom of the corps is, in certain corps at least, equated with failure, for the ambitious and successful have unlimited horizons even after exhausting their career opportunities within the administration. Such a return, as has been officially but discreetly

[17] Unless a member of the Grands Corps actually resigns, his membership in a corps is attached to him very much like a title. The advantages that are gained as a result of entering the Grands Corps are undeniable and have elicited a good deal of criticism.

noted with regard to the Inspection des Finances, "poses in certain cases delicate human problems,"[18] since the scope, importance, and interest of the work within the corps cannot in any sense match what the member of the corps has experienced in the diverse posts he has held during his period of *détachement*. This is perhaps less the case with the Conseil d'Etat, which sees more of its members returning to the corps than is the case for the Inspection des Finances or the Cour des Comptes. It is far more acceptable, or less degrading, for a member of the Conseil d'Etat who has held the highest administrative posts, or who has headed the personal cabinets of the Prime Minister or the President of the Republic, to return to the Conseil d'Etat after his time is up in these posts, than is the case for an Inspecteur des Finances. In fact, no Inspecteur des Finances who has attained such heights would go back to the Inspection.

THE GRANDS CORPS IN MINISTERIAL CABINETS

The ministerial cabinets constitute, as we have seen, crucial centers of power. They also represent an important stage in an upwardly mobile administrative career, so it is not surprising that the various corps should seek to penetrate the inner circles of ministers. The extent to which the major corps (technical and nontechnical) are represented in ministerial cabinets can be seen from Tables 10.3 and 10.4. Table 10.3 shows that of the twenty ministerial cabinets (including those of the Prime Minister and the President of the Republic), seventeen are headed by a member of the six major corps we have listed. Over half of the *directeurs de cabinet* belong to the Inspection des Finances and the Prefectoral corps, and these two corps alone provide 25 percent of the total personnel of ministerial cabinets. The cabinets of the Secretaries of State also illustrate this penetration of the Grands Corps, though to a slightly lesser extent. Almost half of the cabinets of the Secretaries of State are headed by a member of one of the leading corps, with the Prefectoral corps again occupying a preponderant position. Although the members of the four most important nontechnical Grands Corps (the Inspection des Finances, the Conseil d'Etat, the Cour des Comptes and the Prefectoral corps) account for approximately two-thirds of the total

[18] Closon and Filippi, *L'Economie et les finances*, p. 113.

personnel of the cabinets of the twenty ministers (Table 10.3), they account for 25 percent of the total personnel of the cabinets of the Secretaries of State. This disparity is not very significant, and may be explained simply by the lesser importance of the cabinets of the Secretaries of State. We might even wonder why the Grands Corps should attach as much importance as they appear to do to the cabinets of Sub-Ministers, many of whom have no ministries under their control.

Perhaps the most striking feature that emerges from Tables 10.3 and 10.4 is the preponderant role that the Prefectoral corps (prefects and sub-prefects) plays in ministerial cabinets. The traditional function of the Prefect as the representative of the State

TABLE 10.3

Representativity of Grands Corps in Ministerial Cabinets, 1970

Ministry	Total No. in Cabinet	Corps of dir. de Cabinet	I.F.	C.C.	C.E.	Pre-fectoral	Mines	Ponts et Chaussées	To
Presidency of Republic	19	C.C.	1	3	2	3	2	0	1
Prime Minister	29	Prefect.	4	—	2	4	1	1	1
Defense	9	I.F.	2	1	1	1	—	—	
Cultural affairs	11	—	—	1	—	2	—	—	
Relations—Parliament	8	Prefect.	—	—	—	3	—	—	
Justice	10	—	—	—	1	—	—	—	
Foreign affairs	11	I.F.	1	—	1	1	1	1	
Interior	10	Prefect.	—	—	—	4	—	—	
Economy & Finance	17	I.F.	5	2	—	1	1	—	
Education	12	Mines	2	—	—	2	1	1	
Industrial development	11	I.F.	1	1	1	1	2	1	
Equip. & Housing	9	Prefect.	1	—	—	2	—	3	
Post & Telecom.	10	I.F.	1	1	—	—	1	—	
Agriculture	10	C.E.	1	—	1	—	—	—	
Transport	10	—	—	—	—	2	1	1	
Employment	9	I.F.	1	—	1	1	—	1	
Public health	10	C.E.	1	2	1	2	—	—	
Veterans	8	C.E.	1	—	1	1	—	—	
Regional development	6	Ponts et Chaussées	—	—	—	1	1	2	
Overseas territory	10	Prefect.	1	—	—	3	—	—	
Total	229	—	23	11	12	34	11	12	1

(or, perhaps more accurately, of the regime) charged with maintaining order in his *département* has gradually diminished. He is no longer a mere "deliverer of votes." The Prefect today is a civil servant who, like most civil servants, denies vigorously the political aspect of his job, but because of the complex nature of the tasks he performs both as the representative of the State in a *département* and as the ally of the local notables against the central authorities,[19] he comes to acquire a political know-how

TABLE 10.4

Representativity of Grands Corps in Secretariats of State Cabinets, 1970

Secretariats of State	Total No. of Cabinet	Corps of Dir. de Cabinet	I.F.	C.C.	C.E.	Pre-fectoral	Mines	Ponts et Chaus-sées	Total
African affairs	8	—	—	—	—	—	—	—	0
Prime Minister	3	C.E.	—	—	1	—	—	—	1
Youth and sport	6	—	—	1	—	1	—	—	2
Civil service	6	—	—	—	—	—	—	—	0
Prime minister	4	C.C.	—	1	—	—	—	—	1
Defense	4	Prefect.	—	—	—	2	—	—	2
Relations—Parliament	2	—	—	—	—	—	—	—	0
Relations—Parliament	3	Prefect.	—	—	—	1	—	—	1
Foreign affairs	4	—	—	—	—	1	—	—	1
Foreign affairs	6	—	—	—	—	1	—	—	1
Interior	5	Prefect.	—	—	—	2	—	—	2
Economy & Finance	9	—	1	—	1	1	—	—	3
Commerce	4	I.F.	1	—	1	1	—	—	3
Education	5	C.E.	—	—	1	1	—	—	2
Medium & small industry	4	C.C.	—	1	—	—	1	—	2
Industrial development	4	—	—	—	—	—	—	—	0
Tourism	6	—	—	—	—	1	—	1	2
Housing	5	—	—	—	—	—	—	—	0
Agriculture	3	Prefect.	—	—	—	1	—	—	1
Employment	4	—	—	—	—	—	—	—	0
Social affairs	6	—	—	—	—	1	—	—	1
Total	101	—	2	3	4	14	1	1	25

[19] See Jean-Pierre Worms, "Le Préfet et ses notables," *Sociologie du Travail*, Special Number, XIII, no. 3 (1966), 249–275. The collusion of the prefect with the local authorities was recognized and severely attacked more than two decades ago by Michel Debré in his *La Mort de l'Etat républicain* (Paris: Gallimard, 1947), pp. 60–61.

that is unique among civil servants, and perhaps even among politicians. As J.-P. Worms has noted, "The aim of his acts is to obtain agreement, consensus, harmony. It is a role that I would qualify as that of an integrator, and that he defines as that of a synthesizer. Aside from the exhortations that one finds in the great majority of his speeches, the methods that he uses particularly are those of persuasion and arbitration."[20] The Prefect is also sought after by ministers because of his wide contacts in local constituencies and his unsurpassed knowledge of local politics. It is not surprising that members of the Prefectoral corps should most frequently occupy the post in the cabinet (that of *chef de cabinet*) that involves looking after the minister's contacts in his constituency—in effect, incessant contacts with mayors and deputies.

The large-scale presence of civil servants in general, and members of the Grands Corps in particular, in ministerial cabinets is, as was indicated earlier, not a new phenomenon. For both the Third and Fourth Republics there is sufficient evidence to indicate that there were many civil servants in ministerial cabinets, but in the past fifteen years their number appears to have increased. While this fact has been adequately documented, there has as yet been little attention paid to its significance insofar as the functioning of the politico-administrative system is concerned.

Does the ubiquity of higher civil servants and members of the Grands Corps illustrate, as some critics have suggested, the takeover of power by these officials? Does it suggest that civil servants have known, in the words of François Mitterrand, "their finest hour" under the Fifth Republic?[21] Edgar Faure, in applying Galbraith's thesis of *The New Industrial State* to French society, recently suggested that there exists a "technostructure" in France, composed of a group of higher civil servants occupying key posts in the cabinets of the Prime Minister and the President of the Republic, in ministerial cabinets and in the ministries. This group "fixes the options and prepares decisions,"[22] and is thus en-

---

[20] Worms, "Le Préfet," p. 256.

[21] François Mitterrand, *Le Coup d'Etat permanent* (Paris: Plon, 1965), p. 144.

[22] Roger Priouret, "Face à face avec Edgar Faure," *L'Expansion*, no. 22 (September 1969), 101. See also Faure's *L'Ame du combat* (Paris: Fayard, 1970), pp. 54–60.

dowed with the power that politicians ought to have. We shall turn in due course to this important question, but it is necessary first to dwell on certain conflict and consensus patterns that illustrate the role of the corps in the administrative process.

In his interview with Roger Priouret, Faure noted, in a seemingly casual remark, a crucial cause of conflict within the administration. He observed that the "technostructure" does not much like to see foreign elements introduced into it. When, therefore, a cabinet's personnel does not adequately reflect the ministry in which it is acting as the minister's staff—when elements "foreign" to the ministry are brought into the cabinet—there is bound to be conflict between the minister and his cabinet on the one hand and the higher civil servants in the ministry on the other. As Faure put it: "A problem arises . . . for the minister-politician who is impelled by his function, by a certain amount of experience, and by his temperament—most often by all these together —to formulate his own policies, especially when he takes as his *directeur de cabinet*, as was my case at Agriculture with M. Pinchon, at National Education with M. Alliot, someone foreign to the technostructure and even the administration proper. This astonishes the technostructure, which has the impression that the rules of the game are not being observed, and I think that this experience is harder for the *directeur* [*de cabinet*] than for the minister himself."[23]

Faure has pinpointed an important source of conflict between the ministerial cabinet and the Directors in the ministry, although he suggests that cabinet members who are "foreign" to the ministry will have a difficult time in the various decision-making centers of the entire administration. In fact, this conflict exists in almost all ministries. While the administration is composed of corps and while members of the Grands Corps may be ubiquitous in the cabinets, their distribution as between ministries is asymmetrical. In other words, one of the ways by which ministers seek to prevent collusion between the civil servants in their cabinets and those in the ministry is by bringing into their cabinets officials who do not belong to the corps with which the ministry is identified.

We have already noted that ministers are, for all intents and purposes, powerless to remove and replace higher civil servants

[23] "Face à face avec Edgar Faure," p. 103.

despite their legal powers to do so. Consequently they are generally faced, upon taking office, with a situation resembling that of a commander-in-chief who is powerless to change his commanding officers. If they fill their staff with members of the ministry's civil servants, they risk being entirely at the mercy of the ministry's upper command, that is to say, the Directors. In order, therefore, to preserve a certain degree of independence, and to prevent sabotage of their policies, they tend to appoint civil servants from other "administrations" who are total "étrangers à la maison." But so as not to alienate completely the permanent staff of the ministry, they will include a few officials of the ministry in the cabinet. Frequently, of course, such an action is the result of needing someone versed in a particularly technical aspect of the ministry's work rather than a symbolic gesture designed to placate the Directors.

We have already analyzed in detail the nature of the conflict that takes place between the members of cabinets and Directors, and it is necessary now to analyze the mitigating factors, which bear directly on the phenomenon of corps. Table 10.5 shows that each ministry's principal corps has some degree of representation in its cabinet. The degree of representation will, of course, vary. In certain ministries, for example, the representation is generally high. Thus, in the cabinet of the Minister of Interior there is nearly always a strong element of the Prefectoral corps, just as in the cabinet of the Minister of Justice there is likely to be a strong representation of the various legal corps. The clearest example, however, of a ministry that admits few outsiders, either into the highest post in the ministry or into the cabinet, is the Ministry of Finance.

In the ministries where conflicts between Directors and cabinet members are minimal, this has much to do with what I have called the split-loyalty nature of the cabinet. We have already cast some doubt on the hitherto unquestioned assumption that the cabinet is made up of men who owe a personal and political loyalty to the minister, and who are picked because they are personally known to him. We found in our survey that in most cabinets the minister's choice of his principal associates was the result of a number of pressures. A minister will include in his cabinet three or four officials who have long been committed to him; a few others are men he has come to know over the years and whose technical competence he has come to appreciate; still others, who are needed for their technical skills, may be picked by him or by his *directeur de cabinet* in consultation either with the minister's predecessor or with colleagues in the administration. It often happens, for example, that a *directeur de cabinet* will ask a particular corps to suggest someone knowledgeable in a certain sphere. For a jurist he is most likely to consult the Conseil d'Etat, for an engineer the *corps des mines* or the corps of *ponts et chaussées*, and for an expert in financial matters the Inspection des Finances. Nor is it rare for a corps to take the initiative and

TABLE 10.5

Representation of Ministry's Corps in Ministry's Cabinet

Ministry	Principal Corps of Ministry	No. of Members of Ministry's Corps in Cabinet	Total No. of Cabinet Personnel
Justice	Magistrates, judges	5	10
Foreign Affairs	Diplomatic	2	11
Interior	Prefectoral	4	10
Economy & Finance	Inspection des Finances (functionaries of ministry)	5 ⎱ 10 5 ⎰	15
Education	Teaching	1	12
Indust. & Scientific Development	Mines	2	11
Equipment & Housing	Ponts et Chaussées and	3 ⎱ 4	9 ⎱ 19
Transport	Travaux publics	1 ⎰	10 ⎰
Post & Telecommunication	P.T.T.	3	10
Agriculture	Several corps within ministry	1	10
Employment	Several corps within ministry	1	9
Public Health and Social Security	Several corps within ministry	2	10

recommend one of its own to a minister or to his *directeur de cabinet*, without first being asked. It is well known within the administration, for example, that the *corps des mines* and the corps of *ponts et chaussées* have long considered that they were being overwhelmed by, and losing ground to, the graduates of ENA. Since one of the clearest manifestations of this loss has been in the composition of ministerial cabinets, for about the last five years they have undertaken an active campaign to increase their cabinet representation. For the engineers of *ponts et chaussées* the campaign has been a particularly vigorous one, because of a gradual loss of power on a number of fronts.

In certain ministries, out of deference to a powerful Director, a minister will request this Director to suggest his own liaison man in the cabinet. He will not ask the other Directors to do likewise, nor will he see to it that his choice is acceptable to them. In only one ministry, however, can the formation of a cabinet be said to meet with the *general* approval of the Directors. This is the Ministry of Finance. This respect for, or deference to, the Directors occurs because Finance is the only ministry with such a powerful collection of Directors. Thus, after having brought into his cabinet a few officials who have a long-standing commitment to him, the minister will leave to his *directeur de cabinet* the responsibility of choosing the *conseillers techniques*—those responsible for following the work of the *directions*.

The choice of these *conseillers techniques* in the Ministry of Finance is a result of consultation between the *directeur de cabinet*, or the minister, and the Directors. This enables the Directors actually to nominate those who will be responsible for following their work on behalf of the minister, and will be acting as intermediaries between minister and Directors. It should be noted, however, that this consultation takes place only between the *directeur de cabinet* and the Directors of the *directions nobles* (Treasury, Budget, Tax, Public Accounting, Price, and Economic Forecasting). The *conseillers techniques* thus chosen are almost always civil servants pursuing careers in the *direction* that they are now called upon to supervise. By entering the ministerial cabinet they are not terminating these careers but, on the contrary, taking what is regarded not only as an advantageous leave but one that may be indispensable to their future. It is most significant that after their spell in the cabinet is over they will be returning to the same *direction* from which they came. Consequently, to a very considerable extent, their promotion remains in the hands of the Directors under whom they served, whom they are now supposed to supervise, and under whom they will again be serving in the near future. It is this peculiar state of affairs that creates what we have called the split-loyalty nature of cabinets. As a former high-ranking official in the Ministry of Finance has noted:

Every cabinet at Finance is, to a certain extent, the stage for a double game. It contains, first of all, civil servants manifestly chosen to act as links between the important *directions* and the minister, without any doubt obedient to the latter, but maintaining some natural allegiances vis-à-vis their original *directions*, without going so far as to play the role of a fifth column for the administration in the entourage of the citizen charged with supervising it. The cabinet also contains, on the other hand, men long devoted to the person of the minister who, if need be, will assume the role of ambassador for the minister vis-à-vis the *directions*, even as they seek to gain their confidence.[24]

In our analysis of the role conflict that civil servants may experience, we pointed to the French higher civil servant's ability to assume seemingly incompatible roles. Rather than constituting a handicap, the ability to shift from one position to another and to assume roles appropriate to each position was, as we saw, the only practicable solution for the civil servant confronted with contradictory or incompatible tasks. Not all civil servants, however, are fortunate enough to find themselves in situations that call for clearly defined roles. The situation is more complex for a civil servant who, because of his dual allegiance, his short and long-term loyalties and interests, and his clearly defined career goals, finds himself straddling the fence. The *conseiller technique* in the cabinet of the Minister of Finance is in this very situation, for he simultaneously represents the minister vis-à-vis the Directors and, so far as the Directors are concerned, the Directors vis-à-vis the minister. As one *conseiller technique* noted, "Our position in the cabinet is a very delicate one because each Director expects us not to push." Another *conseiller technique* observed: "my job is to prepare the decisions for the minister, but in co-operation with the *direction*. It is they [in the *directions*] who do the preparation. I have to do essentially what the minister requests. Also, it is undeniable that I have a loyalty to my *direction* since I will be returning to it. Because of these circumstances, someone in my position has to be very careful not to burn his bridges." This civil servant's career is clearly mapped out for him; he is able to distinguish between his short-term and long-term interests, and the latter are without any doubt linked to the

[24] Dominique Leca, *Du Ministre des finances* (Paris: Plon, 1966), p. 19.

direction he is now required to supervise. As a higher civil servant of the Ministry of Finance has noted: The *conseillers techniques* "are and remain administratively their [the Directors'] subordinates. At the same time, as members of the cabinet and, as such, wielders of some of the minister's authority, it is up to them to insist in their relationship with the Directors on a particular aspect of the minister's views, on his desire to see a particular reform realized. Such a situation calls for considerable sensitivity and tact on the part of the members of the cabinet as well as on the part of their Directors."[25]

The *conseillers techniques* in the cabinet of the Minister of Finance who come from outside the ministry and owe no loyalty to the Directors whom they have to supervise appear to be in a more comfortable situation. As one of them said: "I am in a more pleasant position than most of my colleagues because I come from outside the ministry and I am not involved in the career syndrome of this ministry. I can call whom I want and I am not under the authority of any Director." This civil servant noted that most of his colleagues in the cabinet could not summon or request Directors to their offices because they lacked the authority to do so. Instead, they go to the Director's office. In the Ministry of Foreign Affairs, where both the cabinet and the *directions* are relatively weak when it comes to substantive policy questions, most Directors refuse to be called in and insist that members of the cabinet come to see them. This sort of tussle occurs in Foreign Affairs because the Directors are determined not to let any further power slip from their hands, and they also seek to establish their authority, for what it's worth, over civil servants who are merely "trespassing."

Why, we may now ask, do ministers leave themselves open to possible collusion between their cabinet members and the Directors? Why do they bring into their cabinets men whose loyalty may be divided between the minister and those whom they are intended to supervise? In the last chapter we discussed the conflicts between cabinet members and Directors; we suggested that such conflicts were inevitable and, to some extent, indispensable if the minister wished to push through some policies of his own. It might be said now, however, that no minister will be able to get his policies implemented if there is an out-and-out conflict be-

[25] In Closon and Filippi, *L'Economie et les finances*, p. 25.

tween his cabinet and the higher officials in his ministry: what occurs in such a case is paralysis of the whole departmental machinery. This is what in fact occurred in the Ministry of Education prior to the events of May 1968. Consequently, a minister is obliged to create a certain balance in the formation of his cabinet so as to demonstrate some respect for the ministry's officials and the skills they have to offer. Even Albin Chalandon, at the height of his battle with the corps of *ponts et chaussées*, had three members of that corps in his cabinet.

A second reason why ministers bring into their cabinets some members of the corps with which the ministry is associated is that their effectiveness as ministers depends, to a very considerable extent, on their ability to succeed in the constant interministerial battles. This entails, above all, insuring a smooth coordinating procedure, which itself depends upon an ability to become an integral part of an informal network, about which more will be said in the next section and in Chapter XII. Suffice it to note here that the members of the ministry's corps that the minister appoints to his cabinet are part of a larger interadministrative network, and their ability to get things done through this network should not be underestimated.

As was noted earlier, however, most ministers resist as much as possible bringing into their cabinets men whose loyalty is likely to be divided. Only in the Ministry of Finance are members of the corps of the Inspection des Finances or the *administrateurs civils* of the ministry to be found occupying almost all the posts in the ministry and in the cabinet. The cabinet members in this ministry are often the Directors' juniors in hierarchy as well as in age. One high-ranking cabinet member in the Ministry of Finance explained that it was "out of courtesy" that the Directors were consulted in the formation of the cabinet. What this meant, as he went on to explain, was that the possibilities of delays and sabotage by the *directions* were too great to risk a clash between the cabinet and the Directors. Consequently, a climate of cooperation has to be established and this entails, primarily, a certain degree of deference to the Directors. In other words, the minister has to risk collaboration between his own advisers and the Directors in order to accomplish his work. Indeed, in certain cases in this ministry, the cabinet members were clearly doing more to represent their Directors—the men whose work they were ostensibly supervising—vis-à-vis the minister than vice versa. This largely explains why the Directors in this ministry, unlike those in all others, did not feel it necessary to criticize the cabinet in vehement terms.

That a minister's success in realizing his projects in the Ministry of Finance depends largely on cooperation between his cabinet and the Directors is premised on the assumption that the minister is reasonably satisfied that the Directors will not oppose him out of principle or as a result of personal and political differences. If this is not the case, the minister will often rid himself of a Director who he believes will remain unalterably opposed to him. For what distinguishes this ministry from the others is that there is generally close contact between the Directors and the minister—the cabinet does not act as a screen between them. Quite apart from the stature and prestige of these Directors, they are regarded as experts in their domains. In the economic crisis of 1969, General de Gaulle convened a special meeting at the Elysée to which were called two Directors from the Ministry of Finance. The President asked each one to present his views of the crisis and to propose concrete solutions ("excluding devaluation," the General added). After each man had presented his analysis and suggested what the government ought to do, the President adopted their proposals. This incident is recounted because Directors were not, under de Gaulle, usually called to the Elysée and asked to propose solutions, even in times of emergency. And the relations between Directors in the Ministry of Finance and the minister follows precisely this line, except that they are much more informal. Consequently, the role of the cabinet in this ministry is not so much the formulation of policy, or even supervising its execution, as it is advising the minister, representing the minister on various interministerial committees and commissions, and coordinating intra- and interministerial economic policy.

In other ministries, where the corps of the ministry is not adequately represented in the cabinet, the Directors approach the cabinet with a good deal of skepticism, if not downright hostility. They see a foreign element being introduced into their "house," an element that has little awareness of and respect for the traditions and mechanisms of this particular administration. When a minister took office in one of the oldest ministries, known for its austere traditions, he brought with him a faithful cabinet that had worked with him in two previous ministries. This cabinet contained an Inspecteur des Finances, a jurist, a doctor, two engineers, and an Inspector of Social Security, a composition so alien to this particular ministry that the Directors were aghast. "Why didn't he bring a psychiatrist with him also?" one Director is supposed to have commented. For the first few months the relationship between the Directors and this cabinet was particularly uncomfortable, with the Directors doing their utmost to pretend that the cabinet did not exist.

We have discussed the closed nature of the corps, of the ministries, and of the *directions* within the ministries. A foreign element is to be resisted because it constitutes a challenge to one's institutional autonomy as well as competition, and competition must at all times be avoided. This explains why, as we noted earlier, coordination becomes a major problem within the French administration. In a system composed of tightly-knit corps, each with its own monopoly over a domain, communication, and hence the coordination of policy, becomes the central problem. The cabinet, by shifting role perceptions and by creating split loyalties, contributes, in part, to the solution of this problem. André Siegfried, subscribing fully to the need for the "purity" of the corps, could argue that the Ministry of Foreign Affairs was weakened after the war as a result of "not having known how to defend its personnel, which now became heterogeneous, against the intrusion of foreign elements, Inspecteurs des Finances, *académiciens*, or mere Resistance fighters."[26]

THE GRANDS CORPS IN THE ADMINISTRATION

It has already been seen how the Grands Corps have gained a hold on some key posts in the administration and the para-administrative sector (Table 10.6 shows the extent of their hold on these posts in the administrative sector). Insofar as administrative posts proper are concerned, I have pointed to certain limitations on the minister's power to nominate the key officials in his ministry. The power to nominate or revoke is regarded as the single most important element in the minister's attempt to establish his authority in the ministry.[27] Everyone recognizes this element of a minister's power; yet, as I have emphasized, only on rare occasions can ministers act in this sphere in accordance with

[26] André Siegfried, *De la IIIème à la IVème République* (Paris: Grasset, 1957), p. 243.
[27] Leca, *Du Ministre des finances*, p. 15.

their legal powers. The fact that the power to hire and fire the highest officials in the ministry can be used only with the greatest discretion partly explains the minister's need to create a cabinet that immerses itself in the ministry's work. It was noted by the Directors on numerous occasions that the cabinet guarantees the stability and permanence of the Directors; without a cabinet, each minister would have to change the Directors as soon as he took office.

In what respects can the Grands Corps be said to maintain a strong foothold in the ministries and thereby circumscribe the

TABLE 10.6

Members of Grands Corps Occupying Directorial Posts, 1969

	Posts												
	Sec. and Delegate Generals Commissioners			Directors			Service Chiefs			Director adjoint Sub-Director			
Ministry	CE	IF	CC	CE	IF	CC	CE	IF	CC	CE	IF	CC	Total
Cultural Affairs	—	—	—	—	—	1	—	—	—	—	—	—	1
Foreign Affairs	1	1	—	1	—	—	—	—	—	—	—	—	3
Social Affairs	—	—	—	2	—	—	—	—	—	—	—	—	2
Veterans	—	—	—	—	—	—	—	—	—	—	—	—	—
Army	1	—	—	—	—	—	—	—	—	—	—	—	1
Caisse des dépots	—	2	—	—	—	—	—	—	—	—	—	1	3
Finance	—	—	—	—	6	—	—	5	—	—	10	—	21
Education	—	—	—	—	—	2	—	—	—	—	—	—	2
Equipment, Housing, Transport	2	—	—	—	3	—	—	—	—	—	—	—	5
Industry	—	—	—	—	1	—	—	—	—	—	—	—	1
Interior	—	—	—	—	1	—	—	—	—	—	—	—	1
Justice	1	—	—	—	—	—	—	—	—	—	—	—	1
Post and Telecommunications	—	—	—	—	—	—	—	—	—	—	—	—	—
Paris Region & Prefecture	1	—	—	—	1	1	—	—	—	—	—	—	3
Prime Minister's Services	4	1	2	3	—	—	—	—	—	—	—	—	10
Total	10	4	2	6	12	4	—	5	—	—	10	1	54

Source: Rapport de la commission d'études des problèmes de l'Ecole Nationale d'Administration, p. 101. Note that error in Ministry of Industry figures in original source has been corrected in this table.

minister's choice of his chief officials? First, there exists an un-quantifiable element, an aura of elitism that attaches itself to the members of the Grands Corps. In the stratified hierarchy that characterizes the French administrative system, the Grands Corps constitute without question the summit. This derives not only from the traditional functions of these corps, but also from their closed nature, their restricted numbers, and their methods of recruitment. It is not surprising that the fierce competition among the students at the Ecole Nationale d'Administration is based on a near-desperate desire to graduate in the top 20 percent so as to be able to enter one of the three major corps. Otherwise one becomes an *administrateur civil*, thus entering into the largest, the least organized, and the most dispersed of all the corps.

While membership in a corps clothes a civil servant with the aura of belonging to a small elite group, it is also, in his eyes, a springboard to the highest administrative posts that would otherwise be unattainable.[28] Now, ministers are not immune to the values of civil servants. They come, now imperceptibly, now out of conviction, to believe in the merits of the Grands Corps and in the high quality of their members. They begin to seek out, not particular civil servants known for their talent, but members of a corps. A majority of the *conseillers techniques* interviewed noted that prior to their entry into the cabinet they neither knew nor had worked with their minister. And most of these cabinet members casually observed that "the minister wanted someone from the Conseil d'Etat," or "the minister was looking for an engineer from the *corps des mines.*" One young associate of a high-ranking minister, who was no more than twenty-five, assured me that the only reason he was in his post was that he was a graduate of the Ecole Normale Supérieure. The minister, it appears, had very specifically sought a *normalien* for this post. The reason, according to this official, was probably the minister's own frustrated desire, many years before, to enter the Ecole Normale. Also, he conceded, "C'est quand même quelque chose pour le ministre d'avoir un normalien dans son cabinet."[29]

[28] Membership in one of the Grands Corps also provides a springboard to the more important and lucrative posts in the private sector.

[29] It is interesting to recall that after his return to Paris in 1944, de Gaulle had sought an *agrégé* for his cabinet. This *agrégé* was Georges Pompidou. The *agrégation* is a diploma granted upon passing a highly competitive na-

In certain technical spheres (transport, aviation, urbanism), members of the Grands Corps were found occupying the highest posts in the administration without having, on their own admission, the requisite technical qualifications. But pure technical know-how, it was contended, was not of crucial importance for nomination to a high administrative post. Clearly, the traditional textbook view of French administrators being "technicians" while their British counterparts are "amateurs" loses much of its credibility in light of this fact. The members of the Conseil d'Etat have no strict legal training, nor are the members of the Inspection des Finances trained in economics. After going through the same course at ENA, the members of the various nontechnical corps obtain their specialized training on the job. But even apart from gaining expertise in the domains for which their corps have primary responsibility, these civil servants are appointed to posts that have little to do with the work for which they have been trained. In a number of cases, for example, it was acknowledged that although the minister could have nominated to the post of Director a civil servant from the ministry, he chose to nominate instead a member of the Grands Corps. That he did so indicates the play of two forces: pressure from the corps of the successful candidate and, on the minister's side, the realization that having a member of the Grands Corps in his ministry augments his inter-ministerial contacts by gaining the ministry entry into a circuit —what Faure would no doubt call the "technostructure."

It is not surprising to find in some traditionally low-prestige ministries (e.g., Employment and Social Security) one or two members of the Grands Corps occupying the post of Director. Since the corps come to consider these posts as "belonging" to them, a minister's choice of Director may appear to be narrowly circumscribed. This limitation, on the minister's part, however, turns out to be a blessing in disguise. Rather than choose a civil servant from the ranks to occupy the post of Director, he is generally only too eager to add some luster to a ministry that does not carry much weight in the government or in the various committees and commissions. One Director in a low-prestige ministry said: "a minister will always request my corps to supply him with a Director because he needs to add some prestige to this

tional examination. It generally leads to a teaching career at either the secondary or the university level.

mediocre administration." The corps, this official made clear, would supply the minister one of its own without his even having to ask, for it would not want to lose its hold on a particular sector, nor see it go to another corps.

In addition to the element of prestige, there is also the important factor of influence. This can perhaps be best explained by a brief description of the relationship that all ministries entertain with the Ministry of Finance. All other ministries are "spending" ministries, and therefore dependent on the Ministry of Finance for their credits. Furthermore, there is in each ministry a Finance Controller, who is a representative of the Ministry of Finance and is not subject to the authority of, nor can he be removed by, the minister in whose ministry he occupies this post. His task is simply that of acting as the watchdog for the Ministry of Finance. He insures that funds are spent for the purposes for which they were allocated and, above all, that there is no overspending beyond the agreed budget. Now, since each ministry is, in a sense, under the tutelage of the Ministry of Finance, it clearly behooves a minister, as a former minister has noted, to maintain good relations with the Finance Controller. Also a minister will be, according to M. Chenot, in a very strong position if he is fortunate enough to have an "understanding man" as Finance Controller.[30] But, above all, it is necessary for the minister to maintain good relations with the Ministry of Finance. Nor does this mean the Minister of Finance. It means establishing permanent contact with the officials of this ministry, so as to be able to exert influence at the right time and at the appropriate places. In order to do this, a minister often feels that he must bring into positions of authority in his ministry civil servants from the Ministry of Finance; he may choose an Inspecteur des Finances with no evident technical qualifications for the post. One Inspecteur des Finances occupying the post of Director in a technical ministry observed that he was one of several candidates considered for this post. "I was the one who finally got the job," he said, "because I wasn't exactly unsupported by my corps and because, let's face

---

[30] Bernard Chenot, *Etre ministre* (Paris: Plon, 1967), p. 69. The Finance Controller, writes Chenot, "is the first guardian of a minister. Such is the situation that led a minister of National Education who, incidentally, resigned, to say that his ministry was in reality placed under the order of a bureau chief at the Budget *direction*" (p. 69).

it, a minister can always use someone with close contacts with the Ministry of Finance."

To increase a ministry's influence with the Ministry of Finance is also to give that ministry a more powerful voice in the interministerial commissions, at Matignon and at the Elysée. This is important because every minister knows that interministerial conflicts, as well as the more important questions of policy, are decided in the committees headed by officials from Matignon. Because the Grands Corps are seen as constituting the most important network within the politico-administrative system, a minister stands to gain a good deal by appointing members of these corps to important posts. This partly explains why so few ministers have ever attempted to appoint to the post of Director, or even to their cabinets, persons from outside the administrative sector. It is not only because a person from the private sector would not be able to gain the confidence of his subordinates, but also because the minister, by not playing according to the rules of the game, would be acting against his own interests: he and his ministry would carry less weight in interministerial battles.

Thus far, we have pointed only to the advantages that accrue to a minister when he recognizes the existence of, and attempts to work within, the informal networks established by the higher civil servants belonging to various corps. These advantages are gained at a price: the network to which he gains entry by a shrewd appointment may work in his favor, but it may also be used to block his projects. For example, an Inspecteur des Finances can promote a project he believes in and thus obtain the necessary credits for his minister. If, on the other hand, this official does *not* believe in his minister's project, he simply has to say, "The Ministry of Finance won't go for this." This, as we noted earlier, was the most frequent argument used to dissuade ministers from pursuing a particular policy. But, coming from one associated with the Ministry of Finance, it will naturally carry greater weight. If the minister persists and continues to cling to his project, "I just pick up the phone, call the appropriate man at Finance, and it is certain that no funds for this project will be forthcoming," said one Director. Thus, gaining entry into the informal network (composed of the institutions indicated in Diagram 10.1) involves the wielding of a double-edged sword. The various types of relationships that constitute this network all take place at the subministerial level and, were it not for the ministerial cabinet, the minister might conceivably have been entirely left out of the decision-making process. As to whether this network constitutes a "technostructure" that makes all decisions, this is a question to which we will return in the concluding chapter. Thus far we have attempted to show that the Grands Corps have

Diagram 10.1
Informal Administrative Network

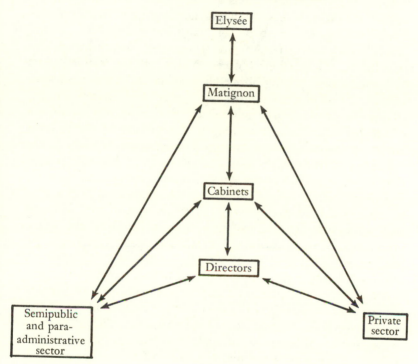

come to occupy the most important posts in the politico-administrative system and we must now turn, once again, to a brief examination of the relationship between politics and administration.

ACTORS IN THE POLITICO-ADMINISTRATIVE SYSTEM

In analyzing some of the implications of the practice of *détachement* from the Grands Corps, we noted the extent to which its members—as well as higher civil servants in general—assume roles that are at once administrative and political. To be sure, civil servants serving in ministries were always quick to deny that their function comprised anything but purely administrative duties. Despite the divergent view of roles that civil servants hold, depending on their positions, we have seen that the tasks they perform involve, by their very nature, political aspects. Politics, as Brian Chapman has noted, is for many civil servants "a rather dirty word." "Its connotations are of some grubby disreputable activity in which the best people do not indulge. This attitude towards 'politics' undoubtedly has many historical overtones, expressing the political resentment of a ruling class challenged by mass forces; of a social elite forced to give way to social inferiors; of conservatives, prizing above all a stable and orderly society, menaced by democrats demanding a new social pattern. Those who prefer the status quo 'administer'; those who wish to change it play politics. The first are engaged in protecting the national interest, the second in advancing sectional interests."[31]

There is undoubtedly a good deal of truth in Chapman's analysis of the connotation of the word "politics" for civil servants, although he appears to miss the functional significance of this connotation. We have attempted, in an earlier part of this study, to analyze the sum of these apolitical or antipolitical beliefs, which may be said to constitute something approaching an ideology. We have shown how this ideology furnishes a framework through which actions are justified and how the constant invocation of the rhetoric of the general interest, which is merely another side to the apolitical rhetoric, is the pivot around which this ideology revolves. Our analysis of the concept of the "general interest" and of the assertions of apoliticism has shown how crucial both are as weapons in delimiting spheres of activity over which civil servants, or the corps to which they belong, come to exercise a monopoly. This will be seen more clearly when we come to examine the relationship between the administration and the deputies. In Chapter XII we will analyze other important aspects of the ideology of the general interest. In particular, it will be seen how important this ideology is, in many instances, in providing a justification for catering to particular interests.

It is not insignificant that the term "politique" in French covers both "politics" and "policy," and to the extent that higher civil

[31] Brian Chapman, *The Profession of Government* (London: Unwin University Books, 1959), p. 274.

servants formulate policies, with all the social and political implications that this entails, if only as a result of choices involved in policy formulation, they engage in politics. As Chapman has noted, the narrow definition of "politics" is apt to be misleading and dangerous.

> Politics means much more than the manoeuvering of parties and their relations with particular clienteles. It is not possible forever to evade questions about "the right kind of society," the purposes of the state, the basis and justification of government business. The determination of ends, the choice of means, the balance of social forces, are the stuff of politics. In these terms it is clear that some civil servants are engaged in politics. The word "policy" is a recognition of this; it is a way of describing what civil servants do when they play a part in determining ends, choosing means and fixing priorities . . . "policy" is then nothing more than the political activity of civil servants.[32]

Chapman has well described the inescapable political role that higher civil servants play in their daily tasks as administrators. We have suggested that higher civil servants play even more openly political roles when they are detached from regular "administrative" duties to serve in ministerial cabinets. In such cases their duties are to prepare the minister's decisions, to inform the minister of the options open to him—the alternatives that are and are not politically viable—to coordinate various choices, and to arbitrate between conflicting policies within the ministry. To accept the contention of members of the Conseil d'Etat who had served in ministerial cabinets that they had been performing a purely technical task is, to say the least, ingenuous.[33] It is, in effect, to share the view that politics is an unwholesome business, whereas administration entails an activity of a higher moral order. Moreover, it is to deny the existence of the more complex and questionable aspects of the practice of *détachement*. Thus, it may happen that a member of the Conseil d'Etat who has taken leave from his corps to enter a ministerial cabinet becomes responsible for elaborating a particular policy, on the legality of which he may find himself ruling at some later point when he has returned to the Conseil. This is evidence of more than the usual interaction

[32] *Ibid.*, pp. 274–275.
[33] Kessler, *Le Conseil d'Etat*, p. 240.

between the domains of politics and administration—indeed, of something approaching a conflict of interest. For either one examines a government's actions as an impartial judge, or one defends those actions as a partisan. One cannot do both. Yet there is no law in France that specifically prohibits a civil servant from engaging in this sort of activity.[34] It is this close relationship between executive and judicial powers that prompted a deputy to address the following questions to the Minister of Justice in the National Assembly in 1961:

> (1) What is the present number of members of the Conseil d'Etat who are *détachés?* (2) What are the posts currently held by these members? (3) Whether it is true that some members of the Conseil d'Etat continue to occupy their posts in the Conseil, and particularly in the *section du contentieux* [judicial section], while they are serving in a ministerial cabinet? (4) Whether he [the minister] does not think that in the case of an affirmative answer to these last questions, there is here a violation of principle, even if this situation is in perfect conformity with the letter of the law insofar as the duties of the members of the Conseil d'Etat are concerned?[35]

The deputy posing these questions was alarmed by an article in *Le Monde* suggesting, by reference to the large number of members of the Conseil d'Etat in ministerial cabinets, that there was an evident incompatibility between the judicial functions of the Conseil d'Etat and the political functions of a ministerial cabinet. This incompatibility has seldom, if ever, been seriously raised, let alone questioned. A further evidence of the close relationship between administrative and political functions is seen by the close link that is maintained between a member of a corps and his

[34] There is merely an "unwritten code" within the Conseil d'Etat which suggests that members who have taken part in the elaboration of a policy which comes before the judicial section of the Conseil ought to disqualify themselves from ruling on that policy. Given, however, that the elaboration of a policy often takes place over several months, or even years, and that one may participate in its formulation at different times and in numerous ways, some more conspicuous than others, it is not always easy to pinpoint the officials who help formulate a policy and then sit in a judicial capacity to determine its legality.

[35] Quoted in Charles Debbasch, *L'Administration au pouvoir: fonctionnaires et politiques sour la Ve République* (Paris: Calmann-Lévy, 1969), pp. 65–66.

corps, even when this member is officially on leave serving in politically sensitive posts: he continues to draw his salary from his corps even while he is officially associated with, and serving under, a particular government. Still more serious is the fact that members of a corps often defend the policies of their minister before their own corps. There are striking examples of members of the Conseil d'Etat who serve under certain ministers, and whose principal duties are to present their minister's policies before the Conseil d'Etat. In effect, they argue briefs on behalf of their ministers and they help, in the words of one such official, "to iron out legal difficulties."

The impartiality of the Grands Corps is always referred to as one of their cardinal traits. Yet the members of these corps continue to benefit from the belief (largely propagated by the corps themselves) that they are impartial, regardless of the posts they happen to be occupying. This aura of impartiality, evidenced in the very designation of the "Grands Corps de l'Etat," has, to a very considerable extent, formed the basis of the remarkable influence that the Grands Corps exercise within the administration. Claiming to be free from the shackles of any particular institution and utilizing the network that they establish within the administrative system, they constantly arbitrate conflicts. They acquire influence as a result of their impartial dispositions, *and* as a result of the network that they constitute. We have already seen that ministers often choose their cabinet members or their Directors with the specific aim of gaining entry into this network. As one member of the Conseil d'Etat put it: "Ministers are always glad to have a member of the Grands Corps around; he can get things done more quickly than an ordinary civil servant; he can arrange, by his contacts, for smooth agreements over knotty problems and, let's face it, it's flattering for the minister."

The members of the Grands Corps thus benefit from an aura of elitism and from a reputation for impartiality; they occupy important positions in the administrative, para-administrative, and private sectors; they form part of a network within and beyond the administration, which enables them to arbitrate conflicts and coordinate policies—all of which means that they are profoundly involved in the decision-making process. Indeed, one student of the decision-making process within the French administration has noted that the Grands Corps seek to avoid having to bring matters before the politicians for arbitration. They consider this a failure on their part. "The members of the Grands Corps thus have means which tend to solve as many problems as possible by 'reasonable' compromises between civil servants; in other words, means that do not upset the power relationships within the higher civil service."[36]

Given the role that the Grands Corps play in the State apparatus, we might well ask how it is possible that administrative and political functions are still seen, by specialists on the French administration, as being separate and separable. The answer lies partly in the ideological predisposition of these specialists and partly in the legal actions which the State itself takes to insure that they remain, at least in theory, separate. Thus members of the Grands Corps draw their salaries from the same account— whether they are executing narrow and laborious tasks in their corps, serving in a ministerial cabinet, or heading the cabinet of the Prime Minister, whether they are in a position to decide the allocation of credits between sectors of society, or overseeing the entire gamut of governmental policies from the Elysée. The belief is thus sanctioned by the State that these functions are not separable and that they all fall within the purview of administration. The civil servants who man the State apparatus are thus the direct beneficiaries of the largely fictitious distinction between politics and administration.

AGENTS OF CHANGE OR FORCE OF STABILITY?

Given the tightly-knit nature of the corps and the networks that they establish within the administration, we must ask whether the Grands Corps constitute elements of change in an otherwise rigid system, or whether they tend to oppose change in the interest of stability. Since there has been little work done on the Grands Corps, we cannot answer this question definitively.[37] From the data presented thus far we may, however, offer a tentative answer.

In the concluding section of *The Bureaucratic Phenomenon*, Crozier argued that the Grands Corps represent the innovative

---

[36] Catherine Grémion, "Les Structures du système de décision de la haute administration française," Groupe de Sociologie des Organisations, mimeo, Paris, November 1969, p. 49.

[37] This is one of the major questions being investigated in my larger study on the Grands Corps.

pinnacle of a bureaucratic system that could not incorporate change within itself, a thesis which has also been accepted by Thoenig and Friedberg.[38] Crozier wrote: "French public administration has set aside special categories of higher civil servants separately recruited and trained, relieved from the usual organizational requirements, who alone can confront these problems and thus become the system's change agents. The role of these members of the Grands Corps has become increasingly important as the gap between the bureaucratic system and its environment has widened, for they have become the necessary mediators between the bureaucracy and the environment, especially at times of crisis."[39]

More recently, Crozier has reiterated his belief that the Grands Corps constitute the element which has gradually "specialized in order to provide the [administrative] system with the agents of change of which the administration has an urgent need, since change can only come from the outside."[40] Now, these corps are not, as we have seen, entities outside the administrative hierarchy, nor are their members "relieved from the usual organizational requirements." These corps and their members are part and parcel of the administrative system. And since the members of the Grands Corps occupy posts throughout the administration, they come to be at the same time members of a corps *and* officials within institutions that have little or no relation to the corps. As the latter they enter into the administration proper, engaging in the defense of their institution, its conflicts and its rivalries. They call on the network of their corps to help them achieve their institutional goals. Since every member *détaché* from his corps comes to owe a certain allegiance to another institution, and since he also operates within an informal network, it becomes somewhat easier to understand why rigid centralization in France does not swiftly produce the coherent policies everyone desires. From this follows an inescapable conclusion: the existence of numerous corps is indissolubly linked with a centralized State. In other words, to the extent that the corps carry out functions on behalf

[38] Jean-Claude Thoenig and Erhard Friedberg, *La Création des directions départementales de l'équipement: phénomènes de corps et réforme administrative* (Paris: C.N.R.S., 1970), p. 219.

[39] Michel Crozier, *The Bureaucratic Phenomenon* (Chicago: The University of Chicago Press, 1964), p. 309.

[40] Michel Crozier, *La Société bloquée* (Paris: Seuil, 1970), p. 113.

271

of the State and to the extent that their responsibilities cover the entire territory of the country, they come to have an interest in denying the virtues of regional or local responsibilities. This largely explains why the reforms of 1945 did not tamper with, but rather reaffirmed belief in the institution of the corps.

Moreover, even given the degree to which conflicts are lessened as a result of the informal communication system established by members of the corps throughout the administrative and para-administrative sectors, we may ask whether such a form of cooperation does not in the end deny access to potentially innovative forces which do not find a place within this network.[41] One of the most remarkable examples, if only because of the conscious creation and maintenance of a network comprising the administrative, para-administrative, and private sectors, is that established by the *corps des mines*. One of the officials responsible for this efficient communication system explained that it was crucial for him to place "my commandos" throughout the administration—and outside it—so as to be able to obtain, without the slightest delay, all the information he desired. This was necessary in order to make his full weight felt where he deemed it necessary and in order to defend the interests of his clientele. These "commandos" are not haphazardly placed in key positions; they are groomed and trained, often in the United States, for very specific posts. Their allegiance to the corps is total and, in return, they gain significant social status as well as remarkably rapid promotion.[42]

[41] The informal network involves, above all, an oral as opposed to written means of communication. This partly explains discontinuities in policy. This method of communication has been praised, however, as being the most efficacious way of solving problems. The former Gaullist minister, Edmond Michelet, at one time in charge of the civil service, noted that "the most insoluble problems are solved generally, it is true, by some telephone call between them [members of the Grands Corps]—those famous telephone calls that lead people to protest that this constitutes a sort of Mafia. But these telephone calls between the *grands commis*, spread all over the Administration, who have not forgotten their common training, have at least one result: it is to accelerate the solution of a certain number of problems and to render the Administration's actions more efficacious." Edmond Michelet, "L'Administration à l'heure des Techniques," *Conférences des Ambassades*, Nouvelle Série, no. 35, November 30, 1967, p. 19.

[42] For example, the average age of the *chefs d'arrondissement* of the engineers of *ponts et chaussées* is thirty, and of Directors is forty. See

A recent study on the *corps des mines* has shown how this corps has gradually implanted itself in all the key sectors of the administration, despite the fact that the mining sector has very much diminished in importance. The main strength of the corps derives from the fact that it trains its own engineers, strictly controlling their type and number; it controls an entire administration, which gives it economic and political advantages and enables it to be represented in the key decision-making centers; and finally, it has career outlets for its members which give it a special type of relationship with the private sectors.[43] (The sectorial distribution of the personnel of the *corps des mines* is indicated in Table 10.7.)

TABLE 10.7

Distribution of Members of the Corps des Mines by Sector

Status or Sector	1949		1961		1970	
	N	%	N	%	N	%
Civil servant in corps (*stricto sensu*)	109	43.4	115	37.1	120	35.9
Public and semi-public sectors (research and teaching included)	69	27.5	98	31.6	109	32.6
Private sector	73	29.1	97	31.3	105	31.5
Total	251	100.0	310	100.0	334	100.0

Source: Friedberg and Dejeux, "Fonctions de l'Etat," p. 569.

This type of network, perhaps best established in the case of the *corps des mines* because of certain advantages, raises certain questions: by whose standards, if not by those of the corps itself, are reforms or innovations judged? How do forces not integrated into this network make themselves felt? How can even potentially new forces manage to grow if they do not constitute part of this

Thoenig and Friedberg, *La Création des direction départementales de l'équipement*, p. 226.

[43] Erhard Friedberg and Dominique Dejeux, "Fonctions de l'Etat et Rôles des Grands Corps: le cas du corps des mines," *Annuaire International de la Fonction Publique*, 1972.

network?[44] It was noted earlier that a minister wishing to enhance his position with the Ministry of Finance or with a particular corps will often appoint an official to a post for which he has but the flimsiest qualifications, simply in order to gain entry into a network without which he may confront insurmountable difficulties in realizing his projects. But who will be the judge of what is "acceptable," of what is "too much," of what "will not pass," of what is "too costly," of what ought to be left "for a later date"? Here again potential reform or new ideas may founder on the opposition of the network.

From this follows the first hypothesis that we should like to advance: the Grands Corps set, in large part, the standards by which the French administrative system functions. To the extent that the system accepts these standards, the desirability as well as the pace of change must necessarily remain the responsibility of the various networks that the corps establish.

Since, however, there exist numerous networks which often work at cross-purposes, the formulation of policy—and this is our second hypothesis—is reduced to the lowest common denominator between the rival corps. This is particularly the case with the technical corps, whose monopoly over a domain is constantly threatened by another corps. Thoenig and Friedberg have shown how the transition from rural to urban life in France has affected the relative power of two technical corps, the corps of civil engineers (*ponts et chaussées*) and the corps of public works engineers (*travaux publics*). The former—the oldest corps in France—had always derived its power and prestige from its rural responsibilities, while the latter, a minor corps by comparison, had had responsibilities in the larger, urban settings which are now offering a more glorious future. The fusion, in 1966, of the Ministry of Construction and the Ministry of Public Works provided the opportunity for the corps of civil engineers to transfer its activity from the countryside to the cities. When this corps encroached on the domain of the public works engineers, the latter saw an opportunity to improve their position vs. the more important and prestigious corps. The civil engineers, on the other hand, sought both to preserve their own hierarchical superiority and to take over the construction of new towns. This corps had

[44] It will be seen (in Chapter XII), for example, how the network of communications between the administration and interest groups can serve to exclude certain groups while giving favored treatment to others.

been, in any case, searching for a field of activity in which it could somehow regain its diminishing power and prestige; it had been losing ground to the more prestigious *corps des mines* and to the other nontechnical corps, and it needed to make an imprint in a decisive area. A "palace revolution" occurred within the corps of civil engineers in 1963. It was led by a handful of young men who demanded that the corps occupy greater positions of responsibility in Paris (hence the campaign to enter ministerial cabinets) as opposed to executive or managerial positions in the provinces, and that the corps extend its monopoly to cover the entire field of urban development.[45] That the civil engineers sought, therefore, to shore up their declining prestige in the area of urban development was partly owing to chance and partly to the extreme importance which urban development had come to assume in France in recent years. The result of this conflict is that urban development has become subordinated to considerations of internecine rivalry. As Thoenig and Friedberg have noted, "In this context, constructing the city becomes a secondary objective. The power relations between corps within the administration impose their logic on the urban policy envisaged by civil servants."[46] To the extent, then, that policies often emanate from rivalry between corps, these corps cannot be said to constitute the elements of change within the administrative system.

Our third hypothesis with regard to the influence of the Grands Corps in the administrative system is that while the corps themselves may not constitute forces of change, their members can initiate change *outside of their corps*. Thus, when a particular agency is created to carry out certain specific tasks, a member of the Grands Corps occupying a chief post in this agency is able, by using the network to which he belongs, to act as an innovative force. The corps itself is bound to act in the interest of preserving stability when it acts solely on its own behalf, and this is especially true with regard to the technical corps. We have seen this to be the case with the *corps des mines*, the corps of *ponts*

---

[45] This explains why, when Pisani proposed the fusion of the Ministry of Construction and the Ministry of Public Works, he received the cooperation of the corps of civil engineers. See Thoenig and Friedberg, *La Création des directions départementales de l'équipement*, pp. 16–20.

[46] J.-C. Thoenig and Erhard Friedberg, "Politique urbaines et strategies corporatives," *Sociologie du Travail*, Special Number, XI (October–December 1969), 388.

et chaussées, and the corps of *travaux publics.* It is precisely the obsession with carving niches, and the imperialism to which this obsession gives rise, that restricts the outlooks of the corps. From their study of two technical corps, Thoenig and Friedberg conclude:

> In the final analysis, the corps appear as a closed and highly structured group which disposes of a monopoly, in fact if not in law, over a particular domain. Access to the group is limited and codified. The creation of professional schools permits the inculcation at once of common values and of an *esprit de corps* to newcomers: it legitimizes the expertise that belongs to the corps and establishes a rigorous selection procedure which restricts the number of the privileged. In order to tighten its hold on a given domain, it sets it up as a recondite activity requiring specialized techniques and modes of thought. It contrives a very highly codified body of knowledge accessible only to the members of the caste. In this way, it aims to maintain adhesion within the peer group and to avoid competition from all other groups.[47]

While Thoenig and Friedberg see the technical corps as being "only one example among others" in the French administrative system,[48] it nevertheless appears that there are certain important distinctions between the technical corps and the non-technical Grands Corps. Foremost among these is the fact that members of the non-technical corps are to be found throughout the administration in positions that have little or no connection with their corps. Nor, in many instances—particularly in the case of the Inspection des Finances—is there any desire on the part of members to return to the bosom of the corps. After he has performed his obligatory service to the corps, an Inspecteur des Finances will not normally return to it (see Table 10.2). He will go on to make an administrative career quite independent of his corps. This is not the case with, say, an engineer of *ponts et chaussées.* The narrowly specialized aspect of his training precludes, in most cases, the achievement of a successful administrative career independent of his corps. The members of the non-technical corps were frequently referred to by members of the technical corps as, pejora-

[47] *Ibid.*
[48] Thoenig and Friedberg, *La Création des directions départementales de l'équipement,* p. 219.

276

tively, "humanists" or "generalists." They are called *polyvalents*, that is, able to undertake diverse tasks because of their general training. In a word, they are akin to the British amateurs. By contrast, of the total number of members of the corps of *ponts et chaussées*, only 14 percent are *détachés* to other ministries,[49] and most of them do not occupy the major directorial posts.

THE CORPS: CULTURAL OR FUNCTIONAL PHENOMENON?

There is one further question that we must attempt to answer: is the phenomenon of corps peculiar to France? The corps have been seen by Crozier, Thoenig and Friedberg, and others as a microcosm of French society, reflecting the particular type of group relations that compels equality within the group and precludes the formation of cross-cutting relationships. If, however, we look at the organization of corps as a means of exerting influence and exercising power over a particular domain, we may find that such a type of organization is not necessarily grounded in a particular culture. The Grands Corps in Spain are replicas of the French ones. Another example, taken from a country often considered very different from France in almost every respect—the United States—may help to give a greater understanding of the corps phenomenon.

The Army Corps of Engineers, created in 1802, has been called "one of the most independent bureaucracies in the federal government"[50] and "the most powerful and most pervasive lobby in Washington."[51] In 1970, the Public Works appropriation bill provided $2.5 billion to the various agencies responsible for public works projects. The Army Corps of Engineers obtained $1.1 billion of this allocation. The Corps is currently working on 275 projects, with an estimated cost of $13.5 billion. To this must be added the 452 projects that Congress has authorized, the (conservatively) estimated cost of which will be $10 billion.[52]

Grant McConnell has analyzed the reasons for the remarkable

---

[49] *Ibid.*, p. 230.

[50] Elizabeth B. Drew, "Dam Outrage: The Story of the Army Engineers," *The Atlantic*, April 1970, p. 53.

[51] Harold L. Ickes in his foreword to Arthur Mass, *Muddy Waters: The Army Engineers and the Nation's Rivers* (Cambridge, Mass.: Harvard University Press, 1951), p. v.

[52] Drew, "Dam Outrage," p. 52.

power that the Army Corps of Engineers has come to exercise. A close look at these reasons suggests that the basis of the Army Corps' power is not very different from that of the corps of *ponts et chaussées*.[53] First, there is the autonomy, within the bureaucracy, of the Army Corps of Engineers. Its responsibility, says McConnell, has not been to a "national constituency" and it has consistently been able to refuse to coordinate its activities with other agencies.[54] It has always sought, like the *ponts et chaussées*, to preserve a monopoly over its domain.

A second reason for the power of the Army Corps of Engineers derives from its close relationship with Congress. The Corps has built up an intricate network that extends to Congress and the congressional committees. "As the prospective builder of large and costly public works in the districts of these elective officers, the Corps has had much to offer to the job security of Congressmen and Senators," so that "the Congressional committees have consistently acted as [the Corps'] especial guardians when moves for reform have been afoot."[55]

A third, and closely related, factor has been the large number of interest groups with which it has allied itself (foremost among these groups are the Chambers of Commerce), and which have always been ready to champion the Corps and the utility of its projects. To this must be added the array of local interests who stand to profit economically from the Corps' projects.

The last and, according to McConnell, the most important factor is the extreme degree of decentralization in the Corps' organization. As McConnell notes, however, "This is only in part a matter of administrative organization; it is as much a matter of outlook and style. . . . This decentralization insures that the head of each District Office is sufficiently close to the communities where work is being done that cordial relationships are maintained with community leaders."[56] Now, decentralized organization and maintenance of close local contacts constitutes the basis of much

[53] Only the top graduates of West Point enter the Army Corps of Engineers.

[54] Grant McConnell, *Private Power and American Democracy* (New York: Vintage, 1970), p. 216.

[55] *Ibid.*, p. 217. As Elizabeth Drew remarks, "There may have been a Corps of Engineers' project that was rejected on the floor of Congress, but no one can recall it." See her "Dam Outrage: The Story of the Army Engineers," p. 55.

[56] McConnell, *Private Power and American Democracy*, p. 219.

of the corps of *ponts et chaussées'* power, as is clearly shown by Thoenig and Friedberg: "The territorial officials, from the chief engineer to the engineer in charge of a sub-division, derive from the exercise of their functions *the status of a local notable.* They constitute part of the local political system; they are elements playing a personal, direct and central role in the management of local collectivities and they are recognized as such by the political class."[57] McConnell's conclusion regarding the importance of a decentralized form of organization is as applicable for the *ponts et chaussées* as it is for the Army Corps of Engineers. "The orientation to localities implied in this decentralized form of organization is directly related to the extreme degree of autonomy the Corps has asserted in the past, and has provided the basis of political support necessary to make good on it."[58]

Thus, the factors that constitute the basis of the Army Corps of Engineers' power—autonomy, extended informal networks, and decentralized organization—have a remarkable similarity to those underlying that of the *ponts et chaussées.* If the latter does not lobby for projects in quite the same way as do the Army Engineers, this is because it already has a virtual monopoly in carrying out work for local collectivities. "As technicians, they exercise, with regard to the local political personnel, the function of general advisers (*conseillers polyvalents*) which places them at the center of political life. Finally, as employees of the State, they assure themselves of additional revenues through their entrepreneurial functions."[59] This also distinguishes technical corps like the *ponts et chaussées* from the nontechnical Grands Corps: the former have deep local roots, the latter have primarily national roots. This certainly affects the role that each plays in the State apparatus and it may also have an effect on the internal relations of each corps. And it indicates, above all, that while the phenomenon of corps is crucial to understanding the French bureaucracy, the corps themselves differ markedly both in their organization and in the power they enjoy within the State system.

Although I have pointed to certain important similarities between the Army Corps of Engineers and the *ponts et chaussées,*

---

[57] Thoenig and Friedberg, *La Création des directions départementales de l'équipement,* p. 39.

[58] McConnell, *Private Power and American Democracy,* p. 219.

[59] Thoenig and Friedberg, *La Création des directions départementales de l'équipement,* p. 40.

it is important not to exaggerate the similarities between the mode of behavior of the officials and the modes of organization in the two societies. For one thing, the corps in France are to be found at every level of the bureaucracy. They are the dominant form of organization and any reform has to meet their challenge. In the United States, on the other hand, the Army Corps of Engineers cannot be regarded as typifying the organization of the American bureaucracy. How different or how similar is the manner in which other parts of the American bureaucracy exert their power and influence is a subject that warrants investigation. Second, the corps in France have strong roots in the society, have official recognition, and are intimately linked to the educational system. This is far from being the case in the United States. Finally, the decentralized Federal structure of the United States may enable certain corps, like the Army Corps of Engineers, to exert a good deal of power, but it undoubtedly prevents others from acquiring a strong grip on the more powerful centers of decision. In France, as I have tried to show, the corps attempt to secure power over a domain by finding themselves a niche within a central ministry. That the Ministry of Industry gradually became less powerful and influential mattered little to the *corps des mines*. In fact, the greater the loss of power of the ministry, the greater was the effort of the *corps des mines* to take it over—and the greater their success. It was a base from which the corps could launch into other activities.[60] It is possible that certain differences in the reactions to political power between the Army Corps of Engineers and the *ponts et chaussées* are of almost no significance. For example, where the French corps are secretive and tend to provide little information to outsiders, the Corps of Engineers achieves the same purpose by providing too much. As former Senator Paul Douglas, an opponent of many of the Corps' projects, said in 1956 when he announced that he was abandoning the fight: "I think it is almost hopeless for any senator to try to do what I tried to when I first came to this body, namely, to consider these projects one by one. The bill is built up out of a whole system of mutual accommodations, in which the favors are widely distributed, with the implicit promise that no one will kick over the applecart; that if senators do not object to the bill

[60] Friedberg and Dejeux, "Fonctions de l'Etat et Rôles des Grands Corps," p. 581.

as a whole, they will 'get theirs.' It is a process, if I may use an inelegant expression, of mutual back scratching and mutual log-rolling. Any member who tries to buck the system is confronted with an impossible amount of work in trying to ascertain the relative merits of a given project."[61]

It is the ubiquity and the number of the French corps, as well as the official sanction with which they are endowed, that enables them to be regarded as an emanation of French culture. Certainly no other country exhibits such an array of corps. But if, on the other hand, the existence of corps is seen as a means of gaining, exercising, and maintaining power, it may be that they will be found to exist in other societies under different guises. This way of looking at the corps in France helps to see them in a more political light. After all, their endurance as well as their resistance to reforms, as certain ministers know only too well, have unquestionable political bases. Consequently their role within the State is a political role, and the reasons for their endurance as well as the question of their eventual reform must be seen as political questions.

[61] Cited in Drew, "Dam Outrage," p. 55.

PART FOUR

The Administration and the Society

CHAPTER XI

The Administration and the Deputy

La permanence du parlement n'est pas nécessaire à la vie de la nation. La nation cesse d'être, au contraire, si les services administratifs s'arrêtent. Tout nous oblige donc à reconnaître que l'administration existe et doit vivre d'une vie propre, en dehors de la politique.

—*Henri Chardon*[1]

If the relationship between the administration and the minister is characterized by a profound mutual mistrust, that between the administrator and the deputy is distinguished by a gulf so wide that it is possible to question the very existence of a relationship. Because the deputy is looked upon by the administrators as the politician *par excellence*, an examination of role perceptions again becomes of crucial importance in attempting to explain the nature of the deputy's relationship to the administration. It has been argued in this study that the politician–administrator distinction of Weber does little to help us understand the relationship between politics and administration, because civil servants are able to assume a number of roles, certain of which place them closer to politicians than to their colleagues. The serious conflict engendered in the relation between Directors and cabinet members (who are almost all higher civil servants themselves) occurs, as was suggested, because the latter adopt outlooks that are far closer to, if not identical with, the minister's. Consequently, civil servants find themselves on both sides of the fence. Although I rejected the distinction between political and administrative types, on the basis of the theoretical and empirical evidence presented in a previous chapter, I have chosen in this chapter to revert to the traditional Weberian scheme, thus appearing, on the face of it, to commit the very error against which I warned. But this is more appearance than reality, since in the earlier chapters

---

[1] Henri Chardon, *Le Pouvoir administratif* (Paris: Perrin, 1911), p. 29.

I treated a triangular relationship that called for interaction on a constant day-to-day basis. The contact between deputies and civil servants, on the other hand, involves two groups and is, at best, intermittent. I will therefore attempt to discuss the manner in which each perceives the other's role, placing by far the greater emphasis on the views of the civil servants.

It is tempting, but entirely wrong, to assert that the Weberian classification of administrators and politicians is simplistic and can have little or no applicability. Like many of Weber's classifications, most notably that concerning the bureaucracy, this one was offered as no more than a framework for analysis. Weber wrote that "to an outstanding degree, politics today is in fact conducted in public by means of the spoken or written word. To weigh the effect of the word properly falls within the range of the lawyer's task but not at all into that of the civil servant."[2] Yet Weber was surely not unaware of the fact that in the Germany of his day (as is the case in present-day Germany), the majority of upper-level administrators had a solid legal training.[3]

Although one of the central preoccupations of this study has been to suggest that a rigid and static distinction between administrative and political types needs in general to be rejected, this should in no way be interpreted as a dismissal of the Weberian framework on which I have relied so heavily. Indeed, as will be gathered from this chapter, Weber's framework is of considerable help in analysis of the relationship between the deputy and the administrator. It should be emphasized that I am not dealing here with all administrators, regardless of the position they occupy within the administrative hierarchy, but only with those who occupy the highest posts in the central administration, the Directors. The question of the relationship between politicians and administrators is far more complex than has hitherto been recognized. It is necessary to take account of *different* types of politicians (ministers, deputies, mayors) and *different* types of civil servants (in ministries, in ministerial cabinets, in para-administrative institutions, in regional services). One would look in vain for two distinct groups of administrators and politicians.

[2] Max Weber, "Politics as a Vocation," in H. H. Gerth and C. Wright Mills, eds., *From Max Weber: Essays in Sociology* (Oxford: Oxford University Press, 1958), p. 95.

[3] See Ralf Dahrendorf, *Society and Democracy in Germany* (New York: Doubleday, 1967), pp. 250–252; Wolfgang Zapf, *Beiträge zur analyse der deutschen Oberschicht* (Munich: Piper, 1965), p. 80.

The Representative and the Administration

There are probably few democratic societies in which the deputy is held in as much disdain by the civil servant as in France. Although the reasons for this have scarcely been analyzed, it has often been maintained that the civil servant's attitude toward the elected official has been characterized by a traditional, now latent, now overt, antiparliamentarianism. This is the most generally accepted view and it has been clearly stated in a recent study:

> The administration is basically antiparliamentarian: it questions the sovereignty of parliament as well as that of the people. It dislikes the political expression of the popular will in all its forms. It detests the predominance of parliament: parliamentary control over the administration is onerous for the general interest . . . and the administration detests equally the party bureaucracies. Ultimately—and in a very Bonapartist tradition—the administration claims to represent the interests of the social group and all aspects of the general interest better than the politicians and parliament who "don't know" the dossiers and who hinder the administration in its actions.[4]

These assertions imply that the administration is basically antidemocratic, although another writer has noted that the administration's antiparliamentarianism "has no homogeneous political content. It expresses the irritation of the technician rather than a hostility based on principle toward democratic institutions."[5] In either case the result is the same: the administrators, whether out of principle or out of technical competence, share an ideology that is fundamentally hostile to or incompatible with democratic norms and institutions. This is a widely accepted thesis, though it has not hitherto been analyzed or explained in a convincing manner. It is a rather simplistic explanation, because it does not take into account the political elements that have entered into and shaped this relationship over a long period. The relationship, as it now exists, between administrators and deputies is the result

[4] Robert Catherine and Guy Thuiller, *Introduction à une philosophie de l'administration* (Paris: Armand Colin, 1969), pp. 222–223. This view is also expressed in Jean Meynaud, *Technocracy* (London: Faber & Faber, 1965), p. 117.

[5] Charles Brindillac, "Les Hauts fonctionnaires," *Esprit*, xxi, no. 6 (1953), 872.

287

of a dialectical process spanning several generations. In other words, neither the deputies nor the administrators developed a hostile "ideology" outside of the specific context of the French political system.

Today, as our survey of the Directors of the central administration indicated, the deputy does not fare well in the eyes of the higher civil servants despite the fact that the influence of the elected official has been sharply curtailed under the Fifth Republic—or perhaps because of it. On a scale that pitted the deputy against the higher civil servant, the member of a liberal profession, and the business executive (Table 11.1), the deputy ranked

TABLE 11.1

Ranking of Deputy vs. Members of Other Professions[1] (percent)

Quality	Superior	Equal	Inferior	Don't know	Total
Prestige	3.7	—	92.6	3.7	100.00
Freedom of action	2.5	—	95.1	2.4	100.00
Importance of task	2.5	—	95.1	2.4	100.00
Preparation for task	2.5	1.2	93.8	2.5	100.00

[1] Other categories with which the Deputy was compared were: the business executive, members of liberal professions, and the higher civil servants.

lowest in the almost unanimous opinion of the higher civil servants with regard to the following: (a) prestige; (b) freedom of action; (c) importance of task; and (d) preparation for task. Only (a)—prestige—and possibly (c)—importance of task—can be regarded as being linked to the particular regime of the Fifth Republic. As many of the higher civil servants interviewed noted, by curtailing the power of parliament the Fifth Republic has also diminished the prestige and the role of the parliamentarian. The remaining two factors on the scale are independent of the regime. I shall, therefore, treat the underlying variables that enter into the relationship between administrators and deputies before turning to the historical antecedents that have affected it.

It should be remarked that the relationship of deputies and civil servants has often been seen as depending on the representativity or unrepresentativity of the bureaucracy. We have already noted this argument with regard to Great Britain, where the social origins of Members of Parliament and of the Administrative Class of the civil service have been more or less homogeneous.[6] Because of this homogeneity it has been concluded that the British higher civil service has been responsive to the politicians. In *The Torment of Secrecy*, Shils treats the antagonistic relationship that exists between legislators and administrators in the United States, and suggests that disparity of background is at the heart of the mutual hostility. In a society more egalitarian than that of Britain, it might have been expected that the bureaucracy would not only be more or less representative of the society as a whole, but would also be representative of the dominant political group. Shils seems to imply, however, that the American Federal bureaucracy (in its upper echelons) does not exhibit the characteristics of what Kingsley has called a representative bureaucracy.[7]

> The particular friction [writes Shils] is, in part, one of the by-products of the merit system. The civil servant . . . will often be more educated and his social and economic origin will probably be higher than the legislators', who are requesting a service from him or interrogating him. . . . Resentment against those whose fortunate accidents of birth gave them educational opportunities which were not available to the legislator is sometimes heightened—it certainly was heightened during the Roosevelt administration—by an attitude of personal, social and intellectual superiority on the part of the administrator. This sense of superiority very often does not exist at all, but is nonetheless often assumed to exist and is as bitterly resented as if it were real.[8]

In the case of France, it has already been shown that the bureaucracy is highly unrepresentative of the society. But how representative is it of the political class? While there are serious gaps

[6] Peter G. J. Pulzer, *Political Representation and Elections: Parties and Voting in Great Britain* (New York: Frederick A. Praeger, 1967), pp. 68–71.

[7] Although Shils himself does not document his argument, there is, as was indicated in Chapter III, sufficient evidence to show that the higher echelons of the Federal bureaucracy are less representative of American society than are the lower ones.

[8] Edward A. Shils, *The Torment of Secrecy* (Glencoe, Ill.: The Free Press, 1956), p. 114. See also E. Pendleton Herring, *Public Administration and the Public Interest* (New York: McGraw-Hill Company, 1936), pp. 385–388.

in the data needed to answer this question, we do possess sufficient evidence to show that the political and administrative elites originate from what may roughly be termed the middle and upper-middle classes. The aristocracy and the working class are pretty much excluded.[9] Mattei Dogan has documented the decline of the nobility in the legislature. He notes that the proportion of deputies from the middle and lower-middle bourgeoisie, which constituted one-third of the legislature in the period 1898–1919, rose to about 70 percent during the Fourth Republic, an increase realized at the expense of the nobility and the upper bourgeoisie. "A veritable silent revolution," writes Dogan, "has occurred in parliamentary representation, as well as in the ministerial personnel. After 'la République des ducs,' after 'la République des notables,' after 'la République de la bonne bourgeoisie,' here, with the Fourth Republic, is the reign of the middle and lower bourgeoisie."[10]

Dogan has also pointed to the preponderance of intellectuals in Parliament. While his classification of the term "intellectual" is really too broad to be very meaningful,[11] it does have the virtue of indicating the educational level attained by the legislators and the degree to which it was a factor contributing to their success. For, as he points out, "the university graduate has been generally better armed for a political career and has had more chances of success than the self-educated."[12]

LOCAL VS. NATIONAL INTERESTS

The civil servant views his role, as has been suggested, as being diametrically opposed to that of the politician. Nowhere is this better illustrated than in the civil servant's view of his own and the deputy's respective constituencies. For a civil servant, a dep-

---

[9] The one significant exception is that deputies representing the Communist party are drawn almost exclusively from the working classes.

[10] Mattei Dogan, "Les filières de la carrière politique en France," *Revue Française de Sociologie*, VIII (1967), 469–470. For a summary of the backgrounds of the parliamentary personnel, see Henry Ehrmann, *Politics in France* (Boston: Little, Brown, 1968), pp. 124–130.

[11] He includes writers, professors, lawyers, journalists, magistrates, doctors, engineers, architects, and school teachers under this rubric.

[12] Mattei Dogan, "Political Ascent in a Class Society: French Deputies 1870–1958," in Dwaine Marvick, ed., *Political Decision-Makers* (Glencoe, Ill.: The Free Press, 1961), p. 77.

uty or a minister is first and foremost a politician. This means that the politician's interests are always segmental, whether they concern the interests of his party, his local constituency or, for a minister, even his ministry. They are not, nor can they be, the general interest. The civil servants, on the other hand, see themselves as the guardians of the general interest—this is a theme that they cling to tenaciously. It has sometimes been taken at face value as an accurate description of reality—it has also been mocked, but it is difficult to exaggerate its importance insofar as the role perception of the higher civil servants is concerned. From the civil servant's point of view, it specifies a role that is distinguishable from the deputy's. Jean-Pierre Worms has analyzed the Prefect's singular attachment to the notion of the general interest: "In effect, his conception of the general interest flows directly from his conception of the State: the general interest is what unites, what assembles; it is the unity of the French people. Being neither the sum of particular interests nor their synthesis, it is, more profoundly, what they have in common. In a way, the Prefect denies the possibility of conflict of interest. If there is conflict, it is due to ignorance of the general interest."[13]

The natural enemies of the general interest are the special interests expressed through the "particularistic demands" that the deputy makes of the administration. When asked what aspect of their work put them in touch with deputies, over 75 percent of the civil servants interviewed replied that contact with deputies came on questions of "cas particuliers." The same proportion of civil servants expressed the belief that the deputy was not concerned with questions of general policy but only with making demands on behalf of his constituents. As Table 11.2 indicates, how-

TABLE 11.2
What Deputies Represent, According to Directors (percent)

The national interest	3.7
Their constituency	85.0
Their party	1.2
Their own careers	33.3

Note: This table does not equal 100% because of multiple choices.

[13] Jean-Pierre Worms, "Le Préfet et ses notables," *Sociologie du Travail,* Special Number, vol. VIII, no. 3 (1966), 256.

ever, the deputy is not seen merely as a cynical politician seeking self-aggrandizemen*r*, although looking after his constituents' interest also promotes his own career.

That the deputy did not concern himself with general questions but only with "cas particuliers" was the most general theme of the civil servants. "I try to have as little contact with deputies as possible. They always come to ask this for this person and that for that person. We do not speak the same language," said one higher civil servant. It is interesting to note, however, that the deputy himself ascribes a greater importance to his national, as opposed to his local activities.[14]

In examining the mail received by a deputy over a three-year period, Marie-Thérèse Lancelot found that of 1,354 letters received 1,261 came from individuals, only fifteen from unions, groups, or associations, and 108 from mayors.[15] Since it is mostly individuals who write to request the intervention of the deputy on their behalf vis-à-vis a public authority, it is not surprising that the deputy should find himself writing or intervening to obtain a post for this constituent, a decoration for that one, requesting that so-and-so receive his pension, that such a family's housing situation is in need of improvement, etc. The type and number of demands made to the deputy (Table 11.4) suggest that the deputy "is far less a dispenser of favors than an intermediary placed between the citizen and the administration in order to alleviate the complexity and rigidity in the functioning of the latter."[16] That the citizens seek to muster all possible influence in their dealings with an all-powerful and remote administration can be seen from the fact that almost one-third do not write directly; they ask the mayor, a friend, or a general councillor to intervene on their behalf and bring a particular matter to the attention of the deputy.

Table 11.3 shows the various channels used by those who chose to contact their deputy indirectly. Two-thirds of the letters analyzed were from individuals writing on their own behalf. Almost

[14] R. Cayrol, J.-L. Parodi and C. Ysmal, "L'Image de la fonction parlementaire chez les députés Français," *Revue Française de Science Politique*, XXI, no. 6 (1971), 1175. I will return to the deputy's view of his own role presently.

[15] Marie-Thérèse Lancelot, "Le Courrier d'un parlementaire," *Revue Française de Science Politique*, XII, no. 2 (1962), 426.

[16] *Ibid.*, p. 429.

all the demands made of the deputy have to do with the administration, which would indicate that "the voters expect the deputy
to protect them and to help them in their relations with the administration"[17] (Table 11.4). This is precisely what the civil servants resent on the part of the deputy because, to them, it indicates a constant preoccupation with trivialities. As one Director

TABLE 11.3
Requests to Deputies by Indirect Channels

Channels Used	Number of Interventions		
	Institutional Circuit	Political and Personal Circuit	%
General councillors	127		33.33
Influential people in the department	—	92	24.35
Deputies	63	—	16.53
Mayors	61	—	16.01
Civil servants	23	—	—
Ecclesiastics	—	8	—
Personal friends	—	4	—
Deputies of other *départements*	—	3	—
Total	274	107	
			71.91
			28.09

Source: Lancelot, "Le Courrier d'un parlementaire," p. 428.

put it, "The deputy comes here and asks for this or that, and he
shows no interest in or understanding of general problems, or of
the policies that we are trying to pursue."

It might be suggested that had the deputy's constituency consisted largely of well-organized groups or associations he might
have fared better in the eyes of civil servants. All available evidence indicates that the well-organized groups do not solicit the
deputy's help—and certainly do not write him letters[18]—in their
relationship with the administration. French higher civil servants
make a fundamental distinction between associational or professional organizations on the one hand, and lobbies and interest
groups on the other. It is a distinction that makes little concession

[17] *Ibid.*, p. 431.   [18] *Ibid.*, p. 426.

to logic, but which reveals an important bias. The deputy does not act on behalf of groups, but on behalf of a disparate mass, that is to say, on behalf of that which is the very antithesis of the general interest. That neither could the professional organization

TABLE 11.4

Types of Demands Calling for Deputy's Intervention

Demands		Number	%
Administrative posts in a private or public enterprise		180	14.27
Pensions and old-age allowances		138	10.94
Change of post (civil servant requesting transfer in a locality or to another region)		124	9.81
Scholarships (secondary, higher and technical education)		76	6.02
Honors		62	4.91
Intervention of deputy in conflicts involving the administration and a private citizen		58	4.59
Promotion in administration		47	3.72
Exemption from, or reduction of, penalties (court records, taxes)		47	3.72
Housing		46	3.64
Information and documents		39	3.09
Intervention of deputy in judicial matters		22	1.74
Reduction of taxes		22	1.74
Obtaining or transferring veterans' payments		22	1.74
Naturalization		18	1.42
Obtaining civil servant status		16	1.26
Reclassification to administrative post		14	1.11
Licenses		13	1.03
Decentralization of firm in deputy's constituency		9	0.78
Work permits		8	0.63
Various favors requested by servicemen		122	9.67
Including retention in metropole or return from Algeria	42		
draft deferment or extension of deferment	31		
Various favors		103	
Including privileged admission to an educational or medical institution	8		
intervention of deputy for (school) examinations	7		

Source: Lancelot, "Le Courrier d'un parlementaire," p. 430.

be equated with the general interest was not always recognized by the civil servants.

Moreover, although the deputy is recognized as an elected official, he is seen not as representing the nation but only a fraction of it. Again this comes out in the interventions that the deputy makes on behalf of the voters: 81 percent of the letters addressed to him come from his own constituency and 9 percent from the immediate vicinity.[19] This fractional representation has been an enduring theme of the French Right, but it has also formed part of the Left's ideology. The point has been most eloquently stated by Tardieu in his trenchant attack on the parliamentary profession: "The representation of France, one and indivisible, is only a fiction. Each deputy represents one six-hundredth of France, and nothing else. Each of these fractions is represented: the country as a whole is not. Each deputy, seeking to be reelected, is passionately interested in what is agreeable to the fraction that he represents, and is indifferent to the needs of the collectivity. Let us say that representation having sacrificed the mandate to the *métier*, the *métier*, in its turn, has killed representation."[20]

The deputy, therefore, is seen as standing at a pole opposite to that of the civil servant. Elected to represent a fraction of the nation, he may not even do that, for this duty is at odds with the legal concept of the sovereignty of the nation. The Burkean notion of representativity has never made much ground in France, so that the very function of the deputy has become almost incompatible with a strong government. A strong executive has always seen parliamentary government as antithetical to the national interest, thus giving rise to what has been called the administrative tradition of government.[21] The adherents of this view have never accepted the representative role of the deputy, regarding it instead as the role of the intermediary (not wholly disinterested to boot), who submerges the public interest beneath the particular interest. "There is no question, be it military, financial or social [wrote Tardieu], that is not first considered from the electoral angle. This means that, in almost all the votes, a

[19] Lancelot, "Le Courrier d'un parlementaire," p. 429.

[20] André Tardieu, *La Révolution à refaire: la profession parlementaire* (Paris: Flammarion, 1932), p. 34.

[21] Nicholas Wahl, "The French Political System," in S. Beer and A. Ulam, eds., *Patterns of Government: The Major Political Systems of Europe* (New York: Random House, 2nd ed., 1963), p. 277.

Cornelian debate can occur between what the public interest requires and what the electoral interests command. The moment this conflict begins, the public interest is in danger."[22]

The legislator's preoccupation with satisfying his constituents, and thereby securing reelection, is an accepted aspect of Anglo-Saxon parliamentary democracy. In the United States, for example, the legislator is "often made into an errand boy or a handmaiden to his constituents";[23] the insecurity of a political career compels him to expend "much of his time and energy running errands for them in Washington and receiving them when they visit the capital for business or for sightseeing purposes."[24] The constant attempt to reconcile national representation with local representation, as well as with the desire for reelection, is simply recognized as what Shils calls "one of the strains of politics." In France, the legislator's preoccupation with the needs of his constituents, aggravated as this is by the centralized system of administration, has been seen as a perversion of democracy. This view emanates, generally, from a contempt not merely for the deputy, but also for his electors who turn him into what he is—a man oblivious to the national interest. "Being reelected is a question of obtaining what the electors demand. And the electors demand all that can be demanded—even a little more."[25]

ADMINISTRATION VS. POLITICS

In addition to the divergent perceptions of constituencies, there is an equally divergent perception, at least in the minds of civil servants, concerning the overall nature of the tasks performed: the deputy, like the minister, engages in politics, whereas the civil servant engages in administration. That this view is at vari-

[22] Tardieu, *La Révolution à refaire*, p. 45.

[23] Shils, *The Torment of Secrecy*, p. 109. The American congressman has also been seen at times in much the same light as the French deputy. Samuel Huntington observes that "Congressmen tend to be oriented toward local needs and small-town ways of thought. The leaders of the administration and of the private national institutions are more likely to think in national terms." See his "Congressional Responses in the Twentieth Century," in David B. Truman, ed., *The Congress and America's Future* (Englewood Cliffs, N.J.: Prentice-Hall, 1965), p. 15.

[24] Shils, *ibid.*, p. 106.

[25] Tardieu, *La Révolution a refaire*, p. 45.

296

ance with anything approaching reality matters very little, for it is a view to which civil servants are ardently attached and it bears heavily on their relationship with deputies. The desire to remain sheltered from politics, to believe passionately that his task is purely technical, leads the higher civil servant to shy away from involvement with deputies. In answer to the question whether he had contact with deputies, one Director replied, "No. And this proves that this administration is not politicized."

What does "politics" represent for the higher civil servants? It connotes, first of all, party politics. Second, it means dealing with segmental interests. It does not mean, as Weber described it, that "interests in the distribution, maintenance, or transfer of power are decisive for the official's sphere of activity."[26] Third, and most significant, to be engaged in politics is to accept the vicissitudes of a hazardous game. In short, it is to risk a loss of power. By the same token, to be totally disengaged from politics is to remain secure in one's monopoly over a domain. Thus a minister could generally be handled relatively easily, if only because he usually lacked sufficient time in which to extract the necessary information from his administration. But what could not be handled by the civil servants was a persistent vulnerability to politics and politicians. Thus have been born, and fiercely defended, such ideologies as the "general interest," "political irresponsibility," "administrative neutrality."

The Directors of the central administration see themselves as doing no more than managing (*gérer*) the affairs which are entrusted to them. Like the French mayor,[27] the Director sees himself as essentially the manager of a large enterprise. Time and again, a Director would observe: "My task here is really the same as that of a director of a large private company. I direct thousands of men; I visit our various divisions. I see that the work gets done, and there is no politics in this." To manage is thus a politically neutral activity. The invocation of the analogy of the "manager" is deeply ingrained, as can be seen from the view expressed by an influential member of the Conseil d'Etat in 1911: "The task of parliament is to supervise the administration of a country, not to administer the country. The ministers who repre-

---

[26] Max Weber, "Politics as a Vocation," p. 78.
[27] Worms, "Le Préfet et ses notables," p. 258.

sent the powers of parliament cannot have other powers than parliament itself; their task is to supervise the public services of the country, not to manage. This job of management and of administration can only be done well by the specialized, permanent civil servant, independent of these [political] fluctuations."[28]

But in order to carry out the apolitical task of "managing," it was necessary that the civil servant should be protected from the (political) vulnerability of the deputy. A casual reading of the writings of civil servants under the Third Republic is sufficient to show the importance attached to this view. And if the contemporary civil servant proclaims these sentiments less loudly and less passionately, it is only because he has largely achieved what his Third Republic ancestors sought so indefatigably to obtain. Addressing a group of civil servants at the beginning of this century, Chardon could declare: "In any case, what is certain is that you can all, little by little and one after the other, conquer, in the interest of public service . . . your independence and the independence of your role vis-à-vis the deputy. The day you will have conquered it, the day that, in every public service, you will have set up an insurmountable barrier to political interventions of any nature whatsoever, that day, not only will France applaud you, but rest assured that the deputies themselves, emancipated and restored to their great and veritable role, will be the first to bless you."[29]

The higher civil servants interviewed noted that the divisiveness of French politics ought not to be reflected in the administration. From this it appeared to follow that permanent contact with the deputies would necessarily lead to a kind of "jeu de pression." And since a government was always—until recently, at least—composed of ideologically disparate elements, the pressure would come from all sides. "One day it would be doing this for this deputy, and the next day it would be doing that for his opponent. That is what would happen. What would happen if we took all the recommendations of deputies seriously? What would happen if they themselves took them seriously?" asked one higher civil servant. It would constitute a loss of authority and it would detract from the real task of the civil servant. But the negation of politics is also the negation of conflict which all civil servants seek, and which accounts for what Worms has called the "rhet-

[28] Chardon, *Le Pouvoir administratif*, p. 14.
[29] *Ibid.*, p. 186.

oric of the general interest,"[30] or what might even be characterized as the ideology of the general interest. To acknowledge the
existence of conflict is to acknowledge the need for shifts in "the
distribution, maintenance and transfer of power," that is to say,
it is to acknowledge a political role. A conflict-free administration is one in which politics has no part and in which politicians
confine themselves to their own arena. Above all, it implies a situation that leaves the civil servant master of his own domain. "In
a great democratic nation like ours [wrote Chardon], the government is infinitely more fragmented. Each civil servant, each employee of the state, no matter how small and modest, is, at the
moment he exercises his functions, the government itself. At this
moment each one, within the limits of his functions, is above all
authority."[31]

Few civil servants would today define their role in so bold and
unequivocal a manner. Yet, in their desire to guard their autonomy and their monopoly over their own domain, they appear to
be echoing Chardon's exhortations. Politics detracts from this
goal in that it is likely to make them more open and, inevitably,
more responsive—hence, also more vulnerable. Consequently,
the French higher civil servant is constantly at pains to draw a
categorical distinction between the domain of administration and
that of politics which, we were repeatedly told, "have nothing to
do with one another."

TECHNICAL COMPETENCE VS. INCOMPETENCE

One of the most persistent criticisms made of politicians in general is their technical incompetence, which civil servants contrast
to their own expertise. The French higher civil servants observed
that they could not communicate with deputies "because we simply do not speak the same language." As one Director in a technical ministry put it, "A deputy understands nothing of what I
deal with. He simply does not have the necessary knowledge.
Should I descend to his level? Such meetings are just a waste of
time." The politician is seen by civil servants as being, at best, a
generalist who lacks technical expertise to understand "the complexities of today's problems." More generally, he is seen as lack-

[30] Worms, "Le Préfet et ses notables," p. 258.
[31] Chardon, *Le Pouvoir administratif*, p. 192.

299

ing the ability and the desire to acquire a grasp of these complexities.

Some writers have interpreted this criticism of the politician as a mere manifestation of a latent antiparliamentarianism on the part of the civil servants, and as sufficient evidence of their "technocratic" predisposition.[32] I have already suggested, however, that the attempt to subsume the complex questions of a civil servant's role and his relationship to the political system under the rubric of an antidemocratic bias is not an approach that is likely to be very rewarding. In the first place, it ascribes to one factor an overwhelming importance that may not be entirely warranted despite the element of truth it may contain. Second, it posits a good–evil distinction that admits of no nuances. Third, because the one factor chosen as an all-inclusive explanation is seen as being more or less a "trait," one is bound to adopt a rather pessimistic attitude toward possible remedies. Finally, this one explanation is basically ahistorical for, as we shall see in the next section, it ignores the historical roots of the very complex dialectical relationship between civil servants and politicians.

If the politician is not well-versed in technical matters, it is the result of three factors: (1) lack of information; (2) lack of time to acquire expertise; and (3) the nature of the political system. Clearly, all these factors are in some way related to one another, and they often leave ministers in charge of a department in the dark about the workings of their administrations.[33] But these factors are certainly not peculiar to France, although they may be somewhat more acute there, given the nature of executive power under the Fifth Republic. In his *The Reform of Parliament*, Bernard Crick laments the decline of the British House of Commons and the concomitant increase of executive power, which he recognizes to be an indispensable element of modern government:

> The declining effectiveness of the House has been paralleled
> . . . by a rising efficiency of the Executive. But there is no necessary contradiction between wanting a strong Executive and

[32] Meynaud, *Technocracy*, p. 219; Brindillac, "Les Hauts fonctionnaires," p. 872.

[33] See the revealing information offered by two former British ministers about the allocation of a minister's time, Patrick Gordon Walker, "On being a Cabinet Minister," and Ernest Marples, "A Dog's Life in the Ministry," both in Richard Rose, ed., *Policy-Making in Britain* (New York: The Free Press, 1969).

wanting a more effective and efficient House of Commons. The more power we entrust to a government to do things for us, the greater the need for it to operate amid a blaze of publicity and criticism. But there is such a contradiction at the moment because Parliament has not improved her own instruments of control, scrutiny, criticism and suggestion to keep pace with the great improvements of efficiency and the increase in size of executive government. Small wonder that public comprehension of Parliament is low and that confidence is declining.[34]

Although Crick refutes effectively the general belief that a strong parliament leads to a weak executive, his arguments would be difficult to apply to France, where the strength of the one *has* usually meant the weakness of the other. The Fifth Republic was determined to rehabilitate the executive, once it had rescued it from the mercy of parliament, and to increase its powers to the detriment of those of parliament. The constitutional checks on parliament's power to review, scrutinize, criticize, and suggest have been so drastically curtailed under the Fifth Republic that the functions of a deputy are no longer self-evident. "Under the new regime," writes Philip Williams, "the parliament of France, once among the most powerful in the world, became one of the weakest."[35] In such a system the deputy is powerless as a representative of public opinion, and utterly powerless to acquire any expertise since information is constantly denied him.

Given the ineffectiveness of parliament, the deputy's role vis-à-vis the bureaucracy shows a corresponding decline. In the first place, he is no longer seen by civil servants as a genuine representative of public opinion. The executive has assumed this role. Second, since he has few powers to question, he remains in perpetual ignorance. Third, and perhaps most important, his limited constitutional powers deny him legitimacy in the eyes of the administration. All this poses serious questions for the future of parliamentary democracy in France. Even in Britain, where parliament's powers to question the Government are greater than in Fifth Republic France, the Fulton Commission emphasized the

[34] Bernard C. Crick, *The Reform of Parliament* (New York: Doubleday, 1965), p. 15.

[35] Philip M. Williams, *The French Parliament: Politics in the Fifth Republic* (New York: Frederick A. Praeger, 1968), p. 21. See also Henry Ehrmann's discussion of the role of parliament in the Fifth Republic in his *Politics in France*, pp. 296–302.

importance of seeing "Members of Parliament more purposively associated with the work of government than they are now. The traditional methods of parliamentary scrutiny have often failed to enlarge Parliament's knowledge of what goes on or to secure for it a proper influence."[36] In Britain, there is a genuine belief that parliamentarians have much to offer by the mere fact of being "professional politicians."[37] In France this is not so. The need to create what Crick has called a "counter-bureaucracy"[38] in parliament, to obtain information from the administration, is anathema in France because to share information is, ultimately, to share power. Moreover, sharing information freely goes against the grain of French institutions, which are known to make a fetish of secrecy. One is reminded of the maintenance workers in Crozier's study, *The Bureaucratic Phenomenon*, who held a privileged position in the plant because they were able jealously to guard their know-how; if other workers in the plant learned to repair the machines, their power and freedom would be lost. Similarly, with regard to the bureaucracy's relationship to the deputy, it is possible to observe this "secrecy principle" at work.

ADMINISTRATIVE VS. POLITICAL LANGUAGE

Administrators, as has been noted, have been wont to insist on the existence of what might be called the two-language syndrome. They claim to be preoccupied with national questions, with the general interest, with efficient management, whereas the deputy is preoccupied, in the main, with a narrow constituency that he is obliged to serve in order to get reelected. The deputies, however, do not perceive their role in the same light. They see themselves as fulfilling both national and local duties (Table 11.5), and they do not regard themselves as mere intermediaries between their constituents and the central administration (Table 11.6).

If we accept this divergence in role perceptions, we must raise

---

[36] The Fulton Commission, *The Civil Service in Britain*, Vol. 1 (London: H.M.S.O., 1968), pp. 92–93.

[37] See *ibid.*, and Crick, *The Reform of Parliament*, p. 184.

[38] *Ibid.*, p. 202. See also David Coombes, *The Member of Parliament and the Administration* (London: George Allen & Unwin, 1966), in which the author shows how M.P.'s, despite the decline of Parliament, can and have been able to scrutinize the administration through the Select Committees.

TABLE 11.5

Local vs. National Activity, According to Deputies

Activity		%
National		22
Rather national		7
Local and national		58
Rather local		6
One local activity		4
Others		2
Total	(N = 381)	100

Source: Cayrol, Parodi, Ysmal, "L'Image de la fonction parlementaire," p. 1175.

the question of whether there is any justification for the claim that administrators and deputies do in fact speak separate languages. If we turn from an examination of role perceptions to the actual means or process of carrying out functions, it may be possible to identify important differences.

The deputy, by the very nature of his task, has never been able to see any of his goals, policies, or desires put into effect without long discussions and long gestation periods. Everything has to be discussed and agreed to by others, which usually means opponents as well as allies. The civil servant has benefited from delegated legislation and has grown accustomed to decrees, ordinances, and circulars; in other words, to a process of policy implementation that is the very opposite of the deputy's. Thus, the "House without Windows," with its long and interminable discus-

TABLE 11.6

Parliamentarian or Intermediary? Deputies' View (percent)

Parliamentary work		37
Intermediary		28
Both		32
No response		3
Total	(N = 381)	100

Source: Cayrol, Parodi, Ysmal, "L'Image de la fonction parlementaire," p. 1176.

sions, has coexisted with what Walter Rice Sharp has referred to as the "regime of decrees."[39] This has been equally true of the Third, Fourth, and Fifth Republics, although the "regime of decrees" predominates under the current Republic as a result of the impotence of parliament.

To the extent that administrators spend a large proportion of their time preparing decrees, their view of the decision-making process comes to be at odds with that of the legislators. The decree-making process is consultative only in a very narrow sense; it involves little conflict, it is secretive, and it allows for rapid implementation of the decision—all of which is in marked contrast to the legislative process.

The amount of time that Directors devote to preparing decrees is far greater than that devoted to preparing and amending legislation (Table 11.7). As a recent critic of the French administra-

TABLE 11.7

Proportion of Directors' Time Spent in Legislative and Regulatory Domains (percent)

Legislative Domain		Regulatory Domain	
All	0.0	All	17.0
3/4	4.9	3/4	57.9
1/2	14.8	1/2	15.8
1/4	59.3	1/4	5.9
0	13.6	0	0.0
Don't know	7.4	Don't know	7.4
Total	100.0	Total	100.0

tion, himself a higher civil servant, has noted: ". . . The civil servant in the central administration cannot, without failing in his own eyes, entrust to another the decision as to how the national will, of which he considers himself the depository, is to be interpreted in applying a directive or observing a vote of the Parliament. But neither can he examine every particular case that comes before him, or hold discussions with every representative

[39] Walter Rice Sharp, *The French Civil Service: Bureaucracy in Transition* (New York: Macmillan, 1931), p. 27.

of the case in question (or with the ninety prefects, or the ninety departmental directors, etc.). There remains to him, therefore, but one means of expression: soliloquy through the *règlement*."[40]

The development and increased use of delegated legislation in France suggests that the political process itself, and the manner in which it has evolved, has contributed to the mutual hostility between administrators and deputies. Rather than seeing this mutual hostility as a "cultural trait," I suggested earlier there were certain historical factors that explain, if only in part, the gulf that separates deputies and administrators. I turn now to a brief examination of the historical roots of this gulf.

An Historical Explanation

The civil servant fulfills a distinct role when he rejects close contact with and demonstrates a scarcely disguised antipathy toward the politician. He is, to a large extent, constrained to act in this manner by norms that are not wholly defined by him. He is thus faced by what Dahrendorf has called "the vexatious fact of society," "one that we cannot ignore or flout without punishment."[41]

What are the constraining forces on the civil servant and who defines them? First, there are his superiors, the politicians who govern the nation—the minister and the government. These politicians are, in addition to being heads of a ministry, members of a government and of a political party with local interests. Their involvement in politics is profound and their success as politicians depends on their ability to balance forces, to compromise, and to be loyal to their government. Their colleagues in the government are also their potential enemies. Now, ministers have always recognized that in order to be masters of their own houses, they need above all the support of their civil servants. But be-

[40] René Mayer, *Féodalité ou démocratie? pour une administration d'un style nouveau* (Paris: Arthaud, 1968), p. 44.

[41] Ralf Dahrendorf, *Essays in the Theory of Society* (Stanford: Stanford University Press, 1968), p. 38. "Social roles," writes Dahrendorf, "are a constraining force on the individual, whether he experiences them as an obstacle to his private wishes or a support that gives him security. The constraining force of role expectations is due to the availability of *sanctions*, measures by which society can enforce conformity with its prescriptions. The man who does not play his role is punished; the man who plays his role is rewarded, or at least not punished" (p. 38).

305

cause civil servants have the power—which they have not infrequently used—to thwart the aims of their minister, there has gradually developed in France a ministerial "domaine réservé," the ostensible aim of which has been to exclude the civil servant from any contact that bore the germs of a possible "stab in the back" for the minister.

Hand in hand with the minister's acquisition of this "domaine réservé" went his powers vis-à-vis the civil servants in his ministry. He could hire and fire as he pleased and he could organize and disorganize the services in his ministry as he willed. This power was deeply resented by the civil servants who, during the early years of the Third Republic, undertook to end the intrusion of politics into administration. "Charged with a mission, could the civil servant at least carry it out conscientiously? Could he expect the well-deserved rewards of his virtues? Was he protected from the abuse of power by others? Appointed at the minister's will, he remained more often than not subject to the ministerial will at every moment of his administrative life."[42]

Civil servants argued that the all-embracing power of ministers played havoc with their lives as well as with the work of the administration. "There was not a single minister who did not believe himself master of 'his' administration. Nor was there one who, wishing to leave behind him traces of his brief stay in power, did not deem it indispensable to upset the work of his predecessor—only to return sometimes to things done away with by the latter some months earlier."[43] In addition to giving rise to administrative syndicalism, which fought long and bitter fights on behalf of the maltreated civil servant, the abuse of power by ministers led to a relentless attack on the whole practice of political intrusion in administrative affairs. It was not surprising, therefore, to see some of the most influential civil servants under the Third Republic championing the cause of administrative autonomy. In fact, many argued that the first step toward attaining this highly desirable end was the abolition of the Prefectoral corps. The prefect, whom Taine had called a mere "deliverer of votes,"[44] had been the backbone of all nineteenth century regimes. It was argued that no serious administrative reform was possible without

[42] Georges Cahen, *Les Fonctionnaires* (Paris: Armand Colin, 1911), p. 10.
[43] *Ibid.*, pp. 12–13.
[44] H. Taines, *Les Origines de la France contemporaine*, Vol. 10 (Paris: Hachette, 1899), 291.

first ridding the country of "prefectoral supervision." "No more of these hybrids living at once on the attributions of politicians and administrators, amalgamating in a more or less occult manner and without any real responsibility politics and administration: consequently, no more prefects."[45]

The administration, it was argued, ought not to be subjected to the daily consequences of politics. It had its own sphere of activity, as did parliament, that admitted of no tampering. It was thus essential to distinguish at all times between politics and administration, for any mingling of the two entailed disastrous consequences for the conduct of the nation's affairs. This has been best expressed by Chardon: "Until we make a more rational distribution of jurisdictions between parliament and the administrators, we will remain in a mess. . . . But if you desire . . . that this rational distribution be called a separation of powers, so be it: I ask you, therefore, to recognize that a democratic republic, like ours, is necessarily composed of two powers: political and administrative; the latter being subordinated to the former, but existing nonetheless and living outside the realm of politics so that in each instance the citizens can easily judge the role of the politicians and the role of the administrators."[46]

The demand for administrative autonomy was not intended to lead to "independence" from politics, nor did it imply unaccountability and irresponsibility for the civil servants. Rather, it was argued that the higher civil servant should not only be held accountable but should also be able to state his own case, when he differed with his minister, publicly.[47] This was, however, the kind of accountability and responsibility that ministers could not accept, since it would be all too likely to undermine their authority. But the demand for administrative autonomy meant different things to different ranks of the civil service: for the lower echelons it was a cry for recognition as employees with rights guaranteed by statute and not subject to the whims of their superiors; for the higher civil servants, who have never shared the lower ranks' desire to regard the state as an ordinary employer, the demand for administrative autonomy was more than a claim on a more secure career. It was a demand for an autonomous function that would not be liable to the hazards and turbulence that characterized French politics.

[45] Chardon, *Le Pouvoir administratif*, p. 35.
[46] *Ibid.*, pp. 19–20.   [47] *Ibid.*, p. 25.

Particularly resented by the civil servants was the by-product of corruption and political patronage in such a convulsive political system. Ministers appointed their friends and political allies to their cabinets only to secure high administrative posts for them later. This ran counter to the embryonic movement of administrative syndicalism and corporatism. As Chardon observes: "Some retired statisticians had the curiosity to calculate the number of recruits that the institution of *chef de cabinet* had furnished in this way to the French administration over the past ten years. The results they arrived at ought to be pinned up in every service. A good number of nominations escaped them. Yet, despite its incompleteness . . . how instructive their picture is! It could be entitled: 'How to climb to the highest post under the Third Republic.' "[48]

Even with regard to those who sought to follow a purely administrative career, promotion was often based on factors that had little to do with administrative capabilities. In the first half of the Third Republic, two of the most important factors determining promotion were religion and republican sympathies. This is adequately revealed in the letters of recommendation and reports by superiors that were included in the dossiers of civil servants. A few typical examples will suffice to give some indication of the nomination and promotion process. In a letter to the Minister of Interior, a prefect writes: "It concerns M. le Guay, general councillor of Randau, to whom a second-class sub-prefecture was promised. I can, in all confidence, point to M. le Guay as a man who honors the administration. He has all the qualities that one is pleased to find in a prefect: intelligence, tact, distinction, excellent manners, a fortune; in politics, principles of the center left. . . ." In a report on this official, the prefect noted that "his republican opinions are firmly placed outside his own interests."[49] The dossiers of civil servants who served under the Third Republic are filled with letters from deputies and senators recommending friends on the basis of their politics. One senator writes to a minister "to recommend M. Emile Demagny, son of the mayor of Issigny, who is one of our firm and devoted friends."[50] Another letter from a deputy to a minister notes, with

[48] Henri Chardon, *L'Administration de la France: les fonctionnaires* (Paris: Perrin, 1908), p. 124.

[49] *Archives Nationales.* F[IB] I. 356.

[50] *Archives Nationales.* F[IB] I. 410.

regard to one who was a Justice of the Peace under the Second Empire: "A liberal mind, sincerely devoted to the actual state of things, he will have no trouble working to make the Republic loved. He knows the law and has wide business experience. Married, father of a family, possessing a certain fortune, he fulfills all the desired conditions of honorability."[51] Religion was also an extremely important consideration, and it figured prominently in all the reports on civil servants made by their superiors.[52] To be sure, the aspiring official's politics and religion counted for more in the more sensitive posts and ministries, but subjective factors played an undeniably important role in all of them. The elected officials—the deputies and senators—had no small hand in emphasizing the subjective factors and influencing the nomination and promotion of the State's officials. And because the civil servants had been denied security of office, their careers were subject to considerable arbitrariness.

The nature of French politics thus gave rise to two distinct forces, whose clashes and antagonisms have produced the mutual hostility that has gradually come to characterize the relationship between politicians and administrators. It is interesting to note that these clashes were not born of divergent views—ultimately, both politicians and administrators sought an administration sheltered from outside interference. On the one hand, politicians imposed on their administrators a strict loyalty which entailed

[51] *Archives Nationales.* FIB I. 307.

[52] The forms that superiors had to fill out periodically called for all kinds of information that pertained to the subordinates' private life and opinions. Here is a typical case of a Director of the central administration who served in the Ministry of the Interior from 1900 to 1907:

Date of birth: December 26, 1850
Place of Birth: Portbail (Manche)
Marital status: Married, 2 children
Father's occupation: notary
Mother's situation: landowner
Fortune: 10,000 francs (1885); 20,000 (1888); 30,000 (1894). Fine fortune.
Social position: Father was a former notary living at Portbail.
Wife: A woman of the world, very charming, and mindful of maintaining
  relations that complement her husband's position. The house is well
  kept and they receive willingly and with fine hospitality.
Religion: Catholic
Politics: Republican

Source: *Archives Nationales.* FIB I. 405.

little contact with the outside world. To protect oneself from
one's political enemies, it was necessary to shelter one's administration. By the same token, ministers tended to use their power
within their ministries rather freely. This was, of course, resented
by the civil servants, if only because each succeeding minister felt
constrained to do likewise. Consequently, even while seeking to
protect his administration from the effects of the unstable and
turbulent political system in which he lived, the minister nevertheless usually succeeded in bringing into his ministry the dis-
equilibrating aspects of this system. On the other hand, the civil
servants sought to reject *all* political intrusion, not just that imposed by the minister himself. The demand for autonomy, the
desire to exist within a clearly defined sphere, the reluctance to
accept constant contact with politicians and groups were born of
this long and unhappy relationship between politicians and civil
servants. When the latter finally acquired their long-sought rights
and guarantees, they gained the upper hand. The consequences
of the civil servant's newly acquired security have transcended
the element of professional self-defense. In many respects, then,
the attitudes of civil servants toward politicians may be seen
partly as a reaction to the era of patronage, political irresponsibility, and second-class status, and partly as an attempt to guard
their autonomy vis-à-vis the outside world.

The Deputy, the Administration, and the Fifth Republic

The relationship between a Director of the central administration
and a deputy is a grossly unequal one, depending as it does always on the deputy's need to be received by a Director. It is a
one-sided relationship, lacking, in most instances, any potential
for collusion. Much of the deputy's bargaining position has been
preempted. This was not the case under the Fourth Republic,
when votes were needed in the National Assembly for the passage of legislation, and many deputies were able to act as spokesmen for particular policies of civil servants. The shift in power
from the legislature to the executive has therefore not been without its impact on the legislators' relationship with the bureaucracy. But there is another factor of even greater importance: the
existence of a majority party that controls the government and
the National Assembly. The impact of this novel development in

the French political system has not hitherto been adequately recognized, and we shall examine its effects on the bureaucracy in Chapter XIII.

Another manifestation of the sharp break in the administration's relationship with deputies is that a civil servant almost never seeks contact with a deputy. Such contact generally takes place only on the deputy's request to be received by a particular Director, or on the minister's request to the Director to receive a particular deputy. In either case, the minister is always kept informed of such meetings—in most cases, he demands to be informed. Instances were encountered in which the minister, upon taking office, issued directives to the effect that civil servants were not to have contact with deputies without first consulting the cabinet; in fact, it was noted by our respondents that ministers considered contact with deputies to fall within their "domaine réservé." In preparing laws or decrees, the Directors rely more on themselves and their subordinates than on the advice of a deputy, even when the deputy might be directly concerned.

Deputies now have to confine themselves to writing letters to the administration. As one Director observed, "The number of letters received by the administration from deputies is probably greater than it was under the Fourth Republic. They no longer have a legislative function, so they have more time to devote to making meaningless demands on the administration." This, in turn, tends to detract from the legitimacy of deputies in the eyes of the administrators. "They write letters, not because they believe in what they are requesting, but in order to be able to show their constituents the letter from M. le Directeur or M. le Ministre in Paris stating that the matter is being looked into." The constitutional loss of influence under the Fifth Republic has forced the deputy to employ means of intervention that cannot but lead to rendering him still more ineffective.[53]

Deputies appear, on the whole, to be aware that it is now best to address themselves either to the minister directly or to his cabinet (Table 11.8). Given the attitude of ministers to their "domaine réservé," Directors prefer not to be approached directly by deputies. They would much prefer not to have to deal with parliamentarians. Why have ministers under the Fifth Republic

[53] Of course, the letter to the deputy from "Monsieur le Ministre" was always important, but it used to be only one of several means of intervention open to the deputy.

done their best to eliminate direct contacts between deputies and Directors? First, and perhaps most important, is the fact that ministers themselves are subject to greater controls and supervision by the Prime Minister and the President of the Republic. The staffs of Matignon and the Elysée have grown enormously under the Fifth Republic, so that the work of ministers and their departments are carefully scrutinized at all times. Second, and not unrelated to this development, is the question of responsibility. It is the minister who is responsible to the Prime Minister and to the President as well as to parliament. It is argued that the

TABLE 11.8

Channels Used by Deputies, According to Directors (percent)

Directors	14.9
Ministerial cabinet	38.3
Minister	72.8

Note: This table does not equal 100% because of multiple choices.

civil servant carries out his task anonymously, that he bears no responsibility for the consequences of his actions and that he is protected by the "umbrella" of the minister. This is the argument that ministers have always used to justify monopolizing contact with deputies. As a former minister wrote:

> It is his task to translate, to expose before parliament, the positions that he has established with the accord of his administration. It is he who can obtain the necessary votes. It is he who is questioned and who has to explain, before the Commissions, his policies.
>
> In the eyes of the public, which often—in all things—seeks a scapegoat, it is he who is responsible. It is he whom the press questions, and criticizes more often than praises.[54]

The implications, for the democratic process, of having the minister solely responsible before the public for the actions carried out by the officials in his ministry are serious—serious enough to have compelled the Fulton Commission to observe that what has

[54] André Morice, "Le Ministre et l'administration," *Promotions*, no. 28 (1954), 15.

for so long been a cardinal principle of British government is no longer tenable. The Commission observed that secrecy has played far too important a role in administrative decision-making, and recommended that parliament come to be associated more purposively in the work of government than it is at present. It concluded:

> Indeed we think that administration suffers from the convention, which is still alive in many fields, that only the minister should explain issues in public and what his department is or is not doing about them. This convention has depended in the past on the assumption that the doctrine of ministerial responsibility means that a Minister has full detailed knowledge and control of all the activities of his department. This assumption is no longer tenable. The Minister and his junior Ministers cannot know all that is going on in his department, nor can they nowadays be present at every forum where legitimate questions go unanswered. In our view, therefore, the convention of anonymity should be modified and civil servants, as professional administrators, should be able to go further than now in explaining what their departments are doing, at any rate as far as concerns managing existing policies and implementing legislation.[55]

This question becomes all the more acute in a regime where the power of parliament to question ministers has been sharply diminished. Indeed, the deputies are so greatly dependent on ministers that open criticism is not likely to be very productive. The consequence is the greater anonymity of the civil servant and the greater ineffectiveness of the deputy, both as a representative of his constituents and as an articulator of public opinion. "By himself he can do nothing for his electors. He appears before a powerful minister as one soliciting favors," wrote a former minister.[56] The political system of the Fifth Republic has conspired to place the deputy in an impotent position, at the mercy of the government and the administration. As one former Fifth Republic minister has noted: "The power relations have changed: parliament does not sit permanently. The minister is no longer at the mercy of a debate. The voting procedure for the finance laws is such

[55] The Fulton Commission, *The Civil Service in Britain*, I, 93.
[56] Bernard Chenot, *Etre ministre* (Paris: Plon, 1967), p. 48.

that a deputy, and especially a senator, has no chance whatever of obtaining the credit he seeks without the agreement of the minister."[57]

That the impotence of parliament has left the minister more time in which to immerse himself in the affairs of his ministry is undeniable. Under the Third and Fourth Republics a minister was obliged to fight most of his political battles in parliament. It therefore became imperative that he maintain a monopoly on all information, for a leak would be bound to have devastating repercussions on him in parliament. Our respondents noted time and again how important it was to weigh one's every word when talking to a deputy. Several of them observed: "The danger is that they can always use the information against you or against the minister." We have already noted how some higher civil servants were able under the Fourth Republic to use deputies to champion their causes in parliament. This was by no means a new situation. André Tardieu wrote in his attack on parliamentarians: "It happens . . . that the deputy can exercise greater power over the civil servants than the ministers to whom they are subordinates. How many times have prefects worked for a deputy against the Minister of Interior! It is the sovereign assembly, and not the government, that commands the civil servants on whom its election depends and who depend on it for their promotion. It is because of this that the deputies, in the budgetary votes, are so generous when it comes to the civil servants. They are both engaged in rendering services to one another."[58]

The Fifth Republic has sought to eradicate what Tardieu called "parliamentary despotism," which meant primarily that deputies were able to undermine the authority of the minister by going over his head directly to the appropriate administration. Senators and deputies, according to Tardieu, used to have their contacts in every bureau of every ministry. "The most important of them have their clientele of Directors, chiefs, sub-chiefs and lower officials."[59] The ministers of the Fifth Republic have sought to "purify" the administration and to protect it from any possible contamination with "politics." But the term "politics" means no more, in this instance, than the political opposition, for the treat-

[57] *Ibid.*

[58] Tardieu, *La Révolution à refaire*, p. 209. See also Brindiallac, "Les hauts fonctionnaires," p. 873.

[59] Tardieu, *ibid.*, p. 208.

ment accorded to deputies by the administration varies according to their place in the political spectrum. The deputies of the majority parties are treated by the administration in a manner usually denied to the deputies of the opposition. This will be explored in greater detail when I take up the question of the relationship between the Gaullist regime and the administration in Chapter XIII.

CHAPTER XII

The Administration and Interest Groups

The administration must be able to resist all pressures. But the administrators must know how to distinguish between groups that are sérieux and those that are not.
— *French higher civil servant*

INTEREST GROUPS AND DEMOCRATIC POLITICS

The role of interest groups in a political system can, and has been, viewed from two distinct perspectives: either it is seen as the basis for the workings of a democratic political system, or it is seen as constituting the corruption of public values. As Georges Lavau has pointed out, there is "a contradiction between the ever more effective action of the interest groups and the democratic fiction according to which elected assemblies have a twofold function: that of representing conflicting interests and of sublimating them, and that of defining in their decisions a general will (if not in each particular concrete decision, at least in the continuity and the aggregate of legislation)."[1] This contradiction points to the differing roles that interest groups have been seen as playing in different political systems. It was Tocqueville who, above all, regarded the existence of voluntary associations as the basis of American democracy. Subsequently, and particularly in our own day, the existence of groups has given rise to the concept of pluralism, which has become the single most important explanation for the working of the American governmental system. The proponents of this concept have come to view the absence of coherent and structured groups in a society as the key to explaining the unviability of a democratic form of government in that society. It is argued that the integration of citizens into organized groups is the surest way of preventing the mobilization

[1] Georges E. Lavau, "Political Pressures by Interest Groups in France," in Henry Ehrmann, ed., *Interest Groups on Four Continents* (Pittsburgh: University of Pittsburgh Press, 1958), p. 62.

of the citizenry for mass politics.[2] Thus, where Marx's proletariat had firmly grounded interests upon which it acted, those susceptible to mass mobilization in a society not divided along class lines have no particular interests to defend. For the Marxian concept of class politics, then, has been substituted the concept of mass politics, the danger of which is said to be that it is the politics of a disparate mass unable to integrate itself within existing groups and unable to form a group of its own, since it has no shared interests in the way that Marx's proletariat does. Thus, in the case of France, it has been argued that the inability of Frenchmen to enter into groups has constituted the greatest obstacle to French democracy, and it has given rise to the "flash" or "surge" party which mobilizes this disparate mass on a temporary basis.[3] But when it was subsequently found that Frenchmen were just as willing and able to join groups as were Englishmen, Germans, and even Americans,[4] it was argued that they entered into groups that reinforced existing divisions.[5] They did not, in other words, exhibit what a leading American pluralist has called "overlapping memberships."[6]

One of the more important hypotheses concerning the extent of interest-group influence in the political system has to do with the strength of political institutions. Where the political institutions are strong, it is held, they will represent the national interest, so that the influence of particular groups will be held in check. Where political institutions are weak and unstable, there will be no firm representative of the general interest, so that the better-organized groups will be able to affect the distribution of power in their favor. At first glance, this appears as— almost—an irrefutable hypothesis. But, as we shall see in this chapter, a strong government will not necessarily arbitrate between groups in favor of the "general interest," and a weak and unstable government may create a fluid situation in which there

[2] William Kornhauser, *The Politics of Mass Society* (New York: The Free Press, 1959).

[3] *Ibid.*, pp. 148–149 and 204–205.

[4] Arnold Rose, "Voluntary Associations in France," in *Theory and Method in the Social Sciences* (Minneapolis: University of Minnesota Press, 1954), pp. 84–85.

[5] Duncan MacRae, *Parliament, Parties and Society in France, 1948–1958* (New York: St. Martin's Press, 1967), p. 29.

[6] David B. Truman, *The Governmental Process* (New York: Alfred A. Knopf, 1965).

317

is a kind of "free-for-all," so that groups that would not normally be able to exert much influence are now able to compete with larger and better-organized groups. The United States, for example, has always been regarded as the epitome of stable government, whose consensus emerges from the conflicts among groups. Yet it has been very forcefully argued that we have permitted "the conquest of segments of formal state power by private groups and associations."[7] The government, argues McConnell, cannot effectively play the role of mediator between different interests because the "government itself is fragmented and the various fragments are beholden to particular interests."[8] We saw in a previous chapter the degree to which the Army Corps of Engineers depended on the decentralized federal structure, to which the Corps had quite willingly, and with considerable benefits, accommodated itself.[9] The solution, as McConnell sees it, is to strengthen "those elements of the political order which tend toward the creation of a constituency of the entire nation,"[10] because the federal structure, coupled with the so-called interest-group pluralism is inherently conservative. "The ideology of 'grass roots democracy' and the gradual growth of power in small units by the institutional processes of accommodation have probably betrayed us into yielding too much of the republic's essential values of liberty and equality. The dangers to democracy in the United States have rarely been anomie and mass movements. The real threats, often adeptly met by cooptation of group leaders, have come from narrowly constituted interest groups. Yet it is all too apparent that often the leaders of such groups have coopted the United States instead."[11]

Thus it is significant to note that in the United States, where the political process has been seen as being no more than the derivative of group behavior, with groups "lying at the heart of the process of government,"[12] it is now seen as being subverted by these group-oriented decisions because "a substantial part of

[7] Grant McConnell, *Private Power and American Democracy* (New York: Vintage, 1970), p. 162.

[8] *Ibid.*, p. 164.

[9] As McConnell notes in another context, "Local elites have become organized nationally, usually on a federal basis, and have then been able to assume the exercise of public authority within significant areas of policy" (*ibid.*, p. 163).

[10] *Ibid.*, p. 368.　　　　　　　　　　[11] *Ibid.*, pp. 358–359.

[12] Truman, *The Governmental Process*, p. 46.

government in the United States has come under the influence or control of narrowly based and largely autonomous elites."[13] The result of administrative decentralization and of interest-group pluralism has been the blurring of the distinction between public and private, the corruption of public values and the public interest, the exclusion of a significant minority from effective representation in the political process, and the identification of the public interest with the interests of particular groups.[14]

In France, on the other hand, most students of the French political system have tended to argue the opposite: namely, that the centralized system of government has created too rigid a distinction between the public and private domains, and that it is the State that has always—if somewhat self-righteously—regarded itself as the sole guardian of the public interest. Consequently, in a system whose philosophical underpinnings deny any virtue to group behavior in the political process, little fear has been evinced regarding the subversion of public values in favor of particular groups. Most students of French interest groups have tended to stress the State's traditional disdain of or contempt for the "intermediary groups"—intermediary, that is, between the citizen and the State—and they have nearly always taken as their point of departure the assertion of Rousseau that "It is essential, if the general will is to be able to express itself, that there should be no partial society within the State and that each citizen should think only his own thoughts." Affirmations concerning the central role of the State and the subversive influences of groups—often including the political parties—have often been heard from French leaders. How strong is the attachment to such statements can be seen from the opening pages of the first volume of de Gaulle's postwar memoirs.[15] Students of French politics, having accepted the philosophical beliefs concerning intermediary groups as an accurate reflection of the actual political process, have not found it necessary to examine the influence that groups do play in the French political system, nor have they examined the attitudes of those who do interact with the groups—the politicians and the administrators. What I am suggesting is that the

[13] McConnell, *Private Power and American Democracy*, p. 339.

[14] All these arguments have been well developed and documented in McConnell, *ibid*.

[15] Charles de Gaulle, *Mémoires d'espoir: Le renouveau, 1958–1962* (Paris: Plon, 1970), pp. 8–11.

role of interest groups in French politics can be seen on two planes: the philosophical and the empirical; it is the former that has been stressed, and taken as an accurate description of reality. As will be seen in this chapter, there is a marked difference between the two.

The centralized system of government in France has recently given rise to proposals that favor the American system of decentralization and interest-group pluralism which, as we have seen, has itself come under severe attack in the United States of late. Wishing to avoid the ills that a centralized administrative system entails, the proponents of decentralization have neglected to consider the equally serious ailments that an administratively decentralized system brings with it. One system appears, in many ways, simplistically opposed to the other. The authors of *Pour nationaliser l'Etat* succumb to this temptation: "To the pluralist world of personal and commercial affairs, of lucrative activities, of the free, competitive market, of the freedom to undertake and to contract, is opposed the centralized and authoritarian hierarchical apparatus of the administration and of the public services with their rules and statutes and the discretionary action of officials."[16] For the proponents of decentralization in present-day France, its consequences entail more than the supposedly obvious advantages of efficiency; they entail a normative judgment concerning participation and democracy. The two are indissolubly linked: "As the example of the Scandinavian and Anglo-Saxon democracies has established, citizens' participation in their responsibilities is not only the breeding-ground of democracy but democracy itself, lived in its totality and reinforced in its foundations."[17] There is an unmistakable tendency on the part of those who wish to see a more decentralized France to idealize the degree of participation that is supposed to characterize the Anglo-Saxon political systems. One reason for this idealization is that political participation is often confused with the efficiency of the functionally decentralized American corporation, which is supposed to allow for diffused decision-making powers.[18]

At the outset of this study we pointed to the undeniable conflict that exists between what we called the *étatistes* and *décen-*

---

[16] C. Alphandery et al., *Pour nationaliser l'Etat* (Paris: Seuil, 1968), pp. 216–217.

[17] *Ibid.*, p. 223.

[18] See J.-J. Servan-Schreiber, *Le Pouvoir régional* (Paris: Grasset, 1971), pp. 68–69.

tralisateurs—one fearing the consequences of interest-group liberalism, the other seeing only the advantages to be derived from such a system. So long as the conflict continues to be seen in such a light, it will remain irreconcilable. It should be noted that the entrenchment of local interests, even under a centralized system, has tended to shift power into the hands of what have become fairly autonomous elites. We have seen this to be the case with regard to local politics and with regard to the power of certain corps.[19] And the studies to which we have referred show fairly clearly what the consequences of interest-group pluralism would be were such a system to be consciously adopted.

While in the United States, therefore, studies of interest groups and interest-group theories abound, in France there has been a dearth of such studies. This may not be so surprising, given the general lack of emphasis on empirical studies in French political science, and given the role of the State in France, where attention is more likely to be directed toward the omnipotence of the State, rather than toward the existence of multitudinous groups within it. Also, the study of groups in general has long been dominated by the works of sociologists, whose concern has focused more on the interpersonal relations of groups than on their political significance or impact.

Quite apart from the analysis of intragroup relations, there is, insofar as the political system is directly concerned, the crucial question of the extent to which groups impinge on political decisions. Here again there has been little fruitful research, although much has been written. Most of the available studies have centered on rather sensational cases—the alcohol lobby, the aid to parochial schools issue, and so on. Without denying the merits of these case studies, it should be noted that they pertain to single issues of major policy where energies are galvanized, on one side or the other, so that once the issue is settled these energies, involving as they do practically the entire society, are dispersed. But, more important, such studies are largely concerned with the outcomes of these particular issues. By way of illustration, we might mention an attempt by one author to answer the question

---

[19] See Pierre Grémion and Jean-Pierre Worms, *Les Institutions régionales et la société locale* (Paris: C.N.R.S., 1969); J.-P. Worms, "Le Préfet et ses notables," *Sociologie du Travail*, Special Number, VIII, no. 3 (1966); and E. Friedberg and J.-C. Thoenig, "Politique urbaines et stratégies corporatives," *Sociologie du Travail*, Special Number, XI, no. 4 (1969).

of whether pressure groups have exerted greater or less influence under the Fifth Republic than they did under the Fourth.[20] The author dwells on the well-known examples of the alcohol lobby, the army, and aid to parochial schools. He deals with each issue separately, detailing the various forces involved and the outcome. But this method of studying the role of interest groups is clearly not very satisfactory—it dwells solely on explosive issues and studies these issues only, to put it somewhat inelegantly, at the time that they explode. Consequently, we are afforded little insight into the role of pressure groups in the French political system, for there is no attempt to comprehend the complex mechanisms and relationships that generally play a role in the groups' attempts to influence decisions. The fact that most of the interest-group battles so far studied were ultimately solved in parliament indicates how unrepresentative they are of what is generally understood by "pressure-group politics," which entails a never-ending attempt by groups to influence the distribution of power. Similarly, in a study of the Fédération de l'Education Nationale, the author discusses the various factors involved in the FEN's attempts to influence decisions on its behalf. But he too concentrates on the dramatic battles concerning aid to parochial schools.[21] Once again, pressure-group politics is portrayed as taking place at one level—parliament—and as being limited to certain explosive issues which readily find solutions. More detailed studies have generally not been undertaken because, as in the case of the bureaucracy, there is a widespread belief that groups would not be willing to participate and cooperate in such studies. The result of this belief, which is only partially correct, is that studies of pressure groups in France have been designed either (as is the case with the useful works of Jean Meynaud) to formulate general hypotheses and make inventories of various types of groups,[22] or to draw generalizations about the role of interest groups in the French political system by reference to some spec-

20 Bernard E. Brown, "Pressure Politics in the Fifth Republic," *Journal of Politics*, xxv (August 1963).

21 James Clark, *Teachers and Politics in France: A Pressure Group Study of the Fédération de l'Education Nationale* (Syracuse: Syracuse University Press, 1967).

22 Jean Meynaud, *Les Groupes de pression* (Paris: Presses Universitaires de France, 1960), and *Nouvelles Etudes sur les groupes de pression en France* (Paris: Armand Colin, 1962).

tacular cases. Hitherto there have been few attempts to study the interaction of interest groups with the political system, which means principally the legislature, the political parties, and the bureaucracy. Ehrmann's fine book, *Organized Business in France*, deals only cursorily with the means by which organized business attempts to influence decisions.[23] In other words, there is as yet no study of the factors governing the relationship of interest groups to the political system in France that attempts to do what La Palombara did in his investigation of Italian interest groups.[24] This chapter will fill only a small part of this lacuna: it will examine the administrator's disposition toward groups and the relationships that ensue as a result.

ADMINISTRATORS AND INTEREST GROUPS

The importance of the bureaucracy in the decision-making process of modern societies has become almost axiomatic. It is true that "the growth of executive power, *de facto* rule-making power in the bureaucracy, growing complexity of rule-making, the emergence of delegated legislation, the burgeoning of welfare state activity, the needs of regulatory and developmental bureaucratic agencies . . . —all help us to understand why a bureaucracy cannot be adequately understood unless we take careful account of the role of interest groups in the bureaucratic process."[25] All these factors are as true of the United States, of Britain, of Italy, of France, and of a number of other countries. It becomes important, therefore, to study the ways in which interactions between interest groups and the bureaucracy differ from one country to another. In France the importance of the bureaucracy, insofar as interest groups are concerned, is probably greater than that of any other branch of governmental activity. While the role of the legislature, the executive, or the political parties may vary from one regime to another, that of the bureaucracy varies least. In France, even when the other political institutions are powerful, they use part of that power to represent interest groups vis-à-vis the bureaucracy. The bureaucracy's

[23] Henry Ehrmann, *Organized Business in France* (Princeton: Princeton University Press, 1957), pp. 219–271.

[24] Joseph La Palombara, *Interest Groups in Italian Politics* (Princeton: Princeton University Press, 1964), chaps. VII, VIII, and IX.

[25] *Ibid.*, p. 257.

323

crucial role derives from the wide *regulatory* powers that it exercises over a wide range of economic and social institutions. These regulatory powers involve more than the preparation of texts, decrees, ordinances, circulars; they involve the application of rules and regulations even when these are handed down in the form of laws passed by parliament (which are almost always initially drawn up by the bureaucracy). Given the paramount role that the bureaucracy plays with regard to interest groups, it appears somewhat curious that this institution figures only cursorily in works attempting to study the role of interest groups in a particular regime.[26] By contrast, we should like to explore still further the role of French higher civil servants by examining the elements that enter into their relationship with—to use a broad term—their clienteles.

If civil servants claim to be the guardians of the general interest, they should be as ill-disposed toward interest groups as they are toward deputies. Such groups, after all, represent the antithesis of the general interest—particularism, segmentalism, selfishness; they are perpetually in conflict with one another, and the civil servant sees himself as arbitrating these conflicts. At first glance, the civil servant is likely to show contempt for the "groupes de pression" and the lobbies. Like the deputy, he would like to have as little contact as possible with them. Table 12.1 indictates that contact between Directors and representatives

TABLE 12.1

Frequency of Directors' Meeting with Groups (percent)

Almost every day	25.9
Very often	44.4
From time to time	2.5
Rarely	8.6
Never	10.6
Total	100.0

26 The reason for this is that probably these works attempt to say more about the nature of the regime than about interest group behavior. The unfortunate consequence of this approach is that no specific patterns, motives, or mechanisms are deciphered. Also, this approach leans heavily on sensational cases and these offer only one kind of documentation, mostly that of newspapers of the day. For example, see Jean Meynaud, "Les Groupes de pression sous la Ve République," *Revue française de science politique,* XII, no. 3 (1962), 672–697.

of interest groups is by no means infrequent, but 34 percent of those Directors who did have contact with interest groups said that it was initiated sometimes by them and sometimes by the groups; the rest (two-thirds) said that any contact they had with interest groups was always the result of the groups' initiative.

The frequency of contacts between the Directors and interest groups gives only a very partial indication of the Directors' attitude or disposition toward groups seeking to influence the administration. In order to probe these attitudes the Directors were asked what they regarded to be the more important advantages and disadvantages of contacts between the administration and interest groups. The responses are shown in Tables 12.2 and 12.3.

TABLE 12.2
Advantages of Contact between
Administration and Interest Groups (percent)

	1st Choice	2nd Choice	3rd Choice	All Mentions as % of total Mentions
1. For the administration such contacts signify contact with the public	8.6	1.2	7.4	7.8
2. Decisions become more rational	1.2	16.0	3.7	9.4
3. Such contact leads to discussion between divers interests and thus facilitates the formulation and application of policy	33.3	19.8	9.9	28.2
4. Such contacts furnish indispensable information to the administration	8.6	14.8	9.9	14.9
5. Because of these contacts, the government is able to foresee opposition	6.2	17.3	22.2	20.3
6. These contacts are without advantage	–	–	–	–
7. Contacts are mostly to give groups information, to inform them of decisions, and to explain decisions[1]	18.6	2.5	1.2	10.0
8. Contacts are for reciprocal exchange of information.[1]	14.8	2.5	3.7	9.4
Total	–	–	–	100.0

[1] Categories not precoded.

325

Perhaps the most striking aspect of these tables is the fairly high rate of no response to the second and third choices, and the fact that the rate of no response is even higher for the first choice in Table 12.3. It was thought that both these questions, being fairly uncomplicated, might elicit straightforward answers. Instead they appeared to cause some bewilderment, which, it must be emphasized, cannot be ascribed to the closed nature of the questions. It will be seen shortly that the responses are as important for what they do not show as for what they do show. Also, the respondents' choices were not limited to the precoded categories: they were at liberty to add, as in fact they did, other advantages or disadvantages to contacts with interest groups. The added categories were carefully noted during the interviews and were later coded. In fact, there may be good reason to assign greater importance to factors spontaneously added by the re-

TABLE 12.3

Disadvantages of Contact between
Administration and Interest Groups (percent)

	1st Choice	2nd Choice	3rd Choice	All Mentions as % of Total Mentions
1. These contacts encourage groups to apply too much pressure on the administration	3.7	3.7	1.2	8.4
2. Constant pressure prevents the administration from making the correct decision	17.3	4.9	3.7	25.0
3. The administration becomes too dependent on interest groups	1.2	7.4	1.2	9.5
4. These contacts encourage every group to demand equal time	7.4	8.6	3.7	19.0
5. These contacts can lead to the corruption of the administration	—	—	1.2	1.2
6. These contacts tend to favor certain groups over others	2.5	6.2	2.5	10.7
7. Information leaks that lead to the mobilization of opponents of administration programs	12.3	9.9	4.9	26.2
Total	—	—	—	100.0

spondents than to those which appear to circumscribe his choice. This does not, of course, mean that one should ascribe little importance to the choices contained in a "closed" question, since a respondent was always free to choose from the list and to add to it, or to discard the list entirely (which a few did) and offer his own categories.

Table 12.2 shows that contacts with interest groups, to the extent that they are regarded as advantageous, are important because they facilitate the formulation and application of policy. Actually, here the Directors tended to put greater stress on "application" than on "formulation."[27] Contacts are also important because they enable the administration to explain its point of view and to convince the groups of the importance of decisions already taken. If the groups do affect decisions taken by administrators, this is likely to be the result, not of a compromise worked out between the administration and the groups, but of the government's awareness of the intensity of opposition to a particular program—one of the more important reasons that Directors considered contacts with interest groups advantageous. Equally important, contacts with interest groups are advantageous because they permit the administration to give information (i.e., explain decisions taken, persuade the groups of the importance of certain decisions) or receive information. What emerges from Table 12.2 is that for the civil servants contacts with interest groups are important more for the communication of policies than for anything to do with the actual substance of these policies.

The responses to the question concerning the disadvantages of contacts with interest groups were even more revealing. The initial reaction of the respondents was to deny outright that there were any disadvantages, since this appeared, in their eyes, to cast doubt on the moral strength of the administration. This is evident in the high rate of no response, particularly to the second and third choices. Again it must be emphasized that this was not because of the "closed" nature of the question. Quite revealing in this respect was the fact that the question itself contained implications that appeared slightly offensive. It implied that the ad-

[27] Unfortunately, no separation was made between "application" and "formulation" in the question. That contacts with groups were considered more important for the application than for the formulation of policy is fairly clear both from the stress that the Directors put on the former and from the responses to the question.

ministration could be diverted from pursuing the "right" policy, that it succumbed easily to diverse pressures, that it was not obedient to the wishes of the government, that its ethics were open to question, and that it did not even have the power and authority to distinguish between "legitimate" and "illegitimate" groups and demands. So great at times was the sensitivity to this question that at various points in the course of the survey, I considered dropping it altogether. The general cooperation and openness of the Directors interviewed made this unnecessary, however, and an attempt was made to take full account of their views. What no doubt rendered the question more palatable and less offensive-sounding was my attempt to phrase it in an impersonal and general manner, thus avoiding any hint that I was after specific experiences of the Director with interest groups. I sought, above all, to dispel the impression that the question itself carried a moral judgment on the administration. Table 12.3 shows clearly how strong is the fear of the administration regarding its ability to act on the information which it alone possesses, unhampered by the claims of these groups on its time.

The reluctance to answer this question is more than compensated for by the answers that the Directors did choose to give. These were later coded and are presented in Table 12.4. Almost two-thirds of the Directors considered that there were no disadvantages—or, to put it more accurately, no fear—in the administration having contacts with interest groups.

TABLE 12.4
Significance of Disadvantages of Contacts with Groups (percent)

1. Time wasted	13.6
2. None of the disadvantages listed in Table 12.3	6.2
3. No disadvantages, because administration chooses the groups it wants to have contact with	9.9
4. No disadvantages, because the purpose of contacts is to explain *faits accompli*	27.2

The Directors stressed that interest groups did not have the strength to cause any of the things suggested by the list of disadvantages that was handed to them. For the Directors this was a question of strength, and it was observed that "the administration is stronger and is able to resist the pressures of groups." To suggest, therefore, that there were certain disadvantages in the administration's contacts with interest groups was to imply that the administration was weak, and that it acted on the desires of some groups against its better judgment. Moreover, the Directors were particularly sensitive to the suggestion that a possible disadvantage of contacts with interest groups might be corruption of the administration. The immediate reaction to this was: "the administration cannot be corrupted," or "this I can say with absolute assurance, there is absolutely no corruption in the French administration." Corruption, it was sometimes suggested by the Directors, was confined to the politicians and to the bureaucracies of underdeveloped countries and of the United States.

Interest (or pressure) groups exist to defend and to champion their interests by means of pressure on the administration. The administration, on the other hand, must resist pressure coming from those who seek particularistic aims. Just as the administration manifests a scarcely disguised antipathy toward the deputy, because of his ability to embroil it in "politics" and his tireless devotion to the petty problems of his constituents, so it sees interest groups as also attempting to embroil the administration in conflicts that revolve around particularistic demands. More important, perhaps, is the fact that conflicts among various interest groups mean, for the administration, that it will be subjected to constant pressures. Therefore its primary task with regard to such groups is to resist them and their pressures. This attitude was clearly expressed by the Directors:

> The administration has to resist pressure from groups, if it's worth its salt.

> It's only the politicians—the minister, the cabinet—that are susceptible to pressures. The Directors do not let themselves be impressed by pressures from groups.

> They [the groups] try to influence politicians rather than us; it's easier.

> It's a question of the quality of the civil servants. The administration isn't at all obliged to accept pressure.

> It all depends on the administration. If it is founded on strong, *sérieux* people, there are no disadvantages to having

contacts with interest groups. If, however, the administration is more fragile, it will not be able to resist and will succumb to pressures.

The Directors do not consider contact with interest groups as being indispensable, or even important, in aiding them to fulfill their tasks. They would just as soon prefer to do without these contacts. From a glance at Tables 12.2, 12.4 and 12.5, it is possible to see more clearly that the Directors of the central administration regard contact with interest groups as more of a burden than a help in allowing them to arrive at decisions. They indicated that after June 1968 the administration had become, at the behest

TABLE 12.5

Utility of Interest Group Demands
for Decision-Making, According to Directors (percent)

Useful	13.6
Useful, even if exaggerated	29.6
Not usually useful	36.0
Not always useless	6.2
Don't know	14.6
Total	100.0

of the government, more open and receptive to groups. In general, these orders were complied with, although not always appreciated. As one Director in the Ministry of Agriculture noted, "If it were just a question of consulting, asking for opinions, that would be fine. But it has gotten to a point where it has become a permanent dialogue. And this starts from the formulation of a law and goes on all the way after the law has been passed. They [the interest groups] make it extremely hard for us to work. As for me, I'm now trying to cut contact with groups to a minimum." Once the euphoric atmosphere of the May–June 1968 uprisings had subsided, many Directors took the view that things ought to go back to normal, which meant "consulting and asking for opinions"—a privilege granted rather than an obligation forced on the administration.

It is interesting to note that, at least in the view of the Directors, interest groups seek to influence decisions at various different levels of the politico-administrative hierarchy (Table 12.6). The fact that the minister himself and his cabinet, according to the Directors, are the most popular targets for interest-group intervention undoubtedly reflects the increasing concentration of power in the hands of the cabinet. This is also true, as we noted, in the case of the deputy, who now confines his contacts to the minister and his cabinet. But Table 12.6 may also reflect the sudden openness to groups of the entire administration, after the May–June uprisings. Above all, however, it shows, as will be seen, that it is those groups which lack a permanent contact within the administration that attempt to influence *particular* policies

TABLE 12.6
*Channels Used by Interest Groups
to Influence Policy, According to Directors (percent)*

The minister	29.6
The ministerial cabinet	28.4
The Directors	15.8
Whoever has most weight in particular decision	14.8
Depends on the group	9.9
Don't know	1.5
Total	100.0

by seeking different targets. The groups which have established close relationships with the administration do not disperse their efforts between the administration proper and the ministerial cabinet; moreover, these are not the groups that burst suddenly on the scene to defend or to oppose a particular policy—the type on which attention has so far been focused in the study of French interest groups. On the contrary, for these groups pressure for or against particular policies is a constant and never-ending process. They are engaged, not in a fight to secure a once-and-for-all gain, but in a continuing attempt to affect the allocation of resources—or the distribution of power—in their favor.

Nevertheless, even the groups who seek the aid of the minister or of his cabinet are often referred to the Directors. In effect, it is the Directors who continue to be responsible for the majority of contacts with interest groups. This is not the case with the deputy, whose contacts with the minister or with his cabinet often, at least in relatively uncomplicated cases, suffice to insure that his requests are fulfilled. But where the demands of interest groups are complex, involving the reorientation of government policy and transcending the powers of a single ministry, the role of the cabinet becomes crucial. This is because the cabinet is responsible for coordination, and because the interministerial communication system passes through the cabinets and involves the Directors only peripherally. Diagram 12.1 shows a slightly simplified outline of the position of the Directors in the governmental system. It shows not only that all extraministerial activities (or communications) are the responsibility of the cabinet, but that the Directors communicate only to the cabinet of their own minister and not to other cabinets.

Diagram 12.1
Intragovernmental Communications

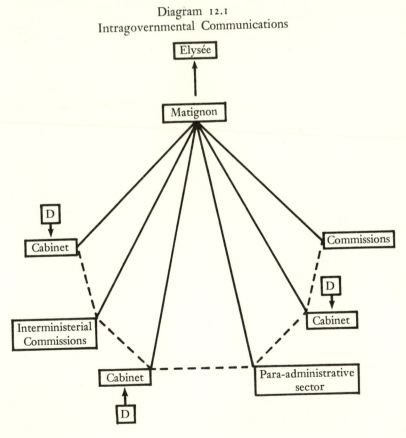

While the diagram appears to show only a small role for the Directors in the intergovernmental communications system, it is important not to minimize their ability to exert influence. Their proposals are often modified or altered by the cabinet, but theirs is the primary responsibility for drawing up decrees, laws, and texts pertaining to all sorts of regulations. It is also the Directors who control and supervise the applications of laws and decrees and regulations. Table 12.7 shows the Directors' inclination to

TABLE 12.7

Frequency of Directors' Consultation with Groups in Preparation of Laws, Decrees, and Reforms (percent)

Often	51.9
From time to time	19.8
Rarely	15.1
Other	14.2
Total	100.0

seek the advice or opinions of interest groups in the preparation of reforms, laws, and decrees. By itself, however, it tells us little: in fact, it even appears to contradict the data presented in Tables 12.2 and 12.3. This is largely because consultation can mean many things and take many different forms—above all, it has many different purposes. The most general view, and one strongly supported by the data presented thus far, is that consultation takes place so that the administration can explain its decisions to the groups affected by them. This view was expressed by Directors in almost all the ministries.

The contact with groups is mostly to inform them, to explain to them. It's true that they can't influence policy.
—Director in Ministry of Industry

Consult by all means, but decisions must come from the *patron.*
—Director in Ministry of P.T.T.

My job is to explain and to inform. I don't think that interest groups contribute anything really constructive. Contacts with them are necessary. But I think I can say that we always manage to have our view prevail. We have to have these contacts to inform the people, to explain to them our intentions.

—Director in Ministry of Equipment and Housing

We always consult. It doesn't mean we listen, but we consult. We don't always reveal our intentions. We reveal only as much as we think it is necessary to reveal.

—Director in Ministry of Education

The Directors thus see interest groups as attempting constantly to harass the administration in order to procure gains for a small minority at the expense of the majority. As such, they cannot be regarded as having much to contribute either to the national good or to the work of the administration. The attempt of one group to outbid the other—"the auctioneering aspect of their demands," as it was put by several Directors—was frequently cited as proof that consultation with interest groups was not a really worthwhile activity. It was, however, a necessary one because it gave the administration the important opportunity of presenting its case, or the *fait accompli*. As one Director in the Ministry of Finance put it: "The one real advantage of contact with interest groups is that it allows the administration to prove its good faith, and gives it a chance to convince. This is a truly political job."

If the task of convincing is a "political job," then it is political in a very special sense: for the Directors to convince interest groups of the validity of what has, in effect, become a *fait accompli* undoubtedly calls for a certain degree of political acumen. An equally plausible manner of looking at this particular function of the Directors is to see it as less "political" and more, perhaps, authoritarian, eschewing the compromises that necessarily take place in any consultative process. But perhaps the line of what is and what is not political is too thin here, since in the very process of consultation Directors must appear, at least, to be making compromises. To carry out this political task, the Directors feel it necessary to invoke the general interest and place less stress on the apolitical nature of their work. In many respects, as was noted earlier, the Directors' task is very much akin to that of the prefect. As the representative of the central government in the provinces, the prefect might be thought to be particularly prone to exhibiting an authoritarian disposition, yet he is especially sensitive to the "political game" and remarkably adept at reconciliation. This goes a long way toward explaining why ministers have come to prize the cooperation of prefects. The Directors are not as devoted to reconciliation and compromises as are the prefects, and they tend to be more categorical in their belief that consultation with interest groups is merely a form to be observed.[28]

The higher civil servants' attitude toward interest groups in general may have a good deal to do with their relationship to civil service unions. Protected by the *Statut des Fonctionnaires* and imposing a severe restriction on the Directors' power to hire and fire, reward and punish civil servants, the unions have become a force to be reckoned with daily. And the fact that civil servants belong to the three major unions (FO, CGT, and CFTC) complicates negotiations and raises problems concerning representation on the *commissions paritaires*. Still a third factor that tends to increase tension between the Directors and the unions is that in a number of cases the unions deal directly with particular *directions*, not with a central office in the ministry. From their experiences with civil service unions is born, to some extent, the Directors' view of interest groups: divided, divisive, obstructive, and a hindrance to the autonomy of the administration. Almost every Director was found to be sharply critical of the guarantees provided by the *Statut des Fonctionnaires*. The administrator's experience with civil service unions also helps to explain his penchant for secrecy and his constant fear (Table 12.3) of information leaks.

The preparation of texts, whether laws, reforms, or decrees, is a process that starts within a tightly-knit group in an atmosphere of total secrecy. The secrecy is lifted very gradually, as those in the unit solicit the adhesion of other interested groups within the ministry. The next step is to seek the agreement of those concerned in other ministries. At the outset, all those not directly involved in the initial preparation are treated as more or less hostile "interest groups," until finally the text is agreed on by the administration. It is only then that the interest groups are approached and "consulted." "To observe complete secrecy is abso-

---

[28] Adhesion to democratic "forms" is important in all democratic societies. As Truman notes with regard to interest groups in the United States: "Open hearings satisfied the forms of the democratic 'rules of the game' even when they did not immediately grant the benefits of real access." See his *The Governmental Process*, p. 373.

lutely essential," explained one Director, "because otherwise there will be opposition over every provision and the text will never get drawn up." This method of arriving at decisions within the administration appears to be a rather general practice, and perhaps derives from the conflicts within the administration itself. That is why each group, in seeking to insure that its own point of view prevails in any final decision, looks at other groups within the administration as suspiciously as it looks at the interest groups. A number of Directors described their method of drawing up texts and their general attitude toward consulting interest groups thus:

> We ask for their [the interest groups'] advice only *after* we have a completely prepared text. And we do this just to make sure that we haven't made some colossal error.
> —Director in Ministry of Equipment and Housing

> First, we make out a report or draw up a text, then we pass it around discreetly within the administration. Once everyone concerned within the administration is agreed on the final version, then we pass this version around outside the administration. Of course, by then it's a *fait accompli* and pressure cannot have any effect.
> —Director in Ministry of Industry

> Interest groups never prevent our view from getting through. Often it's enough to say, "Look, we consulted you." The consultation has nothing to do with following their advice. It's simply a question of form to consult them.
> —Director in Ministry of Education

The administration has been able to adopt these attitudes and procedures because its relationship with interest groups is not one of contending equals. Because of the pervasive role of the State in the economic and social life of the country and because of the diversity and fragmentation of the interest groups, the groups are seen as being at once in conflict with one another and in conflict with the State. Indeed, there is scarcely a conflict, whether it is between the State and its employees or between management and workers in the private sector, that does not in some direct way involve the administration. The administration thus comes to see itself as an arbitrator, and one that must go unchallenged if major social conflicts are to be resolved.

336

LEGITIMATE AND ILLEGITIMATE GROUPS

Thus far, I have tried to show the general attitudes of French higher civil servants toward interest groups: such groups are not looked upon favorably but they are certainly tolerated and consulted, although in a rather special manner. This is because, as was noted, the administration has a number of defense mechanisms at hand. It protects itself by presenting the interest groups with *faits accompli*, or it takes it upon itself to decide which groups it will consult, listen to, or go to for advice. While the administration is theoretically equally open to all interest groups, in practice very careful distinctions are made among them. Nor is this peculiar to French civil servants. One of the respondents in La Palombara's study of Italian interest groups observed, in much the same manner as his French counterparts, "I know of no policy within the Ministry of Industry and Commerce that says that there are certain groups in Italian society whose representatives will not be at least received. It is true that once this has been done we will assign different importance or give varying weight to the proposals made by such groups, but they are free to approach us."[29] On what basis do French higher civil servants make their distinctions between groups?

The term interest group or pressure group—*groupe d'intérêt* or *groupe de pression*—has very specific connotations for the higher civil servants. Such a group is not representative, seeks limited and selfish ends for its members and, by implication, is of highly questionable legitimacy. This type of group is known, with extreme pejorative connotations, as a "lobby," and it is distinguished from professional organizations. An associational or professional organization represents something totally different to the civil servants, who do not consider such organizations as interest groups or lobbies. Such a distinction, which was of course nowhere suggested in the questionnaire, seemed at first quite odd and, to say the least, illogical. But it was repeated so often and in so many ministries that it was decided to examine it and its implications further. "We have no contact with interest groups here. We only have contact with professional organizations," said a Ministry of Justice Director categorically. One of the most influential Directors in the Ministry of Finance stated,

[29] La Palombara, *Interest Groups in Italian Politics*, p. 265.

in answer to a question about contact with interest groups: "One has to make a distinction between interest groups and professional organizations. An interest group—that is, a lobby—is one that defends its specific interests. A professional organization is one that defends not a private interest but a group interest." Another Director, in the Ministry of Equipment and Housing, said: "an interest group or a pressure group has very limited interests, whereas professional organizations represent the interests of a whole profession." One Director who also made this distinction provided some examples: the Chamber of Commerce and the Union of Textile Industries were professional organizations, whereas the PME (the organization of small and medium-sized enterprises) was a lobby. It was pointed out to the Director that the PME also represented a "profession" or a collective group and sought ends for the entire group, much like the unions of mechanical or textile industries, or the organizations of magistrates or notaries. Nevertheless, the Director maintained there *was* a distinction between the two types of groups.

Perhaps the distinction between interest groups and professional organizations makes little concession to logic, but it reveals an undeniable bias in favor of strong, representative organizations. This bias is premised on the administration's choice of groups that *it* considers representative, which in turn affects the type of relationship established between the administration and the favored groups, as well as the latter's method or style of intervention. It was the same Director who made the distinction between the Union of Textile Industries and the PME who noted, in another context: "We've decided to have close contact with *dynamic* groups. The others try to oblige us to take Malthusian decisions. It's obvious for example that certain unions defend the large number of unproductive shopkeepers and not the few productive and dynamic ones. We must not therefore be forced to become intoxicated by the non-dynamic groups. This is what the administration has to guard against." Every administration decides for itself which groups it will have close contact with and which groups will receive less than equal treatment. But what distinguishes "dynamic" from "Malthusian" groups? In the instance in which these terms were used they clearly had an economic connotation. The dynamic groups are those whose economic strength is such that they cannot be ignored. More important, they are considered legitimate because their demands accord with government policy. The Malthusian groups, on the other hand, as the Director in the Ministry of Finance noted, are those whose demands run counter to government policy. Not surprisingly, this Director cited PME several times as an example of a group that constantly attempted to put pressure on the government to take wrong decisions—i.e., to support them in their fight against large-scale business enterprises.

Directors often commented that the major problem with regard to the administration's relations with interest groups was the groups' relative unrepresentativity. "It is hard to negotiate with a group when you don't know how many members it represents," said one Director. It was frequently noted that the fragmentation of interest groups was a decisive factor in their unequal (or inferior) relationship to the administration. This appears to be more than mere rationalization of the administration's own preferences, for the fact that the professional organizations enjoy a far closer relationship with the administration than do other groups has much to do with the relative representativity of and ideological cohesion within these organizations. The previously cited study of Italian interest groups observes, for example, that unions in Italy do not enjoy the same type of favored relationship with the Ministry of Labor and Social Security that Confidustria (the equivalent of the CNPF) has established with the Ministry of Industry and Commerce. To a very great extent, this is owing to the ideological and organizational fragmentation of the unions.[30] In France this is very largely the case also: as one might expect, the industrial organizations are more cohesively organized, can be found to agree on the larger economic issues, and are able to constitute a countervailing power to the administration. By the same token, all this makes the better-organized groups important elements in administrative conflicts, for their power can be marshaled on behalf of one administration against another. This appears, at first glance, to contradict the American pattern in which, as Mancur Olson has very convincingly argued, "small groups will further their common interests better than large groups."[31] But this contradiction is more apparent than real, as will be seen below, because the large associations with which the administration prefers to do business are usually rep-

[30] *Ibid.*, p. 274.
[31] Mancur Olson, *The Logic of Collective Action* (New York: Schocken Books, 1969), p. 52. See also pp. 22–35 and chap. II.

resented, or controlled, by a few dominant firms. These groups thus come to enjoy the advantages of the small groups described by Olson as well as the advantages of large-scale representation, with all the power that this implies.

THE ADMINISTRATION AND LEGITIMATE GROUPS

In the case of the so-called professional organizations there develops a close relationship with a particular administration which becomes reciprocal—each side becomes dependent on the other. Such relationships have generally been referred to in the literature on interest groups as "clientele" relationships. They are generally associated with the practice of cooptation, and there is something to be said for McConnell's assertion that the cautious language of scholars—"clientele relationships" or "clientalism"— "not only confers an aura of professional respectability on the participants in these relationships; it also obscures the fact that they are power relationships and misses the most important facts about them."[32] Perhaps one of the more important facts—and one, it might be added, of the most ignored—is that in a close relationship between the supervisor and the supervised, both sides stand to gain. Cooptation does not work to the advantage of one side, a point that is implicit in Selznick's *T.V.A. and the Grass Roots*,[33] probably the most influential study on the significance of cooptation.

What are the particular aspects of a clientele type relationship and what do they imply insofar as the political process is concerned? In the first place, such relationships exist in administrative agencies organized along vertical lines. Rather than regulating the industries for which they have direct responsibility, these agencies or *directions*, it is often argued, become the spokesmen or lawyers for the industries. Moreover, the private groups that have such privileged relationships with the administration are generally well equipped and well organized, and they are able to provide a good deal of information that is useful, and often indispensable, to the agency. Another basis for the affinity between such groups and administrative agencies is style and working methods: both prefer the secret, informal, and quiet type of deal-

[32] McConnell, *Private Power and American Democracy*, p. 339.
[33] New York: Harper Torchbooks, 1966.

ings to flamboyant and open pressures. Flamboyant tactics may be used occasionally by these groups, but they are used consciously, deliberately, and with the accord of the administrative agency.

With this in mind, it becomes easier to understand the apparently specious distinction between professional organizations and interest groups. The former render as much service to the agency as they receive from it. The latter are seen purely as *demandeurs*, who seek to attain their goals by spectacular means. Since the interest groups are regarded as poorly organized, fragmented, and unrepresentative, they can neither provide the administration with indispensable information, nor can they represent a particular administration in its battles with another administration. As Henry Ehrmann noted some years ago, "In France, as elsewhere, civil servants prefer to deal with large-scale interests or organizations. When faced with their demands most government officials, sometimes precipitately, assume that a satisfactory aggregation of claims has already taken place within the group."[34] But how does the clientele relationship work in practice?

Despite the centralized system of administration in France, there nevertheless exists a multiplicity of what may be called decision centers cutting across the entire administration. Various attempts to group or coordinate some of these loci of decisions by means of horizontal agencies have not proved particularly successful, owing to the autonomy of each decision center. An important such attempt was the creation of the *direction de la politique industrielle* in the Ministry of Industry (now the Ministry of Industrial Development and Scientific Research). The ostensible function of this *direction*, which has now been abolished, was to obtain information in order to analyze, synthesize, and coordinate industrial policy. It was purposely created in the Ministry of Industry because of the vertical and compartmentalized nature of the *directions* in this ministry, because the minister (Olivier Guichard) did not want industrial policy formulation to become the monopoly of the Ministry of Finance, and because the Ministry of Industry had long been in search of a role. But the *direction de la politique industrielle* met with hostility from the other *directions* in the Ministry from the start, not only

[34] Henry Ehrmann, "French Bureaucracy and Organized Interests," *Administrative Science Quarterly*, IV (1961), 547.

because this *direction* was headed by an Inspecteur des Finances but also because the other Directors would not accept any attempt to centralize information. This would have impinged on their autonomy.

The failure of this horizontal *direction* must be seen in the light of the strength of the vertical *directions*, which control a remarkable network of contacts within and outside the administration. The horizontal *direction* could not penetrate this network, could not obtain the information needed for the synthesis of industrial policy, and could not create its own rival network. We have already touched on how some of these networks are created. One Director in the Ministry of Industrial Development explained the strategy of the preservation of the network which, he said, was absolutely indispensable for his work. In the first place, because of the particular position he occupies, this Director has more money at his disposal than do most other *directions*, and this gives him a good deal of liberty. It enables him to train his protégés for specific posts, to have them serve apprenticeships (*stages*) either in France or abroad, and to send them for further study wherever the best training is provided. After this, these young technicians—"my commandos," as the Director called them—are placed in key posts throughout the administration and in the private sector. The purpose of this very carefully planned recruitment and training of the young technicians is to insure that the *direction* can put its hand on all necessary information with a minimum of delay, so as to make its full weight felt in the various decision centers. "Whenever something happens or is about to happen," explained this Director, "I must be able to obtain within minutes all the information. This enables me to react very quickly. Because the training I give to our young recruits is not haphazardly chosen, each one is prepared to undertake a very specific function. The result: there is hardly an important institution inside or outside the administration where I don't have someone representing me."

This network is composed, for the most part, of members of the *corps des mines* and is based on an informal communications system. The informality of relations is discriminatory in that it clearly favors certain groups, or certain firms, over others. This point has also been made with regard to the United States. "To consider formality desirable is perhaps alien to the pragmatism of which Americans boast. Yet formality is a means of limitation and implies a set of bounds upon the possible. It curbs the whimsical and stays the hand of arbitrary action."[35] One Director in the Ministry of Industrial Development noted that although official meetings between the administration and interest groups were increasing, this was not where things really got done. "It's the *officieux* contacts that really count," he observed.

The relations between the vertical *directions* and the industries with which they are daily in contact are characterized by this informal network—the hallmark of the power and influence of these *directions*. The presence of members of the *corps des mines* in these industries, as well as in various sectors of the administration, means that the *direction* itself is able to mobilize the force of the industry in order to exert pressure on its own minister and particularly on the Ministry of Finance. The clientele type of relationship is thus based on an informal system of communication and works to the benefit of both sides.

The vehement attacks by civil servants in the Ministry of Industrial Development on the Ministry of Finance are typical of attacks directed at this ministry by civil servants in all other ministries. The Ministry of Finance is seen as an evil institution, by the civil servants in the Ministry of Industrial Development, because of its control over the financial and economic affairs of the nation. Moreover, the Ministry of Finance, by virtue of its predominant role in setting economic policy, has deprived the Ministry of Industrial Development of any real powers insofar as interventions in the economy are concerned. In the aftermath of World War II the Ministry of Industrial Development enjoyed an influential position because of the various powers with which it was endowed in an economy racked by shortages and rationing, and requiring the urgent allocation of funds to particular sectors. As a result of its means of intervention and its powers to allocate funds, it played a preponderant role in the economy. Today, all that has changed. The ministry no longer has means of intervention by which it can affect the economy. One Director in this ministry went so far as to comment: "because of our lack of real power, which means, really, lack of money, we need the industries more than they need us." The Ministry of Industrial Development, according to the Directors, needs intervention funds, for without these funds the ministry's role remains vague and uncertain. The Directors readily recognized that the original functions of the

[35] McConnell, *Private Power and American Democracy*, p. 361.

343

ministry have long since been superseded, so that in the formulation of industrial policy today the ministry plays only a minimal part. Its main role now appears to be to preserve the close ties it has come to have with the industries it was ostensibly set up to regulate. In a study of one *direction* of a technical ministry (called "X"), Lautman and Thoenig have shown the significance of the external relations of an agency in achieving its goals. They conclude: "The chief assets of an administration are dependent on its system of relations with the environment. X, whose coercive power is by definition limited, cannot restore its position within the administration except by the support of groups under its tutelage and by the effectiveness of the action of its regional services. This in turn would imply, in the last analysis, a modification in the role of the central administration . . . which might establish more fruitful exchanges with its interlocutors both in the private sector and in its local *directions*."[36]

The main purpose of the network that is now established between certain of the *directions* and the industries is to champion the cause of the latter, who reciprocate by supporting their "regulatory agency." In the domains of fuel, petroleum, and chemicals the industries are few and large, so that there is little hope for firms not included in the network to receive equal treatment. To the extent, then, that relations between the *directions* and the industries are dependent on a network of informal relations among members of the *corps des mines*, it follows that the more important firms are also the most favored. Certain of the industries are ideally suited for the close relationships described above. Insofar as chemicals are concerned, for example, it has been noted by two students of French industrial planning that the "key parts of the industry are more a club than contestants in a competitive arena."[37] But where the industries were not as concentrated, as in the case of chemicals, the aim of the Ministry of Industrial Development has been to see to it that these industries do not remain so dispersed. With regard to the mechanical industry, for example, McArthur and Scott note that "the basic idea here [Ministry of Industry], as elsewhere, was that the

[36] Jacques Lautman and Jean-Claude Thoenig, "Conflits internes et unité d'action: le cas d'une administration centrale," *Sociologie du Travail*, Special Number, VIII, no. 3 (1966), 309.

[37] John H. McArthur and Bruce R. Scott, *Industrial Planning in France* (Boston: Harvard Graduate School of Business Administration, 1969), p. 379.

structure of these industries would have to become more concentrated."[38]

This indicates that the relationship between the vertical *direction* and an industry is confined either to a few oligopolistic firms or to a professional organization or association dominated by such firms.[39] My interviews with the Directors in the Ministry of Industrial Development tended to confirm this, as do McArthur and Scott. These authors observed in their detailed study of the State's intervention in key sectors of the economy that the industries involved could be divided into three categories: (a) where State influence was high; (b) where State influence was moderate; and (c) where State influence was low. The State was found to have little or no influence with regard to two types of industries or firms. The first was the group of small firms. "In general, these firms knew relatively little about the shape and direction of national policy, and they expressed considerable frustration concerning their contacts with the State." The attitude of the State officials toward these companies is extremely revealing:

> For their part, the Government officials we met viewed small businesses and businessmen in stereotyped and unsympathetic terms. Indeed, the role, competence, motives, and contribution of small businessmen was often regarded with considerable contempt and suspicion. Even the contributions made by the professional managers of some of the largest companies were sometimes called in question by Government and administration people. It was not uncommon for us to encounter strong value judgments in official circles about the relative social roles. Even so, there was an important difference in attitudes toward large and small businessmen.[40]

The second group of companies that the State appeared to have little interest in "comprised companies in certain industries that seemed to be regarded as falling outside the pale of twentieth-century respectability."[41] The two most important examples were textiles and food, neither of which are characterized by large-

---

[38] *Ibid.*, p. 384.

[39] Ehrmann quotes one Director as saying, "I am in touch with seven or eight persons; through them I reach 29,000 firms which employ a total of one million people." *Organized Business in France*, p. 261.

[40] McArthur and Scott, *Industrial Planning in France*, p. 391.

[41] *Ibid.*, p. 391.

scale firms; they do not have strong organizations, are internally divided, and do not attract the type of skilled management that would gain them entry into the official network.[42]

It seems clear, then, that while the administration evinces a general disdain for interest groups, this does not mean that it is equally disdainful of all groups. It has certain criteria for defining what constitutes a legitimate group or an illegitimate group. Once having defined for itself those groups which it considers legitimate, it proceeds to act upon this definition to the exclusion of other groups whose demands do not receive a hearing. Indeed, again in the case of the Ministry of Industry, those groups who do not fall within the boundaries of respectability and legitimacy *cannot* receive the attention that may be their due. In order to conserve their close ties with the more important firms, in order to offer prestigious and lucrative careers to their recruits, and in order to insure the maintenance of a network within and outside the administration, the Directors in this ministry prefer to deal "man to man"; they prefer to conserve a closely guarded relationship between themselves and the heads of a few firms. I have dwelt, to be sure, on a nearly perfect case of this type of relationship. But to a greater or lesser extent such relationships can probably be found in other ministries.

PRIVATE INTERESTS AND THE GENERAL INTEREST

The type of relationship that I have described between the administration and the *administrés* undoubtedly has the advantage of enabling groups to operate within a framework acceptable to both parties. The groups tend to become more responsible in their demands and more sensitive to the capabilities and limitations of the administration. But this particular form of cooperation also carries with it some serious disadvantages. In the first place, it is highly inegalitarian since it favors the more advantaged group. And because of the emphasis on informal communications, other groups are more or less permanently left out of the network. Second, this type of relationship cannot bode well for overall and long-range planning because, while the information gathered by the *directions* is important and accurate, it is not made available to those who are actually responsible for plan-

[42] See *ibid.*, pp. 392–401.

ning.[43] This is particularly the case with regard to the important *directions* in the Ministry of Industrial Development and their relationship to the agencies responsible for industrial planning. At best, only partial information is made available to other administrative agencies, which may merely serve to distort the planning process. In speaking of his relationship with the minister's cabinet, for example, one Director in the Ministry of Industrial Development noted that he made sure of having his "contact" in the cabinet, and that the cabinet did not have and could not obtain the information that he possessed. "Presenting a project to the cabinet is one thing. You have to know how to do it in such a way that your own plans will not be interfered with," he observed.

Nor is the Ministry of Finance unaware of the profound reluctance of the ministries to hand over important information. It sees, not without justification, although perhaps in an exaggerated manner, the administration as engaged in collusion with certain social and economic groups. One official in the ministry stated that the real function of the Ministry of Finance "is not to have ideas. It is to oppose ideas." He went on to explain that the Ministry of Finance considers the other ministries as spokesmen for particular groups, and it comes to regard conflicts in French society as adequately represented in or reflected by the conflicts among the various ministries. That all social conflicts somehow translate themselves into administrative conflicts may appear to be a startling assertion. But when it is remembered that in this ministry are to be found the Treasury, the Budget Bureau, the Internal Revenue Service, the Comptroller's Office, Customs and Excise, the Office of Price Control, the Foreign Trade Office, and a service for the management of the public debt, it becomes somewhat easier to understand why the administrative system revolves around this ministry and why constant pressure, from the administration and the private sector, is brought to bear on its officials. Also, as was noted earlier, certain sectors of the administration and the private sector collaborate to put greater pressure on this ministry so as to achieve a specific goal. One Director in the Ministry of Finance noted that "some civil servants allow themselves to become lawyers for groups." Another Direc-

[43] Groupe de Sociologie des Organisations, *Le Ministère de l'Industrie et son environnement*, mimeo. (Paris, 1970), p. 51.

347

tor in the ministry stated that "when there is a particularly close contact between the administration and groups, there is usually a tendency to use these groups to oblige a minister to accept a program that the Directors want to get through."

A third evident disadvantage inherent in the close relationship between the administration and certain interest groups is the blurring of the distinction between the public and the private. Even in a centralized system, theoretically given to drawing un-equivocal lines of demarcation between public and private do-mains, symbiotic relationships develop between the two domains. To confuse private and public needs is not a characteristic mere-ly, as McConnell suggests, of decentralized administrative sys-tems. It may also be found in centralized systems. It may be that the multiplicity of decision-making centers—or what has been described as the "authoritarian anarchy"—of the French admin-istration ultimately serves to prevent the creation of what Mc-Connell has called "narrow-interest-centered power structures."[44] But in order to reach any of these decision centers it is necessary, as we have seen, to be endowed with considerable advantages. It is true that in a system with a decentralized administrative structure the decision centers are grouped (or decentralized) at a level that puts them in close touch with groups seeking major benefits from them. But in such a system it is theoretically possi-ble for a group—one not blessed with all the advantages neces-sary to make its weight felt—to attempt to direct its attention to-ward other decision centers. This is less likely to be the case in a centralized system such as exists in France because, unless a group already has a close relationship with a particular adminis-tration, it will not find a representative for its cause within the administration. Consequently, for the groups that are closely linked to an administration, the goals of the one become confused with the other, thus assuring such groups strong representation within the other decision centers. This explains, if it was not al-ready clear, why a Director felt it so necessary to insure that he was well represented by his "commandos" in all the important decision-making centers.

A fourth major disadvantage of the close relationship between interest groups and the administration is the imperceptible dilu-tion of the public interest. It has been suggested that French

[44] McConnell, *Private Power and American Democracy*, p. 339.

higher civil servants are objective and able to resist particularistic demands or pressures because they are guided by the "general interest."[45] The concept of the "general interest" was invoked at various points during our interviews—though not, significantly, when the interview treated the question of the administration's relationship to interest groups. It would be of little help in understanding the administration's relationship to interest groups to know that French higher civil servants are always guided by the notion of the "general interest." Enough has been said in this chapter to indicate that it is simply not so, and, to the extent that this is correct, one arrives at the conclusion that there is an attempt to equate the public interest with certain private interests. The administration's hostility to interest groups, or lobbies, as it chooses to define them, its practice of choosing between the representative, dynamic, or legitimate groups and the unrepresentative, undynamic, or illegitimate groups and, in certain sectors, its identification with the interests of particular groups to the exclusion of all others, suggests only that civil servants are not averse to invoking the general interest while their actions contradict this noble concept. While the general interest is necessarily diluted in a decentralized federal structure such as exists in the United States, it is by no means always kept intact in a centralized system that is always ready to invoke it as a guiding principle.

In the United States the concept of the general interest has never achieved intellectual respectability, and countless have been those ready to deny the existence of an interest transcending that of groups. "In developing a group interpretation of politics, therefore," wrote David Truman, "we do not need to account for a totally inclusive interest, because one does not exist."[46] It seems hardly surprising, then, that the influence of groups—as well as, to a large extent, their open lobbying—has come to be accepted as an integral part of the "governmental process." This process responds to group pressures, which means that few have had any illusions that the government or the bureaucracy would uphold the general interest. It also means that any group with a certain amount of resources can attempt to

[45] Ehrmann, "French Bureaucracy and Organized Interests," p. 545.
[46] Truman, *The Governmental Process*, p. 51. For a similar view, see also Pendleton Herring, *The Politics of Democracy* (Rinehart and Co., Inc., 1940), pp. 424–425.

make its voice heard. This is not a very egalitarian system and one can hardly deny that it favors the stronger groups; at the same time, one must recognize that in such a system there is often more than one avenue through which demands can be made. In France, on the other hand, the concept of the general interest has been marked by an aura of sanctity and the administration has been seen, and has seen itself, as the guardian of the general interest. Consequently, when it favors certain groups above others it associates these groups, even if imperceptibly, with higher and wider interests than they in fact represent. This explains why French administrators feel it so necessary to emphasize the distinction between interest groups and lobbies on the one hand, and professional groups on the other. The former, whatever their claims, are placed by virtue of their designation beyond the pale of respectability. They come to be associated with segmentalism, which is in flat contradiction with the administration's self-defined task.

Does this mean, then, that the French civil servants' invocation of the concept of the general interest is no more than "a handy smoke-screen to cover their decisions, which are actually designed to conciliate the most effectively deployed interests"?[47] The question is complex, if only because the concept of the general interest is always fuzzy and difficult to define, as McConnell's attempts in *Private Power and American Democracy* show only too well. Moreover the administration, as I have tried to show in this study, cannot be regarded as a monolithic organization. Certain parts of it do give favored treatment to some groups, even while invoking the general interest. But there are other parts of the administration that do not maintain close ties with interest groups and whose actions are based on a set of priorities which, if they do not represent the general interest, do not at any rate stand for the strongest groups. I have dwelt on the former case because its implications for the political process, and even its existence, have been largely ignored. There was undoubtedly a need to show that interest groups have played and do play an important role in the governmental system despite the universal invocation and philosophical respectability of the concept of the general interest.

[47] Brian Barry, "The Public Interest," in William E. Connolly, ed., *The Bias of Pluralism* (New York: Atherton Press, 1969), p. 160.

350

CONCLUSION

I have attempted to present in this chapter neither an inventory of interest groups, nor a detailed description of the formal mechanisms of their interaction with the administration. Indeed, I have ignored, perhaps unwisely, the proliferation of joint committees and commissions on which sit representatives of the administration and of interest groups. My aim was not to underestimate the importance of these joint committees—rather, it was to underscore the basic disposition of higher civil servants toward interest groups. To be sure, the picture I have painted is necessarily incomplete, for I have been concerned, as in discussing the relationship between the administration and the deputy, only with the disposition of the higher civil servants and not with that of interest groups. A more detailed study is needed that would take account of the various groups and the different receptions accorded them by the administration; there is need for less concentration on the sensational cases that come and go and that have so far typified the study of French interest groups, and above all there is a need for specific case studies. In this chapter I have done little more than attempt to shed some light on the ways in which the higher civil servants view certain groups, favor others, and justify their distinctions between groups.

CHAPTER XIII

The Bureaucracy and the Fifth Republic

*A un pouvoir nouveau doit correspondre une administra-
tion nouvelle.*

—Michel Debré[1]

*Why give satisfaction to people who in any case will not
vote for us?*

*—Jacques Chirac
(U.D.R. minister)*

TOWARD A PARTY GOVERNMENT

It was suggested in an earlier part of this study that the most
important factor affecting French institutions in the Fifth Republic is the one most neglected by students of French politics. This
is the changed party structure which may ultimately come to
have a far greater impact on the administration and on administrative policies than the much debated phenomenon of technocracy, for it concerns the political control of the bureaucracy—
something that has long been sought and championed but which
may, in the end, turn out to cause greater fears than a "technocratic state."

To the multiplicity of parties have been attributed now the
causes, now the symptoms, of an unstable political system and a
society torn by conflict. For some interpreters of French politics,
the multiplicity of parties is simply the manifestation of an ideologically committed and ideologically divided society.[2] For
others, it is merely an accurate reflection of the unideological and
power-seeking temperament of French politicians.[3] What brought

[1] Michel Debré, *La Mort de l'Etat républicain* (Paris: Gallimard, 1947),
p. 148.

[2] François Goguel, *La Politique des partis sous la troisième République*
(Paris: Seuil, 1946); and Jacques Fauvet, *La France déchirée* (Paris: Fayard,
1957).

[3] Nathan Leites, *On the Game of Politics in France* (Stanford: Stanford

the parties such a degree of prominence, or disrepute, was the turbulent and unstable nature of the French political system as it functioned up to 1958. It has often been observed, however, that the actual number of parties cannot be used to explain the instability of the French political system: other countries, as diverse as Norway and Israel, have numerous parties but are not racked by a seemingly endemic political instability.[4] As Sartori has shown, multiparty systems function in different ways, depending not on the number of parties, but on the distance between the parties—their degree of polarization—and their centripetal or centrifugal drives.[5]

In the case of France, the number of parties has not substantially varied from the Fourth to the Fifth Republic, although there have been important changes in their relative strength, and less important changes in nomenclature. The MRP has vanished, only to give rise to two offshoots, the Centre Démocrate and the Progrès et Démocratie Moderne. The Radical party has lingered on and is now making a desperate attempt, under the new leadership of Jean-Jacques Servan-Schreiber, to dominate the center left of the political spectrum—an attempt about which it is not easy to become optimistic. The SFIO, whose leadership has changed from Mollet to Savary to Mitterrand, appears to have changed only its name (it is now known as the Parti Socialiste). The Communist party remains as entrenched as it was under the Fourth Republic. To this list of major parties that existed under the Fourth Republic must be added the PSU (Parti Socialiste Unifié), a small splinter group of the SFIO whose importance is not accurately reflected by its lack of representation in the National Assembly,[6] and the Gaullist party (the UDR), which appeared and disappeared under various guises in the Fourth Republic, and which is now the single most important party in France.

University Press, 1959); and Constantin Melnik and Nathan Leites, *The House Without Windows* (Evanston, Ill.: Harper and Row, 1958).

[4] Eric Nordlinger, "Democratic Stability and Instability: The French Case," *World Politics*, XVIII, no. 1 (1965), 143.

[5] Giovanni Sartori, "European Political Parties: The Case of Polarized Pluralism," in Joseph La Palombara and Myron Weiner, eds., *Political Parties and Political Development* (Princeton: Princeton University Press, 1966), pp. 138–139.

[6] Michel Rocard, the Secretary General of the party, was the party's only Deputy until March 1973.

Despite the continued existence of numerous parties, the French political system has undergone profound changes since the establishment of the Fifth Republic. Why have these changes taken place? One important explanation invokes the rise of the "technocratic" State run chiefly by the *énarques*. "La République des députés" is seen as having given way to "La République des grands commis." Nevertheless, the ubiquity of the *grands commis* in the administrative, para-administrative, political, and private sectors does not in and of itself suffice to explain the nature of the French political system as it exists under the Fifth Republic; nor does it suffice to explain how the contemporary political system differs from that of the Fourth Republic. It used to be argued by analysts of French politics as diverse as Herbert Luethy and Philip Williams that the levers of power were always in the hands of the higher civil servants, simply because of the weakness and instability of Fourth Republic governments.[7]

Another factor frequently cited to explain the difference between the two regimes is the degree of ministerial stability or instability. This is evidently not nearly as important as it has been thought to be. For one thing, there was not quite as much ministerial instability under the Fourth Republic as might have been deduced from the recurring cabinet crises. Second, certain ministries (Education, Industry, Construction, Public Works) experienced as many, if not more, changes of ministers under the Fifth Republic as under the Fourth.

Still a third popular explanation has centered on the Constitution of the Fifth Republic, which has considerably increased the power of the executive to the detriment of that of the legislature. This argument was perhaps more popular in the early years of the Fifth Republic than it is today, since the changes created by the new Constitution involved a drastic alteration in the distribution of institutional power. Students of de Gaulle's new Constitution saw the shift of power from the legislature to the executive as the result of de Gaulle's need to guarantee executive power while recognizing the need for, and the absence of, a parliamentary majority. "Since there was no chance of a stable parliamentary majority capable of guaranteeing the emergence of

---

[7] The contradictions inherent in this argument have been elaborated in Ezra N. Suleiman, "The French Bureaucracy and Its Students: Toward the Desanctification of the State," *World Politics*, XXIII, no. 1 (1970), 127–129.

a solid and durable Cabinet," wrote Stanley Hoffmann, "Debré's intention could be achieved only by institutional devices or gimmicks. In other words, since there was no organic salvation, there had to be mechanical solutions."[8] It is difficult to deny the importance of the altered institutional arrangements that accompanied the Fifth Republic, but perhaps one should not exaggerate their impact insofar as the working of the political system is concerned.

The fourth, and perhaps most important, explanation concerning the political system of the Fifth Republic has to do with the personality of General de Gaulle, who shaped and dominated its institutions until April 1969. It appeared for a long time only natural to believe that de Gaulle, and hence Gaullism, constituted no more than an ephemeral episode in the political life of France, such as had emerged upon the French scene under different guises several times before, only to disappear and allow the system to shift once again from the administrative to the representative form of government. The Gaullist State was, in Hoffmann's words, "both an exception from and a confirmation of a traditional pattern."[9] The ultimate importance of this analysis resides in the belief that there could be no Gaullism or Gaullist system without de Gaulle: it was seen as indissolubly bound up with his person. It was thus common to believe that the Gaullist party was "hardly likely to survive General de Gaulle," and that "the Gaullists of the Fifth Republic (the UNR) [UDR] are camp followers of the General, not a party, and have no meaning without him."[10] The strength of the party in the Fifth Republic and the concomitant effacement of the other political parties were ascribed to the personality of General de Gaulle. That these parties would return to dominate French politics was a theme propagated by de Gaulle himself, who never ceased to reiterate that the alternative to him was, at best, a return to the "party anarchy" of the "old system," or at worst, communist rule. De Gaulle himself,

[8] Stanley Hoffmann, "Succession and Stability in France," *Journal of International Affairs*, XVIII, no. 1 (1964), p. 87.

[9] Stanley Hoffmann, "Protest in Modern France," in Morton A. Kaplan, ed., *The Revolution in World Politics* (New York: John Wiley, Inc., 1962), p. 88. See also René Rémond, *The Right Wing in France from 1815 to de Gaulle* (Philadelphia: The University of Pennsylvania Press, 1966); and Nicholas Wahl, "The French Political System," in A. Ulam and S. Beer, *Patterns of Government* (New York: Random House, 1966).

[10] Leslie Lipson, *The Democratic Civilization* (New York: Oxford University Press, 1964), p. 432.

therefore, had no small hand in creating the belief or illusion that the political force to which he had, in spite of himself, given rise and which was created with the sole purpose of supporting and sustaining his power could not outlast him. His political opponents, like the students of French politics, took him at his word.

With the resignation of General de Gaulle and the subsequent astounding success of the Gaullists in the June 1969 presidential elections, the significance of the Gaullist party as a political force in its own right came to the fore. Far from foundering on de Gaulle's abrupt retirement, the UDR emerged strengthened. This, more than any other factor, has been responsible for obliging students of French politics to reexamine the relationship of de Gaulle to "his" party, and it now also calls for an examination of the role of the Gaullist party in the politics of the Fifth Republic prior to de Gaulle's resignation. Only recently has the importance of the Gaullist party as a political force manifested itself, but the strength of this force is by no means as recent. The party has been accumulating and solidifying its strength since its creation in 1958. Today for the first time there exists in France a majority party that became dominant in 1962, the date which is seen as a "turning point"[11] in the Fifth Republic because of the remarkable success of the Gaullists both in the Referendum of that year, which pitted the Gaullists against all the other political parties, and in the legislative elections. The existence of a majority party and of cohesive governments has had a more profound impact on French politics than has hitherto been recognized. Its impact has certainly been greater than that of the changed institutional arrangements brought about by the 1958 Constitution. The extent to which the Gaullist party now dominates the Government can be seen from Table 13.1.

To be sure, this situation was in the making over a period of more than a decade, but it could not be clearly comprehended so long as the personality of de Gaulle intruded. Even in 1967 Charlot could write in his excellent study of the then UNR party: "The U.N.R. is indeed a curious party—ignored on principle by General de Gaulle, who is its *raison d'être*, yet endowed with power from its very inception and winning a major electoral victory before it even had the time to become organized. The U.N.R., in effect, is, first, a ministerial team, then a central committee for the

---

[11] Jean Charlot, *Le Phénomène gaulliste* (Paris: Fayard, 1970), p. 22.

selection of candidates for legislative elections, then the largest parliamentary group in the National Assembly, and only lastly a party."[12] Noting that the UNR had a heritage and asking whether it had a future, Charlot asserted with characteristic caution that "it is scarcely possible to reply with certainty to this important question."[13] He concluded by observing that "only the future, that is, circumstances and men, will resolve, in the final analysis, what M. René Remond has aptly called the 'enigma of the U.N.R.' "[14]

TABLE 13.1
Party Representation in Government, 1968-1972

Political Party	Pompidou Gov't 31 May '68		Couve De Murville Gov't. 12 July '68		Chaban-Delmas Gov't. 22 June '69		Chaban-Delmas Gov't 15 May '72		Messmer Gov't 7 July '72	
	Ministers	Sec. of State	Ministers	Sec. of State	Ministers	Sec. of State	Ministers	Sec. of State	Ministers	Sec. of State
UDR	15	4	15	11	12	17	14	17	14	8
Republicains Indépendents	3	–	3	1	4	3	4	3	3	2
Centre Progrès et Démocratie	–	–	–	–	3	–	3	–	3	–
Non-Parliamentarians	5	2	1	–	–	–	–	–	–	–
Total	23	6	19	12	19	20	21	20	20	10

Source: *Le Monde*, 8 July 1972.

With the publication of *Le Phénomène gaulliste*, Charlot has gone a considerable way toward solving this "enigma" and answering the important question that he could only pose in his earlier study. Making extensive use of sample survey and electoral data, he presents, in an extremely convincing manner, the twin theses that the phenomenal rise of the Gaullist party represents "a veritable mutation of the French political system,"[15] so

[12] Jean Charlot, *L'U.N.R.: Etude du pouvoir au sein d'un parti politique* (Paris: Armand Colin, 1967), p. 23.
[13] *Ibid.*, p. 24.   [14] *Ibid.*, p. 310.
[15] Charlot, *Le Phénomène gaulliste*, p. 14.

that it is possible to argue that the French party system has been "qualitatively, *structurally*, modified,"[16] and, second, that there exists a Gaullism that is distinguishable from and wholly independent of de Gaulle. He distinguishes two Gaullisms—a distinction upon which his entire thesis is premised—the "gaullisme gaullien," "Gaullism of national unity around the person of General de Gaulle,"[17] and "party Gaullism, legislative Gaullism—precisely the Gaullism which is at stake in the post-de Gaulle era."[18]

The rise of a majority party in France is as important for its novelty as for its impact on French politics and society. There appears to have been a great reluctance to examine the influence of the Gaullist party on French institutions. This has been owing partly, as I indicated, to the persistence of the view that Gaullism is a mere aberration, and partly to undue emphasis on the more evident, but nonetheless ultimately superficial, factors. After all, the existence of a majority party in Britain is in no small measure responsible for making the political system work as it does. The control of the executive in the United States by a party enables that party to exercise its influence—largely through political appointments—on the governmental (rather than legislative) structure. In France the political system, as it has functioned over the past ten years, has combined the chief elements of the British parliamentary system and the American presidential system. The presidency and the legislature have been in the hands of a single political party, which has been able to govern on its own. We have seen, for example, that ministers are now able to exert greater influence in the administrative and political spheres—not because of the diminished role of parliament or the ministers' relatively long stay in office, but because they have had the support of a dominant political party.

THE GAULLISTS AND THE BUREAUCRACY

It is not possible to cover here the impact that the Gaullist party has had on French institutions, both local and national, in its fifteen-year rule. But a brief look at the influence of the regime in one crucial domain—the administration—may help us to understand the profound importance that the existence of a majority party has had on French politics.

[16] *Ibid.*, p. 38.   [17] *Ibid.*, p. 36.   [18] *Ibid.*, p. 37.

First, a word about the nature of the regime: it is important to stress the extent to which the Fifth Republic has become a presidential regime. This is manifested not merely by the impotence of parliament, but also by the subservience of the prime minister and his government to the president. The president of the Republic, with the aid of his principal associates, has come to oversee the entire gamut of political and administrative institutions, and the important role of his staff in the political process is not unlike that played by the White House staff. It is well known, for example, that when Pompidou called the Elysée in July 1968 to indicate that he was prepared to form a new government, it was Bernard Tricot, General de Gaulle's Secretary General, who informed him that the decision had already been taken to appoint Couve de Murville as the new prime minister. Today Pierre Juillet, President Pompidou's closest adviser, is often called the "real" prime minister (it was largely on his advice that Chaban-Delmas was replaced by Pierre Messmer in July 1972). Perhaps more significant is the extent to which the Elysée can modify a minister's policy, reject it altogether, or induce him to follow a line that the president desires.

Given the movement toward presidential government, it would seem perhaps only logical that the president should become less and less tolerant of the least sign of opposition from within his own government. The removal of prime minister Chaban-Delmas in July 1972 was partly a tactical move designed to give a new image to the Gaullist party and partly a response to the agreements signed by the socialists and communists. It would be a mistake, however, to see the removal of Chaban-Delmas a few months before the legislative elections as a mere tactical move to increase the Gaullist party's chances in the elections. Chaban-Delmas had long been criticized by orthodox Gaullists for his attempts at "ouverture" and dialogue. In his desire to create the "New Society," he made a number of appointments that were anathema to orthodox Gaullists. His appointment of Pierre Desgraupes to the ORTF (state-controlled radio and television), and particularly the appointments of Simon Nora and Jacques Delors, both former associates of Mendès-France and opponents of the Gaullist regime, as his principal advisers on economic and social affairs signaled not only "ouverture" but a considerable degree of independence. Ultimately, it was his policy of "ouverture" and dialogue that brought down the wrath of orthodox Gaullists on his head. And it was his relative independence that brought him into disfavor with the Elysée. The conflicts between the staff of the prime minister and that of the president seemed to pose a challenge to presidential government, at least as it is conceived of by Pompidou.

The choice of Chaban-Delmas' successor showed that Pompidou did not intend France to be ruled by what had been called a two-headed horse. In appointing Pierre Messmer, a military man and ex-colonial service officer, well known for obedience and self-effacement before his superiors, Pompidou and his advisers believed themselves to have found a prime minister who would cooperate with and facilitate the presidential regime. In addition, Messmer had never been known to have strong ideas about social and economic reforms, and was therefore thought unlikely to come up with such grandiose schemes as creating a "New Society." Perhaps most remarkable, however, is the fact that any means of initiative or independence were denied him. Not only did he choose no ministers, but he did not even choose the principal advisers on his staff—this is unprecedented in French politics and may be yet another indication of the strong turn toward presidential government. The Elysée had "suggested" Yves Sabouret and Jacques Friedmann, head of the corps of the Inspection des Finances, as his chief advisers on economic and social affairs. The Elysée had also sent Pierre Doueil, a former prefect, to be Messmer's *directeur de cabinet* (Doueil had been a member of Pompidou's staff when the latter was prime minister). The important point is that Messmer had neither known nor worked with any of these men—they were in fact imposed on him.

The power of the president of the Fifth Republic has been to a very considerable extent based on the support of a political party. (The situation has not as yet arisen in which the president's party was not the one that controlled over 51 percent of the seats in the National Assembly.) As the most influential member of the majority party, the president may feel a duty to promote its members, place its sympathizers in key positions, and generally give it a strong hold on the key institutions in the society. This is in fact what Pompidou who, unlike de Gaulle, is a strong believer in the UDR, has tried to do. He has always been very attentive to his party, so that when de Gaulle resigned in April 1969 and Pompidou forthwith announced his candidacy, the UDR rallied behind him; there was never the slightest possibility that it would back another candidate. In turn, the UDR has assured itself of control over most of the institutions in the public and semipublic sectors and, even at the local level where it is believed to have been unsuccessful at establishing roots,[19] it appears to have a close network with many non-Gaullist mayors and officials, who themselves are closely linked with officials from the central administration.

Insofar as the bureaucracy is concerned, the UDR, as was suggested in an earlier chapter, appears to be moving toward enlisting the bureaucracy in its service. A clear example of this is the attitude of the administration toward deputies. A clear distinction seems to be made between deputies who represent the parties of the majority and those who represent opposition parties. The existence of a dominant political party, coupled with the impotence of parliament, has meant that the field of collusion between deputies of different parties and civil servants has been preempted. The UDR party is gradually coming to have a strong hold on the administration, which no political force had previously been able to secure. One important manifestation of this change is that the administration has become deeply engulfed in partisan politics. In several ministries, contact between the administration and deputies is restricted, by explicit orders from the minister, to the deputies of the parties of the majority. Table 13.2 shows how much more open is the administration to the dep-

TABLE 13.2

*Proportion of Directors' Contact with Majority and Opposition Deputies
(percent)*

	Deputies of		
	Majority Parties		Opposition Parties
	All	13.6	All	0.0
	3/4	46.9	3/4	1.2
	1/2	35.8	1/2	38.3
	1/4	0.0	1/4	16.0
	0	3.7	0	34.5
Total		100.0		100.0

[19] One often comes across the observation that the Gaullists have not been as successful locally as they have been nationally. This usually only takes into account the number of local offices won. It ignores a more subtle kind of penetration at the local level.

uties of the majority parties than it is to opposition deputies. And actually the reception accorded the deputies of the majority is more favorable than Table 13.2 would indicate, because these deputies are generally able to obtain what they want by going directly to the minister or to his cabinet. Also, mere contact between deputies and administrators does not indicate the degree of responsiveness of the administration to the wishes of the elected official—here again, the degree of responsiveness is greater in the case of the deputies of the majority parties. With regard to the opposition deputies, contact with the administration has become less frequent over the past eight or nine years—since the UDR came to have a majority in the National Assembly—and the administration's responsiveness has become less and less assured.

The openness of the administration to deputies of the majority was often ascribed, by the civil servants, to the size of the majority; there was, they said, bound to be more contact with deputies from the majority, given their overwhelming representation in the National Assembly. In fact, however, there is much evidence to indicate that in certain instances the deputies of the opposition were systematically excluded from contact with the administration, which in turn led to their avoiding the administration. They confined themselves to letter-writing. On the administration's side, the usual form-letter to deputies was revised to indicate the degree of the minister's involvement in the problem. The clearest indication, one minister thought, would be in the manner in which the deputy was addressed: for a deputy of the opposition, the form of address was to be "M. le Député," but for a deputy of the majority it was "M. le Député, cher ami."

Thus, although the administration tends, in principle, to have little contact with deputies, it is nevertheless well disposed toward deputies of the majority. The ostracism of the deputies of the opposition varies according to the place of the deputy on the opposition scale. The communist deputies were entirely and systematically excluded from all ministries. In fact, there was no question of a rebuff, since no communist deputy ever attempted to present himself. Nor are communist deputies given to writing letters on behalf of their constituents. Of all the other parties, deputies of the PCF tend to write only a few and occasional letters. The socialist deputies are, in most ministries, only slightly more welcome. The centrists are regarded with varying degrees of hostility and friendliness, depending on their personal contacts. The

UDR deputies are welcomed in every ministry and they have generally been able to obtain what they want by going through the minister or his cabinet, or by having pressure brought on the administration.

The Gaullists have used the administration in a highly partisan way, to attend to their local constituencies as well as to perform a number of political favors designed to engender electoral support for the Gaullists. Because of their persistent efforts to gain a hold on local politics approaching their hold on national affairs, the Gaullist ministers have tended to operate on the premise that their own *départements* were always to be treated as first among equals. Consequently, many Directors observed that they were at times bombarded with notes from the minister and his cabinet to see to affairs that pertained to the minister's *département*. The constitutional requirement for ministers to abandon their seats in the National Assembly has not altered the need for a minister to take care of his constituency. As Chenot has noted: ". . . The separation of the parliamentary mandate and the ministerial function has had only a limited effect: the deputy-minister has remained, in general, the man of his constituency, attentive to the gestures of the shadow who replaces him, present every week in his fief, and consolidating his local power by his post as mayor or general councillor."[20]

Moreover, this partisan use of the administration is particularly accentuated during election periods and referenda. At such times the administration is galvanized into the service of a political party. Its attention is directed toward satisfying claims of groups that have long been denied, toward being open and receptive, making promises, insuring funds for projects, and being less zealous about adherence to the law. In the Presidential election of 1969 Alain Poher, Pompidou's opponent, accused the government of giving orders to its tax collectors not to push the collection of taxes. The accusation, which became a campaign issue, was not an issue pulled out of a hat; it was in fact solidly based. Long before it had become an issue, civil servants in the Ministry of Finance had thought nothing of citing this as an example of the kind of service that they had to perform on behalf of the government at election time. "It's not the kind of thing we like to do. For one thing, how on earth do you send out a circular to thousands

[20] Bernard Chenot, *Etre ministre* (Paris: Plon, 1967), p. 13.

of tax collectors telling them to go easy on their job—yes, telling them, in effect, not to do their job properly because of the impending election. One must always remember that the initial order comes from the government—but the order to execute this order, as well as its precise wording, is the unpleasant task of the civil servant." The civil servant who made this remark also noted that under the Fifth Republic such practice was normal, and that most civil servants tended to accept it as an "occupational hazard." Others noted that serving a political party in this way did not pose grave problems of conscience because it was, for the most part, confined to election times. Others noted that it had become an important part of their job. What appears to be regarded as a general problem is the issuance of an order—like the one on tax collection—that must be filtered down to a large number of civil servants and that is unambiguous in its intentions, coming as it does regularly with elections. This tends to put the higher civil servant in an uncomfortable situation, making him appear in the eyes of his subordinates a political ally of the minister, or a member of the minister's party giving orders to civil servants who do not share the minister's politics and may be manifestly hostile to it.

The use of the administration for specific political ends is by no means a novel situation in France. Under the Third and Fourth Republics ministers made certain that their own ministries were kindly disposed toward deputies of a particular political color. Nor did de Jouvenel exaggerate when he wrote that "there was a time when the bureau chiefs owned copies of the parliamentary yearbooks in which deputies and senators were labeled according to their political persuasion. Those whose names were preceded by a red star were replied to; those whose names were preceded by a blue star never got a reply."[21] There was, however, a certain "fairness" in this game as it was played under the earlier Republics, for no government was controlled by one party. It was therefore tempered by its competitive aspect. Under the Fifth Republic, however, the game has entirely changed, given the existence of a majority party with a strong hold over the State institutions. The bureaucracy is gradually becoming controlled by the UDR party, though it may be too early to suggest that France is now being ruled by a strong exec-

21 Robert de Jouvenel, *La République des camarades* (Paris: Grasset, 1914), p. 46.

utive rather than a strong bureaucracy. The relationship between the UDR and the bureaucracy needs more detailed investigation before any conclusions can be reached about the nature of executive and bureaucratic power in the contemporary political system. But the administration is undoubtedly coming to be identified with the Fifth Republic. One pro-Gaullist Director observed that, in his opinion, a new government—"not a change from de Gaulle to Pompidou, but, say, from Pompidou to the mildest socialist"—would entail mass changes in the personnel of the higher civil service. He believed, as do many non-Gaullist civil servants, that much of the higher civil service is now closely associated with the present regime, and is there precisely for that reason.

It must not be thought, however, that the deputies of the opposition parties have been totally excluded from contact with the administration. Again, to understand the nature of political power in France it is necessary to understand the impact of local politics on national politics. It happens that a deputy of the opposition may also have an *entrée* into the administration, *if he holds a local office*. The deputy-mayor can penetrate the bureaucracy in his role as mayor rather than as deputy, the purpose of his intervention being ostensibly to deal with matters pertaining to his commune. He generally makes it clear that he is coming in his capacity as mayor and not as deputy, and the fact that he happens to be both helps him gain a considerable degree of legitimacy in the eyes of the administration. Also, as mayor, he can always claim that the question at hand is a "technical" one with no political overtones. This will be further substantiated by his having the support of "M. le Préfet." One of the most enduring myths in France, fully shared by civil servants, is, as we noted in an earlier chapter, that the mayoral function is administrative rather than political.

The only deputies of the PCF who had contact with the central administration were those who were also mayors, and the same was true, though to a lesser extent, of socialist deputies. If the opposition gains entry into the central administration, this entry is often limited to *directions* or ministries with regional services. In these cases, the deputy-mayor entertains permanent relations with civil servants representing the central administration in his *département* or commune. The Prefect also plays an extremely important role in facilitating contact between mayors and the

365

central administration. He tends to neutralize the party label of the mayor and may thus be able to have his own point of view championed by the mayor. The mayor and the prefect, as Worms has shown, need each other if they are to accomplish their tasks.[22] This collusion has implications that transcend the affairs of small communes because of the differing political affiliations of the parties concerned.

The deputy-mayor belonging to the opposition may even come to have extremely close contact with a ministry whose minister's local fief happens to be in his *département*. The minister himself may be a mayor in this *département*. In such a case, the one or two officials in the minister's cabinet who are responsible for the minister's local constituency will be as receptive to deputy-mayors, and even simple mayors, of the opposition as they would be to deputies or local officials of the majority. There comes to exist in these cases an imperceptible and tacit alliance between ministers and elected officials, local and national, from the same *départements*. It is not that the sharing of local interests overrides party interests: rather, it is that in according favorable treatment to elected officials of his *département*, the minister is also according favorable treatment to his own *département*. Those members of cabinets responsible for the minister's local constituencies whom we interviewed—generally, the *chefs de cabinet*—noted that one of their most important tasks was to insure the cordial reception of local officials of the minister's *département*. "This [referring to the cabinet] is their most important link with the central administration," said one *chef de cabinet*. This is because the minister is able to exercise his influence not only in his own ministry, but also in the administration as a whole.[23]

[22] Worms, 'Le Préfet et ses notables," *Sociologie du Travail*, VIII, no. 3 (1966), 249–275.

[23] We have already noted the influence exercised on behalf of their *départements* by former Prime Minister Chaban-Delmas and Edgar Faure. In a recent series of articles on politics in the provinces, *Le Monde* pointed to the remarkable case of Faure. "Through his responsibilities in the government and through the intervention of men who are devoted to him in all the ministries, M. Edgar Faure has proven himself remarkably effective. He could allow himself not to be content with mere promises. In every field under consideration, he has resolved the problems hanging in mid-air: paving of roads, supplying of reservoirs and rationalization of the C.E.G.

If I have emphasized so far how favorably disposed the administration is toward the UDR deputies, it has not been merely to indicate that the deputies of the majority party are better able to fulfill the small needs of individual constituents. It happens that all too often they act as representatives of large business enterprises, and sometimes enterprises in which they have a direct financial interest. The UDR deputy's role as the intermediary between these large enterprises and the administration has been a recurring theme for the past three years. As one scandal has succeeded another, charges of corruption, of a regime responsive to special interests, of influence peddling, have been made again and again.

The most recent of the scandals, the so-called Aranda Affair which broke out in September 1972, has probably been the most serious. It centered precisely on the relationship between pressure groups, the UDR and the administration, and it implicated a host of high-ranking UDR officials. In 1971 Gabriel Aranda, a thirty-four year old erstwhile journalist and banker, entered the cabinet of Albin Chalandon, then minister of Equipment and Housing. As a trusted friend of the minister he had the authority to see just about every document. He was struck above all, according to his own accounts, by the "influence traffic," so that when Chalandon was ousted from the government in the July 1972 reshuffle, Aranda felt free to release to the press a series of documents that purported to expose the corruption of the regime and its administration.

The ministry of Equipment and Housing, because of its wide responsibilities for housing and highway construction, for ports, and for public works of all kinds, has fairly extensive contact with interest groups. It is also, as a consequence, a ministry bombarded by political pressure. It appears, for example, that on April 16, three months before the government reshuffle took place, Chalandon had sent a confidential letter to two powerful directors in his ministry in which he drew their attention to the

---

Specific accomplishments win over as many voters as the carefully prepared interventions of electoral agents specializing in certain fields. Thus, an officer is in charge of the section which handles questions of military service. It therefore happens that in cases of deferment, M. Edgar Faure even wins out over the Minister of State in charge of National Defense and that the tribunals rule in his favor." "La politique hors Paris: IV. A la conquête du pouvoir local," *Le Monde*, 18–19 October, 1970.

importance of resisting any pressures that came from the political milieu. Two weeks later Chalandon and Aranda granted an interview to Raymond Barrillon of *Le Monde*, and talked at considerable length about their desire to make public life more ethical.[24]

Chalandon appeared to grasp rather quickly the fact that there was a paradox contained in his policy of allowing greater opportunities to the private sector on the basis of a free, competitive market: it may give rise to greater efficiency, but it weakens the administrator's ability to resist political pressure. "I have been the target of many people's wrath," said Chalandon, "and if I still am I know very well why. In refusing, for example, to slice up the highway construction contracts, awarding them not to small firms but to large ones capable of doing the job better, more quickly and more cheaply, I aroused the dissatisfaction of many and the satisfaction of only a few."[25] It is the large enterprises who are able to mobilize political support more easily than the small ones, so that it becomes necessary, in order not to become a prisoner of a particular group, to ward off both the constant clamor of the small firms and one's own political allies.

Given the preeminent position of the UDR in the contemporary political system, it is not unnatural that almost all the economic groups seeking licenses, contracts, and so forth from the state should go through the UDR. As Aranda himself put it in an interview with *Le Monde*, "very logically, all the careerists and money-seekers veer toward the majority parties. Why should they waste their time in the opposition?"[26] The sanction of the UDR is a sanction of legitimacy bestowed by the state itself. "Just think," said Aranda, "a treasurer of the U.D.R. whose name, to cap it off, is Dr. Fric,[27] wrote to a minister to ask for a contract for a private firm on official U.D.R. stationery. That's just going too far!"[28]

If the groups find it convenient to work through the UDR, the party also comes to rely on their support and resources.[29] It therefore attempts to give them as much satisfaction as possible, and it does so largely by insuring that the state apparatus that it

[24] *Le Monde*, 17–18 September 1972.
[25] *L'Express*, 18–24 September 1972.
[26] *Le Monde*, 17–18 September 1972.
[27] *Fric*: slang for money.   [28] *Le Monde*, 17–18 September 1972.
[29] See the two articles on the financing of political parties in France entitled, "Argent et Politique," *Le Monde*, 12 and 13 October 1972.

controls is more open to them and to their representatives than it is to the opposition. Like the communist party, the UDR claims to be a party "not like the others"; it sees itself as a movement and knows its friends and enemies.

The regime has also encouraged mergers, growth, competitiveness, and it has had little sympathy, save at electoral periods, for the small shopkeeper. The emphasis on "bigness" and on the anachronism of "smallness" suggests that attitudes and policies have undergone a transformation since the days of the Third Republic when every politician had loud words of praise for the small farm, the baker, and the family business that was the backbone of "La petite République." But the acceptance of industrial society has entailed, in part, acquiescence to the power of large, well-organized groups.[30] Their use of this power profoundly affects the political process.

The Aranda Affair, therefore, illustrates not merely the link between "power and money," as most observers in France have suggested. It suggests that pressure groups have strong links with the UDR party, that as a result of these links they have been receiving a more than favored treatment, and that their advocates —the UDR deputies—have an unusually privileged position while the deputies of the opposition parties are shut out of the political system. All this indicates that the Gaullist regime has been able to make the administration responsive to certain groups in the society. As the influential Gaullist Jacques Chirac, currently minister of Agriculture, put it: "Pourquoi donner satisfaction à des gens qui, de toute façon, ne voteront pas pour nous?"[31]

CONCLUSION

If the UDR appears to fit Richard Rose's paradigm of conditions needed for the existence of what he calls "party government,"[32]

---

[30] In his depiction of the planning process of the early 1960's as an "elitist conspiracy between the senior civil servants and the senior managers of big business," Andrew Shonfield may well have detected a trend toward the close association between the administration and large economic groups. See his *Modern Capitalism* (New York: Oxford University Press, 1965), pp. 128–131.

[31] Cited in Hector De Galard, "La Révolution de Juillet," *Le Nouvel Observateur*, 10 July 1972, p. 14.

[32] Richard Rose, "The Variability of Party Government: A Theoretical and Empirical Critique," *Political Studies*, XVII, no. 4 (1969), 416–418.

it also exhibits traits characteristic of what Sartori has called "hegemonic" parties.[33] This is not without its consequences for the political system. In a political system where there is not one, but several oppositions that are bitterly divided among and within themselves and that face a strong and relatively coherent force which holds the levers of power, one either joins the dominating party or one is left out. The relationship between the society and the ruling party begins to mirror the relationship that we have described between the administration and the deputies. In analyzing the *parentela* relationships that exist in Italy between Catholic groups and the Christian Democratic Party, Joseph La Palombara notes that certain groups are unable to bring any influence to bear on the policy-making process. He quotes one respondent as saying: "Those in political power view all of the other groups with which they compete as enemies. . . . The bureaucrats and the functionaries tend to obey the minister and the political party he represents, and they at the same time ignore those parties and those associations that are not instruments of, or representatives of, the parties in power."[34] But the Christian Democratic Party does not have the same position in Italian politics that the UDR has in the French system. As La Palombara himself notes: "If the dominance of the D.C. were absolutely, unqualifiedly unchallenged, we might suppose that certain of Italy's interest groups would be totally excluded from the policy process. Such a consequence would logically follow from the extreme nature of intergroup antagonism and from the discernible widespread tendency of group leaders to assume that to share political power means to keep the 'enemy' completely bereft of it."[35] The fact that this situation does not exist results from the Christian Democrats' need to share power with other groups—a need that the UDR no longer has to endure.

It may well be, therefore, that the bureaucracy in France is finally coming to be, as many have argued that it should be, under the control of the political sector. But one must not suppose that political control of the bureaucracy will lead to a British

[33] Giovanni Sartori, "The Typology of Party Systems—Proposals for Improvement," in Erik Allardt and Stein Rokkan, *Mass Politics: Studies in Political Sociology* (New York: The Free Press, 1970), p. 324.

[34] Joseph La Palombara, *Interest Groups in Italian Politics* (Princeton: Princeton University Press, 1964), pp. 312–313.

[35] *Ibid.*, p. 319.

type of civil service. This is because control is not a neutral control; it is control by and subordination to a particular political force. To the extent, therefore, that the bureaucracy in France is coming to be utilized by and identified with the Fifth Republic, or rather with the UDR, the question arises as to what is likely to happen if the party's preponderant position should be seriously compromised in the near future. How would the political control of the bureaucracy be affected? It is not at all unlikely that were another party to capture power and govern on its own, the myth of administrative continuity would receive a serious blow. François Mitterrand has in fact maintained that if the Left were to come to power it would undertake a veritable purge of the upper echelons of the bureaucracy. If, on the other hand, coalition governments should return to dominate French politics, then it is probable that the bureaucracy would be more equitably "used." At the present moment there can be little doubt that the UDR is aiming to make the bureaucracy responsive, if not to the society, then to those who form the Gaullist ranks. The administration's traditional powers of resistance—compartmentalization, lack of coordination—may yet be seen as the chief virtues of the French State administration.

371

CHAPTER XIV

Bureaucracy, Technocracy,
and the Stalemate Society

I emphasized at the outset that this would be neither a clinical nor a monographic study of the French bureaucracy. The wide-ranging approach I have adopted has particular advantages, especially when it deals with a subject that has scarcely been studied. But it also has an obvious disadvantage: the more it includes, the more it should include, and the less reason there is for leaving this or that out.

Basically, I have dealt with four related themes: the recruitment of higher civil servants, their role perceptions, their relationship to the political sphere and, finally, their relationship to the society. A number of conclusions have emerged from this analysis.

First, the French higher civil service is unrepresentative of the society. Its social basis is extremely narrow and remains so because of the educational system. Knowing the social basis of the administrative elite, however, tells us little about the behavior and attitudes of this elite. Above all, an unrepresentative recruitment need not mean that the elite is unresponsive to the society. This is a crucial point and I shall return to it presently.

Second, one of the most enduring themes of French political analysis has been to place politicians and civil servants in opposition to one another. Our analysis has shown that civil servants have changing perceptions of their role and that, depending on the positions they occupy in the politico-administrative hierarchy, their role perception may sometimes be closer to that of their political chiefs than to that of their colleagues.

Third, this means that they may cooperate with ministers against other higher civil servants, and they do this regardless of the type of regime in existence—regardless of whether there is ministerial stability or instability. In fact, we have shown the degree of ministerial stability to be a relatively unimportant factor. It makes little sense, and serves to distort reality considerably, to

372

speak now of "La République des députés," now of "La République des fonctionnaires." That French higher civil servants are always deeply involved in politics has been shown at length in this study. It is doubtful whether they differ in this respect from their British counterparts.[1]

It would be wrong to imply, however, that the type of regime in existence has no effect on the formulation and implementation of government policy. I have shown that the existence of a majority party has certainly had an impact on the bureaucracy, largely because there has been a greater coherence in governmental policies and a greater cooperation among ministers.

Finally, in examining the bureaucracy's relationship to the society, I have tried to point out the various complexities involved. The administration's hostility to deputies has definite historical roots, but it has also received strong encouragement from the present regime. Politicians today are just as responsible for the administration's hostility to deputies as they were in the nineteenth century, though the reasons and circumstances are wholly different. In their relationship to interest groups, the administrators do have a tendency to support the larger and more powerful groups, with whom they establish networks for mutual benefit. The most striking feature of the bureaucracy's relationship to the society is the degree to which it has come to prefer and to encourage "bigness," with all the bias that this entails.

All this leads to the central question that we must try to answer in this chapter: is the unrepresentative administrative elite undemocratic? Is it a technocratic elite that is unresponsive to the society? Much of the writing on the French administration, whether by specialists, polemicists, or politicians, suggests very strongly that the administration is responsible for France's backwardness. If France is a stagnant society, it is argued, this is owing in large part to a centralized administration, controlled by a homogeneous elite which has few guidelines other than rationality, efficiency, and standardization.[2] One finds that such arguments are hardly ever examined and that they have come to be taken as self-evident truths. In this final chapter we will take a

[1] See Michael R. Gordon, "Civil Servants, Politicians and Parties: Shortcomings in the British Policy Process," *Comparative Politics*, 4, no. 1 (1971), 29–58.

[2] See the works cited in note 54, Chapter 1.

373

brief look at the question of technocracy and at the popular thesis concerning the stalemate society.

BUREAUCRACY OR TECHNOCRACY?

The predominance of civil servants in the key institutions—the State bureaucracy, the nationalized industries, the private sector, and the political posts proper—has given rise to an alarming fear: the rule of the State by a group (or class) of specialists sharing a common social background, a common education, and a common ideology. That the ubiquity of civil servants in all the crucial institutions in France has coincided—at least the awareness of it appears to have coincided—with the Fifth Republic has led, perhaps not unnaturally, to seeing the present regime as responsible for creating conditions conducive to the reign of the technocrats. It is scarcely deniable that the Fifth Republic has considerably facilitated, as well as encouraged, the transfer from an administrative to a political career. Ever since the beginning of the Third Republic civil servants have occupied ministerial posts. Yet prior to the establishment of the Fifth Republic they could become ministers only after relatively long service in parliament, as is the case with British ministers.[3] Today, however, the separation of the parliamentary and ministerial mandates has permitted a number of civil servants to assume ministerial posts without prior political (national or local) experience. Perhaps one should merely interpret "these promotions as a consequence of the limitation, within the framework of a presidential regime, of parliament's prerogatives."[4] Nevertheless, the importance of the "technician" or "specialist" in present-day France raises an important question which no study of the higher civil service can ignore: is France coming to be a "technocratic" state?

The fear of technocracy is premised on the blurring of a fundamental theoretical distinction between the role of the politi-

---

[3] Richard Rose, "Cabinet Ministers in Britain: Their Selection and Consequences," paper delivered at the 8th World Congress of the International Political Science Association, Munich, Germany, August 31–September 5, 1970. See also Bruce Headey, "What Makes for a Strong Minister," *New Society*, 8 October 1970, pp. 624–627.

[4] Jacques Billy, *Les Techniciens et le pouvoir* (Paris: Presses Universitaires de France, 1963), p. 115.

cian and the role of the civil servant. The latter must always be subordinate to the former, but each is endowed with specific talents which the other does not possess. As Weber noted, "All too often the civil servant as a politician turns a cause that is good in every sense into a 'weak' cause, through technically 'weak' pleading. . . . To weigh the effect of the word properly falls within the range of the lawyer's task, but not at all into that of the civil servant."[5]

The politician is thus one who can fight, plead, and convince; but, above all, he is guided by an "ethic of responsibility," which Weber opposed to the "ethic of ultimate ends." The civil servant who replaces the politician is a specialist, guided by rational standards and hence oblivious to the political implications—the sense of responsibility of which Weber spoke so passionately—of his actions. The replacement of the politician by the civil servant gives rise, it is argued, to a technocracy which is seen "as the rise to power of those who possess technical knowledge or ability, to the detriment of the traditional type of politician. The ultimate result, still a long way off, would mean government by technocrats."[6] According to Meynaud, it is technical competence that determines influence. "Technocracy is the combined result of the competence and infiltration of the technocrat at an appropriate point or sector of the deliberation machine. It is this combination of circumstances which favors and permits the technologists' penetration into the political sector."[7]

The fear of technocracy has given rise to passionate debate in France over the past several years. There are a number of reasons why there are so many books on "technocracy" or "énarchie." First, the chief "technocrats" are easily identifiable to their detractors. They are the technical and nontechnical higher civil servants, the graduates of the Ecole Polytechnique and ENA. Since ENA was established only after the war, those who attended the school under the Fourth Republic came to occupy, in increasing numbers, important posts in the State apparatus under the Fifth Republic. Second, the stability of political and administrative personnel under the Fifth Republic has been seen to reflect

[5] Max Weber, "Politics as a Vocation," in H. H. Gerth and C. Wright Mills, eds., *From Max Weber: Essays in Sociology* (New York: Oxford University Press, 1958), p. 95.
[6] Jean Meynaud, *Technocracy* (London: Faber and Faber, 1965), p. 31.
[7] *Ibid.*, p. 70.

375

the authoritarian disposition of the regime. In fact, it is probably the stability of the presidency and the authoritarian disposition of the holder of that office for more than ten years that reflected a greater administrative and political stability than actually existed. Mme. Siwek-Pouydesseau has shown, for example, that the stability of Directors was greater in a number of ministries under the Fourth than under the Fifth Republic. Also, ministerial stability in the Fifth Republic, while greater than in the Fourth, has been highly exaggerated.[8] Third, the reduction in parliament's powers has led many to conclude that power has reverted to the administration. How confused this argument is can be seen from the fact that one writer has restated at great length Luethy's thesis about power falling to the bureaucracy because of the instability of the ministerial personnel, and the consequent inability of this personnel to govern through legislative means, and yet the same author argued a few years later that it is really in the Fifth Republic that the bureaucracy holds power.[9] This shows how dangerous it is to draw general conclusions about the workings of a political system from mere appearances and intuition. The last factor, and in many ways the most important, is the appointment of civil servants as ministers. This is taken as a clear manifestation of the dethronement of the traditional politician by technicians. As Meynaud observes: "Some people believe that such ministers (for example the Governor of the Bank of France becoming Minister of Finance) are not technocrats insofar as they openly and officially acquire political responsibilities. But according to our definition of technocracy, this argument is not entirely convincing: the replacement of politicians by technocrats produces, in fact, a complete dispossession of the former in favor of the latter, and this has nothing to do with the will of the electorate. Is this not a particularly good example—in fact almost the pure example—of technocratic penetration?"[10]

Whether the presence of technicians in ministerial posts consti-

[8] J. Siwek-Pouydesseau, *Le Personnel de direction des ministères* (Paris: Armand Colin, 1969), pp. 73–75.

[9] See Alfred A. Diamant, "The French Administrative System: The Republic Passes But the Administration Remains," in W. J. Siffin, ed., *Toward the Comparative Study of Public Administration* (Bloomington: Indiana University Press, 1957); and "Tradition and Innovation in French Administration," *Comparative Political Studies*, I, no. 2 (1968).

[10] Meynaud, *Technocracy*, p. 60.

tutes a threat to the society is a far more complex question than Meynaud's analysis would lead us to believe. In the first place, the distinction between technicians and politicians is tending to lose some of its force. A former civil servant who is actively engaged in politics, who campaigns for elections, who has been a deputy and becomes a minister, cannot be seen as simply a technician or a politician in any strict sense. He must be seen in the light of the interests he comes to defend. Meynaud's argument, and this is its chief weakness, ignores the problem of shifting loyalties and attachments, a problem that we have felt it necessary to stress; it presupposes a uniform behavior that involves a general attachment to certain ideals, as well as a uniform outlook. There is, after all, a good deal of difference between being Governor of the Bank of France and being Minister of Finance, since the interests of the two institutions are by no means identical. The behavior of officials, as we noted in the case of cabinet members who later become Directors, is determined, not wholly, but to a very considerable extent, by the positions they occupy within the politico-administrative system.

To define technocracy, however, as the rise to power of those with specialized knowledge and to deny the existence of any differences among those occupying the key posts is to ascribe a distinct political orientation to the "technocrats." It is often argued, on the other hand, that technocracy is mainly distinguished by its total lack of ideology. Stephen Cohen notes, for example, that the technocrats "treat ideological arguments with condescending indifference, sometimes with impatience and scorn. For the new technocrats, ideological discussion means endless and sterile debate while the opportunity for action passes. . . . At the center of their system of beliefs is the conviction that social problems are susceptible to technical solutions."[11] While arguing that technocrats are guided by no ideology, Cohen nevertheless writes: "They are far more concerned with raising the level of production than with equalizing its distribution. They favor high profits because they consider profits the motor of capitalist expansion."[12] Is this not a very clear ideology? The evidence at hand suggests that civil servants who engage openly in politics do so as politicians and as members of political parties from across the political

[11] Stephen Cohen, *Modern Capitalist Planning: The French Model* (Cambridge, Mass.: Harvard University Press, 1969), p. 46.
[12] *Ibid.*, p. 50.

spectrum.[13] Meynaud acknowledges "that it is most unusual to find technocrats unanimously on one side and politicians on the other,"[14] though he underestimates the implications of this, just as he underestimates the conflicts among the technocrats because, as he says, "observed differences of behaviour, although not negligible, are, on the whole, purely those of tactics."[15] In fact, he sees the technocrats as being far more united than the working class.[16] It is interesting to observe that in the same section in which Meynaud discusses the homogeneity of technicians, he reverts to their social origins in order to prove his point.[17] And it is this that indicates a basic flaw in his analysis: he makes no allowance for any degree of functional autonomy and thus misconstrues the nature of interests upon which men act. This flaw is common to many of those who have written on technocracy. Alfred Diamant tries, for example, to draw some general conclusions about the behavior of civil servants from an examination of their social origins. He uses the social composition of the French civil service as an example of the French administration's inability "to overcome tradition and to strike out for new ground."[18] Quite apart from the lack of any empirical support for such a conclusion, there is no evidence to indicate that it is social as opposed to structural factors that inhibit innovations. Jacques Lautman has, in fact, argued the very opposite; namely, that in

[13] See Jean-Louis Seurin, "Les Cabinets ministériels," *Revue de droit publique et de la science politique*, no. 6 (November–December 1956), 1293; Jacques Lautman, "Développement économique, priorité accordée à la continuité et communauté des taches et des personnes entre la politique, la fonction publique et l'industrie dans la France actuelle," paper delivered at the 8th World Congress of the International Political Science Association, Munich, Germany, August 31–September 5, 1970, p. 8; and Marie-Christine Kessler, *Le Conseil d'Etat* (Paris: Armand Colin, 1968), p. 237.

[14] Meynaud, *Technocracy*, p. 134.   [15] *Ibid.*, p. 175.
[16] *Ibid.*   [17] *Ibid.*, p. 174.

[18] Diamant, *Tradition and Innovation in French Administration*, p. 263. Present-day Marxists have been particularly prone to assuming a direct relationship between social origins and behavior. They are, and this is certainly not something which Marx would have accepted, more concerned with biographies than with classes or interests. Their unit of analysis is the individual, which was not Marx's unit of analysis. These un-Marxist characteristics are clearly seen in the work of a leading British Marxist. See Ralph Miliband, *The State in Capitalist Society* (New York: Basic Books, 1969), chaps. 2, 3, and 5.

France technical innovations and social conservatism are perfectly compatible.[19]

Because writers like Meynaud attach little significance to "observed differences of behaviour," they fail to take account of the complexity of roles that technicians assume. This also leads them to underestimate the conflicts among the various institutions that these technicians represent, as well as the impact of those conflicts on public policy. To the extent that internecine conflicts often shape policy, as was seen, for example, with regard to urban development, then conflicts among technicians must be accorded greater importance. Sometimes, indeed, policy fails to emerge precisely because the conflicts are so acute. This was the case in the Ministry of Education prior to 1968. Thus, despite the criterion of rationality that technicians supposedly employ and despite their assumed agreement on these criteria, critics of the French administrative system have argued that this system has given rise not to efficiency and rationality but to "centralization minus integration," "authoritarian anarchy," and the "stalemate society." The point is that within any bureaucracy—whether a party or a state bureaucracy—different values and different interests can and do exist. One has only to read Jerry Hough's excellent book on the role of the local party organs in industrial development in the Soviet Union to see how rationality is constantly frustrated by the diversity of interests of the various actors.[20] It is simply an error, as I have emphasized in this study, to regard the French administration as a monolithic organization. It is fairly clear by now that centralized political and administrative systems do not necessarily lead to perfect coordination and coherent decisions. This is shown by the French administration and it was also the case, as Karl Bracher has shown in his study of National Socialism, in Hitler's Germany.[21]

Moreover, it has even been argued by one of the most eloquent critics of technocracy, Edgar Faure, that the politician-technician

[19] Jacques Lautman, "Prestige, inégalités et modernisation de l'organisation bureaucratique," *Esprit*, Special Number (January 1970), 105.

[20] Jerry F. Hough, *The Soviet Prefects: The Local Party Organs in Industrial Decision-Making* (Cambridge, Mass.: Harvard University Press, 1969). See particlarly chaps. xiv and xv.

[21] Karl Dietrich Bracher, *The German Dictatorship* (New York: Praeger, 1970), pp. 330–349.

may be better able to impose his will on the bureaucracy than a "pure" politician. He notes that "it is important to maintain a certain equilibrium between the political element—which ought to be technically competent—and the technostructural element, which ought to be sensitive to political factors." But he goes on to argue that "The entry into the government of men like M. Giscard d'Estaing and M. Duhamel bodes well from this point of view. It is perhaps these men who can have the greatest influence on events. If they have a particular idea of their own, they will know how to shape it so that it can be assimilated by the technostructure. And they will find in this technostructure, because they are part of it, the necessary support."[22] But if it is the politician-technician who is likely to exercise the most influence on his administration, is this because his own thoughts and outlooks are in line with the officials in his ministry, or is it because he is able to impose his will more easily than one who lacks technical competence? Both answers are probably correct, depending on circumstances. For example, Pisani had to impose his reforms on the Ministry of Agriculture, but he was able to solicit the help of the corps of *ponts et chaussées* in carrying out the reforms involved in the fusion of the Ministry of Construction and the Ministry of Public Works. In the former case he was acting against the interests of certain corps; in the latter, his reforms coincided with the interests of the dominant group he had to win over. Any minister, like the President of the United States, must recognize the interests he is up against: all the men and institutions with which he has to deal have responsibilities and interests of their own. And also like the American President, he has "*to induce them to believe that what he wants of them is what their own appraisal of their own responsibilities requires them to do in their interest, not his.*"[23] It may be that ministers who are technicians are better able to convince and persuade. But, and perhaps more

[22] Roger Priouret, "Face à face avec Edgar Faure," *L'Expansion*, XXII, no. 2 (September 1969), 103. There appears to be a slight contradiction in Faure's views since he states, in the same interview, that "the members of the technostructure have an easy influence over ministers who are technicians," while the ministers who are politicians are "embarrassed" by their lack of training and "by their solitude in the face of the alliance between the technicians in the central administration and their own collaborators" (p. 103).

[23] Richard Neustadt, *Presidential Power: The Politics of Leadership* (New York: Signet Books, 1964), p. 53. Italics in original.

important, ministers in the Fifth Republic, whether technicians or politicians, have been immeasurably aided in ruling their departments not so much by their longer tenure as by the support of a dominant political party.

If the politician-technician is better able, as Edgar Faure suggests, to put an idea into practice than a "pure" politician, what of the interests or ideology of the technocratic group as a whole? Given that role perceptions and interests vary according to the positions occupied, it is by now a truism that a member of a group, a class, or a profession, does not necessarily represent his group, class, or profession when occupying an independent position of power. It may well be argued that I have overemphasized the differences and conflicts among the technicians and so, implicitly or explicitly, justified the rule of this group. No one will deny that the technicians, whatever their differences, share with other groups in French society a commitment to the existing political and social system. To the degree that such differences do affect the shape of public policy, however, it is difficult to call them merely differences of tactics.

But there is an equally important factor that militates against the homogeneous reign of technocrats. This is the particular network of power relations that exists at the local level and that is able to thwart reforms imposed from above. I have pointed to some of the more important power relations that exist at the local level (the prefect's relationship to the mayors, the social and political role of the corps of *ponts et chaussées*). These relationships have a considerable degree of autonomy and independence from the central authorities, so that they can continue to exist regardless of reforms envisaged in Paris or of orders handed down. One should not be misled by the legal and apparent subordination of the provinces to the central administration. It is necessary to examine the real or functional autonomy that obtains locally in order to determine the degree of authority exercised by the central government—even if this government is in the hands of a homogeneous group of technocrats—over all forms of activity within the State.

In addition to the imprecision of the concept of technocracy,[24] it has received no clarification from empirical studies. It is merely

[24] For the diverse groups to which the term has been applied, see F. F. Ridley, "French Technocracy and Comparative Government," *Political Studies*, XIV, no. 1 (1964), 36–38.

premised on a priori assertions: (1) that it is synonymous with rationality; (2) that it is based on a common social origin and a common education of the technocrats; and (3) that there is homogeneous behavior among technocrats. We have seen, however, that objective rationality is by no means the chief criterion upon which civil servants act. The alliances formed between certain groups and certain administrations often entail sacrifices of rationality. Similarly, the defense of (administrative) group interests and the public policies that subsequently emanate from these compromises also entail considerable sacrifices of rationality. Moreover, the background and education that civil servants share is, as we have shown in the case of the corps, superseded by the loyalty and attachment of the officials to their particular administrations or corps. Finally, this very loyalty to a particular group within the administration is the chief obstacle to coordination and, hence, to the implementation of a unified policy or a technocratic ideology.

There is yet another factor, one that I have already touched on, that has so far thwarted the establishment of a technocracy. This has to do with the training of the would-be technocrats. It has always been assumed that French civil servants, in contrast to their British counterparts, receive a strictly technical training that qualifies them for particular tasks. It is unfortunate that no attempt has so far been made to examine the precise nature of these officials' training and to link it to the posts that they eventually occupy. It seems clear from the data presented in this study (Chapters III and X), which are by no means exhaustive, that their training is not intended primarily to prepare them for specific tasks. (Obviously, I am not implying that French higher civil servants receive no technical training, only that this training is not, in most cases, linked to their future posts.) The primary purpose of the training is to endow these officials with legitimacy by giving them a much cherished diploma and, ultimately, a title. As with the British civil servants, training and expertise are acquired, for the most part, on the job. In other words, their professionalism, their attachment to criteria of rationality and efficiency, is tempered by their attachment to the requirements and exigencies of particular posts.

Lest my argument be misunderstood, a brief recapitulation is in order. The ubiquity of higher civil servants in the State apparatus and in the private sector may be deplored for a number of reasons. The undemocratic recruitment of the administrative elite may be equally deplorable. But neither necessarily gives rise to a "technocratic" ideology; at least, no empirical evidence has so far been offered to show the existence or content of this ideology. I have not, of course, ignored the existence of informal networks within the administrative system and I have shown at great length the disadvantages of these networks. But such a form of cooperation must be seen against the backdrop of a system that is highly centralized, but nevertheless split into multitudinous groups, each of which pursues its own interests. These interests sometimes include the defense of the small farmer, sometimes that of the big industrialists. It is no wonder that the Ministry of Finance sees itself, however exaggeratedly, as the "arbitrator of social conflicts as they are represented in the various ministries." Ultimately there is a fundamental, perhaps irreconcilable, contradiction between the search for objective, rational policies, and the widespread practice of basing public policies on the compromises that are effected between the various administrations. For if public policy is the lowest common denominator of conflicts among opposing groups within the administration, is this not the surest negation of objectivity and rationality? It could even be said that administrators *fear* rationality because of its possible adverse effects on the autonomy of their institutions. Lautman has very well expressed this rejection of rationality: "The living inequality [of various sectors of the administration], which is fundamental in an administrative system as differentiated as ours and which alone maintains it as a system, forbids that the standard of measure be reduced to simple calculation."[25]

A Stalemate Society?

"That French society is a 'stalemate society' is something everyone admits nowadays," writes Crozier in *La Société bloquée*.[26]

[25] Lautman, "Prestige, inégalités et modernisation de l'organisation bureaucratique," p. 118.

[26] Paris: Seuil, 1970, p. 7. It should be understood that the term "stalemate society" refers here to the popular meaning given it by writers like Michel Crozier. It has nothing to do with the society that Stanley Hoffmann described in his remarkable essay on "Paradoxes of the French Political Community" in *In Search of France* (Cambridge, Mass.: Harvard University

Even the Prime Minister has characterized his own country in these terms. It may well be that the French, despite their supposedly unrivaled chauvinism, are harsher judges of their own society than are foreigners. The recent spate of anti-France books published in France suggests that few people have tried to understand in what way France is more stagnant than other countries. Certainly no one has as yet presented any counterarguments to the universally accepted "stalemate society" thesis. But some such arguments suggest themselves, if only indirectly, from the present study.

In the first place, it is probably no exaggeration to say that, in terms of per capita income, production, and population, France is one of the most developed and dynamic countries in the world, a fact that many people writing about France are apt to ignore. To characterize France as a "stalemate society" is to ignore the condition of most countries in the world.

It is true that old methods and ideas die slowly in France, perhaps more slowly than in other countries. But if progress means, as Crozier suggests, "mobility, competition and negotiation"—i.e., Americanization—then it is difficult to conclude that the French are not catching up. There is a distinct, if at times barely perceptible, feeling in such critical works as *La Société bloquée* and *Pour nationaliser l'Etat* that the trouble with France is that it is not "Americanizing" fast enough in either the political or the economic realm. In the political sphere groups are seen as too ideological and not sufficiently pragmatic to be able really to bargain. Also, the centralized state is seen as hindering participation. As for the economic sphere, it is believed that the rational, no-nonsense management techniques have not made their proper impact on the French businessman. In short, what the critics of the French state admire and wish to see emulated in France is a pluralistic system, both in the political and economic spheres. It is paradoxical, as I have already pointed out, that many French critics have come to view American pluralism as the answer to France's ills at a time when many Americans regard it as the cause of America's present troubles.

Press, 1963). Hoffmann used the term "stalemate society" to refer to a specific situation in a specific historical context. See François Bourricaud, "Michel Crozier et le syndrome de blocage," *Critique*, no. 282 (November 1970), 960–978.

Administrative inefficiency is another perpetual theme of the proponents of the "stalemate society" thesis, a theme very closely related to the plea for decentralization. Here again, there is a tendency among the French to exaggerate the degree of efficiency that exists within the decentralized American governmental structure. One could easily compile an astonishing list of the scandals that are daily uncovered and that reveal waste, arbitrariness, corruption, and mismanagement on a gigantic scale at all levels—federal, state and local—of the American governmental structure. For a public agency, for example, to purchase a desk in New York City, it is necessary to pass through seventy-one different levels of the city government.[27] It is doubtful whether a similar purchase by a public agency in France would take longer. One of course does not prove that a country is dynamic by pointing to the faults of another country, though it helps when the latter is taken as something of a model.

To prove that France is a stalemate society, it is generally thought sufficient to point to its centralized administrative structure. Although I have been less than sanguine about the centralized nature of the French state, I have also shown grave misgivings about the call for decentralization emanating from French liberals. They have tended, I think, to idealize once again the American Federal structure, and hence have exaggerated the degree of citizen participation that actually exists in the United States. French liberals have justified the need for decentralization on a priori grounds and they have failed to elaborate on the theoretical and practical implications of a decentralized state. Having refused to envisage the practical consequences of decentralization, they have not addressed themselves to two crucial questions: first, aside from having greater voting opportunities, how is the citizen actually able to participate in a decentralized system? Second, what means of redress would be available for the inevitable fragmentation of government that ensues from administrative decentralization? In other words, how are the ills of interest-group pluralism, which are undoubtedly accentuated in a decentralized structure, avoided? Since, as we have seen, interest groups play a very important role in the policy-making process and greater consolidation among these groups is occurring, with the encouragement of the administration, these questions should

[27] See the revealing chart in *The New York Times*, January 11, 1971, p. 36.

385

receive some attention. The urgent call for decentralization results, so far as I am able to gather, not from any inherent and
known advantages of decentralization, but from imputing much
of the cause for the stalemate society to the centralized state. If
centralization is bad, then decentralization must be good—a
proposition that requires much thought and proof before it can
be accepted.

Finally, the existence of privileged castes within the public sector has elicited a good deal of justified criticism. The homogeneity in background and education of the administrative elite has
led most writers to conclude that this elite, because it is not representative of the society, cannot by the same token be responsive
to the society. It is certainly true that there are strong a priori reasons for believing that because of class, background, and education, the French administrative elite can be expected to support
the status quo. The data that I have presented would seem to indicate (though considerably more research is required for
proof) that this may in fact be the case. Nevertheless, the administrative elite has probably been more "responsive" to the society
than one might expect from its narrow social base. It is necessary
to bear in mind that a wide spectrum of social classes in a society's elites has by no means always rendered these elites more
democratic or more responsive to the society. The Nazi elites
were considerably more representative of German society than
were the elites of Weimar, yet few would argue that this made
the Nazi elites more democratic. The crucial problem for investigation is, as Karl Mannheim emphasized so strongly, the extent
to which a person "merely tends to absorb the *Weltanschauung*
of [his] particular group and to act exclusively under the
influence of the conditions imposed by his immediate social
situation."[28]

It may well be, as has so often been argued, that all bureaucrats tend, by the very nature of their tasks, to be conservative.
Thus, speaking of British civil servants, one writer recently observed that "the dominating bureaucratic spirit means that
policymaking is predisposed above all toward routine processing,
toward reconciliation of diverse opinions, and toward a harmony

[28] Karl Mannheim, *Ideology and Utopia* (New York: Harcourt, Brace
and World, 1936), p. 156. See also Mannheim's *Man and Society in an Age
of Reconstruction* (New York: Harcourt, Brace and World, 1940), pp.
86–105.

tantamount to an almost unswerving bias in favor of the status quo." This writer goes on to describe the British civil servants very much as their French counterparts have been so often depicted: British civil servants "are virtuosi at the patient, untiring, undramatic processing of problems by means of standard procedures; they take a dim view of experiments or indeed any departure from the habitual and tested practices that have underpinned their organization in the past."[29] If this is an accurate characterization of British civil servants, then it suggests that there are universal principles of organizational behavior rather than unique cultural explanations. The real problem is that when one deals with such questions as the ability of an institution to effect change or to preserve the status quo, one is left with almost no acceptable standard of measurement: what represents change to one person is no more than the defense of the status quo to another.

The term "responsive" is used in a loose manner because it does not lend itself to precision. In most instances it would be difficult to know, much less measure, when an elite was being responsive and when it was being unresponsive. It is only in extreme situations—such as during the New Deal, or in Russia in 1917—that it is possible to see the responsiveness or unresponsiveness of a ruling elite. In the post-World War II era of "routinized" administration, it has become very difficult to apply the criterion of responsiveness to administrative elites with any degree of precision. And when we do speak of responsiveness, it is necessary to specify the groups that are being responded to.

Despite the difficulties inherent in the use of the criterion of "responsiveness," we should not reject it outright. For one thing, it is preferable to the social-background criterion which, as I have repeatedly stressed, cannot be used to gauge the role in society of an administrative elite. If, then, we find it hard to accept the background factor, we must attempt to salvage the criterion of "responsiveness."

The behavior of the administrative elite in a society must be seen in the context of the larger social and political framework of which it is a part. Administration is not an activity that is separate from politics. It becomes all the more difficult to argue, as Crozier and others have done, that the reasons for France's re-

---

[29] Gordon, "Civil Servants, Politicians and Parties," p. 43.

sistance to change are to be found in the French "character," and to argue at the same time that the administration has constituted the chief obstacle to change in the society. The administration is part of the society; it shares the values of the society; it reflects and sometimes exaggerates some of society's defects. The degree to which the UDR has been able to manipulate the administration suggests in fact that the bureaucracy is far more malleable than has hitherto been recognized. It may be that the bureaucracy does no more than reflect the values of the UDR and that it responds to the UDR only. Even so, this would indicate that the bureaucracy is not cut off from the society, that it is susceptible to influence. I have already pointed to some of the reasons for this: the internal contradictions and differences within the French administration, the ability of the administrative elite to assume seemingly incompatible roles and, above all, the involvement of this elite in politics, or in policy formulation, which has probably made it more responsive to the society than has hitherto been thought. If this elite does not behave in quite the same way as does the professional political stratum described by Robert Dahl,[30] it is necessary to bear in mind that this is not its proper or ostensible purpose.

Ultimately, modern administrations differ not in the degree of control they exercise over society but in their professional organization: that is, in their ability to resist reforms aimed at altering the distribution of power between various sectors of the administration. For the most part, the interests of particular bureaucracies lie not so much in defending particular policies as in defending their jurisdiction over specific domains. For example, the Inspection des Finances and the Cour des Comptes cannot be said to have a particular economic or financial policy of their own. Nor does the Conseil d'Etat have a legal policy of its own. What these corps have is a corporate or professional interest that they seek to defend. It is in defending such interests that an administration may prevent the implementation of a particular policy. In other words, civil servants have only a mild commitment to particular policies, but they have a fervent commitment to the interest of their organization. They will willingly exchange one policy for another if the entrenched interest of their organization

[30] Robert A. Dahl, *Who Governs?* (New Haven: Yale University Press, 1966), pp. 305–310.

is left intact. This, I suspect, would be well demonstrated by detailed studies of the various changes that have occurred in France over the past ten years in housing, urban development, and industrial policies.

A problem arises, of course, when a change in policy requires a structural change at the same time. The civil servants who might be affected by the structural change will then fight tooth and claw against both. The members of the Grands Corps in the government, for example, have been willing to pursue policies that ran counter to the wishes of this or that ministry; but they have been unwilling to attack the professional interests of their own corps. Civil servants do not rule by their superior technical knowledge or by their homogeneity or by their opposition to politicians. If they have power, it is based on the establishment of institutions whose chief purpose is to maintain control over a given domain, and to break this hold over a particular sector a determined political will is required. At no point in recent French history have the means to introduce significant structural reforms been as available as they are today; yet at no point has the will to effect such reforms appeared to be so feeble.

APPENDIX: *Questionnaire*

1.1. In some countries, the higher civil servants have a great deal of influence on politics; in others, they only have a little. Would you say that in France the higher civil servants have much, some, little, very little, or no influence on the politics of the country?

_____Much
_____Some
_____Little
_____Very little
_____None
_____Other:
_____Don't know

1.2. Do you think it likely that this influence will increase much, increase a little, remain the same, or decrease in the near future?

_____Increase much
_____Increase a little
_____Remain the same
_____Decrease
_____Other:
_____Don't know

1.3. Why?

1.4. The higher civil servant receives some of the best training in French society. Do you think that his training and his experience create thought processes, work methods, and ways of tackling problems which would prevent him from becoming an accomplished politician?

_____Yes   _____No   _____Don't know

391

1.5. Many higher civil servants and graduates of the Ecole Nationale d'Administration occupy today positions in the government, as well as other purely political positions. Would you say that this phenomenon is inevitable or not?

    ____Inevitable
    ____Not inevitable
    ____Other:
    ____Don't know

1.5a. Would you say that this phenomenon is desirable or not?

    ____Desirable
    ____Not desirable
    ____Other:
    ____Don't know

1.6. As far as the number of officials is concerned, do you believe that in view of the present needs of France there are:

    ____Enough officials
    ____An excessive number
    ____A little more than is strictly necessary
    ____Too few
    ____Other:
    ____Don't know

1.7. (If "an excessive number"): Of what category do you think there is an excessive number?

    ____Those who graduate from ENA
    ____Those of category A
    ____Those of category B
    ____Those of category C
    ____Those of category D
    ____Other:
    ____Don't know

1.8. (If "too few"): Of what category do you think there are too few?

    ____Those who graduate from ENA
    ____Those of category A
    ____Those of category B
    ____Those of category C

_____Those of category D
_____Other:
_____Don't know

1.9. Since the creation of ENA, there has been much discussion of the second *concours*. In your view, what have been the consequences of admitting officials to ENA?

_____It has helped the bureaucracy democratize itself considerably

_____It has helped the bureaucracy to democratize itself a little

_____It has not helped the bureaucracy to democratize itself

_____It has created new divisions within the Administration

_____In general, it has not had a significant effect

_____Other:

_____Don't know

1.10. Do you think that the present system of recruitment of higher civil servants is very democratic, rather democratic, not very democratic, or not democratic at all?

_____Very
_____Rather
_____Not very
_____Not at all
_____Other:

1.11. Several critics have suggested that it would be better to abolish the Grands Corps. Do you think that this would be desirable or not?

_____Desirable
_____Not desirable
_____Other:

1.12. In general, with which of the following opinions do you agree?

_____Officials must *above all* have a training in law
_____It is *necessary* that officials have a training in law
_____It is *preferable* that officials have a training in law

393

_____The study of law is important, *but not more so than other disciplines*

_____Until now there has been too much insistence on the study of law, and not enough on other kinds of training which are more practical and effective

_____A training in law is necessary only for officials who have *juridical functions*

_____Officials have no need at all for training in law

_____Other:

_____Don't know

1.13. Do you think that the training of French higher civil servants today is very adequate, rather adequate, rather inadequate, or quite inadequate to their job?

        _____Very adequate

        _____Rather adequate

        _____Rather inadequate

        _____Quite inadequate

        _____Other:

        _____Don't know

1.13a. (If "rather inadequate" or "quite inadequate"): What reforms would you propose?

1.14. There are countries—the Netherlands, for instance—where civil servants are forbidden from joining extremist political parties. Do you think this is admissible or not?

        _____Admissible

        _____Inadmissible

        _____Other:

        _____Don't know

1.14a. Do you think that this is compatible with democracy?

        _____Yes   _____No   _____Other: _____Don't know

1.15. Do you think that it is good for higher civil servants to have extraprofessional contacts with the political milieu?

        _____Yes   _____No   _____Other: _____Don't know

1.16. Do you think that one can be a higher civil servant at the same time as being:

	Yes	No
A deputy		
A member of a political club		
Conseiller général		
Conseiller municipal		
Mayor		
A member of a political party		

1.16a. Explanation:

1.17. What are, in your view, the factors which most contribute to the promotion of higher civil servants up to the level of "Sous-Directeur" in the French administration? Choose *two* among the following factors in order of importance:

____Seniority
____Hard work
____Having initiative and original ideas
____Extraprofessional activities
____Creating no problems for the superiors
____Personal relations
____Education (degrees)
____Chance
____Being part of a particular group or corps
____Support of a superior
____Other:

1.18. If you were a minister forced to choose between two officials for a high administrative position, which one of these two would you choose: an official who had spent all his life in the Administration, or an official of equal intellectual capabilities, who had spent several years outside the Administration?

____The one who spent all his life in the Administration
____The one who spent several years outside the Administration
____Other:

1.19. If you were a politician—a minister, for example—with a program to be realized, whose collaboration would you pre-

395

fer: that of a higher civil servant with a general training, or that of a higher civil servant with a specialized training?

____That of a high official with a general training
____That of a high official with a specialized training
____Other:
____Don't know

I.20. If you had to introduce administrative reforms, which *three* aspects would you emphasize?

____Simplify or reduce the number of documents
____Improve the training of civil servants
____Reduce public expenditures
____Revise the organization and the competence of Administrative units
____Abolish useless organizations
____Mechanize the work of services
____Plan and coordinate the activities of services
____Improve working conditions
____Other:

I.21. The following is a list of administrative activities. Could you tell me to which ones you give more importance? Choose *three*, in order of importance.

____Giving orders
____Ratifying or controlling others' decisions
____Explaining decisions already taken or to be taken
____Studying technical proposals
____Obtaining information on the activities of your ministry
____Solving conflicts and problems concerning personal relations in your division
____Working on long-term plans and projects
____Establishing norms and general directives
____Obtaining information on activities outside the Administration which concern you
____Other:
____Don't know

I.22. Who, in your view, has more prestige in French society: the director of a large private enterprise, a higher civil servant, or a member of the liberal professions (lawyer, physician, architect, etc.)?

_____Director
_____Higher civil servant
_____Liberal profession

1.23. Who has more freedom of action in his work?

_____Director
_____Higher civil servant
_____Liberal profession

1.24. Whose activity is more important for the life of the nation?

_____Director
_____Higher civil servant
_____Liberal profession

1.25. Who earns more?

_____Director
_____Higher civil servant
_____Liberal profession

1.26. Who is better trained, from a technical point of view, to perform his function?

_____Director
_____Higher civil servant
_____Liberal profession

1.27. How would you compare a deputy in the National Assembly with the man you have chosen in each category?

	Superior	*Equal*	*Inferior*
Prestige			
Freedom of action			
More important activity			
Earns more			
Better trained			

1.28. If a junior official needs information which he cannot obtain in his own office, should he be able simply to call any other office in order to get it?

_____He should be able to call any other office
_____Only the offices in his own ministry

397

_____Only after having obtained permission from his superior

_____Other:

_____Don't know

1.29. As far as the powers of the regional prefects in relation to the Parisian central administrations are concerned, do you think:

_____That it would be desirable to strengthen the powers of the regional prefects

_____That they are sufficient for the time being

_____That, in relation to the central administration, the powers of the regional prefects are already too great

_____Other:

1.30. It has often been said in recent times that the French Communist Party is no longer a revolutionary party. Is this, in your view:

_____Perfectly correct

_____Quite correct

_____Not correct

_____Other:

1.31. How would you react to the participation of the French Communist Party in a left government?

_____I am totally against such participation

_____I would accept such participation in the distant future, but not in the near future

_____I am for such participation

_____Other:

_____Don't know

1.32. Do you think that a democratic regime can function properly without political parties?

_____Yes

_____No

_____Other:

_____Don't know

1.32a. (If "yes") What would be the alternative to political parties?

1.33. In a democratic society, power tends to be divided among certain groups and institutions. In your view, which are the *three* groups or institutions, in order of importance, which have the most power in French society?

——The press   ——The Church
——The political parties   ——The financiers
——The intellectuals   ——The administration
——Parliament   ——The industrialists

1.34. Which is, in your view, the most disadvantaged group in French society today?

1.35. Which is, in your view, the most advantaged group in French society today?

1.36. Do you think that the law of 31 July 1963 concerning the right to strike in the public services has recognized for the first time the right to strike in the public service sector, or has it in fact limited the right to strike in this sector?

——Has recognized the right to strike in public services
——Has limited the right to strike in public services
——Other:

1.37. Do you think that the right to strike in public services should be limited?

——Yes   ——No   ——Other:

Relations between Directors and Ministers

2.1. Recalling the ministers with whom you have worked, could you tell me, in general, under what circumstances you met with them?

——The minister calls you when he has a problem to discuss
——You have regular appointments with him, at a fixed date and hour (Frequency: _____)
——The minister has a joint meeting with all the directors at a fixed date and hour (Frequency: _____)

_____It is possible to get in touch with the minister when one has a problem to discuss

_____Other:

2.2. Could you tell me, according to your experience, to what extent the directors can in general be considered as collaborators of the minister and to what extent, on the contrary, the minister acts independently, i.e. without asking for the directors' advice?

  _____The minister always consults the directors in the subjects of their competence

  _____The minister consults the directors often

  _____The minister consults the directors once in a while

  _____The minister never consults them

  _____Other:

2.3. In order to be successful as a director, would you say that it is necessary, in general, to have the same political opinions and views as the minister; or is this not necessary?

  _____Necessary

  _____Not necessary

  _____Other:

2.4. In your view, should the minister have the same freedom in choosing his directors as he has in choosing the members of his cabinet; or should his choice be limited only to higher civil servants?

  _____He should have as much freedom in choosing his directors as he has in choosing the members of his cabinet

  _____He should choose only among the higher civil servants

  He should choose only among the officials of certain corps

  _____Other:

2.5. It has been suggested that the minister cooperates with the directors above all in the *implementation* and with his cabinet above all in the *formulation* of programs. According to

400

your experience, which of the following statements is more correct?

    ——The minister cooperates with the directors above all in the *implementation* of programs and with his cabinet in their *formulation*

    ——The minister cooperates with the directors in the *formulation* as well as in the *implementation* of programs

    ——The minister cooperates above all with his cabinet, in the *formulation* as well as in the *implementation* of programs

    ——The minister does not "cooperate," rather he has a tendency to give orders

    ——Other:

2.6. Sometimes the directors change when the minister changes. To what do you think this change is attributable?

    ——To the fact that the minister wants his own staff

    ——To the fact that the minister wants collaborators who share his political opinions

    ——Purely personal and nonpolitical factors

    ——Other:

2.7. Which are, in your view, the *two* criteria which tend to guide the minister in making his choice? Please indicate them in order of importance:

    ——Seniority

    ——The corps to which one belongs

    ——The political opinions of the candidates

    ——The professional skills of the candidates and their knowledge of problems

    ——Compatibility of personalities

    ——Contacts established by the candidates in their previous positions (ministerial cabinets, for instance)

    ——Contacts established by the candidates with political parties or political groupings

    ——Authority and prestige of candidates in the ministry

    ——Other:

401

2.8. It has been said that when a minister enters a ministry, he has sometimes precise programs which are more or less utopian and that it is the higher civil servants who make his programs more realistic. Do you think that this description is, in general, valid?

____Yes   ____No

2.9. Which are the *two* arguments among the following which are most effective, in general, in convincing a minister to abandon a specific program?

____Lack of qualified personnel
____Technical difficulties
____Cost of program
____Juridical implications
____Likelihood of strong opposition in Parliament
____Likelihood of strong opposition among interest groups
____Other:

2.10. When a minister is faced by contradictory arguments from his higher civil servants, his political associates, and interest groups with which he is in contact, which arguments, do you think, carry the greatest weight with him?

____Arguments of high officials
____Arguments of political associates
____Arguments of interest groups
____Other:

2.11. It has often been stated that the ministerial instability of the Fourth Republic left the power of formulating programs in the hands of the higher civil servants. According to your experience, would you say that this is absolutely true, quite true, true in some cases, not true?

____Absolutely true   ____Not true
____Quite true   ____Other:
____True in some cases

2.12. (If "true"): Do you think that this situation has changed with the Fifth Republic?

____Yes   ____No

2.12a. (If "Yes"): In what sense and in what direction?

2.13. Do you think that it is preferable, from the point of view of the national interest, that a minister be essentially a professional politician, or should he rather have administrative training and administrative experience?

    ____A minister should be essentially a professional politician
    ____He should rather have administrative training and administrative experience
    ____Other:

2.14. As a higher civil servant who has had contact with several ministers, would you say that you have generally preferred working with a minister who was exclusively a politician, or with a minister who had administrative training and administrative experience?

    ____With a minister who was exclusively a politician
    ____With a minister who had administrative training and administrative experience
    ____Other:

Relations between Directors and Interest Groups

3.1. In your functions as Director, do you have the opportunity to meet with groups, organizations, associations, or individuals representing particular interests?

    ____Almost every day
    ____Very often
    ____Occasionally
    ____Rarely
    ____Never

3.2. Would you say that these contacts depend mainly on the initiative of higher civil servants, on the initiative of the minister, or on the initiative of the groups themselves?

    ____Initiative of higher civil servants
    ____Initiative of minister
    ____Initiative of groups
    ____Other:

3.3. What advantages do you see in constant contacts between the administration and interest groups? Would you choose *three* of the following in order of importance:

____For the administration, such contacts mean in fact contact with the public

____Decisions become more rational

____These contacts lead to discussions among different interests which facilitate the formulation and implementation of programs

____These contacts give indispensable information to the administration

____Because of these contacts the government is in a position to foresee opposition

____These contacts have no advantages

____Other:

3.4. What disadvantages do you see in constant contacts between the administration and interest groups? Would you choose *three* of the following in order of importance:

____These contacts encourage the groups to put too much pressure on the administration

____Constant pressures on the administration prevent the making of necessary decisions by forcing the administration to adopt short-range views

____The administration would be too dependent on interest groups

____These contacts encourage each group, even the smallest, to demand equal time and attention

____These contacts may engender corruption within the administration

____These contacts tend to favor certain groups and disregard others

____Information leaks to the general public which leads to the mobilization of those opposed to a decision

____Other:

3.5. When these groups attempt to influence decisions, would you say that in general their demands are:

____Useful

____Useful, even if exaggerated

____Not always useful

404

———Not always useless
———Useless
———Other:

3.6. When these groups attempt to influence bills, regulations, or reforms, do they tend in general to contact the minister, the ministerial cabinet, or the directors?

———Minister
———Ministerial cabinet
———Directors
———Other:

3.7. In preparing bills, regulations, or reforms do you find it useful or necessary to contact certain groups, associations, or representatives of particular interests in order to obtain information or suggestions?

———Often
———Occasionally
———Rarely
———Never
———Other:

3.8. During the last ten years have contacts between the administration and interest groups increased, decreased, or have they stayed the same?

———Increased
———Decreased
———Stayed the same
———Other:

3.9. (If contacts have changed): What are the reasons, in your view, for this change?

3.10. What proportion of the demands which you receive from interest groups is completely unreasonable?

———100%	———30%
——— 80%	———20%
——— 65%	———10%
——— 50%	——— 0%

3.11. The question of what is commonly called "pantouflage" [going from public to private sector] is often discussed in

405

France. Two arguments are generally used. According to the first, "pantouflage" is not desirable because it produces negative influences on the administration leading, for instance, to favoritism, excessive pressures on the part of the private sector, etc. The other argument, on the contrary, maintains that "pantouflage" has positive results in that contacts between persons having common training and experience lead to a better understanding of the problems on both sides. Which of these two arguments would you consider, in general, as the best description of the consequences of "pantouflage"?

    _____The first
    _____The second
    _____Other:

3.12. Do you think, in general, that the phenomenon of "pantouflage" is:

    _____Very widespread
    _____Widespread
    _____Not very widespread
    _____Rare
    _____Other:

3.13. All in all, do you think that there are more advantages or more disadvantages in contacts between the administration and interest groups?

    _____More advantages
    _____More disadvantages
    _____Other:

Relations between Directors and Deputies

4.1. Does your activity as a director involve much, some, medium, little, or no work on drafting of bills, decrees, or other regulations?

    _____Much   _____Little
    _____Some   _____None
    _____Medium   _____Other:

4.2. (If "little" or "none"): Who is in charge of this work in your ministry?

406

4.3. In the past year, what proportion of your time was devoted to work in the legislative or regulative fields?

——80%   ——20%
——65%   ——10%
——50%   —— 0%
——30%

4.3a. What proportion of this time was devoted to the legislative field (drafting bills) and what proportion to the regulative field (decrees and other regulations)?

Legislative field   *Regulative field*
——75%   ——75%
——50%   ——50%
——25%   ——25%
——10%   ——10%
—— 5%   —— 5%
—— 0%   —— 0%

4.4. Do you have the opportunity, in the course of your work, to meet with deputies?

——Often
——Occasionally
——Rarely
——Never
——Other:

4.5. (If answer is affirmative): In general, what aspect of your work occasions your contacts with the deputies?

4.6. These contacts usually take place:

——On your initiative
——On the minister's initiative
——On the deputy's initiative
——On the initiative of the ministerial cabinet
——Other:

4.7. In your view, what are, in general, the major advantages of contacts between a director and deputies? Please choose *three* among the following:

——For the administration, these contacts mean in fact
     a contact with the public

_____Decisions become more rational

_____These contacts lead to discussions between differ-
ent interests which facilitate the formulation of
programs

_____These contacts give essential information to the
administration

_____These contacts may serve to reduce opposition by
deputies of the majority parties

_____These contacts may serve to reduce opposition by
deputies of the opposition parties

_____These contacts may serve to reduce opposition by
the electors of the deputies

_____Other:

4.8. In general, what are in your view the major disadvantages
of these contacts? Please choose *three* among the following:

_____These contacts encourage the deputies to apply too
much pressure on the administration

_____Constant pressures on the administration prevent
the necessary choices by forcing the administration
to adopt short-term views

_____The administration becomes too dependent in the
long run

_____These contacts may engender the politicization of
the administration

_____Information leaks to the public, which leads to the
mobilization of those opposed to a decision

_____Excessive influence of interest groups on the con-
tents of bills

_____Contacts with deputies of the opposition parties
contribute to destroying the solidarity of the majority parties and the ministers

_____These contacts tend to favor certain groups and
disregard others

_____Other:

4.9. (If answer to question 4.4. is affirmative): Of your contacts
with the deputies, what proportion takes place with deputies

of the majority parties, and what proportion with deputies of the opposition parties?

Majority parties	*Opposition parties*
———All	———All
———Three-fourths	———Three-fourths
———Half	———Half
———Fourth	———Fourth
———None	———None

4.9a. (If there are contacts with opposition parties): Of your contacts with the opposition parties, are there contacts with Communist deputies?

———Yes ———No

4.9b. (If "Yes"): Are your contacts with Communist deputies more numerous, less numerous, or just about equal to your contacts with the other opposition parties?

———More numerous
———Less numerous
———Equal
———Other:

4.10. Do you think that the majority of deputies defend above all

———The interests of the nation
———The interests of their constituency
———The interests of their party
———Their own political career
———Other:

4.11. Do you think that the contacts between the deputies and the administration have increased, decreased, or stayed the same during the past ten years?

———Increased
———Decreased
———Stayed the same
———Other:

4.12. (If there has been change): What do you think this change is due to?

409

4.13. In general, on whom does a deputy call when he wants to discuss a bill, a decree, or a reform?

    ____Directors   ____Minister

    ____Ministerial cabinet   ____Other:

4.14. According to your experience, do you think that a Director *prefers* that a deputy contact the minister, the ministerial cabinet, or the directors?

    ____Minister

    ____Ministerial cabinet

    ____Directors

    ____Other:

4.15. In your contacts with politicians—mayors, deputies—have you found generally that politicians have a tendency to demand political or institutional changes of a general order, *or* do they demand mostly services for their own constituents?

    ____Political or institutional changes

    ____Services for their constituents

    ____Other:

4.16. What proportion of the demands you receive from politicians is totally unreasonable?

    ____100%   ____30%

    ____ 80%   ____20%

    ____ 65%   ____10%

    ____ 50%   ____ 0%

4.17. In your view, is it desirable, not desirable, or indifferent that a higher civil servant become a deputy?

    ____Desirable   ____Indifferent

    ____Undesirable   ____Other:

Relations between Directors and Ministerial Cabinets

5.1. Would you categorize the members of the Cabinet of your Minister as technicians or rather as politicians?

    ____Technicians   ____Both

    ____Politicians   ____Other:

5.1a. (If "both"): What proportion among them are technicians and what proportion are politicians?

5.2. With which members of the cabinet does a Director have the most contacts?

    ____Directeur de cabinet
    ____Conseillers techniques
    ____Chargés de missions
    ____Other:

5.3. How frequent are the contacts between the Directors of your ministry and the cabinet members you just mentioned?

5.4. It has been said that the cabinet of a minister concerns itself mainly with political issues (elections, the minister's reputation, passage of bills by Parliament, etc.) and that the higher civil servants concern themselves mostly with administrative and technical questions. Do you think that this analysis is generally:

    ____Correct   ____Not correct
    ____Quite correct   ____Other:

5.5. A French Ambassador wrote ten years ago that during the Third Republic the ministerial cabinet was but "a liaison organ between the minister and his administration and between the minister and parliament"; in his view, the ministerial cabinet "hardly intervened in the functioning of the administration." However, since the Liberation the cabinet, according to the same Ambassador, has become "the brains of the minister and, in relation to the administration, the eye of the master" which "short-circuits" the administration. Do you find this description valid?

    ____Yes   ____No   ____Other:

5.6. (If "Yes"): Would you say then that the ministerial cabinet has become a screen between the minister and the administration, or do you think it is a useful intermediary?

    ____Screen
    ____Useful intermediary
    ____Other:

5.6a. (If "No"): Why?

5.7. How would you define the role of the director of the cabinet?

5.8. Would you say that the functions of the members of the ministerial cabinet are so well defined that in general they do not conflict with the functions of the directors?

    ____Yes   ____No

5.8a. (If "No"): At what level of the ministerial cabinet do the functions of the directors and those of the cabinet conflict more often?

    ____Level of directeur de cabinet
    ____Level of conseillers techniques
    ____Level of chargés de missions
    ____Other:

5.9. France is one of the few countries where there are ministerial cabinets. Do you think that the existence of a ministerial cabinet is essential from the point of view of the minister?

5.9a. Why?

5.10. Do you think that the existence of ministerial cabinets is essential from the point of view of the administration?

5.10a. Why?

5.11. In your view, what should be the main function of a ministerial cabinet?

5.12. Does this happen in reality?

5.13. Do you think that serving in a ministerial cabinet tends to politicize a higher civil servant?

    ____Yes
    ____No
    ____Depends on the ministry
    ____Other:

5.13a. (If "depends on the ministry"): Could you give me some examples of ministerial cabinets which tend to politicize a higher civil servant?

5.14. Do you think that serving in a ministerial cabinet is useful for the career and training of a higher civil servant?

    ____Useful for both
    ____Useful only for career
    ____Useful only for training
    ____Useless for both
    ____Other:

Personal Questions

6.1 (For the officials who were in a profession before entering the administration): In what year did you enter the administration?

6.1a. (Same as for 6.1.): What profession were you in at that time?

6.2. (For the officials who began their career in the administration): How old were you when you began thinking about a career in the administration?

6.2a. (Same as for 6.2.): Did you consider other careers at that time?

    ____Yes   ____No

6.3. (If "yes"): Which ones?

    ____Private enterprise
    ____Public enterprise
    ____Entrepreneur
        ____Family enterprise
        ____Founder of an enterprise
    ____Academic
        ____College level
        ____High school level
    ____Journalism
    ____Politics
    ____Liberal profession: which one? ____
    ____Other:

6.4. What considerations pushed you towards a career in the administration? Please choose *two* among the following, in order of importance:

    ____Because it offers all sorts of possibilities
    ____Pleasant, interesting work

_____Political vocation
_____Possibilities of promotion
_____Job security
_____Desire for public service
_____Prestige of administration
_____Salary
_____Family tradition
_____Other:

6.5. What was your high school (*lycée*)?

6.6. Where did you go to university?

6.7. Where was your father born?

6.8. What was (is) your father's occupation?

6.8a. Is he (or was he) a civil servant?

_____Yes   _____No

6.9. What is (was) your father-in-law's occupation?

6.10.   What was the occupation of both your grandfathers?
Paternal:
Maternal:

6.11. Do you have any brothers?

_____Yes   _____No

6.11a. What are their occupations?

6.12. What is the level of education of your father?

_____University
_____High school
_____Elementary

6.12a. (If "university"): Did your father graduate from a Grande Ecole? Which one?

_____Yes: _____
_____No

6.12b. (If "no"): What university did he go to?

6.13. What is your family's religion?

6.14. Is (was) your father very religious, fairly religious, or not religious?

       ____Very
       ____Fairly
       ____Not
       ____Other:

6.15. Are you very religious, fairly religious, or not religious?

       ____Very
       ____Fairly
       ____Not
       ____Other:

BIBLIOGRAPHY

Works on French Administration

Armand, Louis. "Conversations sur l'avenir de l'administration." *Promotions*, no. 60 (1962).

———. "Grands Corps et Grands Commis: Les Corps d'ingénieurs." *La Revue des deux mondes*, November 15, 1958.

Belorgey, Gérard. *Le Gouvernement et l'administration de la France*. Paris: Armand Colin, 1967.

Bertrand, A., and Long, M. "L'Enseignement supérieur des sciences administratives en France." *Revue Internationale des Sciences Administratives*, no. 1 (1960).

Billy, Jacques. *Les Techniciens et le pouvoir*. Paris: Presses Universitaires de France, 1963.

Blanc, Laurent. *La Fonction publique*. Paris: Presses Universitaires de France, 1971.

Blanc-Gonnet, Pierre. *La Réforme des services extérieurs du ministère de l'agriculture*. Paris: Editions Cujas, 1969.

Bonin, Georges, and Lelong, Pierre. "Inspecteurs des finances et administrateurs civils au Ministère des Finances." *Promotions*, no. 55 (1960).

Bottomore, T. B. "Higher Civil Servants in France." *Transactions of the Second World Congress of Sociology*, vol. II, 1954.

Bouffard, Pierre. "Le Recrutement des cadres de la nation: l'école nationale d'administration." *Revue de défense nationale*, x (January 1950).

Boyer, Michel. "M. Albin Chalandon s'en prend au corps des ponts et chaussées." *Le Monde*, 12 May 1969.

Braibant, Guy. "Libres opinions sur l'Ecole Nationale d'Administration." *Promotions*, no. 35 (1955).

Brindillac, Charles. "Décoloniser la France." *Esprit*, xxv (December 1957).

———. "Les Hauts fonctionnaires." *Esprit*, xxi (June 1953).

Cahen, Georges. *Les Fonctionnaires*. Paris: Armand Colin, 1911.

Catherine, Robert. *Le Fonctionnaire français.* Paris: Albin Michel, 1961.

———, and Thuiller, Guy. *Introduction à une philosophie de l'administration.* Paris: Armand Colin, 1969.

Cayrol, R., Parodi, J.-L., and Ysmal, C. "L'Image de la fonction parlementaire chez les députés français," *Revue française de science politique*, xxi, no. 6 (1971).

Chalandon, Albin. "Comment je conçois le rôle de l'Etat." *Preuves*, 2ème trimestre (1970).

Chardon, Henri. *L'Administration de la France: les fonctionnaires.* Paris: Perrin, 1908.

———. *Le Pouvoir administratif.* Paris: Perrin, 1911.

———. *Les Travaux publics.* Paris: Perrin, 1904.

Chatenet, P. "The Civil Service in France." *The Civil Service in Britain and France*, edited by W. A. Robson. London: Hogarth Press, 1956.

Chenot, Bernard. *Etre ministre.* Paris: Plon, 1967.

Cheverny, Julien. "Le Mode autoritaire de l'anarchie." *Esprit*, Special Number (January 1970).

Closon, F.-L., and Filippi, J. *L'Economie et les finances.* Paris: Presses Universitaires de France, 1968.

Club Jean Moulin. *Les Citoyens au pouvoir.* Paris: Seuil, 1968.

———. *L'Etat et le citoyen.* Paris: Seuil, 1961.

———. *Quelle réforme? quelles régions.* Paris: Seuil, 1969.

Cohen, William. *Rulers of Empire: The French Colonial Service in Africa.* Palo Alto, Cal.: The Hoover Institution Press, 1971.

Crozier, Michel. *La Société bloquée.* Paris: Seuil, 1970.

———. *The Bureaucratic Phenomenon.* Chicago: University of Chicago Press, 1964.

Darbel, Alain, and Schnapper, Dominique. *Les Agents du système administratif.* Paris: Mouton, 1969.

Debbasch, Charles. *L'Administration au pouvoir: fonctionnaires et politiques sous la Vᵉ République.* Paris: Calmann-Lévy, 1969.

Debré, Michel. "Naissance et perspectives d'une institution." *Promotions*, no. 35 (1955).

———. *Réforme de la fonction publique.* Paris: Imprimerie Nationale, 1946.

Demartial, G. *Le Personnel des ministères.* Paris: Berger-Levrault, 1911.

Déroche, Henri. *Les Mythes administratives*. Paris: Presses Universitaires de France, 1966.

Deroy, Henri. "Grands Corps et Grands Commis—III. L'Inspection des Finances." *La Revue des deux mondes*, August 1, 1958.

Deschanel, Paul. *La Décentralisation*. Paris: Berger-Levrault, 1895.

Diamant, Alfred. "The French Administrative System: The Republic Passes But the Administration Remains." *Toward the Comparative Study of Public Administration*, edited by W. J. Siffin. Bloomington, Ind.: Indiana University Press, 1959.

———. "Tradition and Innovation in French Administration." *Comparative Political Studies*, I, no. 2 (1968).

Ehrmann, Henry. "French Bureaucracy and Organized Interests." *Administrative Science Quarterly*, IV (1961).

Escoube, Pierre. "Grands Corps et Grands Commis—V. La Cour des Comptes." *La Revue des deux mondes*, October 1, 1958.

———. *Les Grands Corps de l'Etat*. Paris: Presses Universitaires de France, 1971.

Friedberg, Erhard, and Thoenig, J.-C. "Politique urbaines et stratégies corporatives." *Sociologie du Travail*, XI, no. 4 (1969).

———, and Desjeux, Dominique. "Fonctions de l'Etat et rôles des Grands Corps: le cas du corps des mines," *Annuaire International de la Fonction Publique*, *1972–1973*.

Gournay, Bernard, Kesler, J.-F., and Siwek-Pouydesseau, J. *Administrations Publiques*. Paris: Presses Universitaires de France, 1967.

Gournay, Bernard. "Un Groupe dirigeant de la société française: les grands fonctionnaires." *Revue française de science politique*, XIV, no. 2 (1964).

Grégoire, Roger. *La Fonction publique*. Paris: Armand Colin, 1954.

Grémion, Pierre, and Worms, J.-P. *Les Institutions régionales et la société locale*. Paris: C.N.R.S., 1969.

———, and D'Arcy, François. *Les Services extérieurs du Ministère de l'Economie et des Finances dans le système de décision départemental*. Paris: C.N.R.S., 1969.

Kesler, François. "Les Anciens élèves de l'Ecole Nationale d'Administration." *Revue française de science politique*, XIV, no. 2 (1964).

Kessler, Marie-Christine. *Le Conseil d'Etat*. Paris: Armand Colin, 1968.

Lalumière, Pierre. *L'Inspection des finances.* Paris: Presses Universitaires de France, 1959.

Lamothe, A. Dutheillet De. "Ministerial Cabinets." *Public Administration*, XLIII (Winter 1965).

Lancelot, Marie-Thérèse. "Le Courrier d'un parlementaire." *Revue française de science politique*, XII, no. 2 (1962).

Langrod, Georges. "La Science de l'administration publique en France au 19ème et au 20ème siècle." *Revue Administrative*, no. 79 (January–February 1961).

Lanza, Albert. *Les projets de réforme administrative en France de 1919 à nos jours.* Paris: Presses Universitaires de France, 1968.

Lautman, Jacques. "Prestige, inégalités et modernisation de l'organisation bureaucratique." *Esprit*, Special Number (January 1970).

————, and Thoenig, J.-C. "Conflits internes et unité d'action: le cas d'une administration centrale." *Sociologie du Travail*, VIII, no. 3 (1966).

————. "Développement économique, priorité accordée à la continuité et communauté des taches et des personnes entre la politique, la fonction publique et l'industrie dans la France actuelle." Paper delivered at the 8th World Congress of the International Political Science Association. Munich, Germany, August 31–September 5, 1970.

Leca, Dominique. *Du Ministre des finances.* Paris: Plon, 1966.

Léonard, Roger. "La Haute administration et ses problèmes." *Revue des deux mondes*, April 1, 1959.

Loppin, Paul. "Grands Corps et Grands Commis—IV. La Magistrature." *La Revue des deux mondes*, September 1, 1958.

Mandrin, Jacques. *L'Enarchie, ou les mandarins de la société bourgeoise.* Paris: La Table Ronde du Combat, 1967.

Maspetiol, Roland. "Grands Corps et Grands Commis.—I. Le Conseil d'Etat." *La Revue des deux mondes*, June 15, 1958.

Mignot, Gabriel, and d'Orsay, P. *La Machine administrative.* Paris: Seuil, 1968.

Morice, André. "Le Ministre et l'administration." *Promotions*, no. 28 (1954).

Mounier, Henri. "L'Ecole et l'administration." *Promotions*, no. 35 (1955).

Noëll, H. *Les Ministères.* Paris: Berger-Levrault, 1911.

Ormesson, Wladimir De. "Grands Corps et Grands Commis—II. La carrière diplomatique." *La Revue des deux mondes,* July 1, 1958.

Pelletier, Emile. "Grands Corps et Grands Commis: Le corps préfectoral." *La Revue des deux mondes,* December 1, 1958.

Piquemal, Marcel. *Le Droit syndicale en France.* Paris, 1962.

Richardson, Nicholas. *The French Prefectoral Corps, 1814–1830.* Cambridge: Cambridge University Press, 1966.

Ridley, F. F. "French Technocracy and Comparative Government." *Political Studies,* XIV, no. 1 (1964).

——, and Blondel, J. *Public Administration in France.* New York: Barnes and Noble, 1965.

Robson, W. A., ed. *The Civil Service in Britain and France.* London: The Hogarth Press, 1956.

Seurin, Jean-Louis. "Les Cabinets ministériels." *Revue de droit publique et de la science politique,* no. 6 (November–December 1956).

Sharp, W. R. *The French Civil Service: Bureaucracy in Transition.* New York: Macmillan, 1931.

Silvera, Victor. "De quelques réflexions sur certains aspects de la stabilité gouvernementale et de l'exercise de l'action administrative sous la Vᵉ République." *Actualité Juridique,* XXIII (February 1967).

——. *La Fonction publique et ses problèmes.* Paris: Éditions de l'Actualité Juridique, 1971.

Siwek-Pouydesseau, J. *Le Personnel de direction des ministères.* Paris: Armand Colin, 1969.

Suleiman, Ezra N. "The French Bureaucracy and Its Students: Toward the Desanctification of the State." *World Politics,* XXIII, no. 1 (1970).

——. "Sur les limites de la mentalité bureaucratique: conflits des rôles entre cabinets ministériels et directeurs." *Sociologie du Travail,* XIV, no. 4 (1972).

——. "L'Administrateur et le député en France." *Revue Française de Science Politique,* XXIII, no. 4 (1973).

Thoenig, Jean-Claude, and Friedberg, E. *La Création des directions départementales de l'équipement: phénomènes de corps et réforme administrative.* Paris: C.N.R.S., 1970.

Thorez, Maurice. *Le Statut Général des Fonctionnaires.* Paris, n.d.

Worms, Jean-Pierre. "Le Préfet et ses notables." *Sociologie du Travail*, VIII, no. 3 (1966).

WORKS ON FRENCH POLITICS AND SOCIETY

Archives Nationales. *Série FBI.*

Alphandéry, C., and others. *Pour nationaliser l'Etat.* Paris: Seuil, 1968.

Aron, Raymond. *La Révolution introuvable.* Paris: Fayard, 1968.

Avril, Pierre. *Le Gouvernement de la France.* Paris: Editions Universitaires, 1969.

Beau de Loménie, E. *Les Responsabilités des dynasties bourgeoises.* 4 vols. Paris: Denoël, 1947–1954.

Bisseret, Noëlle. "La 'naissance' et le diplôme: les processus de sélection au debut des études universitaires," *Revue Française de Sociologie*, IX (1968).

Blum, Léon. *La Réforme gouvernementale.* Paris: Grasset, 1936.

Bouère, Jean-Pierre. *Le Droit de grève.* Paris: Librairie Sirey, 1958.

Bourdieu, Pierre, and Passeron, J.-C. *Les Héritiers.* Paris: Editions de Minuit, 1964.

Brown, Bernard. "Pressure Politics in the Fifth Republic." *Journal of Politics*, XXV (August 1963).

Buron, Robert. *Le Plus beau des métiers.* Paris: Plon, 1963.

Caillaux, Joseph. *Mes mémoires.* Vol. 1, *Ma jeunesse orgueilleuse, 1863–1907.* Paris: Plon, 1942.

Castel, Robert, and Passeron, J.-C. *Education, développement et démocratie.* Paris: Mouton, 1967.

Charlot, Jean. *Le Phénomène gaulliste.* Paris: Fayard, 1970.

──────. *L'U.N.R.: étude du pouvoir au sein d'un parti politique.* Paris: Armand Colin, 1967.

Cheverny, Julien. *Ces Princes que l'on gouverne.* Paris: Juillard, 1966.

Clark, James. *Teachers and Politics in France: A Pressure Group Study of the Fédération de l'Education Nationale.* Syracuse, N.Y.: Syracuse University Press, 1967.

Clemenceau, Georges. *Sur la démocratie.* Paris: Larousse, 1930.

Cohen, Stephen. *Modern Capitalist Planning: The French Model.* Cambridge, Mass.: Harvard University Press, 1969.

Cohen, William. "The Colonial Policy of the Popular Front," *French Historical Studies*, VII, no. 3 (1972).

Debré, Michel. *Au service de la nation*. Paris: Edition Stock, 1963.

———. *Ces princes qui nous gouvernent*. Paris: Plon, 1957.

———. *La Mort de l'Etat républicain*. Paris: Gallimard, 1947.

———. *La République et son pouvoir*. Paris: Nagel, 1950.

———. *Une Certaine idée de la France*. Paris: Fayard, 1972.

De Gaulle, Charles. The Complete War Memoirs of Charles De Gaulle. New York: Simon and Schuster, 1967.

———. *Mémoirs d'espoir: le renouveau, 1958–1962*. Paris: Plon, 1970.

Dioguardi, Giuseppe. *Le Droit de grève: étude de droit constitutionnel comparé*. Paris, 1961.

Dogan, Mattei, and Campbell, Peter. "Le Personnel ministériel en France et en Grande Bretagne." *Revue française de science politique*, VII, no. 2 (1957).

———. "Les Filières de la carrière politique en France." *Revue française de sociologie*, VIII (1967).

———. "Political Ascent in a Class Society: French Deputies 1870–1958." *Political Decision-Makers*, edited by Dwaine Marvick. Glencoe, Ill.: The Free Press, 1961.

———. "Political Cleavage and Social Stratification in France and Italy." *Party Systems and Voter Alignments*, edited by S. M. Lipset and Stein Rokkan. New York: The Free Press, 1967.

Durkheim, Emile. *Sociology and Education*. Glencoe, Ill.: The Free Press, 1956.

Earle, Edward M., ed. *Modern France: Problems of the Third and Fourth Republics*. Princeton, N.J.: Princeton University Press, 1951.

Ehrmann, Henry, ed. *Interest Groups on Four Continents*. Pittsburgh, Pa.: University of Pittsburgh Press, 1958.

———. *Organized Business in France*. Princeton, N.J.: Princeton University Press, 1957.

———. *Politics in France*. Boston: Little, Brown & Co., 1968.

Elgey, Georgette. *La République des illusions*. Paris: Fayard, 1965.

Faure, Edgar. *L'Ame du combat*. Paris: Fayard, 1970.

Fauvet, Jacques. *La France déchirée*. Paris: Fayard, 1957.

423

Ferrat, André. *La République à refaire*. Paris: Gallimard, 1945.

Gelinier, Octave. *Le Secret des structures compétitives*. Paris: Hommes et Techniques, 1966.

Girard, Alain. *La Réussite sociale*. Paris: Presses Universitaires de France, 1967.

———. *La Réussite sociale en France*. Paris: Presses Universitaires de France, 1961.

Girardet, Raoul, *La Crise militaire française, 1945–1962*. Paris: Armand Colin, 1964.

Goguel, François. *La Politique des partis sous la troisième république*. Paris: Seuil, 1946.

Gravier, Jean-Francois. *Paris et le désert français*. Paris: Flammarion, 2nd ed., 1958.

———. "Les Parisiens sont-ils colonialistes?" *La Table Ronde*, Special Number, no. 245 (June 1968).

Greenstein, Fred, and Tarrow, Sidney. "The Study of French Political Socialization: Toward the Revocation of Paradox." *World Politics*, XXII, no. 1 (1969).

Grosser, Alfred. *La IVᵉ République et sa politique extérieure*. Paris: Armand Colin, 1961.

Hoffmann, Stanley. "The Areal Division of Powers in the Writings of French Political Thinkers." *Area and Power: A Theory of Local Government*, edited by Arthur Mass. Glencoe, Ill.: The Free Press, 1959.

———. "Paradoxes of the French Political Community." *In Search of France*, by S. Hoffmann and others. Cambridge, Mass.: Harvard University Press, 1963.

———. "Protest in Modern France." *The Revolution in World Politics*, edited by Morton A. Kaplan. New York: John Wiley, Inc. 1962.

———. "Succession and Stability in France." *Journal of International Affairs*, XVIII, no. 1 (1964).

Hugues, Philippe De, and Peslier, Michel. *Les Professions en France: évolution et perspectives*. Paris: Presses Universitaires de France, 1969.

Jouvenel, Robert De. *La République des camarades*. Paris: Grasset, 1914.

Kesselman, Mark. *The Ambiguous Consensus: A Study of Local Government in France*. New York: Alfred A. Knopf, 1967.

Kriegel, Annie. *Les Communistes français*. Paris: Seuil, 1968.

Laski, Harold J. *Authority in the Modern State*. New Haven, Conn.: Yale University Press, 1919.

Lavau, Georges. "Political Pressures by Interest Groups in France." *Interest Groups on Four Continents*, edited by Henry Ehrmann. Pittsburgh, Pa.: University of Pittsburgh Press, 1958.

Leites, Nathan. *On the Game of Politics in France*. Stanford, Cal.: Stanford University Press, 1959.

Luethy, Herbert. *France Against Herself*. New York: Meridian Books, 1954.

MacRae, Duncan. *Parliament, Parties and Society in France, 1948–1958*. New York: St. Martin's Press, 1967.

McArthur, John, and Scott, Bruce R. *Industrial Planning in France*. Boston: Harvard Graduate School of Business Administration, 1969.

Marx, Karl. *The 18th Brumaire of Louis Bonaparte*. New York: International Publishers, 1963.

Massigli, René. *Sur quelques maladies de l'Etat*. Paris: Plon, 1958.

Mayer, René. *Féodalité ou démocratie? pour une administration d'un style nouveau*. Paris: Arthaud, 1968.

Melnik, C., and Leites, N. *The House Without Windows*. Evanston, Ill.: Harper and Row, 1958.

Mendès-France, Pierre. *A Modern French Republic*. New York: Hill and Wang, 1963.

Meynaud, Jean. *Les Groupes de pression*. Paris: Presses Universitaires de France, 1960.

———. *Nouvelle Etudes sur les groupes de pression*. Paris: Armand Colin, 1962.

———. *Technocracy*. London: Faber and Faber, 1965.

———. "Les Groupes de pression sous la Ve République." *Revue française de science politique*, XII, no. 3 (1962).

Mitterrand, François. *Le Coup d'Etat permanent*. Paris: Plon, 1965.

Nordlinger, Eric. "Democratic Stability and Instability: The French Case." *World Politics*, XVIII, no. 1 (1965).

Ollé-Laprune, Jacques. *La Stabilité des ministres sous la troisième république, 1879–1940*. Paris: Librairie Générale de Droit et de Jurisprudence, 1962.

Priouret, Roger. "Face à face avec Edgar Faure." *L'Expansion*, no. 22 (September 1969).

———. *La République des députés*. Paris: Grasset, 1959.

Remond, René. *The Right Wing in France from 1815 to De Gaulle*. Philadelphia, Pa.: University of Pennsylvania Press, 1966.

Scheinman, Lawrence. *Atomic Energy Policy in France under the Fourth Republic*. Princeton, N.J.: Princeton University Press, 1965.

Servan-Schreiber, Jean-Jacques. *Le Pouvoir régional*. Paris: Grasset, 1971.

Siegfried, André. *De la IIIème à la IVème République*. Paris: Grasset, 1956.

———. *France: A Study of Nationality*. New Haven, Conn.: Yale University Press, 1930.

Paris: Receuil Sirey, 1939.

Taine, H. *Les Origines de la France contemporaine*. Paris: Hachette, 1899.

Tardieu, André. *La Révolution à refaire: la profession parlementaire*. Paris: Flammarion, 1932.

Tocqueville, Alexis De. *The Old Regime and the French Revolution*. New York: Doubleday, Anchor Books, 1955.

Vedel, Georges, ed. *La Dépolitisation: mythe ou réalité*. Paris: Armand Colin, 1962.

Waterman, Harvey. *Political Change in Contemporary France*. Columbus, Ohio: Charles E. Meril Co., 1969.

Williams, Philip M. *Crisis and Compromise: Politics in the Fourth Republic*. New York: Doubleday, Anchor Books, 1966.

———. *The French Parliament: Politics in the Fifth Republic*. New York: Frederick A. Praeger, 1968.

OTHER WORKS

Allardt, Erik, and Rokkan, S. *Mass Politics: Studies in Political Sociology*. New York: The Free Press, 1970.

Ammassari, Paolo, and others. *Il Burocrate di Fronte Alla Burocrazia*. Milan: Giuffre, 1969.

Anales de Moral, Social y Economica. Sociologiá de la Administración Pública Española. Madrid: Raycar, 1968.

Barker, Ernest. *The Development of Public Services in Western Europe, 1660–1930*. Hamden, Conn.: Archon Books, 1966.

Barry, Brian. "The Public Interest." *The Bias of Pluralism*, edited by William E. Connolly. New York: Atherton Press, 1969.

Birnbaum, Norman. *The Crisis of Industrial Society*. New York: Oxford University Press, 1969.

Bracher, Karl Dietrich. *The German Dictatorship*. New York: Praeger, 1970.

Chapman, Brian. *British Government Observed: Some European Reflections*. London: George Allen and Unwin, Ltd. 1963.

———. *The Profession of Government*. London: Unwin University Books, 1959.

Connolly, William E. *The Bias of Pluralism*, New York: Atherton Press, 1969.

Coombes, David. *The Member of Parliament and the Administration*. London: George Allen and Unwin, 1966.

Crick, Bernard C. *The Reform of Parliament*. New York: Doubleday, 1965.

Dahl, Robert A. *After the Revolution?* New Haven, Conn.: Yale University Press, 1971.

———. *Who Governs?* New Haven, Conn.: Yale University Press, 1966.

Dahrendorf, Ralf. *Essays in the Theory of Society*. Stanford, Cal.: Stanford University Press, 1968.

———. *Society and Democracy in Germany*. New York: Doubleday and Co., 1967.

De Castro, De la Oliva A., and Reñón, Alberto. "Los Cuerpos de Funcionarios." *Sociología de la Administración Pública Española*. Madrid: Raycar, 1968.

Deutsch, Karl, and Edinger, Lewis. *Germany Rejoins the Powers*. Stanford, Cal.: Stanford University Press, 1959.

Domhoff, G. William. *Who Rules America?* Englewood Cliffs, N.J.: Prentice-Hall, Inc. 1967.

———. *The Higher Circles*. New York: Vintage Books, 1971.

———, and Ballard, H. E. ed. *C. Wright Mills and the Power Elite*. Boston: Beacon Press, 1969.

Drew, Elizabeth B. "Dam Outrage: The Story of the Army Engineers." *The Atlantic* (April 1970).

Edinger, Lewis J. *Politics in Germany*. Boston: Little, Brown & Co., 1968.

———, and Searing, D. S. "Social Background in Elite Analysis: A Methodological Inquiry." *The American Political Science Review*, LXI (June 1967).

Frey, Frederick W. *The Turkish Political Elite*. Cambridge, Mass.: The M.I.T. Press, 1965.

Fry, Geoffrey K. "Some Weaknesses in the Fulton Report on the British Home Civil Service." *Political Studies*, XVII, no. 4 (1969).

Godine, M. R. *The Labor Problem in the Public Service*. Cambridge, Mass.: Harvard University Press, 1951.

Gordon, Michael. "Civil Servants, Politicians, and Parties: Shortcomings in the British Policy Process." *Comparative Politics*, IV, no. 1 (1971).

Guttsman, W. L. *The British Political Elite*. New York: Basic Books, 1963.

Herring, Pendleton. *Public Administration and the Public Interest*. New York: McGraw-Hill Co., 1936.

———. *The Politics of Democracy*. New York: Rinehart and Co., 1940.

Hoffmann, Stanley, et al. *In Search of France*. Cambridge, Mass.: Harvard University Press, 1963.

Hough, Jerry F. *The Soviet Prefects*. Cambridge, Mass.: Harvard University Press, 1969.

Huntington, S. "Congressional Responses in the Twentieth Century." *The Congress and America's Future*, edited by David B. Truman. Englewood Cliffs, N.J.: Prentice-Hall, Inc., 1965.

Kaplan, Morton A., ed., *The Revolution in World Politics*. New York: John Wiley and Sons, Inc., 1962.

Kelsall, R. K. *Higher Civil Servants in Britain*. London: Routledge and Kegan Paul, Ltd., 1955.

Kingsley, J. Donald. *Representative Bureaucracy*. Yellow Springs, Ohio: The Antioch Press, 1944.

Kornhauser, William. *The Politics of Mass Society*. New York: The Free Press, 1959.

La Palombara, Joseph. *Interest Groups in Italian Politics*. Princeton, N.J.: Princeton University Press, 1964.

———, and Weiner, M. *Political Parties and Political Development*. Princeton, N.J.: Princeton University Press, 1966.

Linz, Juan, and De Miguel, Amando. "La Elite Funcionarial Española Ante la Reforma Administrativa." *Sociología de la Administración Pública Española*, ed. *Anales de Moral Social y Economica*. Madrid, 1968.

Lippmann, Walter. *A Preface to Morals*. New York: Macmillan, 1929.

Lipset, S. M. *Political Man*. New York: Doubleday Anchor, 1963.

428

Mackintosh, I. P. *The Devolution of Power*. Middlesex: Penguin Books, 1968.

Mann, Dean E. *The Assistant Secretaries*. Washington, D.C.: The Brookings Institution, 1965.

Mannheim, Karl. *Ideology and Utopia*. New York: Harcourt, Brace and World, 1936.

————. *Man and Society in an Age of Reconstruction*. New York: Harcourt, Brace and World, 1940.

Marvick, Dwaine, ed. *Political Decision-Makers*. Glencoe, Ill.: The Free Press, 1961.

Mass, Arthur. *Muddy Waters: The Army Engineers and the Nation's Rivers*. Cambridge, Mass.: Harvard University Press, 1951.

McConnell, Grant. *Private Power and American Democracy*. New York: Vintage Books, 1970.

Merton, Robert K. "The Role-Set: Problems in Sociological Theory." *The British Journal of Sociology*, VIII, no. 2 (1967).

Michels, Roberto. *Political Parties*. New York: Dover Publications, 1959.

Miliband, Ralph. *The State in Capitalist Society*. New York: Basic Books, 1969.

Mills, C. Wright. *The Power Elite*. New York: Oxford University Press, 1959.

Mosher, Frederick C. *Democracy and the Public Service*. New York: Oxford University Press, 1968.

Neustadt, Richard. *Presidential Power*. New York: The New American Library, 1964.

————. "White House and Whitehall." *Policy-Making in Britain*, edited by Richard Rose. New York: The Free Press, 1969.

Olson, Mancur. *The Logic of Collective Action*. New York: Schocken Books, 1969.

Parris, Henry. *Constitutional Bureaucracy*. London: George Allen and Unwin, Ltd., 1969.

Pulzer, Peter G. J. *Political Representation and Elections: Parties and Voting in Great Britain*. New York: Frederick A. Praeger, 1967.

Rose, Arnold. *Theory and Method in the Social Sciences*. Minneapolis, Minn.: University of Minnesota Press, 1954.

Rose, Richard, ed. *Policy-Making in Britain*. New York: The Free Press, 1969.

Rose, Richard. "The Variability of Party Government: A Theoretical and Empirical Critique." *Political Studies*, XVII, no. 4 (1969).

Rustow, Dankwart, A. "The Study of Elites: Who's Who, When and How." *World Politics*, XVIII (July 1966).

Sampson, Anthony. *The Anatomy of Britain Today*. New York: Harper and Row, 1966.

Sartori, Giovanni. "European Political Parties: The Case of Polarized Pluralism." *Political Parties and Political Development*, edited by Joseph La Palombara and M. Weiner. Princeton, N.J.: Princeton University Press, 1966.

Selznick, Philip. *T.V.A. and the Grass Roots*. New York: Harper Torchbooks, 1966.

Shils, Edward A. *The Torment of Secrecy*. Glencoe, Ill.: The Free Press, 1956.

Shonfield, Andrew. *Modern Capitalism*. New York: Oxford University Press, 1965.

Silver, Allan. "Social and Ideological Bases of British Elite Reactions to Domestic Crisis in 1829–1832." *Politics and Society*, I (February 1971).

Sisson, C. H. *The Spirit of British Administration*. London: Faber and Faber, 1959.

Stanley, David T., Mann, Dean E., and Doig, James W. *Men Who Govern*. Washington, D.C.: The Brookings Institution, 1967.

Subramaniam, V. "Representative Bureaucracy: a Reassessment." *The American Political Science Review*, LXI, no. 4. (1967).

Taradel, Allessandro. "La Burocrazia Italiana: provenienca collocazione dei direttori generali." *Tempi Moderni*, no. 13 (April–June 1963).

The Fulton Commission. *The Civil Service in Britain Today*. London: H.M.S.O., 1968.

Truman, David B., ed. *The Congress and America's Future*. Englewood Cliffs, N.J.: Prentice-Hall, 1965.

———. *The Governmental Process*. New York: Alfred A. Knopf, 1965.

Ulam, A., and Beer, S., eds. *Patterns of Government: The Major Political Systems of Europe*. New York: Random House, 2nd ed., 1963.

Waldo, Dwight. *The Administrative State.* New York: The Ronald Press, 1948.

Warner, Lloyd, and Abegglen, James C. *Big Business Leaders.* New York: Harper and Row, 1955.

————, and Abegglen, James C. *Occupational Mobility in American Business and Industry.* Minneapolis, Minn.: University of Minnesota Press, 1955.

————, and others. *The American Federal Executive.* New Haven, Conn.: Yale University Press, 1963.

Weber, Max. *Economy and Society: An Outline of Interpretative Sociology.* Edited by Guenther Roth. 3 vols. New York: Bedminster Press, 1968.

————. *From Max Weber: Essays in Sociology.* Edited by C. Wright Mills and H. H. Gerth. New York: Oxford University Press, 1958.

Zapf, Wolfgang. *Beiträge zur Analyse der deutschen Oberschicht.* Munich: Piper, 1965.

INDEX

433

LIBRARY OF CONGRESS CATALOGING IN PUBLICATION DATA

Suleiman, Ezra N   1941-
    Politics, power, and bureaucracy in France.

    Bibliography: p.
    1. France—Politics and Government—20th century.
2. France—Executive departments. 3. Cabinet officers—France.
4. Government executives—France. I. Title.
JN2728.S94   354'.44'01   72-6524
ISBN 0-691-07552-2
ISBN 0-691-1022-5 (pbk.)